Religio Romana Handbook

A Guide for the Modern Practitioner

Modern Roman Living Series,

Vol. I, 2nd Edition

L. VITELLIUS TRIARIUS, Ed.

LVCIVS VITELLIVS TRIARIVS

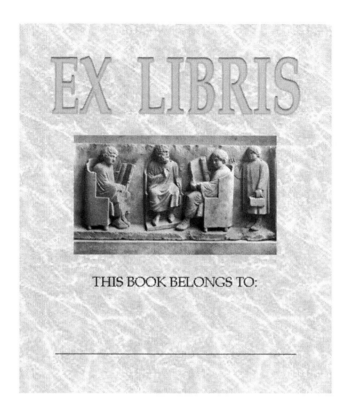

Copyright © 2014
L. Vitellius Triarius, Ed.

All rights reserved. 2nd Edition.

ISBN-13: 978-1493595990
ISBN-10: 1493595997

VISIT US ONLINE AT:
MASONICPRESS.COM

Available from Amazon.com, CreateSpace.com, and other retail outlets

www.CreateSpace.com/4499194

Printed by CreateSpace, Charleston SC
An Amazon.com Company

DEDICATIO

*Romans, though you're guiltless, you'll still expiate
your fathers' sins, till you've restored the temples,
and the tumbling shrines of all the gods,
and their images, soiled with black smoke.*

~Horace, Odes, III, 6

This handbook is dedicated to my old friend and Pontifex, Gnaeus Cornelius Lentulus, who has given much to the efforts required by Horace's Ode above and been a great inspiration to me for the last eight years.

LVCIVS VITELLIVS TRIARIVS

TABLE OF CONTENTS

    Acknowledgments   i

1 Introduction to Roman Religion   1
    Rites, Rituals and Ceremonies   4
    No Salvation, No Forgiveness   8

2 Monotheism vs. Polytheism   11
    For Monotheists   11
    For Polytheists   13
    God or the Gods: A Comparison   14

3 Declaration of Roman Religion   18

4 On Roman Reconstruction   21
    Roman Reconstructionist Organizations Today   22

5 Religion of the Home   23
    The Penates   25

6 Worshipping the Gods at Home   27
    The Basic Outline of Household Worship   28
    The Lararium   28
    Tools Used at the Lararium   29
    Making a Lararium   31

7 Your First Prayer to the Gods   33
    Libation   33
    Libation of Wine to a Male Divinity   34
    Libation of Wine to Multiple Male Deities   34

	Libation of Milk to a Female Divinity	35
	Libation of Milk to Multiple Female Deities	35
8	**Ancestral and Household Worship**	**36**
	Offering Sacrifice to the Manes, Lares and Penates	36
	Simple Request to a Deity	37
9	**Daily Rituals**	**40**
	Ablutio Before Performing Rituals	41
	Daily Lararium Ritual (ritus Graecus)	42
	Morning Lararium Ritual (ritus Graecus)	43
	Evening Lararium Ritual (ritus Graecus)	44
	Daily Lararium Ritual (ritus Romanus)	45
	Morning Lararium Ritual (ritus Romanus)	47
	Evening Lararium Ritual (ritus Romanus)	49
10	**Kalends Ritual**	**51**
11	**Nones Ritual**	**54**
12	**Ides Ritual**	**56**
13	**Other Rituals**	**58**
	Ritual for the New Year	59
	Dies Natalis Ritual	61
	Rite of Marriage Ritual (Coemptio)	63
	Wedding Anniversary Ritual (by Officiant)	87
	Wedding Anniversary Ritual (by Pater familias)	92
	Pregnancy Ritual (by Mother)	97
	Pregnancy Ritual (by Sacerdos/Priestess)	101
	Birth of a Child Ritual	108

	Naming of a Child Ritual	114
	Loss of a Child Ritual	117
	Liberalia Ritual and Ceremony (Son)	119
	Liberalia Ritual and Ceremony (Daughter)	122
	Travel Ritual	125
	New Business Ritual	127
	Funeral Ritual	130
14	**On Domestic Roman Sacrifice**	**136**
	Template and Guidelines	136
	Praeparatio	137
	The Two Forms of Sacrifice	138
	The Six Types of Sacrifice	142
	Oblationes	143
	Guide for Oblationes	44
	Votives	148
	Praefatio	155
	Precatio	157
	Immolatio	158
	Redditio	160
	Profanatio	162
	Epulum	162
	Table of Traditional Offerings and Sacrifices	163
15	**Posture and Gesture in Roman Prayer**	**172**
	Written Sources	172
	Depictions	178

16	**Foreign Cults in Ancient Rome**	**181**
	Greco-Roman Cults	181
	Roman-Persian Cults	182
	Roman-Egyptian Cults	182
17	**Gods and Goddesses of Rome**	**183**
	Introduction to the Gods	183
	Dii Consentes	186
	Dii Familiaris	189
	Dii Indigetes	191
	Dii Novensiles	191
	Dii Inferi	192
	The Roman Pantheon & Associated Deities	192
18	**Roman Festivals and Ludi (Games)**	**273**
	Keeping the Feriae	274
	List of Festivals by Month	275
	Feriae conceptivae	283
	Feriae imperativae	284
	Mercatus	285
19	**Roman Beliefs about the Afterlife**	**287**
	Preparation	287
20	**The Roman Virtues**	**289**
	Personal Virtues	289
	Public Virtues	291
21	**Glossary of Roman Religious Terms**	**294**
	About the Author	**397**

ACKNOWLEDGMENTS

This work is derived from the writings, articles, opinions and beliefs from many practitioners of the Religio Romana in antiquity and from Nova Roma, the global Roman Reconstruction effort in our modern age, and other sources.

It has been compiled to assist those interested in learning more about the Cultus Deorum Romanum and related Roman culture, both ancient and modern, and has been designed to be of practical use by the religio practitioner and a reference guide for the non-practitioner.

It is the desire of the author that this handbook touch on those people who have lost their faith in the social aspects, confusing interpretation, and practice of modern religion, and who desire to return to a system of faith that was grounded in common sense, personal, and not punitive to those who chose to see and relate to the divine in their own way and be responsible through their own actions.

Special Thanks goes out to the Collegium Pontificum and Senate of Nova Roma, M. Cassius Iulianus, L. Equitius Cincinnatus Augur, Cn. Cornelius Lentulus, C. Petronius Dexter, Ti. Iulius Sabinus, Q. Fabius Maximus, Marcus Horatius Piscinus, Gryllus Graecus, Salvius Austur, and the other Pontifices, Augurs, Flamens, and Sacerdotes of Nova Roma, past and present, whose insights into the ancient world of the Romans and personal initiatives led to a resurgence of interest of the old ways in the modern age. May the gods watch over you, your families, and your housholds.

LVCIVS VITELLIVS TRIARIVS

1 INTRODUCTON TO ROMAN RELIGION

The Religio Romana, or cultus deorum Romanum, is the practice of spiritual traditions and rites of the ancient Roman peoples in our modern age. It is composed of that set of orthopraxic beliefs and practices that for centuries guided the Romans in their daily life, before the orthodox beliefs and practices, promising salvation or the eternal damnation of the soul, arrived from the East in the latter 1st Century B.C.E. To understand the evolution of the religious system in ancient Rome, let us first go back to primitive man on the Italian Peninsula.

In the beginning there were spirits, called *numens*, which governed Nature and all things in it. There were no holy books or scrolls that guided man on his journey through life. Man walked outside every day, looked up to the heavens, and prayed to the spirits that guided him and the rest of the world around him.

Over time, the hunters and gatherers and farmers developed into the Etruscan natives and the Latin invaders to the Italian Peninsula, who began to cultivate a relationship with these different spirits, which represented the differents aspects of society, nature and the world. These spirits had no names, but rather were referred to as "the spirits that guide newborn children" or "the spirits of that cause the crops to grow" or "the spirits that bring the rain."

In time, man on the peninsula categorized these spirits into different groups of more important spirits and less important spirits, and they became named deities. The deities were, however, gods and goddesses without a face.

As time progressed, rituals were developed to appease these gods and goddesses. Most were in agreement that the gods were neutral, but leaning more to the benevolent side than the malicious side. They believed that these gods walked among them and could affect their daily lives, successes, fortunes, and fates; therefore, it was of the utmost importance that offerings and tributes be made in their names to make and keep them happy, averting ill will, anger, and any retribution which might be laid down upon the family, community, or state for their irregular actions.

During the Regal Period, religious practices were set up which forbade portraying or depicting these gods in human form. Later in the Republican Period, the stories of the Greek Gods were introduced into the Roman world, and these gods and goddesses took on human forms. Many of the original deities, who held common roles with each other, from different tribes on the peninsula were merged together to form one deity with a specific role or roles.

Religious beliefs among the Roman peoples were much as they are today: some believed that these gods were separate entities, some believed that they were individual aspects of a single spiritual guiding force in the universe, and some believed the stories, myths and gods themselves were purely hogwash meant for entertainment venues of the individual's mind. Thus, we find polytheistic, monotheistic, and atheistic personal belief systems throughout the religious world of the ancient Romans.

During these pre-Imperial times, we find no religion of the individual. The basis of the ancient Roman Religion began in the household with the Paterfamilias and the family. It was a religion of the household. There was also a religion of the gens (extended family), of the tribe, of the community, and of the state.

Religion was a dual system of private and public rites, which differed with the private being more informal and completely unstructured and the public being more formal and wrought with strict observance of repetitive ritual work to ensure that the gods received their proper respect in due form.

As we approach the latter end of the Republican Period, we see the populace more and more trending to worship somewhat monotheistically toward Iuppiter Optimus Maximus, with a preference to him as the best and greatest of the gods.

By the end of the 1st century, the Eastern religions found their way into the western world, bringing with them their orthodox doctrines and the promise of eternal salvation for the individual soul, whereby, the religious belief systems of the masses abandon the traditional role of the Roman religion as a family and household form of worship to adopt the religion of the individual.

No longer could your good works "get you into Heaven." Now, it was no longer what you did, but what you believed. The foreign cults of Mithras, Christ and others provided the Roman with an individual option, which previously was unavailable.

Confusing as it was to the Romans, these new religions overtook mainstream religious thought and eventually won out over the old ways. It was much easier to pray to one single deity than to pray to many, plus, there was the new concept of salvation of the soul.

Many Romans thought that the old ways were no longer working for them, and opted for a new system, and, in time, the gods and goddesses of antiquity became shelved antiques. No longer was the deity walking side by side with you during the course of your day. He now sat on a throne high above all and became somewhat unapproachable, guarded by seraphim and cherubim.

With modern congregational religion, the home is no longer a temple, the respect for and guidance from the spirits of the ancestors are no longer relevant, and the world suffers much from indifference.

As the Religio Romana resurfaces in our modern world, the gods and goddesses of old shake the dust of their togas and stolas, peer down upon us, smile, and say, "You remember us." Or, at least, that is what some of us dare to believe.

Within the daily practices of the Religio Romana, we find that ancient and simple form of worship that was for centuries practiced as an integral part of the family and state. Its revival in our modern age does not subject it to become a "New Age" religion.

It is an "Old Age" religion, and new practitioners should keep that in mind, for we do not wish to offend the gods and goddesses of old, lest they fear we may be trying to assert superiority over them as we engage them with the complexities of our modern technology, notions of absurdity, and vanilla irrelevances of modern thought and practice.

While individual practices will vary from cultor to cultor, it is important that we respect the ways of old and not use the religio Romana as an experimental forum for new perspectives and interpretations to the extent the cultus deorum Romanum is morphed into the "new religion of the week," for it is not.

It is a gift from old given to us to remember, respect, and revive for the good of our descendants.

Rites, Rituals and Ceremonies

According to M. Horaius Piscinus, former Pontifex Maximus of Nova Roma and the Societas Via Romana:

The Latin term ritus means means a rite that is performed in the customary and usual Roman manner (Festus s. v.). More specifically ritus refers to a Roman rite where prayers are correctly spoken, and the customary gestures and actions of Roman ritual are used. It is a marriage of prayer and action where the words giving meaning to an action and the action gives substance to the words. Furthermore a Roman ritus can be said to be composed of four parts:

- The Approach
- The Gesture and Prayer
- The Request
- The Reply

One ought to know which God or Goddess he is calling upon, what are appropriate offerings to bring for the deity, how to address a particular God or Goddess, when and where to perform the ritual and other considerations. This can be a little complicated in any polytheistic tradition, but there is always a certain internal logic in a tradition that aids a worshiper when approaching a God. In the Roman tradition there is even a traditional manner of approach when you do not know what God or Goddess might be present in a place.

The prayer and gesture is generally specific to the kind of rite being performed, where as a request may be more specific to the occasion or desire. Not always, but during a formal Roman rite one also takes a moment to see whether any sign appears to indicate whether one's offerings have been accepted or reject in reply to your request. This sounds more complicated than it actually is in practice.

A relatively simple rite is called the adoratio. It may involve a simple greeting such as saying "Ave, Ave, Di parenti." This greeting is coupled with a gesture where in one kisses the back of the right hand just behind the knuckle of the index finger, and then touches the finger tips onto an altar or an image. It is specifically used when addressing one's ancestors, so one approaches a family member's tomb, or the family lararium within the home, or sometimes it might be a tree or other outdoor shrine. The adoratio was so closely associated with rites for deceased family members, that is could be used interchangeably for the annual ritual owed to the dead in a parentatio. An adoratio can also be used with certain celestial deities when They are approached in a parental way.

One example from Roman literature is where a woman would stop by each shrine and image of Venus, calling upon the Goddess to lend her daughter beauty and poise. In word and action the mother both promised Venus sacrifices in the future while reminding Her of past sacrifices, while at the same time she was including Venus as a parental figure to her daughter and thereby asked Venus to take a special interest in the welfare of her daughter.

The gestures, prayers, and particular manner in which a Roman pours incense or wine as an offering on an altar can be called a "rite." A Roman ritual is then composed of a series of rites. As we move forward, I shall break down a Roman ritual into its component parts and it is easiest to think of a ritual as having been built up from little ritual moments.

The Latin term caeremonium means "ritual" in the sense I gave above. But I shall use it instead to mean "ceremony" in the sense of a sequence of rituals. Roman celebrations could extend over several days, with a variety of rituals performed for several deities. For our purpose, then, "rite" or ritus will refer to a ritual act, like a building block, for a Roman ritual, which in turn serves as a building block for a formal Roman ceremony.

There are two modes of performing Roman ritual. The first is called ritus Romanus that Romulus brought from Alba Longa to Rome. Ritus Romanus was performed in the Latin fashion with the toga pulled tightly around the torso (cinctus Gabinus) and drawn up to veil the head (capite velato). For certain rituals conducted in ritus Romanus, animal sacrifices were prohibited. In others, animal victims were selected according to the deities for whom they were meant as offerings. In general, white victims were selected for celestial deities, black victims for deities of the Underworld, while red victims were preferred for Vulcanus and Robigo. Goddesses generally received female victims.

There were always exceptions, with each temple having its own rules on sacrifice. Gods received male victims that were first castrated, except in sacrifices for Mars, Neptunus, Janus, or a genius. How the animal was decorated was another consideration, depending on the deity and the particular festival – whether gilt horns were to be used, the color of ribbons (red, white or black in most instances, blue for Neptune), a wreath of bread at some festivals, otherwise a wreath of flowers and fruits in some cases, and the embroidered dorsuale was draped over the flanks of oxen. Other kinds of offerings were likewise selected according to the particular deity or the particular festival. Milk was used as a libation in the oldest rites. Generally Goddesses received milk libations, although there are exceptions here too. Venus is one Goddess Who usually receives wine as a libation. Where wine is the libation commonly used in Roman ritual, wine is prohibited in some rites. All of the rules of ritual were once kept in the pontifical books. Commentaries on these lost books have since preserved some of the requirements of Roman ritual for us.

In spite of its name ritus Graecus is wholly a Roman style of performing ritual. Legend held that before Romulus came to Rome a Greek named Evander had established a settlement in the area. Legend also told how Hercules had come to Italy and first established the rites conducted at the Ara Maxima. Thus ritual held for Hercules and for Saturnus, among others, was conducted in ritus Graecus. Also when some Greek deities were adopted into the Roman pantheon, Their festivals could be celebrated in ritus Graecus, although, once again, there were exceptions like Castor and Pollux. Ritus Graecus was performed without the head being veiled. Instead wreaths were worn, usually made from woven laurel branches or flowers. When women took part, they are sometimes mentioned as having been barefoot. The same prescriptions on sacrifices used in ritus Romanus would seem to have applied as well in ritus Graecus. Perhaps more closely identified with ritus Graecus were other types of offerings.

Music, dance, theatrical performances were always performed at festivals as an offering to the Gods, not as entertainment for the public. Special hymns would be composed for the Gods, sung as an offering, just as poetry and theatrical contests were held in Their honor. Certain dances performed by mimes that were introduced from Campania were more closely associated with ritus Graecus than with ritus Romanus. But then, there were celebrations such as those conducted by the Salii who danced in celebrations of Mars and sacrificed in ritus Romanus. Horse races seem to have been associated more with ritus Romanus; chariot races more often with ritus Graecus. Ritus Graecus is also more closely associated with certain kinds of ceremonies called lectisternia, sellisternia, and supplicationes. The prayers used in ritus Romanus are more direct, sometimes becoming contractual, where as prayers associated with ritus Graecus might tend towards hymns of praise or invocations that recall myths and titles and honors of the deity. Along with a different style of prayer, the gestures used in ritus Romanus may have been distinct from those used for ritus Graecus.

By the Late Republic such distinctions made little difference. Caeremonia were composed of several rituals, and as Roman ritual grew more elaborate, with sacrifices offered to several deities, a caeremonia might pass from ritus Graecus to ritus Romanus and back again several times as each God and Goddess received what was most appropriate. Also adopted during the Late Republic and into the Imperial periods were foreign ceremonies that, although performed in Rome, were still held separate from the religio Romana. Such celebrations were thus conducted in a ritus peregrines, or in a foreign manner.

Every family, every clan or gens, every temple, shrine, and altar had their own traditional rituals, many of which changed over time. If anything can be said about Roman practice it is that is vastly diverse and that it was continually evolving throughout time. Trying to condense it all down into something understandable for a modern practitioner will thus overlook some things even as I try to develop some of the details that cultores Deorum Romanorum follow today.

No Salvation, No Forgiveness

Piscinus further states: A self-described "born-again" Christian once told me that what distinguishes Christians from people of all other religious faiths is that "Christians are forgiven."

As Cultores Deorum Romanorum, we are not forgiven. We are responsible for all of the actions we take and all of the words we speak aloud. We are responsible for not taking action when we ought, and for words left unspoken when we should. We can try to make amends. We can try to correct wrongs. We may ever afterwards do right. But we are always responsible for our words and deeds. This is required by Virtus of all those who worship the Goddesses and Gods.

In the end, you are the sum of all you have ever done or said. Our indiscretions, misadventures and misfortunes are all part of life, making us who we are just as much as our wise and virtuous words and good deeds. People always act on the impression that what they do is right. If they act from a false impression, they have deceived themselves. If they instead act falsely, unjustly, or out of malice, then they have only harmed themselves. On the other hand, through the practice of virtues we may approach the divine.

"It is right," Cicero said, "that Good Sense (Mens), Piety (Pietas), Moral Excellence (Virtus), and Good Faith (Fides) should be deified; and in Rome temples have long been publicly dedicated to those qualities, so that those who possess them, and all good people do, should believe that actual gods have been set up in their souls (Legg. 2.28)." Other virtues that Cicero included were Salus, Goddess of Health and Safety, Honor, Helpfulness, and Spes, Goddess of Good Hope. Among other divine qualities honored at Rome were Justice, Liberality, Concord, Fecundity, Freedom, Patience, Tranquility, Modesty, Goodness, Equity, Frugality, Happiness, Peacefulness, and the Nourishment of Children. Instilling such qualities in ourselves makes us into better people and provides a better society. Taking on such divine qualities as the virtues, we become more pleasing to the Gods, who are then more inclined to propitious to us when we call upon Them for Their assistance.

Further still, the ancients held that by practicing divine virtues we may become similar to the Gods and set ourselves on a pathway towards godhood.

> **"The solution is in understanding the virtues and what each has to give; thus the man will learn to work with this or that (virtue) as every several need demands. And as he reaches to loftier principles and other**

standards these in turn will define his conduct; . . . (until) he will live, no longer the human life of a good man, such as Civic Virtue commends, but, leaving this beneath him, will take up instead another life, that of the Gods (Plotinus Enneads I.2)."

Right conduct and prudence makes this life less contentious. Virtue improves the quality of the life we live now, a good life on earth. Virtue can also prepare us for the life to come by advancing our spiritual evolution in a manner that Plotinus addresses. We do not hold that doing good in this life is necessarily rewarded in an afterlife or that not abiding in virtue will necessarily bring punishment on you. You are your own person, made from the choices you make, and it is by becoming the person that you are at the time of your death that will determine what happens to you in the next life.

Though your body may be imprisoned, crippled, or diseased in this life, although others may do misdeeds to you, though you may be stripped of all your possessions and lose everything else to uncertain fortune, your true Authentic Being cannot be harmed by anyone other than yourself. Only you can choose a path towards becoming a God or a Goddess. Thus there are no excuses for what we make of ourselves either in this life or the next. With clear judgment we do not shrink from doing what ought to be done.

Acting rightly, we are not swayed by the censure of others, but remain steadfast in our resolve to do right. At the end of each day we examine the actions we took, judging what were done rightly, what were amiss, what was left undone, faulting the wrong we do and rejoicing in the right. Each day brings new adventures, new challenges, and more decisions to make. Each decision places another brick in the person we are becoming. Then, on whatever day the Fates have determined shall be the last day of your life, you shall be the person that only you have determined. Whatever kind of person we have made ourselves into at that our last moment, whether spiritually evolved or regressed, we are not forgiven.

You may visit M. Horatius Piscinus' blog for further reading at:
http://www.patheos.com/blogs/religioromana/

2 MONOTHEISM VS. POLYTHEISM

Of the three religious belief systems, Atheism will not be discussed here, as it would be a mute point, so we focus on the other two: Monotheism and Polytheism.

For Monotheists

As a new practitioner of the cultus deorum Romanum, it is most likely that you come to the religio seeking an alternative faith system, probably from one of the monotheistic world religions. There are a million and one reasons we find you knocking on the door of the temples of Rome, and the reasons are irrelevant. If you have made the decision to practice the ancient Roman faith, or are at last thinking about it and/or are curious, then we welcome you as a new or soon-to-be practitioner.

Having a monotheistic view of the divine is absolutely acceptable, however, you must be willing to accept that all the gods and goddesses of Rome are the individual aspects of the one supreme ruler of the universe, and that a hierarchy exists among these spiritual forces, just like that of the Judeo-Christian-Muslim angels and the pantheon of the Hindu Brahmans.

Of course, you may see the Almighty Divine Force of the Universe as Iuppiter Optimus Maximus, or as Ianus the creator god, or as Apollo the Son. This is a personal belief that begins with your basic household worship. Understand there is no salvation or vehicle to salvation here. Different belief system, different time period. That time period was yesterday. Today is today.

When you study and research the religio, you may find the Lars and Penates have something in common with your prior learning about guardian angels. If you come to us from the Roman Catholic faith, you may find that the Saints and the gods and goddesses bear a striking resemblance to each other. You may find that there are three major Flamines (High Priests, if you will) that form a trinity, and other similarities. You may find that the ancient Roman festivals fall on the same days as current church holidays, bearing the same or strikingly similar purposes.

Regardless of how you interpret the religio, you must understand that it is your decision on how you practice the faith and what you believe. The Religio Romana places no restriction, rules or regulations on your personal beliefs. Should you come to the decision to become a public priest or priestess, understand there is no congregation. The religio is not a congregational religion. There are temples, but no congregations. There are cultus groups, but no congregations. There are public rites, but there is no sermon. There are public sacrifices, but there are no communions.

The basis of your worship and foundation of your religious practice is in the home, not the temple. The temples are the dwelling places of the gods, where the public priests make their offerings and sacrifices, conduct special rites, and keep their records. The role of the public priest is to advise cultores and conduct public rites to keep the populace in good favor amongst the deities of Rome.

If you are the head of your household, then you become the priest or priestess of your own household. You are the paterfamilias (male) or materfamilias (female). It becomes your responsibility to "make and keep things right" between the gods and your household and keep it that way. The later chapters of this book will explain how you do that, so do not worry or fret over this task. It really is not so hard a task or responsibility. But, it does take a little practice and some memory work, which you will gain over time.

There are no sacred or apocryphal books or texts. There are myths and stories to explain things, but no divine texts to refer to. There are historical writings that discuss the role of the religio, but not religious writings, per se. Many opinions and decisions on the public rites are based on historical precedence, and private religious decisions are based on family or household traditions and practices.

For Polytheists

We welcome you into our merry band of practitioners! While you may or may not have come recently from a monotheistic faith, we hold that you understand that a relationship exists between the gods and man, and understand that relationship. If you are a practicing polytheist, you understand the concept of pantheon, so there stands no reason to explain the nature of the gods from that perspective. Becoming a practitioner of the cultus deorum Romanum is a little different from same of the other polytheistic religious systems.

First, the Greek gods and Roman gods are not seen in the same light. The role of the gods in these two religious systems have different aspects and expectations. Roman society evolved around the relationship with the gods and man, walking through this world together, with man charged with doing what was necessary to maintain a good, positive relationship with the divine entities, who were generally regarded to be neutral-leaning mostly toward benevolent.

The Roman gods do not "toy" with man, as was in the Greek religious system. If a Roman's household suffered a plague, it was of his own doing that brought that plague about, not from the whimsical desires of a bored or angry god or goddess for their own personal reasons or pleasures. Not to make any attempt at bashing the Greek system, it is just important to point out that the two systems are different. Neither are necessarily right or wrong, just different.

For Wiccans, the Roman religious system considers witchcraft and other related and associated belief systems to be taboo, and therefore, is not compatible with cultus practice.

We believe in a system where the gods rule and can determine our fates—should they choose—and not in a belief system that allows you to manipulate nature to your own ends, good or bad. If this be the case, you could theoretically manipulate the gods, and no one can manipulate the gods. That is why they are gods.

Of the modern religions of man, practitioners of the Shinto religion may find a closeness to the Religio Romana, more so that others.

There are many discourses that have been written over time that provide a good, solid argument for polytheism over monotheism, and vice versa, but that determination is left up to the individual practitioner within his own belief system.

God or the Gods: A Comparison

No human has demonstrable or irrefutable proof for or against a belief in a divinity or a lack thereof. All theories regarding the divine are based on faith, supposition, and individual experience. That being the case, we should focus instead on the ramifications and practical usefulness of the various theological conceptualizations on the people who hold them as well as on the rest of the world. Among the most ancient of these concepts is polytheism.

"Polytheism" (from the Greek polutheos, "many gods") denotes a theological system involving a belief in and worship of multiple divinities. The term was first popularized in the writings of eighteenth century European ethnographers as they encountered, then sought to identify and label the religious beliefs of "primitive" peoples they studied. "Polytheism" was used to contrast these beliefs with Judeo-Christian monotheism. Nowadays, the term is essentially used to refer to any belief system in which multiple spirit beings are worshiped. These may include gods, goddesses, semi-divine beings, good or evil spirits, or the spirits of departed ancestors. Depending upon the tradition, there may be an established and recognized hierarchy of worshipped beings or they may be seen to act independently. They may work in conjunction with one another or at cross purposes.

There are several significant characteristics typically found in nearly all polytheistic traditions. Among these are a belief that each divinity or spirit being has a specific function (such as healing, protection in travel, etc.), that it controls a particular realm (such as a spirit realm or a specific location in the physical world), or that it possesses a specific power or range of powers.

The latter can include forces of nature, such as rain, thunder, a celestial body, the seasons, or may involve dominion over characteristics of human personality, like love, devotion, compassion, jealousy, revenge, and so forth. Another common belief is that spirits possess or adopt a specific form, often human-like, and are endowed with human-like characteristics, such as love and compassion, but also jealousy and revenge. Other forms that spirits may embody include those of animals, of aspects of nature like a volcano, or a combination of several, thus making reverence toward and worship of both human-like and non-anthropomorphic forms commonplace. Finally, singular devotion to one specific divinity is not necessary. Simultaneous propitiation of several deities tends to be common and accepted. In some cases, this is seen as practical and necessary, since different spirits control different realms or powers.

Reflecting on how this approach can be understood on a human level, it parallels in many ways the functioning of democratic society in which power exists in the hands of various individuals who can be approached in turn or simultaneously for assistance. In conceptualizing such a theology, then, the adherents obviously drew upon their own human experiences. In the Jewish creation story, the gods (elohim) say "Let us make man in our image, in our likeness." What may be more accurate is that humans create the gods in their image and likeness, believing that what happens on earth must be a reflection of what happens in the heavens.

Polytheism, then, often mirrors the human experience of family, village, and state. It is frequently found in cultures with a clearly stratified social and/or political hierarchy, where power is held in the hands of different individuals based on their position within the hierarchy, and that these powers are there to benefit those who approach the various divinities seeking assistance.

Different divinities, like different bureaucrats, have different powers. One then approaches and propitiates the being with the requisite power to fulfill his or her needs or desires. Additionally, one can choose to focus exclusively on a divinity who appeals to one's own personality. At the same time, one can choose to ignore all deities. While such individuals are then believed to not receive divine assistance, they are typically not understood to be punished for this choice. Thus, in many ways polytheism is a pragmatic theological view that, as mentioned above, reflects aspects of a democratic style system.

If one looks at the monotheistic concept, in which there is a solitary omnipotent divinity, on the other hand, we find a very different approach to the divine and also to the likely world experience of those who formulated it. In monotheism, especially as expressed in the Abrahamic religions, ultimate power is in the hands of a single male divinity. He is all knowing, all powerful, and ever present. Like with the gods in polytheistic traditions, he has human personality traits. Unlike what is found in most polytheistic traditions, he demands allegiance and punishes those who do not worship him exclusively. On the human level, one typically finds such a being in monarchies, dictatorships, and societies run by a ruling tribal leader or warlord like those currently found in many Middle Eastern countries. While such systems may be comforting to those who "belong" to the right tribe or belief system, a solitary all-powerful ruler is a threat to those who do not. The vast majority of individuals in such societies remain weak and powerless unless they observe strict adherence to the being in power and do whatever they are told. This is seen as the only means of survival.[1]

Polytheists divide their world up into a variety of domains and assign gods to each: a god of the sea, a god of the sun and so forth. In their efforts to cover their bases, polytheists end up with conflicting gods. A god of war and a god of peace, a god of virginity and a god of fertility, a god of creation and a god of destruction. Things that might please the god of war, would upset the god of peace. Rites of fertility would be directly opposed to rites of virginity. In short, pretty much anything a person can do might please one god and anger another. This may seem a recipe for chaos, but we must remember that life, and indeed the world itself, is chaotic. In a world without science, when nature itself seems unpredictable, a variety of gods allows for flexibility. Since no one action is inherently good or bad, one is free to do what one must to get through the day. If everything you do or don't do will anger a deity, it doesn't so much matter what you do, as much as how much you do it. In this way, polytheism encourages moderation. Rather than seeking unwavering devotion to a single value system, ancient people instead looked for balance. By contrast, monotheism establishes a single authority. To make this authority cover the countless complexities of life, monotheistic religions create large bodies of holy law. The law of Moses would add over 600 laws to the original ten.

The result is a very restrictive belief system, one that the Israelites clearly chafed under. Moreover, holy laws end up contradicting each other. For example, the sixth commandment quite clearly states, thou shalt not kill, yet there are hundreds of sins in Mosaic law that carry a sentence of death. Such contradictions would not be a problem if the laws were not, as it were, set in stone.

References

1. Ramdas Lamb, Professor of Religion, University of Hawai'i.
2. Max Pfingsten. "What's the Difference Between Polytheism and Monotheism?" http://education-portal.com

3 DECLARATION OF ROMAN RELIGION

In the course of spiritual practice, it is necessary for persons aspiring to common ideals to form a clear foundation for their religion. It is also proper that they should declare their religious tenets to the world for consideration and remembrance.

We hold the ideals expressed herein to be basic and integral to our faith, that Roman Pagans may be united both in act and spirit. Pagan religion provides a spiritual heritage which embodies the basic nature of Western Civilization. It is both a historical faith and a living faith, which preserves the spiritual past even as it progresses into the future. Here we establish the structure and basic nature of Roman Pagan Religion so that it may be preserved, while allowing for future growth and freedom of individual expression.

We hold that a Roman Pagan may be defined as a person who actively performs rites, rituals, and/or prayers to any or all of the gods and goddesses of ancient Pagan Rome as the majority of their spiritual involvement. We acknowledge also that individuals may at times work with Roman deities without considering themselves as Roman Pagans.

We affirm that the Roman Pagan Religion embodies the spiritual beliefs, practices, virtues and philosophies of ancient Pagan Rome. These constitute and express a clear and separate form of religion and spirituality that is unique and different from all other spiritual paths. We hold that our practices today are the spiritual successor of the ancient ways, reborn anew.

We affirm that the historical basis of our spirituality comes from the Pagan religions of the ancient Roman Republic and Empire. The core of this history proceeds from the founding of Rome in 753 BC, to the removal of the Altar of Victory from the Roman Senate in 394 AD. Our historical basis also includes pre-Roman Latin and Etruscan roots, and Pagan survivals into later periods of history.

We hold that the Roman Pagan Religion is open to all people, regardless of nationality, race, gender, sexuality, spiritual affiliation or other individual circumstance. We affirm that the Roman Pagan Religion belongs to no one race or nationality, but is instead a common founding heritage of all Western civilization. It is further a universal spiritual current which throughout the centuries has influenced all peoples and nations of the world, either directly or by the legacy of its history, philosophies and practices.

We also affirm that the Roman Pagan Religion is compatible with, and may be practiced alongside all other forms of religion and spiritual expression, without diluting or diminishing its basic ideals and spiritual identity.

In the ancient world Roman religion was practiced alongside Celtic, German, Greek, Egyptian, Persian, and Oriental faiths, to the enhancement of all. This syncretistic approach to other religions remains basic to the Roman Pagan spiritual world view.

We affirm that the Roman Pagan Religion itself embodies many forms of rite and worship. These include the ancient Roman festivals, the rites of both Roman state and private religion, cults of the various deities, divination, the ancient Mystery religions, and Roman Pagan philosophy as well as other forms of ancient religious expression.

We further affirm that rites and worship within the Roman Pagan may be approached in many ways. In this manner the spiritual needs of all practicing individuals may be fulfilled. These various approaches may include group or individual worship, philosophical practice focusing on prayer and contemplation, purely historical reconstruction of ancient ritual form, as well as forms of modern rites and worship that adapt ancient practices and ideals.

We affirm that the Roman Pagan Religion shall be an organized and structured faith. In addition to purely individual involvement and the organization of autonomous groups, its form may contain the reestablishment of historical religious institutions. These may include established physical temples, mystery schools, priesthoods and religious colleges, and coordinating bodies such as a Senate formed among practitioners of Roman Pagan Religion.

We affirm that the Roman Pagan Religion was and is a civilized faith, empowering family, community and state to positive virtue and beneficial effect. The rites, virtues and philosophies of Roman Pagan Religion are by nature benign and lawful, serving to facilitate piety toward the gods, and understanding and cooperation among all people.

We affirm that the spiritual duty of the Roman Pagan Religion is to restore, maintain and promote the worship of the ancient Roman Goddesses and Gods. We seek to rebuild their influence in the world, and through piety and action preserve the sacred link between the ancient deities and humanity.

We affirm that the earthly responsibility of the Roman Pagan Religion is to preserve the basic ideals of Classical spirituality and civilization, that they may continue to be a positive force in society. We seek to renew the principles, philosophies, history and culture of the ancient Roman Pagan world, and make them available to all persons wishing to incorporate them as a modern spiritual path.

These religious ideals and tenets are set forth and adopted under the approval of the gods and goddesses of ancient Rome, and in remembrance of our ancient Roman Pagan spiritual forebears. Through them we are focused and united. Let them stand as an affirmation of our intent, faith and practice.

4 ON ROMAN RECONSTRUCTIONISM

While individuals are, of course, free to pursue whatever personal religions their hearts and souls commend them to, part of the mission of Nova Roma and other similar Roman organizations is the reconstruction of the public rites of the Religio Romana, or pagan Roman religion. As such, the concept of Reconstructionism entails that there be the following:

- There must be a reverence for the pre-Christian Roman deities and Mysteries. This includes a connection with the ancestors and the Lares and Di Penates. In a modern context, this means a concern for the importance of family, in its broadest sense.

- There must be a connection with the Roman past. We strive to be as historically (and mythologically) accurate as the state of the evidence allows. When gaps in the evidence, or the realities of modern life, make it necessary to create something new it should be as consistent as possible with what we do know about the classical-era Romans and their legacy. It should be clearly presented as a recent innovation. We frown on attempts to advertise something modern and invented as ancient and historical in order to give it an authority (and marketability!) it does not deserve.

- There must be a balanced approach to understanding classical Roman religion which relies on both sound scholarship and poetic inspiration without mistaking one for the other, remembering also that the divine was the realm of religion, whereas, the moral and ethical was the realm of the philosophers. The Roman religion was unlike today's modern congregational forms of religion. It was a two-part system of belief, one side the public rites, the other the personal or private rites.

- It must be inclusiveness. While we have the Roman fascination with genealogy, we do not rely on genealogy or geography to determine who is Roman.

- We must forego the ills of antiquity and hold an utmost respect for women.

- There must be a moral code which stresses truthfulness, honor, personal responsibility, and the other Roman Virtues.

- As we are concerned with historical accuracy, the public rites of the Religio Romana do not include ceremonial Magick or traditions influenced by it, such as Wicca. Nor, Italian witchcraft, or Stregha (an indigenous Italian form of witchcraft with some classical elements, but with its origins in the 14th Century). Nor, Eclecticism as opposed to historical syncretism; combining classical Roman religion with other cultural traditions that weren't combined historically; Romano-Celtic worship is certainly appropriate, sacrifice to Mercurius-Quetzalcoatl probably isn't.

Roman Reconstructionist Organizations Today

Nova Roma ~ novaroma.org
SVR, the Societas via Romana ~ societasviaromana.net
CDR ~ cultusdeorumromanorum.blogspot.com
The Maestrum of Cybele ~ gallae.com
The Julian Society ~ juliansociety.org
ADF ~ adf.org/rituals/roman

5 RELIGION OF THE HOME

"The family as we know it today bears little of no relation to that ancient institution of which the Lares were the Keepers of the Gate....In those early days the title to the land was possession and use. Because it was to him the source of his life, because its cultivation gave him occupation, because upon the land he build his house and in the land he made his grave, therefore the land to the archaic man was sacred; for not only was it the home of the living, it was also the place of the dead. And it was the dead ancestors in their graves who really possessed the land and, as the Lares, were the Keepers of the Gates.

"The belief of the ancient man in the ghosts of his fathers, with their unknown power to help and harm, was better than a title deed to secure each man in the possession of his land. Every man feared the Lares of every other man. The earth in those days was peopled with a host of spiritual beings — unseen, unheard, smiting with the pestilence, and killing with the plague. If any untoward accident befell a man, or sickness came to him after he had trespassed on his neighbor's land, then he, as well as his neighbor, ascribed his misfortune to the wrath of the Lares of that land. Thus each man had a wholesome fear of the ghosts of his neighbor. He was ready to fight his neighbor, whom he could see, but not his neighbor's ghosts, whom he could not see. In the good old days every house was haunted and every field bewitched, and it was the haunt and the bewitchment that was the safety of the house and the land. Domestic religion was the keeper of domestic wealth and life. It was the fear of the Lares that gave sacredness to property and made theft and trespass not only a crime but a sacrilege.

"This sacredness of property was religion in its origin. It existed for centuries before it gave rise to the civil laws that are now its security... Long before the reign of the law we had the reign of Lar. Each House-Father, absolute lord and master of his own house and land, was under the protection of his Lares; the fear of them and the dread of them was upon all the country-round about. If his lands were seized by a stronger man than he, his Lares were expelled from the land, the graves of his ancestors violated, and he and his household were either killed or reduced to slavery.

"This relation of the family to the land, and of the House-Father to the family, classified ancient society as master and slave, patron and client, patrician and plebeian... With the institution of the family, there came into existence a class of out-family men and women: runaway slaves, prodigal sons, remnants of broken families, -men and women without land, without Manes, without Lares, having no place at any family altar... Private property in land, the basic principle of the family, was the fruitful cause of poverty, with the wretchedness and degradation that always follow in its camp. That same poverty is today destroying the family and changing the face of civilization.

"Private property in land has, in the course of time, passed out of the keeping of the family Lares into the care of the civil law; what man had once to do for himself society now does for him. The Keepers of the Gates are no longer the Lares but the lawyers....

"The Lares of the archaic world, if they still haunt the earth and hover in the air, must look down in sad, bewildered wonderment upon the modern world, which to them must seem a mad world, wherein all sane principles have been driven out by crazy notions.

Here are millions upon millions of landless men with wives and children combining to secure the title of a few landlords to their land; these landlords doing nothing with or for the land but to take from it rents and profits. These two things, idle landlords and starving people, condemn the world as it is and call for a new race of Lares to visit the vengeance of the gods upon these profaners of the land."

The Penates

"The hearth is the heart of the family life. To keep the fire alive on the hearth is the bounden duty of the family gods. We of the modern world have lost altogether those conception that made "hearth' and "altar" sacred words. Domestic religion sanctified domestic life. The Penates, who were the Spirits of Ancestors, were the Keepers of the Fire and of the Store....

"It was the domestication of fire that changed man from a savage, living upon roots and raw flesh, into a civilized being, feasting on roast beef and baked potatoes. It was the capture and taming of fire that made possible the home and the family. Because of this, the Penates, the Keepers of the Fire, are the best beloved of the family gods.

With them the family was intimate as it gathered around the hearth when the day's work was over; they were present when the House-Father and House-Mother gave bread and meat to the children and the slaves, and after the dinner was over the Penates inspired the members of the household to speak words of love and wisdom one to another.

The husband could have a secret from his wife, the wife from the husband, but to the Penates all secrets were open. The light of their fire penetrated to the marrow to the bones. All profanation of family life was an offense to the Penates, to be punished by the heat of fever and the cold of the chill.

"While the family slept, the Penates watched; all through the night the dull glow of their life was seen in the slow-burning brand lying in the ashes, that kept the fire alive on the hearth. If that fire died out, the Penates were disgraced, and the family shamed; for the life of the fire once gone was not easily restored.

In these days of matches and electricity the smoldering brand has lost its usefulness and, therefore, its sacredness....Our modern improvements have improved these lovely gods out of existence.

"The Penates were not only Keepers of the Fire, they were also the Guardians of the Store. It was their duty to inspire the cook with skill to make delicate dishes for the family able, to watch the meat before the fire, to scare the rats from the cupboard. In the archaic world the gods were more useful than ornamental.

The men and women of that world would laugh our gods to corn and think of them with pity, — gods shut up in churches, having nothing to do but to listen to the droning of prayers and the confessions of sins; gods who pass their dreary existence away from the warmth of the hearth, the smell of the cooking, the chatter of the maids and the stir of the family life!

A god upon a great white throne, with cherubim and seraphim bowing before him, may have power and dignity, but for comfort and good-fellowship one must go to the god who sits by the fire, inhales the odor of spice, and the flavor of the bread and the cake and the meat that are cooking in the kitchen.

Such a god can understand the tribulations of the cook and the annoyances of the mistress; he knows by experience that fire burns and ginger is hot in the mouth. All other religion is cold and formal beside this intimate religion of the hearth."

Quoted from: Crapsey, Algernon Sidney. The Ways of the Gods. New York: The International Press, 1920. (Out of Print)

6 WORSHIPPING THE GODS AT HOME

Private worship was the foundation of religion in ancient Rome. Although the public rites have received the most attention from historians, such things as the grand temples and many festivals were possible only because of the pietas which grew from household and family rites.

Each household in Rome was in a sense a temple to the gods. All Roman homes had a household altar, or "lararium", at which the family interacted with the goddesses and gods on a personal level each day. The rites of the home and family were so important to the Romans that such worship persisted into very late antiquity, surviving centuries longer than the public manifestations of the cultus deorum, which were officially banned in the late 4th century CE.

The reasons that household worship was important are understandable even today. The family is the basis of Roman culture, and the household is the "center" of a family's existence. Inviting the gods into one's house helps to ensure that one's property, relatives, and worldly efforts are blessed by the Roman deities, and that the positive powers of the goddesses and gods will enrich one's daily life. Such a sharing of life between humans and the gods is the essence of the Pax Deorum, or "Peace of the Gods."

The Basic Outline of Household Worship

The basics of cultus deorum household worship are simple and easy to do. A lararium is set up in the home, at which both the deities that are responsible for the home and the patron deities of the family are worshipped. Historically, there are two simple rites done at the lararium each day: in the morning and in the evening. During these rites the gods are honored, and asked to watch over the affairs of the family. The lararium was of course also a place where individuals could worship the gods privately, and make small offerings to them.

The Lararium

The Lararium (pl. lararia) altar is the sacred place of the home where offerings and prayers are made to the Gods. In more affluent Roman homes, such as private villas, the main Lararium altar was usually set in the Atrium (front reception room, near the front door). In smaller Roman homes which might not have an atrium, such as insula apartments, the Lararium was most often located near the hearth (the kitchen or place of a central fire). But a house could have several minor Lararia as well, indoors (especially in the bedrooms) or outdoors.

The forms of Lararium varied greatly. Rich homes might have a huge affair of carved marble which looked rather like a temple in miniature. In other homes the Lararium might only be a simple wooden cabinet or wall shelf. Big or small, the important thing about a Lararium is that it should be permanent rather than something to be put away when the rites are not being held.

A lararium, properly speaking, is a shrine for the Lares. During the Republic there does not seem to have been any statues used to represent the Lares, since they were considered more as ancestors. The death masks of ancestors were stored in boxes, hung on a wall near the entrance of the house, and it might possibly be that lararium meant something like a foyer where these were kept.

Today it would be comparable to having photographs of your ancestors at your lararium. Beginning in the fourth century BCE certain patrician families assumed divine heritages and thus may have begun to include images of a Lar familiaris such as Venus, but these would still have been regarded there as an ancestor.

Tools used at the Lararium

Acerra - Container for incense. The acerra is a special container for sacred incense. As with the turibulum, in the ancient Roman world the acerra could be made from a variety of materials and designs. An acerra for your home altar should be some sort of covered container that will keep your incense "fresh." Resins such as frankincense can sometimes absorb too much moisture, or even lose some of their scent if left uncovered for weeks at a time. A pottery container with a lid, or a decorated metal or wood box can make a fine acerra.

Salinum - Container for salt.

Gutus - Container for milk or wine. The gutus is a container for sacred milk or wine that is offered to the gods. As with the acerra and the salinum, the gutus is used to keep a sacred offering substance clean and protected. Any of a variety of materials may be used, such as pottery, glass, stone or metal. Liquid from the gutus is poured into the patera when it is being offered to the gods. If you are offering milk to the gods it should be placed in the gutus only a short time before the rite in which you will offer it, and the gutus should be emptied afterward. Wine may be left in the gutus for a longer time, although care should be taken if your gutus is made from metal. (The acid in wine may corrode the metal if left there for days.)

Patera - Offering dish. The patera or offering dish was used at the lararium throughout all periods of Roman religion. The patera is used to offer bits of food or wine from household meals to the gods. The Romans thought it important to symbolically share the sustenance of life with deity, as honored members of the home. In ancient times there were many different forms of paterae. Most often it was a clay or metal saucer-like dish, shallow and perhaps half an inch deep at best. The patera was usually round or oval in shape. The patera is an easy tool to use. A small bit of food from the family table, or liquid such as wine or milk is placed into it so that the gods may share with the members of the household. The offerings placed in a patera need only be left for an hour or two, although they can be left from meal to meal if one wishes. The patera should be kept spotless when not in use.

Incense - An offering to the gods. The ancient Romans burned a wide variety of incenses. Usually they were resins, powdered substances or herbs, or a mixture of the three. Resins such as frankincense or myrrh were very popular, as were substances such as sandalwood. Powdery incense was stored in the acerra and then sprinkled the coals of the turibulum to make offerings to the gods. It is because the incense was considered a sacred offering that the acerra is a sacred lararium "tool."

Turibulum - Incense burner. The turibulum or incense burner was used in household worship throughout Roman history. The turibulum is used both to create sacred scents pleasing to the gods, and also to change things from solid form into an ethereal form by consuming them with fire. The turibulum holds hot coals, and powdered or resin incense is put on them to give off smoke. The coals were also used to burn small offerings such as bits food or flowers and other sacred plants. In the ancient Roman world, the turibulum was made from a variety of materials depending on a person's needs or monetary status. The form varied as well. To add a turibulum to your home lararium, you will need a non-burnable container, (clay, stone or metal), and fill it with some sort of non-burnable substance for the coals to rest on so that they won't make the turibulum too hot to hold or leave on the surface of an altar. A simple pottery bowl filled with an insulating substance such as sand (so that the coals won't overheat and crack the bowl) will work fine, as can a metal or stoneware vessel. The turibulum may be decorated or plain. Incense burners are of course commercially available in religious shops, etc. The material for the inside of the incense burner should be both non-burnable, and also something that doesn't conduct heat. Sand is perfect. Clay based granular "kitty litter" will work as well. Dug up earth won't work well unless it is very, very dry, as anything organic in it tends to be burned by the charcoal and give off a smell. In the ancient world, the coals for the turibulum were wood charcoal. Today it is easy enough to buy "incense burner charcoal." This can be purchased at many different stores including church supply stores, religious shops, new age shops, and of course on-line. Outdoor "charcoal briquettes" for your backyard grill should not be used at all in any ritual and definitely not indoors as they give off poison gasses that can be very dangerous if inhaled inside a closed space.

Lucerna - Sacred lamp. The lucerna, "Loo-KAIR-na", or sacred lamp, was most usually the source of sacred flame at the Lararium altar. This was an oil lamp made of clay or metal that was lit during the rites in honor of deity. There are companies which make reproductions of ancient Roman oil lamps, but one can use a small modern oil lamp just as well. It is the flame that's important, not the container. Even more easily, a white votive or taper candle in a holder may be used. The tallow candle was invented by Romans and certainly was used in ancient times. A lucerna or candle should be on the lararium altar always, but it needs only be lit during the rites or when an offering of food, flowers, etc. is made to the gods.

Before statues were used in the household rites, the home altar centered around a sacred fire. This fire was a representation of the goddess Vesta, but also it was a combination of offering to the gods, and a representation of the power of the gods. In all eras of the Religio Romana, a sacred flame was part of household worship.

Making a Lararium

The easiest way to set up a lararium is to reserve a small one-tier wall shelf, or a table or cabinet as an altar. A trip to a hardware store, a department store or an antique shop will usually yield something workable. A lararium may be decorated to taste in classical style if one wishes, but it need not be any special style or color. One doesn't really need a lot of surface space. A square foot of space or so is about the average, as long as there is room for a candle, incense, and an offering dish. Space for statuary or wall space to hang pictures on is nice but not critical. It is well if one can place the lararium in a front room or near the kitchen area as was done in antiquity, but this is not essential. The important thing is that the lararium be placed somewhere that isn't so remote that it will be ignored or forgotten, or in a place so obtrusive it gets bumped into and knocked about during the course of the day. The lararium should be kept clean. The acerra, the salinum and the gutus can be stored near or under your lararium depending on its design, and need only be present before the gods during the rites.

7 YOUR FIRST PRAYER TO THE GODS

There is no special initiation into Roman religion like Christian baptism. You can start honoring Roman deities at any moment with any prayer. But if you want some advice or a little help with your first Roman prayer, we suggest that you start with offering libations at occasions when you feel appropriate.

While the public rites followed a strict formula in their construction and delivery, THERE ARE NO FORMAL OR SPECIAL REQUIREMENTS FOR PRIVATE RITES; however, many cultores, both ancient and modern, probably did not stray far from the standard prayer and offering template, so as to stay within the standard and acceptable "legal framework" when dealing with the gods. In other words, one cannot necessarily "do it the wrong way."

Libation

If you want to show your respect towards a deity, or if you want to assure they keep you in their continuous favor, you can offer a libation. This is the simplest formula you can use at any occasion, for example, during your meal, or while drinking at a party, or at home, when you feel like it.

Libation of wine to a male divinity

Take some wine and pray the following words aloud:

Latin

**(Name of god in vocative), macte hoc vino libando
esto fito volens propitius
mihi domo familiae!**

English

**(Name of god), blessed by the libation of this wine,
be benevolent and propitious
to me, to my household and to my family!**

Then pour the libation to fire, or to the ground, and drink the rest of the wine.

Libation of wine to multiple male deities

Take some wine and pray the following words aloud:

Latin

**(Name of gods in vocative), macte hoc vino libando
estote fitote volentes propitii
mihi domo familiae!**

English

**(Name of gods), blessed by the libation of this wine,
be benevolent and propitious
to me, to my household and to my family!**

Then pour the libation to fire, or to the ground, and drink the rest of the wine.

Libation of milk to a female divinity

Take some wine and pray the following words aloud:

Latin

(Name of goddess), macte hoc lacte libando
esto fito volens propitia
mihi domo familiae!

English

(Name of goddess), blessed by the libation of this milk,
be benevolent and propitious
to me, to my household and to my family!

Then pour the libation to fire, or to the ground, and drink the rest of the milk.

Libation of milk to multiple female deities

Take some wine and pray the following words aloud:

Latin

(Name of goddesses), macte hoc lacte libando
estote fitote volentes propitiae
mihi domo familiae!

English

(Name of goddesses), blessed by the libation of this milk,
be benevolent and propitious
to me, to my household and to my family!

Then pour the libation to fire, or to the ground, and drink the rest of the milk.

8 ANCESTRAL AND HOUSEHOLD WORSHIP

Worship of deceased ancestors and household deities is the core of Roman religious life. If you want to be a pious Roman, which must be the most important goal of all true Romans, you have to start to honor your ancestors, the Manes, and your household deities, the Lares and Penates by prayers and sacrificial offerings. Read more about Roman household worship...

As for now, we will offer you here some very basic & simple rites just to get started with it.

Offering sacrifice to the Manes, Lares and Penates

You may offer many things, but typical offerings are: incense, wine, milk, sacrificial cakes, flower.

Approach the lararium, perform a simple adoratio by kissing your right hand and touching the lararium.

Cover your head, preferably with your toga or palla, but anything will do it and will be acceptable.

You can pray to the Manes, Lares and Penates at once, or separately. You can also invoke any of them personally, by on his or her name. If you wish, invoke your deceased ancestors, parents or relatives using their names. Invoke your personal household Lar by using the words "Lar familiaris". Invoke your personal god of the penates by using the god's name, e.g. Apollo, Minerva, Furrina etc.

Pray the following words aloud:

Latin

Manes/Lares/Penates/NN, macte
(a) hoc vino/lacte/libo libando
(b) hoc thure obmovendo
(c) hoc flore dato
estote fitote volentes propitii
mihi domo familiae!

English

Manes/Lares/Penates/NN, blessed
(a) by the libation of this wine/milk/cake
(b) by the offering of this incense
(c) by giving you this flower
be benevolent and propitious
to me, to my household and to my family!

Then pour the libation and put the sacrifices into the fire of the lararium, or if you cannot burn them, place the items on a plate on your lararium for that day, and when you can, bury or place them under an arbor felix.

Simple request to a deity

Since you are a starter and probably don't know Latin, you can formulate your special request to a deity in your own native language. Ideally, it should be in Latin, and we encourage you to learn this wonderful language of our spiritual ancestors, but it is not forbidden to use another language when you pray and you don't know Latin.

Such prayers consist of two main parts: the formulation of your request, and the offering of sacrifice in order to convince the deity to fulfill your request. It may contain a third part, a vow, in which you offer another sacrifice in the case if the god completes your request.

Invoke the god or gods whom you want to ask something. An effective invocation is to chant the divine name(s) three times aloud.

Formulate your request in your native language if you don't know Latin. Make sure that your prayer is essentially short, concise, very precise and accurate, and use synonyms and repetitions (e.g.: "I ask you, I pray you, I beseech you...", "...give me, lend me, allow me that..."; "...save me from any harm, any damage, any danger...").

When you finished the prayer with your request, use the following Latin formula to offer your sacrifice:

Latin

(1.a) **Cuius rei ergo, macte**
(1.b) **Quarum rerum ergo, macte**
(2.a) **hoc vino/lacte/libo libando**
(2.b) **hoc thure obmovendo**
(2.c) **hoc flore dato**
(3.a) **esto fito volens propitius**
(3.b) **esto fito volens propitia**
(3.c) **estote fitote volentes propitii**
(3.d) **estote fitote volentes propitiae**
(4) **mihi domo familiae!**

English

(1.a) **For the sake of this request, blessed**
(1.b) **For the sake of these requests, blessed**
(2.a) **by the libation of this wine/milk/cake**
(2.b) **by the offering of this incense**
(2.c) **by giving you this flower**
(3.a) **be benevolent and propitious (praying to a male god)**

(3.b) be benevolent and propitious (praying to a goddess)
(3.c) be benevolent and propitious (praying to many gods)
(3.d) be benevolent and propitious (praying to many goddesses)
(4) to me, to my household and to my family!

Then pour the libation and put the sacrifices into the fire of the lararium, or if you cannot burn them, place the items on a plate on your lararium for that day, and when you can, bury or place them under an arbor felix.

In Latin or not in Latin...that is the Question?

There is amongst the members of the cultus deorum Romanum a question of whether the deities of Roman hear and consider any prayers spoken in languages other than Latin. Some say yes, and some say no. The Author poses this scenario:

You are a Celt or a Briton, born at the time of Roman occupation. You choose to accept the gods of Rome. You do not speak Latin yet, but in the last battle of your village and tribe with Legio II Adiutrix, your village did not win...you got whipped...and badly!

As a result, it is your personal belief that the Roman gods are stronger and more powerful than your tribal gods...otherwise, your village would have won, so you accept the Roman gods into your personal pantheon.

Now, can you offer prayers and sacrifices to the Roman dieties...or do you have to wait until you become fluent in Latin, both in the spoken and written word?

The nature of this scenario eliminates the NO option, as most people of that time NEVER learned to read or write Latin, and only a minority learned to speak the language. The Gods hear ALL languages in the opinion of the Author You have to decide the answer to this question on your own.

9 DAILY RITUALS

These rituals, as well as the ones that follow, are presented in English, with the Latin translations omitted. As you become educated in the Latin language, you may choose to make your offering in Latin, but a lack of proficiency in the Latin language should not be a hindrance in performing your religious obligations. The rituals presented here are from the Author's own book of household rituals, and serve as a guide and example for the practitioner. In most cases, the author uses stick incense in the traditional scents (Frankincense, Myrrh and Sandalwood), broken into small pieces for ritual use, instead of resin incense as to be economical.

You may choose to offer wine, milk, honeyed milk, flowers, etc., depending on the deity honored. As a member of the private cultus, you are welcomed and encourage to formulate your own rituals, should you so desire. In the *sacra private*, or private rites, there are NO required formulae for the offering of prayers and devotions to the gods and goddesses of Rome. You may formulate your prayers and devotions as you wish, but you should make an offering of some kind as a gesture of your faithfulness and household duty and responsibility. Again, for private rites, there are NO set or required formulae. Rites may be simple or elaborate, based on your own beliefs, time requirement, economic resources, etc. You may choose the more formal ritus Romanus, or the leff formal and creative approach with the ritus Graecus. You are building your own personal traditions in you household.

In the ancient Roman world, it was traditional to make an offering twice daily, in the Morning and in the Evening. Given our modern schedules and commitments, this is not always possible, so the Daily Lararium Ritual is provided and should be used, or your own variation, when you choose to offer one single daily ritual, instead of the Morning and Evening Lararium Rituals.

Ablutio Before Performing Rituals

Wash both hands in clean water and in capite velato (covered head) pray:

May this water cast out all impurities from my substance as from lead to gold.

May this water cleanse my body of impurities, as the rain cleanses the air.

Purify my mind.

Purify my body.

Purify my heart.

It is so.

DAILY LARARIUM RITUAL
(ritus Graecus)

Incense is placed in the focus of the altar.

Be you well and blessed, O Father Ianus, O Household Gods, and all Gods immortal! I offer incense and pray good prayers to you, Father Ianus, so that the incense find favor with You that all things beneficent and auspicious may be with us in beginning this day; Father Apollo, that You watch over the health and healing of me, my family, and my household, and grant us good health and long life; Mother Iuno, that You watch over our family and guide us down the correct path; Mother Vesta, that Your flames always guide us to the Gods, may Your flames always warm our home and our hearts, and may all be well this day and night in the House of the (Your Family Name); Manes, Lares et Penates, may You always preserve and maintain our house and household, and may You watch over us this day and bless us with a restful sleep this night. Genius of the Paterfamilias, may You guide us to all things joyous and fortunate this day, blessing us this night with fortuitous dreams of the coming day; and, that you be benevolent and propitious to me, to my family to my household.

Other prayers offered here.

O Father Ianus, O Household Gods, and all Gods Immortal by whatever name I may call you: as by offering to you the incense virtuous prayers were well prayed. If anything in this ceremony was displeasing to you, with the sacrificial incense I ask forgiveness and expiate my fault. May everything I do and say this day bring honor and happiness on me, on my family, and on the Gods.

Incense is placed in the focus of the altar.

It is done!

MORNING LARARIUM RITUAL
(ritus Graecus)

Incense is placed in the focus of the altar.

Be you well and blessed, O Father Ianus, O Household Gods, and all Gods immortal! I offer incense and pray good prayers to you, Father Ianus, so that the incense find favor with You that all things beneficient and auspicious may be with us in beginning this day; Father Apollo, that You watch over the health and healing of me, my family, and my household, and grant us good health and long life; Mother Iuno, that You watch over our family and guide us down the correct path; Mother Vesta, that Your flames always guide us to the Gods, may Your flames always warm our home and our hearts, and may all be well this day in the Domus of the (Your Family Name); Manes, Lares et Penates, may You always preserve and maintain our house and household, and may You watch over us this day. Genius of the Paterfamilias, may You guide us to all things joyous and fortunate this day; and, I pray and beseech you to be benevolent and propitious to me, to my family to my household.

Other prayers offered here.

O Father Ianus, O Household Gods, and all Gods Immortal by whatever name I may call you: as by offering to you the incense virtuous prayers were well prayed. If anything in this ceremony was displeasing to you, with the sacrificial incense I ask forgiveness and expiate my fault. May everything I do and say this day bring honor and happiness on me, on my family, and on the Gods.

Incense is placed in the focus of the altar.

It is done!

EVENING LARARIUM RITUAL
(ritus Graecus)

Incense is placed in the focus of the altar.

Be you well and blessed, O Father Ianus, O Household Gods, and all Gods immortal! I offer incense and pray good prayers to you, Father Ianus, so that the incense find favor with You that all things beneficient and auspicious may be with us in the coming Morrow; Father Apollo, that You watch over the health and healing of me, my family, and my household, and grant us good health and long life; Mother Iuno, that You watch over our family and guide us down the correct path; Mother Vesta, that Your flames always guide us to the Gods, may Your flames always warm our home and our hearts, and may all be well this night in the Domus of the (Your Family Name); Manes, Lares et Penates, may You always preserve and maintain our house and household, and may You watch over us and bless us with a restful sleep this night. Genius of the Paterfamilias, may You guide us to all things joyous and fortunate in the coming Morrow, blessing us this night with fortuitous dreams of the coming day; and, I pray and beseech you to be benevolent and propitious to me, to my family to my household.

Other prayers offered here.

O Father Ianus, O Household Gods, and all Gods Immortal by whatever name I may call you: as by offering to you the incense virtuous prayers were well prayed. If anything in this ceremony was displeasing to you, with the sacrificial incense I ask forgiveness and expiate my fault. May everything I do and say this day bring honor and happiness on me, on my family, and on the Gods.

Incense is placed in the focus of the altar.

It is done!

DAILY LARARIUM RITUAL
(ritus Romanus)

(ABLUTIO)

Wash both hands in clean water and in capite velato pray:

May this water cast out all impurities from my substance as from lead to gold. May this water cleanse my body of impurities, as the rain cleanses the air. Purify my mind. Purify my body. Purify my heart. It is so.

(PRAEFATIO)

Be you well and blessed, O Father Ianus, O Household Gods, and all Gods immortal! By offering you this incense, I pray good prayers so that you may be benevolent and propitious to me, my family, and my household.

Incense is placed in the focus of the altar.

(PRECATIO)

Be you well and blessed, O Father Ianus, O Household Gods, and all Gods immortal! I offer incense and pray good prayers to you, Father Ianus, so that the incense find favor with You that all things beneficent and auspicious may be with us in beginning this day; Father Apollo, that You watch over the health and healing of me, my family, and my household, and grant us good health and long life; Mother Iuno, that You watch over our family and guide us down the correct path; Mother Vesta, that Your flames always guide us to the Gods, may Your flames always warm our home and our hearts, and may all be well this day and night in the House of the (Your Family Name); Manes, Lares et Penates, may You always preserve and maintain our house and household, and may You watch over us this day and bless us with a restful sleep this night. Genius of the Paterfamilias, may You guide us to all things joyous and fortunate this day, blessing us this night with fortuitous dreams of the coming day; and, that you be benevolent and propitious to me, to my family to my household.

Other prayers offered here.

Incense is offered in the focus of the altar.

(REDDITIO)

O Father Ianus, O Household Gods, and all Gods Immortal, as by offering to you the incense virtuous prayers were well prayed. For the sake of this be honoured by this incense.

Incense is offered in the focus of the altar.

It is so.

(PIACULUM)

O Father Ianus, O Household Gods, and all Gods Immortal by whatever name I may call you: if anything in this ceremony was displeasing to you, with the sacrificial incense I ask forgiveness and expiate my fault. May everything I do and say this day bring honor and happiness on me, on my family, and on the Gods.

Incense is placed in the focus of the altar.

It is done!

MORNING LARARIUM RITUAL
(ritus Romanus)

(ABLUTIO)

Wash both hands in clean water and in capite velato pray:

May this water cast out all impurities from my substance as from lead to gold. May this water cleanse my body of impurities, as the rain cleanses the air. Purify my mind. Purify my body. Purify my heart. It is so.

(PRAEFATIO)

Be you well and blessed, O Father Ianus, O Household Gods, and all Gods immortal! By offering you this incense, I pray good prayers so that you may be benevolent and propitious to me, my family, and my household.

Incense is placed in the focus of the altar.

(PRECATIO)

Be you well and blessed, O Father Ianus, O Household Gods, and all Gods immortal! I offer incense and pray good prayers to you, Father Ianus, so that the incense find favor with You that all things beneficient and auspicious may be with us in beginning this day; Father Apollo, that You watch over the health and healing of me, my family, and my household, and grant us good health and long life; Mother Iuno, that You watch over our family and guide us down the correct path; Mother Vesta, that Your flames always guide us to the Gods, may Your flames always warm our home and our hearts, and may all be well this day in the Domus of the (Your Family Name); Manes, Lares et Penates, may You always preserve and maintain our house and household, and may You watch over us this day. Genius of the Paterfamilias, may You guide us to all things joyous and fortunate this day; and, I pray and beseech you to be benevolent and propitious to me, to my

family to my household.

Other prayers offered here.

Incense is offered in the focus of the altar.

(REDDITIO)

O Father Ianus, O Household Gods, and all Gods Immortal, as by offering to you the incense virtuous prayers were well prayed. For the sake of this be honoured by this incense.

Incense is offered in the focus of the altar.

It is so.

(PIACULUM)

O Father Ianus, O Household Gods, and all Gods Immortal by whatever name I may call you: if anything in this ceremony was displeasing to you, with the sacrificial incense I ask forgiveness and expiate my fault. May everything I do and say this day bring honor and happiness on me, on my family, and on the Gods.

Incense is placed in the focus of the altar.

It is done!

EVENING LARARIUM RITUAL
(ritus Romanus)

(ABLUTIO)

Wash both hands in clean water and in capite velato pray:

May this water cast out all impurities from my substance as from lead to gold. May this water cleanse my body of impurities, as the rain cleanses the air. Purify my mind. Purify my body. Purify my heart. It is so.

(PRAEFATIO)

Be you well and blessed, O Father Ianus, O Household Gods, and all Gods immortal! By offering you this incense, I pray good prayers so that you may be benevolent and propitious to me, my family, and my household.

Incense is placed in the focus of the altar.

(PRECATIO)

Be you well and blessed, O Father Ianus, O Household Gods, and all Gods immortal! I offer incense and pray good prayers to you, Father Ianus, so that the incense find favor with You that all things beneficient and auspicious may be with us in the coming Morrow; Father Apollo, that You watch over the health and healing of me, my family, and my household, and grant us good health and long life; Mother Iuno, that You watch over our family and guide us down the correct path; Mother Vesta, that Your flames always guide us to the Gods, may Your flames always warm our home and our hearts, and may all be well this night in the Domus of the (Your Family Name); Manes, Lares et Penates, may You always preserve and maintain our house and household, and may You watch over us and bless us with a restful sleep this night. Genius of the Paterfamilias, may You guide us to all things joyous and fortunate in the coming Morrow, blessing us this night with fortuitous dreams of the coming day; and, I pray and beseech you to be benevolent and propitious to me, to my family to my household.

Other prayers offered here.

Incense is offered in the focus of the altar.

(REDDITIO)

O Father Ianus, O Household Gods, and all Gods Immortal, as by offering to you the incense virtuous prayers were well prayed. For the sake of this be honoured by this incense.

Incense is offered in the focus of the altar.

It is so.

(PIACULUM)

O Father Ianus, O Household Gods, and all Gods Immortal by whatever name I may call you: if anything in this ceremony was displeasing to you, with the sacrificial incense I ask forgiveness and expiate my fault. May everything I have done and said this day bring honor and happiness on me, on my family, and on the Gods.

Incense is placed in the focus of the altar.

It is done!

10 KALENDS RITUAL

Preparation

This ritual is performed in clean clothing; if possible, a clean tunica and toga are best, even better if they are white. The toga should be worn capite velato (with the head covered), so as to veil the performer from any and all ill omens that might present themselves in the course of the ritual. **Performed on Jan 1, Feb 1, Mar 1, Apr 1, May 1, Jun 1, Jul 1, Aug 1, Sep 1, Oct 1, Nov 1 & Dec 1.**

Ritual

(ABLUTIO)

Wash both hands in clean water and in capite velato pray:

May this water cast out all impurities from my substance as from lead to gold. May this water cleanse my body of impurities, as the rain cleanses the air. Purify my mind. Purify my body. Purify my heart. It is so.

(PRAEFATIO)

Be you well and blessed, O Father Ianus, O Mother Iuno Limentina, O Lar familiaris, on these Kalends! By offering you this incense, I pray good prayers so that you may be benevolent and propitious to me, my family, and my household.

Incense is placed in the focus of the altar.

(PRECATIO)

O Father Ianus, O Mother Iuno Limentina, O Lar familiaris, on these Kalends, with this offering of wine I pray, worship, ask and beseech you so that you may confirm, strengthen and help my family and household and save it from all discord; Listen, You Gods and Goddesses of our ancestors, who cherish this City, this neighborhood, and sacred places within it. Gods and Goddesses of our forefathers, I make this offering of wine to You and pray with a sincere heart that You will look favorably upon us and our children, on our house and on our household; and so that my family and household may always flourish and prosper, and so that you may be benevolent and propitious to my friends, to me, to my household and to my family.

A libation of wine is poured on the altar.

(REDDITIO)

O Father Ianus, as by offering to you the incense virtuous prayers were well prayed. For the sake of this be honoured by this humble offering of wine.

A libation of wine is poured on the altar.

O Mother Iuno Limentina, as by offering to you the incense virtuous prayers were well prayed. For the sake of this be honoured by this humble offering of wine.

A libation of wine is poured on the altar.

O Lar familiaris, as by offering to you the incense virtuous prayers were well prayed. For the sake of this be honoured by this humble offering of wine.

A libation of wine is poured on the altar.

It is so.

(PIACULUM)

O Mother Iuno Limentina, O Lar familiaris, and all Gods Immortal by whatever name I may call you: if anything in this ceremony was displeasing to you, with the sacrificial incense I ask forgiveness and expiate my fault.

Incense is placed in the focus of the altar.

Good Days and Bad Days

The first day of every month is the Kalends, sacred to Juno. The Kalends ritual is usually celebrated early in the morning (before breakfast) by the head of the household. Bathe and offer incense and prayers to Iuno at your lararium. The Nones is on the 5th day and the Ides, sacred to Jupiter, is on the 13th day of every month except March, May, July and October. They are on the 7th and 15th of these months. The day following each of the Kalends, Nones and Ides is an unlucky day (dies ater, plural, dies atri). On these days:

- **Gods or Goddesses should not be invoked by name while indoors**

- **No celestial God or Goddess should be invoked by name while outdoors.**

- **Sacrifices and religious rites should not be made.**

- **You should avoid doing anything risky or making journeys.**

- **New projects should not be started on these days since any new project would necessarily begin by performing a rite calling for the assistance of the gods.**

11 NONES RITUAL

Preparation

This ritual is performed in clean clothing; if possible, a clean tunica and toga are best, even better if they are white. The toga should be draped in capite velato, so as to veil the performer from any and all ill omens that might present themselves in the course of the ritual. **Performed on Jan 5, Feb 5, Mar 7, Apr 5, May 7, Jun 5, Jul 7, Aug 5, Sep 5, Oct 7, Nov 5 & Dec 5.**

Ritual

(ABLUTIO)

Wash both hands in clean water and in capite velato pray:

May this water cast out all impurities from my substance as from lead to gold. May this water cleanse my body of impurities, as the rain cleanses the air. Purify my mind. Purify my body. Purify my heart. It is so.

(PRAEFATIO)

Be you well and blessed, O Lar familiaris, on these Nones! By offering you this incense, I pray good prayers so that you may be benevolent and propitious to me, my family, and my household.

Incense is placed in the focus of the altar.

(PRECATIO)

O Lar familiaris, on these Nones, with this offering of wine I pray, worship, ask and beseech you so that you may confirm, strengthen and help my family and household and save it from all discord; so that my family and household may always flourish and prosper, and so that you may be benevolent and propitious to me, my family, and my household.

A libation of wine is poured on the altar.

(REDDITIO)

O Lar familiaris, as by offering to you the incense virtuous prayers were well prayed. For the sake of this be honoured by this humble offering of wine.

A libation of wine is poured on the altar.

It is so.

(PIACULUM)

O Lar familiaris, and all Gods Immortal by whatever name I may call you: if anything in this ceremony was displeasing to you, with the sacrificial incense I ask forgiveness and expiate my fault.

Incense is placed in the focus of the altar.

It is done!

12 IDES RITUAL

Preparation

This ritual is performed in clean clothing; if possible, a clean tunica and toga are best, even better if they are white. The toga should be draped in capite velato, so as to veil the performer from any and all ill omens that might present themselves in the course of the ritual. **Performed on Jan 13, Feb 13, Mar 15, Apr 13, May 15, Jun 13, Jul 15, Aug 13, Sep 13, Oct 15, Nov 13 & Dec 13.**

Ritual

(ABLUTIO)

Wash both hands in clean water and in capite velato pray:

May this water cast out all impurities from my substance as from lead to gold. May this water cleanse my body of impurities, as the rain cleanses the air. Purify my mind. Purify my body. Purify my heart. It is so.

(PRAEFATIO)

Be you well and blessed, O Father Iuppiter, O Lar familiaris, on these Ides! By offering you this incense, I pray good prayers so that you may be benevolent and propitious to my friends, to me, to my household and to my family.

Incense is placed in the focus of the altar.

(PRECATIO)

O Father Iuppiter, O Lar familiaris, on these Ides, with this offering of wine I pray, worship, ask and beseech you so that you may confirm, strengthen and help my family and household and save it from all discord; so that my family and household may always flourish and prosper, and so that you may be benevolent and propitious to me, my family, and my household.

A libation of wine is poured on the altar.

(REDDITIO)

O Father Iuppiter, O Lar familiaris, as by offering to you the incense virtuous prayers were well prayed. For the sake of this be honoured by this humble offering of wine.

A libation of wine is poured on the altar.

It is so.

(PIACULUM)

O Father Iuppiter, O Lar familiaris, and all Gods Immortal by whatever name I may call you: if anything in this ceremony was displeasing to you, with the sacrificial incense I ask forgiveness and expiate my fault.

Incense is placed in the focus of the altar.

It is done!

13 OTHER RITUALS

The following rituals are provided for your use and are just a portion of those possible that one might offer during the year. They are written in ritus Romanus format, but you may simplify them to ritus Graecus format, should you choose:

- **Ritual for the New Year**
- **Dies Natalis Ritual**
- **Rite of Marriage Ritual (Coemptio)**
- **Wedding Anniversary Ritual (by Officiant)**
- **Wedding Anniversary Ritual (by Pater familias)**
- **Pregnancy Ritual (by Mother)**
- **Pregnancy Ritual (by Sacerdos/Priestess)**
- **Birth of a Child Ritual**
- **Naming of a Child Ritual (Solemnitas nominalium or Dies lustricus)**
- **Loss of a Child Ritual**
- **Liberalia Ritual & Ceremony (Son)**
- **Liberalia Ritual & Ceremony (Daughter)**
- **Travel Ritual**
- **New Business Ritual**
- **Funeral Ritual**

RITUAL FOR THE NEW YEAR

Performed on the Kalends of Ianuarius (Jan. 1)

(ABLUTIO)

Wash both hands in clean water and in capite velato pray:

May this water cast out all impurities from my substance as from lead to gold. May this water cleanse my body of impurities, as the rain cleanses the air. Purify my mind. Purify my body. Purify my heart. It is so.

(PRAEFATIO)

Father Ianus, God of the New Beginning, by offering you this incense I pray good prayers so that you be benevolent and propitious to me, to my friends, to my household and to my family.

Incense is placed in the focus of the altar.

_____ (name of another deity – repeated for each deity invoked), by offering you this incense I pray good prayers so that you be benevolent and propitious to me, to my friends, to my household and to my family.

Incense is placed in the focus of the altar.

(PRECATIO)

Father Ianus, God of the New Beginning, Most Sacred Guardian of the future and past, on this first day of the New Year, Kalends of January, I pray and ask you so that you give gladness and fortune, a good and prosperous, successful and most happy progress of events, peace and concord to the Roman peoples, the Quirites, and to my own family; and that you be benevolent and propitious to the Roman peoples, the Quirites, to my friends, to me, to my household and to my

family. For this reason, thou blessed by offering this wine, by offering this incense be benevolent and propitious to the Roman peoples, the Quirites, to my friends, to me, to my household and to my family.

Incense is placed in the focus of the altar.

(REDDITIO)

Father Ianus, God of the New Beginning, as by offering to you the incense virtuous prayers were well prayed.

Incense is offered in the focus of the altar.

_____(name of other deity invoked – repeated for each deity invoked), as by offering to you the incense virtuous prayers were well prayed.

Incense is offered in the focus of the altar.

It is so.

(PIACULUM)

Father Ianus, God of the New Beginning, _____(names of all other deities invoked), Lares, Manes, Penates, Iuppiter, Iuno, Minerva, All Gods Immortal, by whichever name: if something in this ceremony was unpleasant to you, by this wine I do apogize and expiate my mistake.

Incense is placed in the focus of the altar.

It is done!

DIES NATALIS RITUAL

Performed on One's Birthday

(ABLUTIO)

Wash both hands in clean water and in capite velato pray:

May this water cast out all impurities from my substance as from lead to gold. May this water cleanse my body of impurities, as the rain cleanses the air. Purify my mind. Purify my body. Purify my heart. It is so.

(PRAEFATIO)

Be you well and blessed, O Father Ianus, on this, my Dies natalis, by offering you this incense, I pray good prayers so that you may be benevolent and propitious to me, my family, and my household.

Incense is placed in the focus of the altar.

Be you well and blessed, O Genius paterfamilias (Iuno materfamilias), on this, my Dies natalis, by offering you this incense, I pray good prayers so that you may be benevolent and propitious to me, my family, and my household.

Incense is placed in the focus of the altar.

(PRECATIO)

O protectors, I pray and beseech thee that you may be gracious and favorable to me, my family, and my household, for which course I have ordained that the offering of this (wine/milk) and incense should be made in accordance with my own vows; that you may avert, ward off, and keep afar all disease visible and invisible, all barrenness, waste, misfortune, and ill weather; that you may cause my family, affairs and business to come to prosperity; and that you grant health and strength to me, my home and my household.

A libation of wine/milk is poured on the altar.
Incense is placed in the focus of the altar.

(REDDITIO)

O Father Ianus, as by offering to you the incense virtuous prayers were well prayed. For the sake of this be honoured by this humble wine.

A libation of wine is poured on the altar.

O Genius Paterfamilias (Iuno Materfamilias), as by offering to you the incense virtuous prayers were well prayed. For the sake of this be honoured by this humble (wine/milk).

A libation of wine/milk is poured on the altar.
End of the sacrifice.

It is so.

(PIACULUM)

O Father Ianus, O Genius Paterfamilias (Iuno Materfamilias), and all Gods Immortal by whatever name I may call you: if anything in this ceremony was displeasing to you, with the sacrificial incense I ask forgiveness and expiate my fault.

Incense is placed in the focus of the altar.

It is done!

RITE OF MARRIAGE RITUAL (Coemptio)

*Ceremony adapted from **The Private Life of the Romans** by Harold Whetstone Johnston and Mary Johnston, and **Roman Antiquities** by Alexander Adam.*

Coemptio was one of three (3) types of marriage ceremonies. Elements of the coemptio ceremony were borrowed from the older Patrician Confarreatio Ceremony, which required the presence of the Pontifex Maximus and Flamen Dialis and is thus not possible to perform this confarreate ceremony today. The third form of wedding ceremony, that is, the ceremonies preliminary to Usus, probably admitted of more variation than either of the others, but no description has come down to us. We may be sure that the hands were clasped, the words of consent spoken, and congratulations offered, but we know of no special customs or usages. It was almost inevitable that the three forms should become more or less alike in the course of time, though the cake of spelt could not be borrowed from the confarreate ceremony by either of the others, or the scales and their holder from the ceremony of coemptio.

DEVELOPMENT AND PRACTICES OF ROMAN MARRIAGE

Early Forms of Marriage. Polygamy was never sanctioned at Rome, and we are told that for five centuries after the founding of the city divorce was entirely unknown. Up to the time of the Servian constitution (traditional date, sixth century B.C.) patricians were the only citizens and intermarried only with patricians and with members of surrounding communities having like social standing. The only form of marriage known to them was called confarreatio. With the consent of the gods, while the pontifices celebrated the solemn rites, in the presence of the accredited representatives of his gens, the patrician took his wife from her father's family into his own, to be a mater familias, to bear him children who should conserve the family mysteries, perpetuate his ancient race, and extend the power of Rome. By this, the one legal form of marriage of the time, the wife passed in manum viri, and the husband acquired over her practically the same rights as he would have over his own children and other dependent members of his family. Such a marriage was said to be cum conventione uxoris in manum viri.

During this period, too, the free non-citizens, the plebeians, had been busy in marrying and giving in marriage. There is little doubt that their unions had been as sacred in their eyes, their family ties as strictly regarded and as pure as those of the patricians, but these unions were unhallowed by the national gods and unrecognized by the civil law, simply because the plebeians were not yet citizens. Their form of marriage, called usus, consisted essentially in the living together continuously of the man and woman as husband and wife, though there were probably conventional forms and observances, about which we know absolutely nothing. The plebeian husband might acquire the same rights over the person and property of his wife as the patrician, but the form of marriage did not in itself involve manus. The wife might remain a member of her father's family and retain such property as he allowed her by merely absenting herself from her husband for the space of a trinoctium, that is, three nights in succession, each year. If she did this, the marriage was sine conventione in manum, and the husband had no control over her property; if she did not, the marriage, like that of the patricians, was cum conventione in manum.

Another Roman form of marriage goes at least as far back as the time of Servius. This was also plebeian, though not so ancient as usus. It was called coemptio and was a fictitious sale, by which the pater familias of the woman, or her tutor, if she was subject to one, transferred her to the man matrimonii causa. This form must have been a survival of the old custom of purchase and sale of wives, but we do not know when it was introduced among the Romans. It carried manus with it as a matter of course, and seems to have been regarded socially as better form than usus. The two existed for centuries side by side, but coemptio survived usus as a form of marriage cum conventione in manum.

Iūs Cōnūbiī. Though the Servian constitution made the plebeians citizens and thereby legalized their forms of marriage, it did not give them the right of intermarriage with the patricians. Many of the plebeian families were hardly less ancient than the patricians, many were rich and powerful, but it was not until 445 B.C. that marriages between the two Orders were formally sanctioned by the civil law. The objection on the part of the patricians was largely a religious one: the gods of the State were gods of the patricians, the auspices could be taken by patricians only, the marriages of patricians only were sanctioned by heaven. Their orators protested that the unions of the plebeians were not marriages at all, not iustae nuptiae; the plebeian wife, they insisted, was only taken in matrimonium: she was at best only an uxor, not a mater familias; her offspring were "mother's children," not patricii.

Much of this was class exaggeration, but it is true that for a long time the gens was not so highly valued by the plebeians as by the patricians, and that the plebeians assigned to cognates certain duties and privileges that devolved upon the patrician gentiles. With the extension of the ius conubii many of these points of difference disappeared. New conditions were fixed for iustae nuptiae; coemptio by a sort of compromise became the usual form of marriage when one of the parties was a plebeian; and the stigma disappeared from the word matrimonium. On the other hand, patrician women learned to understand the advantages of a marriage sine conventione in manum, and marriage with manus grew less frequent, the taking of the auspices before the ceremony came to be considered a mere form, and marriage began to lose its sacramental character. With these changes came later the laxness in the marital relation and the freedom of divorce that seemed in the time of Augustus to threaten the very life of the commonwealth.

It is probable that by the time of Cicero marriage with manus was uncommon, and consequently that confarreatio and coemptio had gone out of general use. To a limited extent, however, the former was retained into Christian times, because certain priestly offices (those of the flamines maiores and the reges sacrorum) could be filled only by persons whose parents had been married by the confarreate ceremony, the sacramental form, and who had themselves been married by the same form. Augustus offered exemption from manus to mothers of three children, but this was not enough, for so great became the reluctance of women to submit to manus that in order to fill even these few priestly offices it was found necessary under Tiberius to eliminate manus from the confarreate ceremony.

Iustae Nuptiae. There were certain conditions that had to be satisfied before a legal marriage could be contracted even by citizens. The requirements were as follows:

(1) The consent of both parties should be given, or that of the pater familias if one or both were in patria potestate. Under Augustus it was provided that the pater familias should not withhold his consent unless he could show valid reasons for doing so.

(2) Both of the parties should be puberes; there could be no marriage between children. Although no precise age was fixed by law, it is probable that fourteen and twelve were the lowest limit for the man and the woman respectively.

(3) Both man and woman should be unmarried. Polygamy was never sanctioned at Rome.

(4) The parties should not be nearly related. The restrictions in this direction were fixed by public opinion rather than by law and varied greatly at different times, becoming gradually less severe. In general it may be said that marriage was absolutely forbidden between ascendants and descendants, between other cognates within the sixth (later the fourth) degree, and between the nearer adfines.

If the parties could satisfy these conditions, they might be legally married, but distinctions were still made that affected the civil status of the children, although no doubt was cast upon their legitimacy or upon the moral character of their parents.

If the conditions named above were fulfilled and the husband and wife were both Roman citizens, their marriage was called iustae nuptiae, which we may translate by "regular marriage." The children of such a marriage were iusti liberi and were by birth cives optimo iure, "possessed of all civil rights."

If one of the parties was a Roman citizen and the other a member of a community having the ius conubii but not full Roman civitas, the marriage was still called iustae nuptiae, but the children took the civil standing of the father. This means that, if the father was a citizen and the mother a foreigner, the children were citizens, but, if the father was a foreigner and the mother a citizen, the children were foreigners (peregrini), as was their father.

But if either of the parties was without the ius conubii, the marriage, though still legal, was called iniustae nuptiae or iniustum matrimonium, "an irregular marriage," and the children, though legitimate, took the civil position of the parent of lower degree. We seem to have something analogous to this today in the loss of social standing which usually follows the marriage of one person with another of distinctly inferior position.

Betrothals. Formal betrothal (sponsalia) as a preliminary to marriage was considered good form but was not legally necessary and carried with it no obligations that could be enforced by law. In the sponsalia the maiden was promised to the man as his bride with "words of style," that is, in solemn form. The promise was made, not by the maiden herself, but by her pater familias, or by her tutor if she was not in patria potestate. In the same way, the promise was made to the man directly only in case he was sui iuris; otherwise it was made to the Head of his House, who had asked for him the maiden in marriage. The "words of style" were probably something like this:

"Spondesne Gaiam, tuam filiam (or, if she was a ward, Gaiam, Luciī filiam), mihi (or filio meo) uxorem dari?"

"Di bene vortant! Spondeo."

"Di bene vortant!"

At any rate, the word spondeo was technically used of the promise, and the maiden was henceforth sponsa. The person who made the promise had always the right to cancel it. This was usually done through an intermediary (nuntius); hence the formal expression for breaking an engagement was repudium renuntiare, or simply renuntiare. While the contract was entirely one-sided, it should be noticed that a man was liable to infamia if he formed two engagements at the same time, and that he could not recover any presents made with a view to a future marriage if he himself broke the engagement. Such presents were almost always made. Though we find that articles for personal use, the toilet, etc., were common, a ring was usually given. The ring was worn on the third finger of the left hand, because it was believed that a nerve (or sinew) ran directly from this finger to the heart. It was also usual for the spōnsa to make a present to her betrothed.

The Dowry. It was a point of honor with the Romans, as it is now with some European peoples, for the bride to bring to her husband a dowry (dos, Modem French dot). In the case of a girl in patria potestate this would be furnished by the Head of her House; in the case of one sui iuris it was furnished from her own property, or, if she had none, was contributed by her relatives. It seems that if they were reluctant she might by process of law compel her ascendants at least to furnish it. In early times, when marriage cum conventione prevailed, all the property brought by the bride became the property of her husband, or of his pater familias, but in later times, when manus was less common, and especially after divorce had become of frequent occurrence, a distinction was made. A part of the bride's possessions was reserved for her own exclusive use, and a part was made over to the groom under the technical name of dos. The relative proportions varied, of course, with circumstances.

Essential Forms. There were really no legal forms necessary for the solemnization of a marriage; there was no license to be procured from the civil authorities; the ceremonies, simple or elaborate, did not have to be performed by persons authorized by the State. It has been remarked that the pater familias could refuse his consent for valid reasons only; on the other hand, he could command the consent of persons subject to him. Parental and filial affection (pietas) made this hardship much less rigorous than it now seems to us.

But, though this consent was the only condition for a legal marriage, it had to be shown by some act of personal union between the parties, that is, the marriage could not be entered into by letter or by messenger or by proxy. Such a public act was the joining of hands (dextrarum iunctio) in the presence of witnesses, or the bride's act in letting herself be escorted to her husband's house, never omitted when the parties had any social standing, or, in later times, the signing of the marriage contract. It was never necessary to a valid marriage that the parties should live together as man and wife, though, as we have seen, this living together of itself constituted a legal marriage.

The Wedding Day. It will be noticed that superstition played an important part in the arrangements for a wedding two thousand years ago, as it does now. Especial pains had to be taken to secure a lucky day. The Kalends, Nones, and Ides of each month, and the day following each of them, were unlucky. So was all of May and the first half of June, on account of certain religious ceremonies observed in these months, in May the Argean offerings and the Lemuria, in June the dies religiosi connected with Vesta. Besides these, the dies parentales, February 13-21, and the days when the entrance to the lower world was supposed to be open, August 24, October 5, and November 8, were carefully avoided. One-third of the year, therefore, was absolutely barred. The great holidays, too, and these were legion, were avoided, not because they were unlucky, but because on these days friends and relatives were sure to have other engagements. Women being married for the second time chose these very holidays to make their weddings less conspicuous.

The Wedding Garments. On the eve of her wedding day the bride dedicated to the Lares of her father's house her bulla and toga praetexta, which married women did not wear, and also, if she was not much over twelve years of age, her childish playthings. For the sake of the omen she put on before going to sleep the tunica recta, or tunica regilla, woven in one piece and falling to the feet. It was said to have derived the name recta from being woven in the old fashioned way at an upright loom, though some authorities have thought it so called because it hung straight, not being bloused over at the belt. This same tunic was worn at the wedding.

On the morning of the wedding day the bride was dressed for the ceremony by her mother. The chief article of dress was the tunica recta already mentioned, which was fastened around the waist with a band of wool tied in the knot of Hercules (nodus Herculaneus), probably because Hercules was the guardian of wedded life. This knot the husband only was privileged to untie. Over the tunic was worn the bridal veil, the flame-colored veil (flammeum). So important was the veil of the bride that nubere, "to veil oneself," is the word regularly used for the marriage of a woman.

Especial attention was given to the arrangement of the hair. It was divided into six locks by the point of a spear, or comb of that shape, a practice surviving, probably, from ancient marriage by capture; these locks, perhaps braided, were kept in position by ribbons (vittae). As the Vestals wore the hair thus arranged, it must have been an extremely early fashion, at any rate. The bride had also a wreath of flowers and sacred plants gathered by herself. The groom wore, of course, the toga and had a similar wreath of flowers on his head. He was accompanied to the home of the bride at the proper time by relatives, friends, and clients, who were bound to do him every honor on his wedding day.

The Ceremony. In connection with the marriage ceremonies it must be remembered that only the consent was necessary, with the act expressing the consent, and that all other forms and ceremonies were nonessential and variable. Something depended upon the particular form used, but more upon the wealth and social position of the families interested. It is probable that most weddings were a good deal simpler than those described by our chief authorities. The house of the bride's father, where the ceremony was performed, was decked with flowers, boughs of trees, bands of wool, and tapestries. The guests arrived before the hour of sunrise, but even then the omens had been already taken. In the ancient confarreate ceremony these were taken by the public augur, but in later times, no matter what the ceremony, the haruspices merely consulted the entrails of a sheep which had been killed in sacrifice.

After the omens had been pronounced favorable, the bride and groom appeared in the atrium, the public room of the house, and the wedding began. This consisted of two parts:

(1) The ceremony proper, varying according to the form used (confarreatio, coemptio, or usus), the essential part being the consent before witnesses.

(2) The festivities, including the feast at the bride's home, the taking of the bride with a show of force from her mother's arms, the escorting of the bride to her new home (the essential part), and her reception there.

WEDDING CEREMONY

The coemptio begins with the fictitious mutual sale, carried out in the presence of no fewer than five witnesses, between the bride and the groom (Cic. Orat. i. 57). The purchase money is represented by a coin each from both the Bride and the Groom, which are laid by the Bride and Groom in the scales held by a iībripens. The bride and groom are brought together by the pronuba, a matron but once married and living with her husband in undisturbed wedlock, and presented to the Officiant at the altar.

They join right hands in the presence of the five witnesses.

Then followed the dextrarum iuctio and the words of consent spoken by the bride:

BRIDE: Quando tu Gaius, ego Gaia *(When and where you are Gaius, then and there I am Gaia)*

OFFICIANT: In silence, you will each make your vows to each other.

Once the Bride and Groom have silently made their vows, they then ask for a solemn commitment from each other (Boeth in Cic. Topic. 3; Serv. in Virg. G. i. 31).

GROOM: An sibi mater familias esse vellet? *(Do you wish to be the Mother of the House?)*

BRIDE: Se velle. *(I will.)*

BRIDE: An sibi pater familias esse vellet? *(Do you wish to be the Father of the House?)*

GROOM: Se velle. *(I will.)*

MODERN: The Bride and Groom exchange rings.

ANCIENT: Traditionally, this was not done by the ancients. The Bride only received an engagement ring, which sealed the marriage contract when she accepted it.

The bride and groom then take their places side by side at the left of the altar and facing it, where the officiant offers prayer and sacrifice.

(ABLUTIO)

Officiant washes both hands in clean water and in capite velato pray:

May this water cast out all impurities from my substance as from lead to gold. May this water cleanse my body of

impurities, as the rain cleanses the air. Purify my mind. Purify my body. Purify my heart. It is so.

(PRAEFATIO)

O Ianus, by offering this incense to you I pray good prayers, so that you may be benevolent and propitious to me, my family, and my household.

Incense is placed in the focus of the altar.

O Iuno, by offering this incense to you I pray good prayers, so that you may be benevolent and propitious to me, my family, and my household.

Incense is placed in the focus of the altar.

O Tellus, by offering this incense to you I pray good prayers, so that you may be benevolent and propitious to me, my family, and my household.

Incense is placed in the focus of the altar.

O Picumnus, by offering this incense to you I pray good prayers, so that you may be benevolent and propitious to me, my family, and my household.

Incense is placed in the focus of the altar.

O Pilumnus, by offering this incense to you I pray good prayers, so that you may be benevolent and propitious to me, my family, and my household.

Incense is placed in the focus of the altar.

[LONG VERSION ADDITIONAL VERSES– OPTIONAL]

O Domiduca, by offering this incense to you I pray good prayers, so that you may be benevolent and propitious to me, my family, and my household.

Incense is placed in the focus of the altar.

O Domitius, by offering this incense to you I pray good prayers, so that you may be benevolent and propitious to me, my family, and my household.

Incense is placed in the focus of the altar.

O Unxia, by offering this incense to you I pray good prayers, so that you may be benevolent and propitious to me, my family, and my household.

Incense is placed in the focus of the altar.

O Cinxia, by offering this incense to you I pray good prayers, so that you may be benevolent and propitious to me, my family, and my household.

Incense is placed in the focus of the altar.

O Virginiensis, by offering this incense to you I pray good prayers, so that you may be benevolent and propitious to me, my family, and my household.

Incense is placed in the focus of the altar.

O Subigus, by offering this incense to you I pray good prayers, so that you may be benevolent and propitious to me, my family, and my household.

Incense is placed in the focus of the altar.

O Prema, by offering this incense to you I pray good prayers, so that you may be benevolent and propitious to me, my family, and my household.

Incense is placed in the focus of the altar.

O Pertunda, by offering this incense to you I pray good prayers, so that you may be benevolent and propitious to me, my family, and my household.

Incense is placed in the focus of the altar.

O Venus mater, by offering this incense to you I pray good prayers, so that you may be benevolent and propitious to me, my family, and my household.

Incense is placed in the focus of the altar.

O Priapus, by offering this incense to you I pray good prayers, so that you may be benevolent and propitious to me, my family, and my household.

Incense is placed in the focus of the altar.

O Perficia, by offering this incense to you I pray good prayers, so that you may be benevolent and propitious to me, my family, and my household.

Incense is placed in the focus of the altar.

O Maturna, by offering this incense to you I pray good prayers, so that you may be benevolent and propitious to me, my family, and my household.

Incense is placed in the focus of the altar.

(PRECATIO)

O Father Janus, who was before all the Gods, the god of new beginnings, to whom our parents first invoked in their prayers, from whom all things proceed, be well and blessed. I pray good prayers, offer this wine, and ask that you grant the blessings of a harmonious and successful beginning in the

marriage of (Name of Bride) and (Name of Groom); and, I pray that you may be benevolent and propitious to them, to their household and to their family.

A libation of wine is poured in the focus of the altar.

O Mother Iuno, queen of the gods and protector of women, marriage and birth, be well and blessed. I pray good prayers, offer this wine, and ask that you watch over, guide and direct, and grant the blessings of a happy marriage and long fruitful life together for (Name of Bride) and (Name of Groom), and that healthy children be borne unto them, their family and their household; and, I pray that you may be benevolent and propitious to (Name of Bride) and (Name of Groom), to their household and to their family.

A libation of wine is poured in the focus of the altar.

O Terra mater, Holy Goddess, Mother of all Nature, engendering all things and regenerating them each day, as You alone bring forth from Your womb all things into life, be well and blessed. I pray good prayers, offer this honeyed milk. I call upon Your power, come. Make what I ask to be readily and easily accomplished, and draw my thanks, Mother Earth, that, in fidelity, You do rightly watch over, protect and bless the marriage of (Name of Bride) and (Name of Groom), and grant unto them the fruits of their labors; and, I pray that you may be benevolent and propitious to (Name of Bride) and (Name of Groom), to their household and to their family.

An offering of honeyed milk is placed in the focus of the altar.

O Brothers Pilumnus and Picumnus, be well and blessed. I pray good prayers, offer this wine, and ask you to stimulate the growth of the children to come from this union, avert all sickness, protect mother and unborn child, prevent the mischievous intrusion of Silvanus into the house of the (Family Name) thus representing the triumph of civilization over the wild forest life; and accept this offering of corn, ground on the pilum first offered to man by you; and, I pray that you may be benevolent and propitious to (Name of Bride) and (Name of Groom), to their household and to their family.

A libation of wine is poured in the focus of the altar.

An offering of ground corn (wheat & barley) is placed in the focus of the altar.

[LONG VERSION ADDITIONAL VERSES– OPTIONAL]

O Domiduca, who safely lead the bride to her husband's house, be you well and blessed. I pray good prayers, offer this wine, and, I pray that you may be benevolent and propitious to (Name of Bride) and (Name of Groom), to their household and to their family.

A libation of wine is poured in the focus of the altar.

O Domitius, who keeps the bride at her new home, be you well and blessed. I pray good prayers, offer this wine, and, I pray that you may be benevolent and propitious to (Name of Bride) and (Name of Groom), to their household and to their family.

A libation of wine is poured in the focus of the altar.

O Unxia, who anoints the doorposts of the bride's new home, be you well and blessed. I pray good prayers, offer this wine, and, I pray that you may be benevolent and propitious to (Name of Bride) and (Name of Groom), to their household and to their family.

A libation of wine is poured in the focus of the altar.

O Cinxia, who ties and loosens the bride's girdle, be you well and blessed. I pray good prayers, offer this wine, and, I pray that you may be benevolent and propitious to (Name of Bride) and (Name of Groom), to their household and to their family.

A libation of wine is poured in the focus of the altar.

O Virginiensis, overseer of the bride's virginity, be you well and blessed. I pray good prayers, offer this wine, and, I pray that you may be benevolent and propitious to (Name of Bride) and (Name of Groom), to their household and to their family.

A libation of wine is poured in the focus of the altar.

O Subigus, who tames the bride, be you well and blessed. I pray good prayers, offer this wine, and, I pray that you may be benevolent and propitious to (Name of Bride) and (Name of Groom), to their household and to their family.

A libation of wine is poured in the focus of the altar.

O Prema, the mother goddess, who overpowers the husband by holding the bride, be you well and blessed. I pray good prayers, offer this wine, and, I pray that you may be benevolent and propitious to (Name of Bride) and (Name of Groom), to their household and to their family.

A libation of wine is poured in the focus of the altar.

O Pertunda, along with Venus and Priapus and Perficia, who oversee the act of consummation of marriage on the first night, be you well and blessed. I pray good prayers, offer this wine, and, I pray that you may be benevolent and propitious to (Name of Bride) and (Name of Groom), to their household and to their family.

A libation of wine is poured in the focus of the altar.

O Maturna, who sees that the bride and groom remain together, be you well and blessed. I pray good prayers, offer this wine, and, I pray that you may be benevolent and propitious to (Name of Bride) and (Name of Groom), to their household and to their family.

A libation of wine is poured in the focus of the altar.

(REDDITIO)

O Father Ianus, as by offering to you the incense virtuous prayers were well prayed. For the sake of this be honoured by this humble wine.

A libation of wine is poured in the focus of the altar.

O Mother Iuno, as by offering to you the incense virtuous prayers were well prayed. For the sake of this be honoured by this humble wine.

A libation of wine is poured in the focus of the altar.

O Mother Tellus, as by offering to you the incense virtuous prayers were well prayed. For the sake of this be honoured by this humble honeyed milk.

A libation of honeyed milk is poured in the focus of the altar.

O Brothers Picumnus and Pilumnus, as by offering to you the incense virtuous prayers were well prayed. For the sake of this be honoured by this humble wine.

A libation of wine is poured in the focus of the altar.

It is so. [Omit this phrase, if using Long Version]

[LONG VERSION ADDITIONAL VERSES– OPTIONAL]

O Domiduca, as by offering to you the incense virtuous prayers were well prayed. For the sake of this be honoured by this humble wine.

A libation of wine is poured in the focus of the altar.

O Domitius, as by offering to you the incense virtuous prayers were well prayed. For the sake of this be honoured by this humble wine.

A libation of wine is poured in the focus of the altar.

O Unxia, as by offering to you the incense virtuous prayers were well prayed. For the sake of this be honoured by this humble wine.

A libation of wine is poured in the focus of the altar.

O Cinxia, as by offering to you the incense virtuous prayers were well prayed. For the sake of this be honoured by this humble wine.

A libation of wine is poured in the focus of the altar.

O Virginiensis, as by offering to you the incense virtuous prayers were well prayed. For the sake of this be honoured by this humble wine.

A libation of wine is poured in the focus of the altar.

O Subigus, as by offering to you the incense virtuous prayers were well prayed. For the sake of this be honoured by this humble wine.

A libation of wine is poured in the focus of the altar.

O Prema, as by offering to you the incense virtuous prayers were well prayed. For the sake of this be honoured by this humble wine.

A libation of wine is poured in the focus of the altar.

O Pertunda, as by offering to you the incense virtuous prayers were well prayed. For the sake of this be honoured by this humble wine.

A libation of wine is poured in the focus of the altar.

O Venus mater, as by offering to you the incense virtuous prayers were well prayed. For the sake of this be honoured by this humble wine.

A libation of wine is poured in the focus of the altar.

O Priapus, as by offering to you the incense virtuous prayers were well prayed. For the sake of this be honoured by this humble wine.

A libation of wine is poured in the focus of the altar.

O Perficia, as by offering to you the incense virtuous prayers were well prayed. For the sake of this be honoured by this humble wine.

A libation of wine is poured in the focus of the altar.

O Maturna, as by offering to you the incense virtuous prayers were well prayed. For the sake of this be honoured by this humble wine.

A libation of wine is poured in the focus of the altar.

It is so.

(PIACULUM)

[SHORT VERSION]

O Father Ianus, O Mother Iuno, O Mother Tellus, O Brothers

Picumnus and Pilumnus, and all Gods Immortal by whatever name I may call you: if anything in this ceremony was displeasing to you, with the sacrificial incense I ask forgiveness and expiate my fault. May everything I have done and said this day bring honor and happiness on me, on my family, and on the Gods.

Incense is offered in the focus of the altar.

It is done!

[LONG VERSION]

O Father Ianus, O Mother Iuno, O Mother Tellus, O Brothers Picumnus and Pilumnus, O Domiduca, O Domitius, O Unxia, O Cinxia, O Virginiensis, O Subigus, O Prema, O Pertunda, O Venus mater, O Priapus, O Perficia, O Maturna, and all Gods Immortal by whatever name I may call you: if anything in this ceremony was displeasing to you, with the sacrificial incense I ask forgiveness and expiate my fault. May everything I have done and said this day bring honor and happiness on me, on my family, and on the Gods.

Incense is offered in the focus of the altar.

It is done!

(CONCLUSION)

At this point, the Groom may kiss the Bride.

(CLOSING)

Quirites, the ceremony is ended, and I present to you the newly-wed couple.

GUESTS: *(Congratulate the newly-weds by shouting)* **Feliciter!**

After the conclusion of the ceremony came the wedding feast (cena nuptialis), lasting in early times until evening. There can be no doubt that this was regularly given at the house of the bride's father and that the few cases when, as we know, it was given at the groom's house were exceptional and due to special circumstances which might cause a similar change today. The feast seems to have concluded with the distribution among the guests of pieces of the wedding cake (mustaceum).

After the wedding feast the bride was formally taken to her husband's house by the Bridal Procession. This ceremony was called deductio, and, since it was essential to validity of the marriage, it was never omitted. It was a public function, that is, anyone might join the procession and take part in the merriment that distinguished it; we are told that persons of rank did not scruple to wait in the street to see a bride. As evening approached, the procession was formed before the bride's house with torch-bearers and flute-players at its head.

When all was ready, the marriage hymn (hymenaeus) was sung and the groom took the bride with a show of force from the arms of her mother. The Romans saw in this custom a reminiscence of the rape of the Sabines, but it probably goes far back beyond the founding of Rome to the custom of marriage by capture that prevailed among many peoples.

The bride then took her place in the procession. She was attended by three boys, patrimi et matrimi; two of these walked beside her, each holding one of her hands, while the other carried before her the wedding torch of white thorn (spina alba). Behind the bride were carried the distaff and spindle, emblems of domestic life. The camillus with his cumera also walked in the procession.

During the march were sung the versus Fescennini, abounding in coarse jests and personalities. The crowd also shouted the ancient marriage cry, the significance of which the Romans themselves did not understand. We find it in at least five forms, all variations of Talassius or Talassio, the name, probably, of a Sabine divinity, whose functions, however, are unknown. Livy derives it from the supposed name of a senator in the time of Romulus.

On the way the bride, by dropping one of three coins which she carried, made an offering to the Lares Compitales, the gods of the crossroads; of the other two she gave one to the groom as an emblem of the dowry she brought him, and one to the Lares of his house.

The groom meanwhile scattered nuts through the crowd. This is explained by Catullus that the groom had become a man and had put away childish things, but the nuts were rather a symbol of fruitfulness. The custom survives in the throwing of rice in modem times.

When the procession reached the groom's house, the bride wound the door posts with bands of wool, probably a symbol of her own work as mistress of the household, and anointed the door with oil and fat, emblems of plenty. She was then lifted carefully over the threshold, in order, some say, to avoid the chance of so bad an omen as a slip of the foot on entering the house for the first time.

Others, however, see in the custom another survival of marriage by capture. She then pronounced again the words of consent: **Ubi tu Gaius, ego Gaia**, and the doors were closed against the general crowd; only the invited guests entered with the newly-married pair.

The husband met his wife in the atrium and offered her fire and water in token of the life they were to live together and of her part in the home. Upon the hearth was ready the wood for a fire; this the bride kindled with the marriage torch, which had been carried before her. The torch was afterwards thrown among the guests to be scrambled for as a lucky possession. A prayer was then recited by the bride and she was placed by the pronuba on the lectus genialis, which always stood in the atrium on the wedding night. Here it afterwards remained as a piece of ornamental furniture only.

On the next day there was given in the new home the second wedding feast (repotia) to the friends and relatives, and at this feast the bride made her first offering to the gods as a matrona. A series of feasts followed, given in honor of the newly-wedded pair by those in whose social circles they moved.

WEDDING ANNIVERSARY RITUAL (By Officiant)

(ABLUTIO)

Officiant washes both hands in clean water and in capite velato pray:

May this water cast out all impurities from my substance as from lead to gold. May this water cleanse my body of impurities, as the rain cleanses the air. Purify my mind. Purify my body. Purify my heart. It is so.

(PRAEFATIO)

O Ianus, by offering this incense to you I pray good prayers, so that you may be benevolent and propitious to me, my family, and my household.

Incense is placed in the focus of the altar.

O Iuno, by offering this incense to you I pray good prayers, so that you may be benevolent and propitious to me, my family, and my household.

Incense is placed in the focus of the altar.

O Tellus, by offering this incense to you I pray good prayers, so that you may be benevolent and propitious to me, my family, and my household.

Incense is placed in the focus of the altar.

O Picumnus, by offering this incense to you I pray good prayers, so that you may be benevolent and propitious to me, my family, and my household.

Incense is placed in the focus of the altar.

O Pilumnus, by offering this incense to you I pray good prayers, so that you may be benevolent and propitious to me, my family, and my household.

Incense is placed in the focus of the altar.

(PRECATIO)

O Father Janus, who was before all the Gods, the god of new beginnings, to whom our parents first invoked in their prayers, from whom all things proceed, be well and blessed. I pray good prayers, offer this wine, thank you for the blessings to our marriage and household for the previous year, and ask that you grant the continued blessings of a harmonious and successful marriage of (Wife) and (Husband) in the coming year; and, I pray that you may be benevolent and propitious to them, to their household and to their family.

A libation of wine is poured in the focus of the altar.

O Mother Iuno, queen of the gods and protector of women, marriage and birth, be well and blessed. I pray good prayers, offer this wine, and ask that you watch over, guide and direct, and grant the continued blessings of a happy marriage and long fruitful life together for (Wife) and (Husband), and that their family and their household be granted the benefits of good health and well-being; and, I pray that you may be benevolent and propitious to (Wife) and (Husband), to their household and to their family.

A libation of wine is poured in the focus of the altar.

O Terra mater, Holy Goddess, Mother of all Nature, engendering all things and regenerating them each day, as You alone bring forth from Your womb all things into life, be well and blessed. I pray good prayers, offer this honeyed milk. I call upon Your power, come. Make what I ask to be readily and easily accomplished, and draw my thanks, Mother Earth, that, in fidelity, You do rightly watch over, protect and bless the marriage of (Wife) and (Husband), and grant unto them the fruits of their labors in the coming year and offer thanks for those rewards thus received; and, I pray that you may be benevolent and propitious to (Wife) and (Husband), to their household and to their family.

An offering of honeyed milk is placed in the focus of the altar.

[IF NO CHILDREN]

O Brothers Pilumnus and Picumnus, be well and blessed. I pray good prayers, offer this wine, and ask you to stimulate the growth of the children to come from this union, avert all sickness, protect mother and unborn child, prevent the mischievous intrusion of Silvanus into the house of the (Family Name) thus representing the triumph of civilization over the wild forest life; and accept this offering of corn, ground on the pilum first offered to man by you; and, I pray that you may be benevolent and propitious to (Wife) and (Husband), to their household and to their family.

A libation of wine is poured in the focus of the altar.

An offering of ground corn (wheat & barley) is placed in the focus of the altar.

[IF CHILDREN]

O Brothers Pilumnus and Picumnus, be well and blessed. I pray good prayers, offer this wine, and ask you to stimulate the growth of the children from this union, avert all sickness, protect mother and unborn child, prevent the mischievous intrusion of Silvanus into the house of the (Family Name) thus representing the triumph of civilization over the wild forest life; and accept this offering of corn, ground on the pilum first offered to man by you; and, I pray that you may be benevolent and propitious to (Wife) and (Husband), to their household and to their family.

A libation of wine is poured in the focus of the altar.

An offering of ground corn (wheat & barley) is placed in the focus of the altar.

(REDDITIO)

O Father Ianus, as by offering to you the incense virtuous prayers were well prayed. For the sake of this be honoured by this humble wine.

A libation of wine is poured in the focus of the altar.

O Mother Iuno, as by offering to you the incense virtuous prayers were well prayed. For the sake of this be honoured by this humble wine.

A libation of wine in the focus of the altar.

O Mother Tellus, as by offering to you the incense virtuous prayers were well prayed. For the sake of this be honoured by this humble honeyed milk.

A libation of honeyed milk is poured in the focus of the altar.

O Brothers Picumnus and Pilumnus, as by offering to you the incense virtuous prayers were well prayed. For the sake of this be honoured by this humble wine.

A libation of wine is poured in the focus of the altar.

It is so.

(PIACULUM)

O Father Ianus, O Mother Iuno, O Mother Tellus, O Brothers Picumnus and Pilumnus, and all Gods Immortal by whatever name I may call you: if anything in this ceremony was displeasing to you, with the sacrificial incense I ask forgiveness and expiate my fault. May everything I have done and said this day bring honor and happiness on me, on my

family, and on the Gods.

Incense is offered in the focus of the altar.

It is done!

(CLOSING)

Quirites, the ceremony is ended, and I present to you the honoured couple thus renewed to begin a new year together!

GUESTS: *(Congratulate the couple by shouting)* **Feliciter!**

WEDDING ANNIVERSARY RITUAL
(By Pater familias)

(ABLUTIO)

Wash both hands in clean water and in capite velato pray:

May this water cast out all impurities from my substance as from lead to gold. May this water cleanse my body of impurities, as the rain cleanses the air. Purify my mind. Purify my body. Purify my heart. It is so.

(PRAEFATIO)

O Ianus, by offering this incense to you I pray good prayers, so that you may be benevolent and propitious to me, my family, and my household.

Incense is placed in the focus of the altar.

O Iuno, by offering this incense to you I pray good prayers, so that you may be benevolent and propitious to me, my family, and my household.

Incense is placed in the focus of the altar.

O Tellus, by offering this incense to you I pray good prayers, so that you may be benevolent and propitious to me, my family, and my household.

Incense is placed in the focus of the altar.

O Picumnus, by offering this incense to you I pray good prayers, so that you may be benevolent and propitious to me, my family, and my household.

Incense is placed in the focus of the altar.

O Pilumnus, by offering this incense to you I pray good prayers, so that you may be benevolent and propitious to me, my family, and my household.

Incense is placed in the focus of the altar.

(PRECATIO)

O Father Janus, who was before all the Gods, the god of new beginnings, to whom our parents first invoked in their prayers, from whom all things proceed, be well and blessed. I pray good prayers, offer this wine, thank you for the blessings to our marriage and household for the previous year, and ask that you grant me and my wife the continued blessings of a harmonious and successful marriage in the coming year; and, I pray that you may be benevolent and propitious to me, to my household and to my family.

A libation of wine is poured in the focus of the altar.

O Mother Iuno, queen of the gods and protector of women, marriage and birth, be well and blessed. I pray good prayers, offer this wine, and ask that you watch over, guide and direct, and grant the continued blessings of a happy marriage and long fruitful life together for my wife and I, and that our family and our household be granted the benefits of good health and well-being; and, I pray that you may be benevolent and propitious to me, to my household and to my family.

A libation of wine is poured in the focus of the altar.

O Terra mater, Holy Goddess, Mother of all Nature, engendering all things and regenerating them each day, as You alone bring forth from Your womb all things into life, be well and blessed. I pray good prayers, offer this honeyed milk. I call upon Your power, come. Make what I ask to be readily and easily accomplished, and draw my thanks, Mother Earth, that, in fidelity, You do rightly watch over, protect and bless our marriage, and grant unto us the fruits of our labors in the coming year and offer thanks for those rewards thus received; and, I pray that you may be benevolent and propitious to me, to my household and to my family.

An offering of honeyed milk is placed in the focus of the altar.

[IF NO CHILDREN]

O Brothers Pilumnus and Picumnus, be well and blessed. I pray good prayers, offer this wine, and ask you to stimulate the growth of the children to come from this union, avert all sickness, protect mother and unborn child, prevent the mischievous intrusion of Silvanus into the house of the (Family Name) thus representing the triumph of civilization over the wild forest life; and accept this offering of corn, ground on the pilum first offered to man by you; and, I pray that you may be benevolent and propitious to me, to my household and to my family.

A libation of wine is poured in the focus of the altar.

An offering of ground corn (wheat & barley) is placed in the focus of the altar.

[IF CHILDREN]

O Brothers Pilumnus and Picumnus, be well and blessed. I pray good prayers, offer this wine, and ask you to stimulate the growth of the children from this union, avert all sickness, protect mother and unborn child, prevent the mischievous intrusion of Silvanus into the house of the (Family Name) thus representing the triumph of civilization over the wild forest life; and accept this offering of corn, ground on the pilum first offered to man by you; and, I pray that you may be benevolent and propitious to me, to my household and to my family.

A libation of wine is poured in the focus of the altar.

An offering of ground corn (wheat & barley) is placed in the focus of the altar.

(REDDITIO)

O Father Ianus, as by offering to you the incense virtuous prayers were well prayed. For the sake of this be honoured by this humble wine.

A libation of wine is poured in the focus of the altar.

O Mother Iuno, as by offering to you the incense virtuous prayers were well prayed. For the sake of this be honoured by this humble wine.

A libation of honeyed milk is poured in the focus of the altar.

O Mother Tellus, as by offering to you the incense virtuous prayers were well prayed. For the sake of this be honoured by this humble honeyed milk.

A libation of honeyed milk is poured in the focus of the altar.

O Brothers Picumnus and Pilumnus, as by offering to you the incense virtuous prayers were well prayed. For the sake of this be honoured by this humble wine.

A libation of wine is poured in the focus of the altar.

It is so.

(PIACULUM)

O Father Ianus, O Mother Iuno, O Mother Tellus, O Brothers Picumnus and Pilumnus, and all Gods Immortal by whatever name I may call you: if anything in this ceremony was displeasing to you, with the sacrificial incense I ask forgiveness and expiate my fault. May everything I have done and said this day bring honor and happiness on me, on my

family, and on the Gods.

Incense is offered in the focus of the altar.

It is done!

PREGNANCY RITUAL (BY MOTHER)

Performed to Encourage Pregnancy in a Woman

(ABLUTIO)

Wash both hands in clean water and in capite velato pray:

May this water cast out all impurities from my substance as from lead to gold. May this water cleanse my body of impurities, as the rain cleanses the air. Purify my mind. Purify my body. Purify my heart. It is so.

(PRAEFATIO)

O Lar familiaris, O Alemonia, O Decima, O Parcae, O Facunditas, O Iuno, O Lucina, O Mutinus Mutunus, O Nascio, O Nixi, O Prorsa Postverta and Vitumnus, by offering this incense to you I pray good prayers, so that you may be benevolent and propitious to me, my family, and my household.

Incense is placed in the focus of the altar.

(PRECATIO)

Be you well and blessed, O Lar familiaris, on this day, I pray good prayers and ask and beseech you, so that you will grant me a child, born healthy and safely without harm or illness; that my pregnancy shall be without complication, well, healthy and successful; that you may continue to confirm, strengthen and help my household, and save it from all discord, so that my houshold may always flourish and prosper; and, that you may be benevolent and propitious to my unborn child, to me, to my household and to my family.

O Alemonia, be well and blessed and adequately feed the unborn child from the day of its conception until the day of its birth, that it may be healthy and not in want of proper nutrition; and, I pray that you may be benevolent and propitious to my child, to me, to my household and to my family.

O Decima, be well and blessed and grant me, my family and my household the favor of a healthy child; and, I pray that you may be benevolent and propitious to my child, to me, to my household and to my family.

O Parcae, be well and blessed and let it be my good fate to bring forth into this world a child into my family and household; and, I pray that you may be benevolent and propitious to my child, to me, to my household and to my family.

O Facunditas, be well and blessed and grant fertility that I may bear a child of good health and wellbeing; and, I pray that you may be benevolent and propitious to my child, to me, to my household and to my family.

O Iuno, queen of the gods and protector of women, marriage and birth, be well and blessed, and grant the blessings of a child to be borne unto me, my family and my household; and, I pray that you may be benevolent and propitious to my child, to me, to my household and to my family.

O Lucina, be well and blessed and at the appointed time of childbirth, ease my pain and ensure all goes well. Bring my child into the light; and, I pray that you may be benevolent and propitious to my child, to me, to my household and to my family.

O Mutinus Mutunus, be well and blessed and hear my plea to invoke thee as I seek to bear children; and, I pray that you may be benevolent and propitious to my child, to me, to my household and to my family.

O Nascio, be well and blessed and protect and guide my pregnancy and grant the healthy birth of my child.

O Nixi, be well and blessed and at the appointed time of my labor with child, I promise to invoke thee to assist in giving birth to my child; and, I pray that you may be benevolent and propitious to my child, to me, to my household and to my family.

O Prorsa Postverta, be well and blessed and at the appointed time of my labor, guard over the position of the child in the womb, that it may be safe and correct for the birth; and, I pray that you may be benevolent and propitious to my child, to me, to my household and to my family.

O Vitumnus, be well and blessed and I pray you to give life to the child in my womb; and, I pray that you may be benevolent and propitious to my unborn child, to me, to my household and to my family.

Other prayers are offered here.

I pray these good prayers and offer this wine and honeyed milk that you may be benevolent and propitious to my unborn child, to me, to my household and to my family.

Libations of wine and honeyed milk are poured on the altar.

(REDDITIO)

O Lar familiaris, O Alemonia, O Decima, O Parcae, O Facunditas, O Iuno, O Lucina, O Mutinus Mutunus, O Nascio, O Nixi, O Prorsa Postverta and Vitumnus, as by offering to you the incense virtuous prayers were well prayed. For the sake of this be honoured by this humble wine and honeyed milk.

Libations of wine and honeyed milk are poured on the altar.

It is so.

(PIACULUM)

O Lar familiaris, O Alemonia, O Decima, O Parcae, O Facunditas, O Iuno, O Lucina, O Mutinus Mutunus, O Nascio, O Nixi, O Prorsa Postverta and Vitumnus, and all Gods Immortal by whatever name I may call you: if anything in this ceremony was displeasing to you, with the sacrificial incense I ask forgiveness and expiate my fault.

Incense is placed in the focus of the altar.

It is done!

PREGNANCY RITUAL (BY SACERDOS/PRIESTESS)

Performed to Encourage Pregnancy in a Woman

(ABLUTIO)

Wash both hands in clean water and in capite velato pray:

May this water cast out all impurities from my substance as from lead to gold. May this water cleanse my body of impurities, as the rain cleanses the air. Purify my mind. Purify my body. Purify my heart. It is so.

(PRAEFATIO)

O Lar familiaris, by offering this incense to you I pray good prayers, so that you may be benevolent and propitious to me, my family, and my household.

Incense is placed in the focus of the altar.

O Alemonia, by offering this incense to you I pray good prayers, so that you may be benevolent and propitious to me, my family, and my household.

Incense is placed in the focus of the altar.

O Decima, by offering this incense to you I pray good prayers, so that you may be benevolent and propitious to me, my family, and my household.

Incense is placed in the focus of the altar.

O Parcae, by offering this incense to you I pray good prayers, so that you may be benevolent and propitious to me, my family, and my household.

Incense is placed in the focus of the altar.

O Facunditas, by offering this incense to you I pray good prayers, so that you may be benevolent and propitious to me, my family, and my household.

Incense is placed in the focus of the altar.

O Iuno, by offering this incense to you I pray good prayers, so that you may be benevolent and propitious to me, my family, and my household.

Incense is placed in the focus of the altar.

O Lucina, by offering this incense to you I pray good prayers, so that you may be benevolent and propitious to me, my family, and my household.

Incense is placed in the focus of the altar.

O Mutinus Mutunus, by offering this incense to you I pray good prayers, so that you may be benevolent and propitious to me, my family, and my household.

Incense is placed in the focus of the altar.

O Nascio, by offering this incense to you I pray good prayers, so that you may be benevolent and propitious to me, my family, and my household.

Incense is placed in the focus of the altar.

O Nixi, by offering this incense to you I pray good prayers, so that you may be benevolent and propitious to me, my family, and my household.

Incense is placed in the focus of the altar.

O Prorsa Postverta, by offering this incense to you I pray good prayers, so that you may be benevolent and propitious to me, my family, and my household.
Incense is placed in the focus of the altar.

O Vitumnus, by offering this incense to you I pray good prayers, so that you may be benevolent and propitious to me, my family, and my household.

Incense is placed in the focus of the altar.

(PRECATIO)

Be you well and blessed, O Lar familiaris, on this day, I pray good prayers and ask and beseech you, so that you will grant (full name of mother) a child, born healthy and safely without harm or illness; that her pregnancy shall be without complication, well, healthy and successful; that you may continue to confirm, strengthen and help the House of (Last Name of Mother), and save it from all discord, so that the House of (Name of Mother) may always flourish and prosper; and, that you may be benevolent and propitious to her unborn child, to her, to her household and to her family.

O Alemonia, be well and blessed. I pray good prayers, offer this wine, and ask that you adequately feed the unborn child from the day of its conception until the day of its birth, that it may be healthy and not in want of proper nutrition; and, I pray that you may be benevolent and propitious to to her unborn child, to her, to her household and to her family.

A libation of wine is poured on the altar.

O Decima, be well and blessed. I pray good prayers, offer this wine, and ask that you grant her, her family and her household the favor of a healthy child; and, I pray that you may be benevolent and propitious to to her unborn child, to her, to her household and to her family.

A libation of wine is poured on the altar.

O Parcae, be well and blessed. I pray good prayers, offer this wine, and ask that you let it be her good fate to bring forth into this world a child into her family and household; and, I pray that you may be benevolent and propitious to her unborn child, to her, to her household and to her family.

A libation of wine is poured on the altar.

O Facunditas, be well and blessed. I pray good prayers, offer this wine, and ask that you grant fertility that she may bear a child of good health and wellbeing; and, I pray that you may be benevolent and propitious to her unborn child, to her, to her household and to her family.

A libation of wine is poured on the altar.

O Iuno, queen of the gods and protector of women, marriage and birth, be well and blessed. I pray good prayers, offer this wine, and ask that you grant the blessings of a child to be borne unto her, her family and her household; and, I pray that you may be benevolent and propitious to her unborn child, to her, to her household and to her family.

A libation of wine is poured on the altar.

O Lucina, be well and blessed. I pray good prayers, offer this wine, and ask that you at the appointed time of her childbirth, ease her pain and ensure all goes well. Bring her child into the light; and, I pray that you may be benevolent and propitious to her unborn child, to her, to her household and to her family.

A libation of wine is poured on the altar.

O Mutinus Mutunus, be well and blessed. I pray good prayers, offer this wine, and ask that you hear her plea to invoke thee as she seeks to bear children; and, I pray that you may be benevolent and propitious to her unborn child, to her, to her household and to her family.

A libation of wine is poured on the altar.

O Nascio, be well and blessed. I pray good prayers, offer this wine, and ask that you protect and guide her pregnancy and grant the healthy birth of her child; and, I pray that you may be benevolent and propitious to to her unborn child, to her, to her household and to her family.

A libation of wine is poured on the altar.

O Nixi, be well and blessed. I pray good prayers, offer this wine, and declare that at the appointed time of her labor with child, she promises to invoke thee to assist in giving birth to her child; and, I pray that you may be benevolent and propitious to her unborn child, to her, to her household and to her family.

A libation of wine is poured on the altar.

O Prorsa Postverta, be well and blessed. I pray good prayers, offer this wine, and ask at the appointed time of her labor, guard over the position of the child in the womb, that it may be safe and correct for the birth; and, I pray that you may be benevolent and propitious to her unborn child, to her, to her household and to her family.

A libation of wine is poured on the altar.

O Vitumnus, be well and blessed. I pray good prayers, offer this wine, and pray you to give life to the child in her womb; and, I pray that you may be benevolent and propitious to her unborn child, to her, to her household and to her family.

A libation of wine is poured on the altar.

(REDDITIO)

O Lar familiaris, as by offering to you the incense virtuous prayers were well prayed. For the sake of this be honoured by this humble offering of wine.

A libation of wine is poured on the altar.

O Alemonia, as by offering to you the incense virtuous prayers were well prayed. For the sake of this be honoured by this humble offering of honeyed milk.

A libation of honeyed milk is poured on the altar.

O Decima, as by offering to you the incense virtuous prayers were well prayed. For the sake of this be honoured by this humble offering of honeyed milk.

A libation of honeyed milk is poured on the altar.

O Parcae, as by offering to you the incense virtuous prayers were well prayed. For the sake of this be honoured by this humble offering of honeyed milk.

A libation of honeyed milk is poured on the altar.

O Facunditas, as by offering to you the incense virtuous prayers were well prayed. For the sake of this be honoured by this humble wine and honeyed milk.

A libation of wine or honeyed milk is poured on the altar.

O Iuno, as by offering to you the incense virtuous prayers were well prayed. For the sake of this be honoured by this humble offering of milk.

A libation of honeyed milk is poured on the altar.

O Lucina, as by offering to you the incense virtuous prayers were well prayed. For the sake of this be honoured by this humble offering of milk.

A libation of honeyed milk is poured on the altar.

O Mutinus Mutunus, as by offering to you the incense virtuous prayers were well prayed. For the sake of this be honoured by this humble offering of wine.

A libation of wine is poured on the altar.

O Nascio, as by offering to you the incense virtuous prayers were well prayed. For the sake of this be honoured by this humble wine and honeyed milk.

A libation of wine or honeyed milk is poured on the altar.

O Nixi, as by offering to you the incense virtuous prayers were well prayed. For the sake of this be honoured by this humble wine and honeyed milk.

A libation of wine or honeyed milk is poured on the altar.

O Prorsa Postverta, as by offering to you the incense virtuous prayers were well prayed. For the sake of this be honoured by this humble offering of honeyed milk.

A libation of milk is poured on the altar.

O Vitumnus, as by offering to you the incense virtuous prayers were well prayed. For the sake of this be honoured by this humble offering of wine.

A libation of wine is poured on the altar.

It is so.

(PIACULUM)

O Lar familiaris, O Alemonia, O Decima, O Parcae, O Facunditas, O Iuno, O Lucina, O Mutinus Mutunus, O Nascio, O Nixi, O Prorsa Postverta and Vitumnus, and all Gods Immortal by whatever name I may call you: if anything in this ceremony was displeasing to you, with the sacrificial incense I ask forgiveness and expiate my fault.

Incense is placed in the focus of the altar.

It is done!

BIRTH OF CHILD RITUAL

Performed After Birth of a Child

ANCIENT: As soon as the birth of a child had taken place began a series of ceremonies, which are of particular interest, as they seem to belong to a very early stage of religious thought, and have a markedly rustic character. Immediately a sacred meal was offered to the two field-deities, Picumnus and Pilumnus, and then the Roman turned his attention to the practical danger of fever for the mother and child. At night three men gathered round the threshold, one armed with an axe, another with a stake, and a third with a broom: the two first struck the threshold with their implements, the third swept out the floor. Over this ceremony were said to preside three numina, Intercidona (connected with the axe), Pilumnus (connected with the stake, pilum), and Deverra (connected with the act of sweeping). Its object was, as Varro explains it, to avert the entrance of the half-wild Silvanus by giving three unmistakeable signs of human civilisation; we shall probably not be wrong in seeing in it rather an actual hacking, beating, and sweeping away of evil spirits.

MODERN: A special offering of ground corn (wheat & barley) is served to the brother deities. A small extra bed/bedroll is made next to the child's bed to ensure the help of these gods.

(ABLUTIO)

Wash both hands in clean water and in capite velato pray:

May this water cast out all impurities from my substance as from lead to gold. May this water cleanse my body of impurities, as the rain cleanses the air. Purify my mind. Purify my body. Purify my heart. It is so.

(PRAEFATIO)

O Lar familiaris, O Candelifera, O Carmenta, O Lucina, O Cuba, O Decima, O Fabulinus, O Febris, O Iuno, O Levana, O

Nascio, O Paventia, O Brothers Pilumnus and Picumnus, O Potina, O Quiritis, O Vitumnus, O Volumna, by offering this incense to you I pray good prayers, so that you may be benevolent and propitious to me, my family, and my household.

Incense is placed in the focus of the altar.

Father lifts the child from the ground/crib and places it next to the Mother.

(PRECATIO)

Be you well and blessed, O Lar familiaris, on this day of the birth of our child, I pray good prayers, offer this wine, and ask and beseech you, so that you will safeguard our newborn child, (full name), and see him (her) safely back home without harm or illness; that the lives of our new child and his (her) mother be well, healthy and successful; that you may continue to confirm, strengthen and help my household, and save it from all discord, so that my household may always flourish and prosper; and, that you may be benevolent and propitious to my child, (first name/praenomen), to me, to my household and to my family.

A libation of wine is poured on the altar.

O Candelifera, Carmenta and Lucina, be well and blessed. I pray good prayers, offer this wine, and I thank you for the birth of the child; and, I pray that you may be benevolent and propitious to my child, to me, to my household and to my family.

A libation of wine is poured on the altar.

O Cuba, be well and blessed. I pray good prayers, offer this wine, and ask that you protect the child in their crib and send them to sleep in gentle peace each night; and, I pray that you may be benevolent and propitious to my child, to me, to my household and to my family.

A libation of wine is poured on the altar.

O Decima, Nona and Morta, the Parcae goddesses of fate, be well and blessed. I pray good prayers, offer this wine, and ask that you seal the fate of the child with good health, wisdom and success; and, I pray that you may be benevolent and propitious to my child, to me, to my household and to my family.

A libation of wine is poured on the altar.

O Fabulinus, be well and blessed. I pray good prayers, offer this wine, and ask that you teach the child to utter their first word, in which I will make an offering to you on that day; and, I pray that you may be benevolent and propitious to my child, to me, to my household and to my family.

A libation of wine is poured on the altar.

O Febris, be well and blessed. I pray good prayers, offer this wine, and ask that you protect the child from fevers; and, I pray that you may be benevolent and propitious to my child, to me, to my household and to my family.

A libation of wine is poured on the altar.

O Iuno, queen of the gods and protector of women, marriage and birth, be well and blessed. I pray good prayers, offer this wine, and ask that you watch over the child and mother; and, I pray that you may be benevolent and propitious to my child, to me, to my household and to my family.

A libation of wine is poured on the altar.

O Levana, be well and blessed. I pray good prayers, offer this wine, and ask that you protect and recognize the child who is lifted by its father in your honor; and, I pray that you may be benevolent and propitious to my child, to me, to my household and to my family.

A libation of wine is poured on the altar.

Father lifts the child from the ground/crib and places it next to the Mother.

O Nascio, be well and blessed. I pray good prayers, offer this wine, and ask that you for your assistance and guidance in the birth of the child; and, I pray that you may be benevolent and propitious to my child, to me, to my household and to my family.

A libation of wine is poured on the altar.

O Paventia, be well and blessed. I pray good prayers, offer this wine, and ask you to protect the child against sudden fright and terrors; and, I pray that you may be benevolent and propitious to my child, to me, to my household and to my family.

A libation of wine is poured on the altar.

O Brothers Pilumnus and Picumnus, be well and blessed. I pray good prayers, offer this wine, and ask you to stimulate the growth of the child and avert all sickness, and accept the offering of ground corn; and, I pray that you may be benevolent and propitious to my child, to me, to my household and to my family.

A libation of wine is poured on the altar.

O Potina, be well and blessed. I pray good prayers, offer this wine, and ask you aid and assist in the first drink of mother's milk by the child; and, I pray that you may be benevolent and propitious to my child, to me, to my household and to my family.
A libation of wine is poured on the altar.

O Quiritis, be well and blessed. I pray good prayers, offer this wine, and ask you watch over the mother of the child; her safety, recovery and wellness; and, protect and guide the

mother well, wisely and safely through motherhood; and, I pray that you may be benevolent and propitious to my child, to me, to my household and to my family.

A libation of wine is poured on the altar.

O Vitumnus, be well and be blessed, thou who gave life to the child in the mother's womb; blessed. I pray good prayers, offer this wine, and ask that you may be benevolent and propitious to my child, to me, to my household and to my family.

A libation of wine is poured on the altar.

O Volumna, be well and blessed. I pray good prayers, offer this wine, and ask you to protect the nursery of our household; and, I pray that you may be benevolent and propitious to my child, to me, to my household and to my family.

A libation of wine is poured on the altar.

(REDDITIO)

O Lar familiaris, O Candelifera, O Carmenta, O Lucina, O Cuba, O Decima, O Fabulinus, O Febris, O Iuno, O Levana, O Nascio, O Paventia, O Brothers Pilumnus and Picumnus, O Potina, O Quiritis, O Vitumnus, O Volumna, as by offering to you the incense virtuous prayers were well prayed. For the sake of this be honoured by these humble offerings of wine and honeyed milk.

Libations of wine and honeyed milk is poured on the altar.

It is so.

(PIACULUM)

O Lar familiaris, O Candelifera, O Carmenta, O Lucina, O Cuba, O Decima, O Fabulinus, O Febris, O Iuno, O Levana, O

Nascio, O Paventia, O Brothers Pilumnus and Picumnus, O Potina, O Quiritis, O Vitumnus and Volumna, and all Gods Immortal by whatever name I may call you: if anything in this ceremony was displeasing to you, with the sacrificial incense I ask forgiveness and expiate my fault.

Incense is placed in the focus of the altar.

It is done!

NAMING OF A CHILD RITUAL
(Solemnitas nominalium or Dies lustricus)

ANCIENT: On the ninth day after birth, in the case of a boy, on the eighth in the case of a girl, occurred the festival of the naming (solemnitas nominalium). The ceremony was one of purification (*dies lustricus* is its alternative title), and a piacular offering was made to preserve the child from evil influences in the future. Friends brought presents, especially neck-bands in the form of a half-moon (lunulae), and the golden balls (bullae) which were worn as a charm round the neck until the attainment of manhood.

MODERN: This ceremony should be performed on the 9th day after birth for boys and on the 8th day after birth for girls.

(ABLUTIO)

Wash both hands in clean water and in capite velato pray:

May this water cast out all impurities from my substance as from lead to gold. May this water cleanse my body of impurities, as the rain cleanses the air. Purify my mind. Purify my body. Purify my heart. It is so.

(PRAEFATIO)

O Lar familiaris, by offering this incense to you I pray good prayers, so that you may be benevolent and propitious to me, my family, and my household.

Incense is placed in the focus of the altar.

O Mother Nundina, by offering this incense to you I pray good prayers, so that you may be benevolent and propitious to me, my family, and my household.

Incense is placed in the focus of the altar.

(PRECATIO)

Be well and blessed, O Lar familiaris, on this ninth day after the birth of my child, I pray good prayers, offer this wine, and ask and beseech you, so that you will watch over the safety and wellbeing of my child and safeguard the child from harm, fever, illness, and disease; that you confirm, strengthen and help my household, and save it from all discord, so that my household may always flourish and prosper; and, so that you may be benevolent and propitious to me, to my household and to my family.

Be well and blessed, O Mother Nundina, goddess of the ninth day. I pray good prayers, offer this milk, and ask that my child, who shall from this day forth be called (Full Name of Child), shall be blessed with good health, happiness, success, wellbeing and receive all the blessings of a good life through her name and the name of our family; that the child be preserved from evil influences in the future; that (his/her) name be acceptable to you; and that that you may be benevolent and propitious to me, to my household and to my family.

(REDDITIO)

O Lar familiaris, as by offering to you the incense virtuous prayers were well prayed. For the sake of this be honoured by this humble wine.

A libation of wine is poured on the altar.

O Mother Nundina, as by offering to you the incense virtuous prayers were well prayed. For the sake of this be honoured by this humble milk.

A libation of milk is poured on the altar.

Bulla is ceremoniously presented to the mother for the child.

It is so.

(PIACULUM)

O Lar familiaris, Mother Nundina, and all Gods Immortal by whatever name I may call you: if anything in this ceremony was displeasing to you, with the sacrificial incense I ask forgiveness and expiate my fault.

Incense is placed in the focus of the altar.

It is done!

LOSS OF A CHILD RITUAL

Performed After the Loss of a Child

(ABLUTIO)

Wash both hands in clean water and in capite velato pray:

May this water cast out all impurities from my substance as from lead to gold. May this water cleanse my body of impurities, as the rain cleanses the air. Purify my mind. Purify my body. Purify my heart. It is so.

(PRAEFATIO)

O Lar familiaris, by offering this incense to you I pray good prayers, so that you may be benevolent and propitious to me, my family, and my household.

Incense is placed in the focus of the altar.

O Mother Orbona, by offering this incense to you I pray good prayers, so that you may be benevolent and propitious to me, my family, and my household.

Incense is placed in the focus of the altar.

(PRECATIO)

Be you well and blessed, O Lar familiaris, after the loss of my child, I pray good prayers, offer this wine, and ask and beseech you, so that you will grant me the benefit of another child; that you confirm, strengthen and help my household, and save it from all discord, so that the My household may always flourish and prosper; and, so that you may be benevolent and propitious to me, my household, and my family.

A libation of wine is poured on the altar.

O Mother Orbona, after the loss of my child, I pray good prayers, offer this milk, and ask and beseech you, so that you will grant me the benefit of another child; that you confirm, strengthen and help my household, and save it from all discord, so that the My household may always flourish and prosper; and, so that you may be benevolent and propitious to me, my household, and my family.

A libation of milk is poured on the altar.

(REDDITIO)

O Lar familiaris, as by offering to you the incense virtuous prayers were well prayed. For the sake of this be honoured by this humble wine.

A libation of wine is poured on the altar.

O Mother Orbona, as by offering to you the incense virtuous prayers were well prayed. For the sake of this be honoured by this humble milk.

A libation of milk is poured on the altar.

It is so.

(PIACULUM)

O Lar familiaris, Mother Orbona, and all Gods Immortal by whatever name I may call you: if anything in this ceremony was displeasing to you, with the sacrificial incense I ask forgiveness and expiate my fault.

Incense is placed in the focus of the altar.

It is done!

LIBERALIA CEREMONY & RITUAL (SON)

Performed on March 17 in the year of One's Sixteenth Birthday

WELCOME TO GUESTS & INTRODUCTORY REMARKS BY HOST

(ABLUTIO) [PARENT AND SON]

Both Parent and Son wash both hands in clean water and in capite velato pray:

May this water cast out all impurities from my substance as from lead to gold. May this water cleanse my body of impurities, as the rain cleanses the air. Purify my mind. Purify my body. Purify my heart. It is so.

(PRAEFATIO) [PARENT]

Be you well and blessed, O Lar familiaris! By offering you this incense, I pray good prayers so that you may be benevolent and propitious to my son (name), to me, to my family, and my household.

Incense is placed in the focus of the altar.

Be you well and blessed, O Father Liber, on this Liberalia! By offering you this incense, I pray good prayers so that you may be benevolent and propitious to my son (name), to me, to my family, and my household.

Incense is placed in the focus of the altar.

(PRECATIO) [PARENT]

O Lar familiaris, accept this offering from my son, (full Roman name), and by offering you this incense, I pray good prayers so that you may be benevolent and propitious to my son (first name/praenomen).

Lock of son's hair is placed in the focus of the altar.
Incense is placed in the focus of the altar.

O guardian of maturation, Father Liber, I pray good prayers, offer this wine, and ask that you guide him as he dons the toga virilis of manhood; that you watch over and protect him on the pathways of his future; that you protect him as he progresses through the trials and tribulations of young adulthood; that you give him courage to face and conquer those fears and enemies, beset upon his trail of life, that in due course, shall cause him to fail if caution and common sense not be his watchwords; that you bless him with wisdom to know the difference between right and wrong, and the knowledge to act upon each situation with the forethought of an adult and not the foolishness of a child. Grant him many successes and few failures as he grows from a boy into a man.

A libation of wine is poured on the altar.
Bulla is removed.

Toga praetexta is shed and toga virilis is donned by son.

[SON]

O Father Liber, be well and blessed. I pray good prayers, offer this wine, and beseech Thee that you may be gracious and favorable to me, my home and my household on this my first occasion of sacrifice, for which course I have ordained that the offering of this incense should be made in accordance with my own vows; that you may avert, ward off, and keep afar all disease visible and invisible, all barrenness, waste, misfortune, and ill weather; that you may cause my family, affairs, business and education to come to prosperity; and that you grant health and strength to me, my home and my household.

A libation of wine is poured on the altar.

(REDDITIO) [SON]

O Father Liber, as by offering to you the incense virtuous prayers were well prayed. For the sake of this be honoured by this humble wine.

A libation of wine is poured on the altar.

It is so.

(PIACULUM) [SON]

O Lar familiaris, O Father Liber, and all Gods Immortal by whatever name I may call you: if anything in this ceremony was displeasing to you, with the sacrificial incense I ask forgiveness and expiate my fault.

Incense is placed in the focus of the altar.

It is done!

REMARKS BY GUESTS

REMARKS BY PARENT

REMARKS BY SON

CELEBRATORY FESTIVITIES COMMENCE

LIBERALIA CEREMONY & RITUAL (DAUGHTER)

Performed on March 17 in the year of One's Sixteenth Birthday

WELCOME TO GUESTS & INTRODUCTORY REMARKS BY HOST

(ABLUTIO) [PARENT AND DAUGHTER]

Both Parent and Daughter wash both hands in clean water and in capite velato pray:

May this water cast out all impurities from my substance as from lead to gold. May this water cleanse my body of impurities, as the rain cleanses the air. Purify my mind. Purify my body. Purify my heart. It is so.

(PRAEFATIO) [PARENT]

Be you well and blessed, O Lar familiaris! By offering you this incense, I pray good prayers so that you may be benevolent and propitious to my daughter (name), to me, to my family, and my household.

Incense is placed in the focus of the altar.

Be you well and blessed, O Mother Libera, on this Liberalia! By offering you this incense, I pray good prayers so that you may be benevolent and propitious to my daughter (name), to me, to my family, and my household.

Incense is placed in the focus of the altar.

(PRECATIO) [PARENT]

O Lar familiaris, accept this offering from my daughter, (full Roman name), and by offering you this incense, I pray good prayers so that you may be benevolent and propitious to my daughter (first name/praenomen).

Lock of daughter's hair is placed in the focus of the altar.
Incense is placed in the focus of the altar.

O guardian of maturation, Mother Libera, I pray good prayers, offer this honeyed milk, and ask that you guide her as she dons the stola of womanhood; that you watch over and protect her on the pathways of her future; that you protect her as she progresses through the trials and tribulations of young adulthood; that you give her courage to face and conquer those fears and enemies, beset upon her trail of life, that in due course, shall cause her to fail if caution and common sense not be her watchwords; that you bless her with wisdom to know the difference between right and wrong, and the knowledge to act upon each situation with the forethought of an adult and not the foolishness of a child. Grant her many successes and few failures as she grows from a girl into a woman.

A libation of honeyed milk is poured on the altar.

Bulla is removed.

Garland crown of flowers is placed upon the daughter's head.

[DAUGHTER]

O Mother Libera, be well and blessed. I pray good prayers, offer this honeyed milk, and beseech Thee that you may be gracious and favorable to me, my home and my household on this my first occasion of sacrifice, for which course I have ordained that the offering of this incense should be made in accordance with my own vows; that you may avert, ward off, and keep afar all disease visible and invisible, all barrenness, waste, misfortune, and ill weather; that you may cause my family, affairs, business and education to come to prosperity; and that you grant health and strength to me, my home and my household.

A libation of honeyed milk is poured on the altar.

(REDDITIO) [DAUGHTER]

O Mother Libera, as by offering to you the incense virtuous prayers were well prayed. For the sake of this be honoured by this humble honeyed milk.

A libation of honeyed milk is poured on the altar.

It is so.

(PIACULUM) [DAUGHTER]

O Lar familiaris, O Mother Libera, and all Gods Immortal by whatever name I may call you: if anything in this ceremony was displeasing to you, with the sacrificial incense I ask forgiveness and expiate my fault.

Incense is placed in the focus of the altar.

It is done!

REMARKS BY GUESTS

REMARKS BY PARENT

REMARKS BY DAUGHTER

CELEBRATORY FESTIVITIES COMMENCE

TRAVEL RITUAL

Performed before Departing on a Journey

(ABLUTIO)

Wash both hands in clean water and in capite velato pray:

May this water cast out all impurities from my substance as from lead to gold. May this water cleanse my body of impurities, as the rain cleanses the air. Purify my mind. Purify my body. Purify my heart. It is so.

(PRAEFATIO)

O Lar familiaris, by offering this incense to you I pray good prayers, so that you may be benevolent and propitious to me, my family, and my household.

Incense is placed in the focus of the altar.

(PRECATIO)

Be you well, O Lar familiaris, on this day that I depart to travel, I pray good prayers, offer this wine, and ask and beseech you, so that you will safeguard me (and those who travel with me), seeing me (us) safely to my (our) destination without harm, illness, ill weather, inconvenience, nor misdirection; that the trip be well and successful to the completion of its purpose; that you may confirm, strengthen and help my household, and save it from all discord in my absence, so that my household may always flourish and prosper; and, so that you may be benevolent and propitious to me, to my household and to my family.

A libation of wine is poured on the altar.

(REDDITIO)

O Lar familiaris, as by offering to you the incense virtuous prayers were well prayed. For the sake of this be honoured by this humble wine.

A libation of wine is poured on the altar.

It is so.

(PIACULUM)

O Lar familiaris, and all Gods Immortal by whatever name I may call you: if anything in this ceremony was displeasing to you, with the sacrificial incense I ask forgiveness and expiate my fault.

Incense is placed in the focus of the altar.

It is done!

NEW BUSINESS RITUAL

Performed before starting a New Business Veture.

(ABLUTIO)

Wash both hands in clean water and in capite velato pray:

May this water cast out all impurities from my substance as from lead to gold. May this water cleanse my body of impurities, as the rain cleanses the air. Purify my mind. Purify my body. Purify my heart. It is so.

(PRAEFATIO)

O Iane pater, by offering this incense to you I pray good prayers, so that you may be benevolent and propitious to me, my family, and my household.

Incense is placed in the focus of the altar.

O Mercurius, by offering this incense to you I pray good prayers, so that you may be benevolent and propitious to me, my family, and my household.

Incense is placed in the focus of the altar.

(PRECATIO)

Father Ianus, be you well and blessed, on this day that I begin anew in business, and I pray good prayers, offer this wine, and ask and beseech you, so that you will grant the blessings of a new and successful beginning to my business venture. I pray for your continued strength that you may confirm, strengthen and help my business and my household, and save it from all discord, so that my business and my household may always flourish and prosper; and, so that you may be benevolent and propitious to me, to my household and to my family.

A libation of wine is poured on the altar.

Be you well and blessed, O Mercurius, on this day that I begin a new business venture of (Business Venture), and I pray good prayers, offer this wine, and ask and beseech you, so that you will safeguard me along the way. Nothing more ample do I pray, O Maia's son, save that You will make these my gifts last throughout my life.

O Mercurius Cyllenius, principle author of all sacred knowledge, at times within Heaven, at other times travelling within the starry signs to open the celestial paths to the highest parts above and the lowest paths beneath the earth. You stitch together the stars in the empty void of space into constellations, name them and determine their course; may it have been for us to reverently use the greater powers of the universe that You make, pondering them, not in all matters, but in the potential of things in themselves, and to learn of the divine plan set for the greatest nations. Guide and rotect me, O Great One, as I travel the land and help me to understand, as you communicate to me, the messages of the gods as they offer me opportunities for abundance, but that which I might not hear, see or understand without your divine help and assistance

May You, O Mercurius, make plump the riches of my house and all else there, spare my natural talents in any case, and as usual, may You remain the primary guardian over me.

Grant that I may profit, grant joy in making a profit, grant that I may enjoy once more enjoy success in my venture! Help me in my business affairs and quadruple my fortune with profit.

I pray for your continued strength that you may confirm, strengthen and help my business and my household, and save it from all discord, so that my business and my household may always flourish and prosper; and, so that you may be benevolent and propitious to me, to my household and to my family.

A libation of wine is poured on the altar.

(REDDITIO)

O Iane pater, as by offering to you the incense virtuous prayers were well prayed. For the sake of this be honoured by this humble wine.

A libation of wine is poured on the altar.

O Mercurius, by all names, as by offering to you the incense virtuous prayers were well prayed. For the sake of this be honoured by this humble wine.

A libation of wine is poured on the altar.

It is so.

(PIACULUM)

O Iane pater, O Mercurius, and all Gods Immortal by whatever name I may call you: if anything in this ceremony was displeasing to you, with the sacrificial incense I ask forgiveness and expiate my fault. May everything I have done and said this day bring honor and happiness on me, on my family, and on the Gods.

Incense is placed in the focus of the altar.

It is done!

FUNERAL RITUAL (ritus Romanus)

May be performed at the graveside for inhumation or at a memorial service after cremation.

Adapted from the Roman Memorial Service by Kirk Thomas at adf.org. Myrrh is also used, as it is a funerary incense.

Quirites, we are here to celebrate the life of (Name of Deceased). While this is a time of grief, it is also a celebration of Life!

(LAUDATIO)

Dis Manibus Sacrum. (Name of Deceased), who lived ___ years and whose spirit is attended here today by his/her family and friends, we remember you.

Adoratio is performed and the image of the deceased is touched by the Sacerdos.

(INVOCATIO)

O Manes, who claimed him;
Mercury who conveyed him;
Charon who ferried him;
And Dis Pater who welcomed him;
O Powers of paths where the newly dead go,
We pray to You now – hear us!
Your spirits are great, Your powers intense,

We ask that you join Yours with ours.
Let the barriers standing between this world and Yours
Dissolve in our hearts – hear us!

With love and with joy, we humbly pray
For our dearly departed friend to join us here now.
As our newest Ancestor to cross the divide
We welcome you home – hear us!

Newest Ancestor, (Name of Deceased), we welcome you here!
And though we shall miss you here in this world,
We take comfort in knowing that you are quite near,
Just beyond the veil of this world.

When the veil is thin and the Gates open wide,
We will welcome you here once again!
One day we will pass to the Land of the Dead
We hope that you'll welcome us, too.

Quirites, this is also the time of the living!

We now call on those who have cared for (Name of Deceased) and who miss him, To come forward and speak, sharing a memory of happy times. And in days of old, offerings were made to the newly dead to accompany them on their way.

We invite all family members to bring up their Grave Goods and Offerings, that they may honor our new Ancestor.

Individuals come up, make sacrifices and tell stories about the deceased.

We invite all others to bring up Grave Goods for sacrifice, that we may make offering to our new Ancestor.

The People come up one at a time, and leave an offering (such as silver or beer or other food) on the altar for later burial or disposal, or put it in the grave or the well or pour it on the ground.

After an offering is made, the person may speak for a time about the deceased. When each person is finished speaking, the Sacerdos will say:

So shall it be!

When everyone who wishes to speak has spoken of the Dead, the Sacerdos performs the sacrifice.

(ABLUTIO)

Wash both hands in clean water and in capite velato pray:

May this water cast out all impurities from my substance as from lead to gold. May this water cleanse my body of impurities, as the rain cleanses the air. Purify my mind. Purify my body. Purify my heart. It is so.

(PRAEFATIO)

Be you well and blessed, O Manes, O Father Mercury, O Charon, O Dis pater, and all Gods immortal! By offering you this incense, I pray good prayers so that you may be benevolent and propitious to me, my family, and my household.

Incense is placed in the focus of the altar.

(PRECATIO)

Palms turned downward.

O Manes, spirits of the ancestors of (Name of Deceased), we make offering to You! We thank you for meeting (Name of Deceased) at his/her bedside, remaining with him/her until he/she was ready, offering him/her comfort, allaying his/her fears, preparing his/her soul for its journey.

O Manes, accept this sacrifice!

A libation of wine is poured onto the ground.
Incense (myrrh) is offered in the focus of the altar.

Palms turned upward.

O Mercury Pater, Fleet-footed Soul Carrier, we make offering to You! We thank You for conducting (Name of Deceased) through the Worlds to the shores of the River Styx! Offerings are made at the riverbank! For (Name of Deceased) has reached the Land of the Dead.

O Fleet-Footed Mercury Pater, accept this sacrifice!

A libation of wine is poured in the focus of the altar.
Incense (myrrh) is offered in the focus of the altar.

Palms turned downward.

O Charon, the Dark Ferryman, we make offering to You! We thank you for conveying (Name of Deceased) across the dark river to the Underworld, offerings are made to the Mouth of the Earth to pay for Your sacred duty.

O Faceless Charon, accept this sacrifice!

Coins are placed in the grave or in the offerings receptacle.
Incense (myrrh) is offered in the focus of the altar.

Palms turned downward.

O Dis Pater, Lord of the Dead and Ruler of Hades, We make offering to You! We thank you for accepting (Name of Deceased) among the Mighty Dead, That he/she might join

his/her Ancestors and receive these humble sacrifices of the Living, and for opening the Doors of Dis that we may commune with him.

O Somber Dis Pater, accept this sacrifice!

A libation of wine is poured onto the ground.
Hematite is placed in the grave or in the offerings receptacle.
Hemlock is offered in the focus of the altar.
Incense (myrrh) is offered in the focus of the altar.

(REDDITIO)

O Manes, O Father Mercury, O Charon, O Dis pater, and all Gods Immortal, as by offering to you the incense virtuous prayers were well prayed. For the sake of this be honoured by this incense.

Incense (Myrrh) is offered in the focus of the altar.

It is so.

(PIACULUM)

O Manes, O Father Mercury, O Charon, O Dis pater, and all Gods Immortal by whatever name I may call you: if anything in this ceremony was displeasing to you, with the sacrificial incense I ask forgiveness and expiate my fault. May everything I have done and said this day bring honor and happiness on me, on my family, and on the Gods.

Incense (Myrrh) is offered in the focus of the altar.

It is done!

(CLOSING)

Quirites, though grieving continues, now is the time to let go.

O Manes, Fleet-footed Mercury, Faceless Charon and Somber Dis Pater, We thank you for your aid. Departed Friend, our love and thanks go with you on your way. Now look we deep within our hearts and closing Gates discern. We know that death is but a door And loved-ones will return!

Valete.

Go forth and walk with wisdom, Quirites, this rite has ended.

Illicet.

There are many rituals that may be performed each year and periodically from time to time.

As you progress and become more familiar with the Religio Romana, you will develop the skills needed to perform your own celebrations...be they daily ones or festival days from the calendar.

These examples have been provided for your use, as well as serving as a basis for you to create your own. There is no "correct" prayer formula for private rites. That is between you and the gods.

It is the express desire and hope of the Author that these examples will spur your own creativity, thereby, improving yourself as a practitioner of the *cultus deorum Romanum*.

14 ON DOMESTIC ROMAN SACRIFICE

Template and Guidelines

The main source for the study of domestic Roman sacrifices is no doubt Cato in his work *De Agricultura*. Comparison with surviving descriptions of public sacrifices reveals that private and public sacrifices followed much the same set of guidelines, which allow us to fill the gaps left open by Cato with elements that survived in the descriptions of public sacrifices. In fact, several public sacrifices were originally private to some families, the state having decided to preserve them (e.g. after the lineage of the family was broken) because of their importance to the city of Rome as a whole. We can even go further and state that the public cult in Rome was nothing more than a domestic cult adapted to the scale of the city. Just like any private household, the city had its own hearth (the Temple of Vesta) where Vesta and the Penates Publici (Public Penates) were honored.

In this chapter we will provide a template for a standard traditional domestic roman sacrifice, as well as information about the correct offerings to give to the main deities. Non-standard sacrifices (e.g. *lectisternia, sellisternia, devotiones*) or sacrifices with special mysterious rites performed at specific occasions and/or stemming from a long tradition (the meaning of many being already forgotten by the time of the Republic), fall out of the span of the present work. On the other hand, most simple daily rites and offerings can be considered as consisting on a small subset of the procedures described below (e.g. libation of wine, daily offering of incense).

The provided template will be illustrated with the original description of a simple offering to Iuppiter Dapalis [**Cato, *De Agricultura*, 132**], as well as other sources when needed.

We can divide the standard sacrificial procedures in several parts or moments:

1. Praeparatio
2. Praefatio
3. Precatio
4. Immolatio
5. Redditio
6. Profanatio
7. Epulum

The page finishes with an appendix which presents a table with the sacrificial details for specific deities. For any doubts or information on deities not included in the table feel free ask the Collegium Pontificum. You can also join the Religio Romana mailing list to discuss these and other related matters.

Praeparatio

In domestic sacrifices the preparation is easier. The sacrifice takes place in front of the *Lararium* usually placed near or above an hearth or fireplace (*focus*). If it is a blood sacrifice, it can be made on an outdoor *Lararium* or on a *focus* prepared on purpose outside the house.

The sacrificer is usually the paterfamilias, but the materfamilias can also sacrifice in some occasions (e.g. she sacrifices to her Iuno - guardian spirit or female equivalent of the Genius - on her birthday). Other members of the household can help to carry the offerings or other objects. In order to ensure that the words are correctly spoken, one of the assistants may be charged to read the words and whisper them to the sacrificer [Plinius, Naturalis Historia, 28.3.10]. The sacrificer should also bath himself before the sacrifice [Livius, Ab Urbe Condita, 1.45].

Once the time comes, the officiants approach the Lararium where an image of the deity honored in the sacrifice is placed among the Penates (deities worshiped in the household). The sacrificer faces the Lararium, while the assistants and audience remain on his back.

For more information regarding the preparation of the Lararium and the sacrificial tools, please refer to Lararium section of Chapter 4, Worshiping the Gods at Home.

The two forms of sacrifice

In general there can be said to have been two forms of sacrifice previously practiced in the religio Romana: bloodless offerings and blood sacrifice. While recognizing that blood sacrifices were made in the past and may be regarded as part of the tradition, there is more precedence in the tradition that rejects the use of blood sacrifice. At different places in the Fasti, Ovid mentions that "Formerly what served to conciliate gods and men was spelt and pure salt's glistening grain," Sabine juniper and laurel, and garlands of flowers alone [1] , and that blood sacrifices were a later introduction. Later offerings of incense from distant lands were begun by Liber, these being myrrh, frankincense, and Indian nard, and also that he introduced libations of milk and honey, and special liba cakes (3.727-736). Still later, after the introduction of the vine, libations of wine were made to some of the gods, while milk was retained as the appropriate libation for the gods and goddesses of an older tradition. Pliny mentions that rites established by Romulus continued the custom of using milk libations, and that Numa had forbidden wine libations on funeral pyres [2] . Tradition held that Pompilius Numa was the second king of Rome, succeeding Romulus. That same tradition credited Numa with having founded most of the institutions of the religio Romana, including its calendar and priesthoods. The rites instituted for the state religio by Numa did not include the use of blood sacrifices, and explicitly disallowed their use. Plutarch too mentions that blood sacrifices were uncommon in the time of Numa, and that grain was the most frequently used offering (Numa 8.8). We should understand this to mean then that blood sacrifices continued in private practices, although not in the tradition of the public rites. This tradition forsaking blood sacrifices goes back further, to Pythagoras, and this was recognized in Roman traditions by making Numa a student of Pythagoras. This story may trace back to Aristoxenus who is said to have written that Romans were among Pythagoras' followers. The story continued at least until 186 BCE, and although officially abandoned later, it is still found with Ovid into the early empire (Cicero, Republica 2.28, Tusculum 4.3; Livy 1.18, 40.29.9-14; Dionysius of Halicarnassus 2.59; Plutarch, Numa 18; Ovid, Metamorphoses 15.4.481, Fasti 3.153; Pliny, Natural History XIII.87). From Pythagoras and Numa, through Seneca and in a broader sense Apollonius of Tyana as well, there was within the religio Romana another, older tradition which not only rejected the use of blood sacrifices, but which also made vegetarianism a pious choice in private practice.

The first blood sacrifice, that of a sow, is said to have been ordered for Ceres [3] . In Rome the Aventine Temple of Ceres had a strong association with Greek influences arriving from southern Italy. Cicero considered the worship of Ceres at Rome to have derived from the Greeks (pro Balbo 55; In C. Verrem 72.187). He states that the rituals were Greek in origin and in name, and that even the priestesses who conducted the rituals in his time were Greek and performed their rites in Greek. But we should understand these Greek rites to have been the later introduction brought to Rome when priestesses from Capua were invited in 196 BCE to perform the ritus Graecus. The earlier Temple of Ceres, dedicated in 494 BCE, was also associated with Sabellian Capua and may have had some Greek influences, but was distinctly an Italic cult. The Temple of Ceres was also dedicated to Liber and Libera in 494 BCE. The assimilation of Dionysus with Liber did not occur until 186 BCE, however, and so the cultus deorum of Ceres, Liber, and Libera was Italic at the time of its initial introduction. It cannot therefore be said that Ceres was introduced to Rome by Greeks in the same manner that the Magna Mater arrived from Asia; only that certain aspects of Her worship was derived from Greek influences. These traditions on the cultus Cereri suggest that the adoption of blood sacrifice was a foreign introduction to the religio Romana originally established by Pompilius Numa, but not that blood sacrifices were necessarily of Greek origin.

We should recall, also, that human sacrifices were made in an earlier period. The Senate outlawed the practice in 454 BCE (Pliny N. H. XXX.12; the Twelve Tablets), although we know of some later instances. The Senate again outlawed human sacrifices in 97 BCE when Licinius Crassus was consul. In certain Roman rites puppets were substituted for human victims. There is the well-known example of the Argei. These straw puppets were tossed by the Vestal Virgins into the River Tiber on 14 (15) May, who Ovid and Cicero mention as substitutes for old men that were sacrificed in an earlier age (Ovid, Fasti 5.621-662; Cicero, pro Roscio Amerino, 35.100 mentions the sexagenarios de ponte). Similarly at the Feriae Sementiva and Paganalia in January, and at the Feriae Latinae in April, puppets (oscillae) were hung in trees in substitution of an earlier practice of sacrificing boys (Probus and Servius commenting on Georgic II.389, where Virgil wrote, "invoke Thee with glad hymns, O Bacchus, and to thee hang puppet-faces on tall pines to swing." Macrobius 1.7.34). One legend held that Remus had been sacrificed to purify the pomerium wall, and recently (summer 2000) there was discovered a pomerium wall around the Palatine under which the remains of four sacrificial victims had been placed. These are believed to have been sacrificed at the time when Servius Tullius built the walls of Rome, expanding the pomerium. When Augustus rededicated the city, four pillars were buried, one inscribed in memory of Remus, either commemorating or in substitution of the Servian sacrifices. Recalling ancient practices, yet substituting puppets of straw, wax, or bread in the religio Romana may be compared to the practices of other religions. The main celebration of Christian churches is that of a human sacrifice and a cannibalistic meal, where bread is substituted for the flesh of their founder. Among the Chinese objects made of paper are burned in sacrifice as substitutes for what they represent.

In a similar fashion the attitude towards the use of animals for blood sacrifices changed over time. In the Republican era pontifical regulations permitted wax figures or animal forms made of dough to be substituted for animal victims. In the time of Nero, the philosopher and miracle-worker Apollonius of Tyana spoke out against not only human sacrifices, but also against any of the traditional blood sacrifices. "I am not," he said, "the sort of person who prays with his eye on a knife or offers these kind of sacrifices...and if I had...I would become guilty of murder and operate with entrails that are an abomination to me and wholly unacceptable to the gods (Philstratus, Life of Apollonius of Tyana 8.7.9-10)." Blood sacrifices of all kinds were then banned by an imperial decree on 24 February, 391 CE. Modern practitioners of the religio Romana, rejecting the use of blood sacrifices, have thus returned to honoring the practices first instituted by Pompilius Numa. The reasons for sacrifices

The rites of the religio Romana employ the use of sacrifices in conjunction with prayers offered up to the gods and goddesses. The reasons for including sacrifices are given by the fourth century Neoplatonist Cynic Sallustius.

1. First is the matter of giving thanks to the gods and goddesses for all they have provided. One gives back a portion of what they have received. As such, what is appropriate to sacrifice to any deity depends upon what specific providence is under the deity. An appropriate sacrifice to Ceres, the goddess of grain, would therefore be grain or bread; for Pomona, the goddess of fruiting plants, the appropriate sacrifice would be the fruits She has provided.

2. "Prayers offered without sacrifices are only words, with sacrifices they are live words; the wording gives meaning to the life while the life animates the words." The religio Romana promotes the growth and development of the whole person, in body, mind and soul. Thus in every rite we perform, these three components of ourselves must be involved. It is with our physical actions that we involve the use of the body, our mind in the thoughts and words we use, and our soul is in the sincere intent and devotion of the performance of our rites. The words of a prayer voices the meaning and intent, the sacrifice gives it substance, but there must also be the third portion to conjoin our soulful essence with our actions.

The essence of our actions is then carried along with the essence of the sacrifice back to its divine source.

3. "The happiness of every object is its own perfection, and perfection for each is communion with its own cause." Everything proceeds from the gods and shall return to the gods in its own time. Or as Proclus stated, "Every effect remains in its cause, proceeds from it, and reverts upon it (Elements of Theology, Prop. 35). Having lived its life, performed its purpose in life, each constituent part of an object shall return to its source, its being perfected in the completion of its entire cycle of life. That is true for humans, animals, and plants, and even, it may be said, for inanimate objects as well. In the first reason given above, the perspective was from that of the deities, returning what is already under their providence. Here Sallustius looked at sacrifice from the perspective of what is being offered, that is, its returning to its divine source alone, to achieve its perfection of being. Reverting back to its origin, returning through each stage of its procession from the source, and thus returning towards the divine, a sacrifice reverts upon its own perfection in the Divine (Proclus Elements of Theology Prop. 37).

The six types of sacrifices

There are six types of sacrifices that may be made in the religio Romana.
1. First is to honor the gods and to commemorate certain events such as the dedication of a temple.
2. To propitiate the gods when some disaster has occurred or other event whereby the gods demand a sacrifice.
3. Similarly, if divination, dreams or visions reveal a requirement that a sacrifice needs to be made.
4. By far though, most sacrifices made by individuals are performed in thanks, after a contract was met by the gods. A vow (nuncupatio) is first made that a sacrifice will be offered, or that an altar will be erected, or a temple built or renovated, or some other action that will be taken to fulfill the vow, on condition that the

god perform some request. If the request is fulfilled, the deity having accepted the vow, then one is obliged to fulfill the vow (ex voto); failure to do so would make that person sacer.

5. Sometimes, in expectation that prayers will be answered, a sacrifice is made, but there is no obligation on the part of the deity. Most often these types of sacrifices would be dedicated pro salute in hopes of being healed of some illness.

6. Lastly there are those sacrifices made, not to honor the gods or to fulfill a vow, but made instead as part of a purification rite.

Oblationes

In ancient times ludi were established to honor the gods and goddesses. The Ludi plebii of November, established in 220 BCE, and the Ludi Taurei Quinquennales conducted every five years in June, first established in 186 BCE, consisted of chariot races and horse races. The Ludi Apollinares of July, established in 212 BCE, and the Ludi Florales of April, established in 173 BCE, consisted of theatrical performances and chariot races. While the Ludi Saeculares of May and June consisted of three days and three nights of continuous theatrical performances. At other times poetry contests were held in honor of gods and goddesses. Composing poetry for the gods and goddesses, especially odes to the deities, is still an accepted form of offering made today.

Another ancient practice was to hold a feast in honor of the gods, a lectisternitum. Couches (lecti) were set outside in front of temples, upon which were placed their images, representing that the gods and goddesses join with the celebrants at the feast. Offerings of food were placed on tables before them. In private homes this practice was also made for the Lares, not unlike at the Seder of Judaism, or the Sicilian practice for St. Joseph's Day. Today bringing the images of the gods from the lararium to a dinner table to share in the family meal continues this practice, or otherwise food is set before the lararium. Such offerings of food are left for only as long a time as the meal takes place, and then are properly disposed.

By far the most common form of sacrifice made in ancient times was the erection of altars to the gods and goddesses of Roma antiqua. These were small column-like altars with a hallow (focus) in the upper surface for a flame in which to make offerings of incense. Such arae are inscribed with the name of the deity (in dative case) to whom it is offered, the name of the practitioner (in nominative) who erected the ara, followed by a statement of the reason. The reasons usually given were: pro salute for health, ex visu following a vision, ex voto following a vow or VSLM (votum solvit libens merito, "kept his vow freely to the god who deserved it"), or simply to say dono dedit ("He gave this gift"). Such arae were erected at roadside shrines or in front of temples. Today grottoes and arae are set up either in a family garden or inside the home.

Following the erection of arae then, the most common offerings used on them, ancient or modern, is that of incense or the burning of aromatic herbs. Herbs used for all gods and goddesses are myrtle, bay laurel and juniper, while frankincense, myrrh, nard, gum Arabic and orris root are common incenses. Cut flowers and floral wreaths are another common offering. Certain herbs and flowers are more closely associated with certain goddesses and gods than others.

Working together over the past ten years, pontiffs Gryllus Graecus, Salvius Austur, and Marcus Horatius developed a guide on oblations for specific Gods and Goddesses, a summary of which is provided below:

GUIDE FOR OBLATIONES

- **Adonis**: barley, fennel, roses, release of white doves.

- **Apollo**: bay laurel, calendula, hyacinth, wheat, crowns of laurel, cheese, honey, parsley, wine.

- **Asclepius**: butterfly weed, milkweed, mustard, thin-leaf parsnip.
- **Carna**: beans mixed with spelt and bacon.

- **Castor and Pollux**: frankincense.

- **Ceres**: barley, bread, crown of wheat (corona spicea), crown of oak leaves, dittany of Crete, flour, honey combs mixed in milk, hyacinth, incense, oak leaves, pennyroyal, poppies, spelt cakes, salt, storax, violets, wheat, first sampling of ears of wheat, wine.

- **Chiron**: chiron vine, greater centaury, St. John's wort, wormwood, yarrow.

- **Diana**: cakes of cheese, cakes of honey, cakes of parsley, hazel, jasmine, lavender, mandrake, rosemary, wormwood.

- **Dis Pater**: hemlock tree.

- **Faustus**: ivy, pine.

- **Hecate**: garlic, hemlock, mandrake, rue.

- **Hercules**: Aconite, black poplar tree, henbane, herb Robert, monkshood, opopanax, oregano, water lilies.

- **Genius or Juno**: incense, liba wheat cakes, wine.

- **Janus**: incense, strues cakes, wine.

- **Juno**: blue flag iris, cypress tree, incense, lily, orris root, saffron, silver, wild fig, wine.

- **Juno Lucina**: cakes of cheese, cakes of honey, cakes of parsley.

- **Juppiter**: bay laurel, beans and greens, beech tree, benzoin, cassia, cinnabar, cinnamon, far cakes, fertum cakes, fluorspar, frankincense, fruits, holm oak, marjoram, oak, saffron, sage, verbena, wine.

- **Lares**: bread, flour, flowers, fruit, incense, juniper, milk, myrtle, salt, water, wine.

- **Liber and Libera**: honey, ivy, liba cakes, libations of must, mint, pennyroyal, wine.

- **Manes**: black beans, milk, roses, salt, violets, water, wheat corns, wheat mixed in wine.

- **Mars**: bacon fat, cinnamon, clover, fertum cakes, iron, peony, strues cakes.

- **Mater Larum**, Mania, Mater Manua: garlic, poppyheads.

- **Mercury**: beans and greens, crocus, cypress, dill, frankincense, hellebore niger, herb mercury (mercurialis annua), marjoram, myrtle.

- **Minerva**: ampelos or chiron vine, dogbur mixed with plantain and yarrow, olive, rosemary, silver.

- **Neptune**: beans with greens, incense, scaled fish, sea shells, wine.

- **Pales**: basil.

- **Priapus**: liba cakes, lotus tree, milk.

- **Proserpina**: hemlock tree, hyacinth, mandrake, mint, myrtle, parsley, pennyroyal, poppies, rosemary, rue, violets.

- **Quirinus**: juniper, milk.

- **Saturnus**: costus, storax, violets.

- **Venus**: ambergris, anemone, fennel, incense, jewelry, lily, marjoram, mint, myrtle, pearls, rose, wine.

- **Vesta**: bay laurel, incense, juniper, violets, wine. An incomplete list of these associations is given below:

Libations of unmixed wine may be offered to any of the goddesses and gods, with the exception of Ceres, Tellus, and Pales, to whom only milk, or honey mixed in water or in milk is offered. Milk, or honey mixed in water or in milk may also be offered to female deities. Wine offered in a libation to Fauna, the Bona Dea, may be made, provided it is referred to only as milk and to its container as a honey pot, while no myrtle may be offered to Her. One may also note a passage from Virgil, (Eclogue 7.33-34): Sinum lactis et haec te liba, Priape, quotannis exspectare sat est: custos es pauperis horti. (A bowl of milk, Priapus, and these cakes, yearly, it is enough for you to claim; you are the guardian of a poor man's plot.) Following in the tradition of Numa, milk is a more acceptable general libation.

Often mentioned as an offering to the gods is libum, a special cake made for religious rituals. See Cato's De Agricultura 75 for a recipe. The libum is cut into small squares, then piled into a neat stack. Honey may be dripped over the liba, which is then served into a fire with a knife, as a burnt offering. Any offering or sacrifice, once dedicated to a god or goddess, should not be touched or profaned in any manner. Other special breads used for sacrifices are known. Cato also offers a recipe for placenta at De Agricultura 76, and mentions fertum at other places, although the recipe is not given.

Special moulds were used to make a sacrificial bread for Quirinus that had a wheel impressed into the top. Some had deep indentations to facilitate breaking the bread. Another specially prepared offering is moretum, described in a poem by that name and attributed to Virgil. Ovid mentions moretum as an offering to Magna Mater [4] . This is an herb salad, made with garlic, celery, rue, and coriander combined with cheese to form a pate (some oil and vinegar can be added to help smooth it into a paste). It may be molded into a round form and covered with a flour and water paste, then baked and used like libum. In modern practice any home baked bread may be substituted, with perhaps a foccaccia being the best to use. These may be drizzled with honey or oil before offering.

It was duty of the Vestal Virgins to make the mola salsa used in sacrifices. Spelt was dry roasted in ovens, then crushed into course flour and combined with pure salt. The mola salsa was then drizzled over the backs of sacrificial animals. Today mola salsa may be drizzled directly into a fire as an offering, or used to season other offerings. If a wax or dough figure is being used in substitution of an animal sacrifice then it would be treated in the manner employed in the past. Some hairs would be made into the figure's forehead, which would be cut and fed to a flame first. Its head would then be anointed with wine and mola salsa drizzled over its back. The figure would then be sliced into and the whole figure fed into a flame. For the use of vegetable substitutes for animal sacrifices, see the contest between Jupiter and Numa given by Ovid (Fasti 3.337-348). Similar to the mola salsa was the februa or pium far made for the purification rituals of the house and curiae that took place in February. This too was made of spelt roasted in an antique fashion, but salt is not mentioned in its preparation. The spelt was then pounded into rude cakes and offered to Juno on crude tables (mensae). Roman lictores carried februa for use in purifying houses, believed to have been used by strewing it on a doorsill of a house where someone had died and also as an incense (Ovid Fasti 2.24-5). There was also the salsamina "made by mixing four kinds of fruit" (Arnobius Adversus Gentes 7.24), i.e. four kinds of grains.

Votives

Another type of offering is the use of votives. These may be made of wood, terracotta, silver, copper or bronze. They can be coins or figurines of the gods and goddesses. They may be miniature tools or weapons, or models of feathers or leaves. Often miniature parts of the body, such as hands and feet or specific organs, were used as votives in sacrifices made for assistance in healing. Plaques with triangular handles were also used, either made with a relief depicting the gods or inscribed with a special request. Votives were then broken and buried in special deposits beneath arae or near or under templa.

Unique sacrificial terms for offerings of various kinds are known to us only from Arnobius (Adversus Gentes 7.24). These include a number of consecrated cakes formed into different shapes: africia,

gratilla, catumeum, cumspolium, and cubula. Prior to bread making Romans ate grain in pottages, and two these, differing only in quality, were retained in sacrifices – fitilla and frumen. There are several other specialized terms referring to blood sacrifices, such as the taedae that is animal fat cut into very small pieces like dainties. These specialized terms for different offerings, and instruction on how to prepare them, were kept in the Libri pontificales. Other strictures gave the specific animals that were to be offered to various deities, along with their markings, such as the use of a goat for Liber, a virgin calf for Minerva, or a special breed of oxen for Jupiter. There were also specialized terms for the instruments used in sacrifices, and the archaic utterances to be recited, all the details to be followed to the letter. But all of these strictures were meant for the formalized rituals of the state religio. In private practice there was greater variance and the same pontifical books provided for substitutions by using images made of wax or flour dough. Cato's lustratio is an example of a private rite, that mentions that a piglet, lamb, and calf may be substituted in a suovitaurilia which required matured animals be sacrificed, provided that they were not referred to as such (De Agricultura 141). A modern practitioner of the religio Romana who researches ancient rites for their own rites should bear this in mind. While attention to detail and exactness is emphasized in the religio Romana, more attention should be given to pious devotion than to outward performances.
Performing a Sacrifice

Daily prayers and offerings are made before the lararium. At the main meal of the day a portion of wine is offered to Jupiter by pouring it onto the ground, or otherwise in a small bowl which can later be poured on soil, with a simple prayer, Jupiter Pater macte vino in ferio esto. Other simple rites may be performed in a similar fashion.

A sacrifice however is a more formal rite and requires some preparation. First the practitioner should prepare himself or herself through fasting, purification, and prayer. Usually this will involve a period of days, five to nine days being common. One should fast, abstaining from meats, grain products, sweets and any heavy foods, and instead eat fruits and light foods. Alcohol, caffeine, drugs and preservatives should also be avoided. Herbal teas and tonics are taken as drink. Bathing, fumigations with sulphur or vervain, and anointings with oil are made in this period; the hair and beard should not be cut, nor should the nails be trimmed in this period. Daily rites of prayer and offerings should be maintained. On the day the sacrifice will be made, the celebrant should eat no food and drink only a small amount of vervain tea; bathe, anoint with oil, and dress in white. Other precautions may be warranted when approaching certain deities, or when sacrificing to a deity whose identity is unknown.

An area is then prepared in which to perform the sacrifice. The area should be swept, then aspersed with vervain water and incensed with frankincense. The altar is scrubbed with fresh vervain or mints, and wound with woolen filaments three times. A fire is then lit upon the altar and incense of vervain or frankincense is offered. (Pliny, Natural History 25.59; Virgil, Eclogue VIII. 64-66.) Facing south, auguries should then be taken for any sign of an ill omen before proceeding (see On Auguries).

If no signs appear which prohibit the sacrifice from being made at that time, then the sacrifice must be ordered. This is an important step as it signifies what action is about to be made. In De Agricultura 141 Cato states this ordering of the sacrifice as "Impera suovitaurilia circumagi, and then gives an example of the instructions one gives in ordering a sacrifice to be made. Another example is found in Plautus (Pseudolus 326-7), Ei accerse hostias, victumas, lanios, ut ego sacrificem summo Jovi ("Go, fetch offerings, victims, and those who slay them, that I may sacrifice to Jove most high"). Usually a sacrifice is promised to the deity on some previous occasion. One must fulfill such a promise, but a specific time when it is to be performed is not generally given. Now however, having then ordered the sacrifice, one is committed to begin performing the sacrifice. Failure to perform the sacrifice beyond this step would place a person in sacer. The sacrifice that is to be made will depend upon the occasion and the deity to whom it is offered. Every precaution should be taken to follow exactly what a formula requires in a particular ritual. Here we will consider the various steps required in making sacrifices, speaking only in general terms.

1) One should always begin with an invocation in the manner of "Jane, Jupiter, Mars Pater, Quirine." Other deities may be called

upon in addition to, or substituted for these deities, however Janus should always be included, and should always be named first to begin a formal sacrifice. In general, a priest would face east when invoking Janus and the other deities. Gods of the sea are invoked by facing in the direction of the largest nearby body of water. Certain other deities may be traditionally thought of as living in other directions. The Dii Inferi and chthonic goddesses and gods like Tellus and Ceres are generally invoked with the palm of the right hand placed on the earth or otherwise facing downward (Sallustius: pecora quae natura prona finxit; Varro: puerum imponere equo pronum in ventrem, postea sedentem). Most of the Dii Consentes are invoked with the palm of the right hand raised to the sky, the fingers bent slightly backward (supinas manus ad caelum tendere). The gods invoked in this first step are called to witness the sacrifice. In addition to the invocation, they are also given offerings individually, beginning with Janus. The manner of making these offerings is the same as in a daily ritual. Cato offers an example (De Agricultura 134): Iano pater, te hac strueo ommovendo bonas preces precoruti sies volens propitius mihi ("Father Janus, in offering you this heap of cakes, I pray with virtuous prayers, in order that you may be favorable and gracious to me.") And again, Iano pater, uti te strue ommovenda bonas preces bene precatus sum, eiusdem rei ergo macte vino inferio esto ("Father Janus, as in offering you the heap of cakes prayers were well spoken, for the sake of the same things, be honored by this humble wine.") After offerings have been made in turn to each deity who has been invoked aloud, the formal sacrifice may proceed. At the conclusion of the sacrifice itself, a prayer and offering should be made to Vesta in the same manner to conclude the ceremony.

2) The invocation that will be made to the deity to whom the sacrifice is offered is performed a little differently. This invocation is made in two parts, the manner of which is described on the Iguvium Tavolo, in Umbrium, as Sevum kutef pesnimu arepes arves, or in Latin, Formulam clare precator tostis granis. The instruction given here is that the prayer is to be spoken over each offering (in the example given, over each pile of grain), and that it is to be made according to ritual formula. This indicates that the invocation is first to be made aloud, and it is to be intoned, not simply spoken. Further, the particular phrasing used here,

formulam clare, means that the invocation is to be murmured. The reason why both forms of invocation are inferred here is simple. At a public sacrifice such as is described on the Iguvium Tavolo the names of gods who are invoked aloud are for the benefit of those witnessing the ceremony. But the names of the gods who are invoked to sanctify the sacrifice, and thus are spoken by formula over the sacrifices themselves, are murmured because the names which will be used are known only to the attending priests. The deity is first addressed aloud in a formula that is more elaborate than used above. An example from Plautus for Jupiter is, Iovi opulento, inculto, Ope gnato, supreme, valido, viripotenti, Opes, spes bonas, copias commodenti, lubens disque omnibus ago gratias virtulorque merito...(O Jove, opulent, glorious son of Ops, supreme God, powerful and mighty, bestower of wealth, good hopes and bounty, gladly I give thanks and rightly praise you and all the gods...) (Persa 251-4). Or again in Plautus, Iuppiter, qui genus colis alisque hominem, per quem vivimus aevom, quem penes spes vitae sunt hominum omnium, ... (O Jupiter, you who cherish and nurture the human race, through who we live and draw the breath of being, in who rests the hopes and lives of all mankind...) (Poenulus 1187-88). This initial address of the deity may call upon Him with several references to myths about Him, His titles and His attributes, in a manner that is found among the Orphic Hymns. Offerings of incense and libations are made along with the invocation.

3) The sacrifice is first led to the altar. The altar is approached with the right hand raised to waist level, palm up, either by the individual carrying the sacrifice, or the one who leads the procession. Taking position at or near the altar along with the celebrant will be the priest (popa) who will perform the ceremony, certain assistants (gemelli, flamines, and victimi) and the flute players (tibiae) or other musicians who are to play throughout the ceremony.

A) The ceremony begins with the celebrant invoking the deity aloud, as described above.

B) Then is followed a ceremony in the manner described by Livy (A.U.C. 1.24). The popa requires of the chief celebrant, "Do you order me to make this sacrifice to (the name of the deity)?" Upon an affirmative answer, the popa then says, "I demand of thee, (name or title), some tufts of grass." The celebrant then replies, "Take those that are pure." (For the meaning of the 'grass' see Ovid, Fasti 3.27-28.) A small portion of the sacrifice is then cut away and offered into the fire on the altar. In ancient times tufts of hair would be cut from the forehead of a sacrificial animal. One rite described by Cato involves a sacrifice of leeks to Jupiter, in which he specifies that the tops are first cut from the heads, and that both are offered. The popa next asks, 'Do you constitute me as the representative of (those on whose behalf the sacrifice is made), sanctioning also my vessels and assistants?' To which the celebrant replies, 'So far as may be without hurt to myself and (those named above), I do.'

C) The popa takes the portion of the sacrifice that was removed and touches it to the forehead of the celebrant. Whatever else is being sacrificed, this first portion represents the whole, and is connected to the person authorizing the sacrifice. This portion is then offered to the flames before it is sanctified. Observance is made to see that the selected sacrifice is acceptable to the invoked deity. Were the sacrifice made to Jupiter or any of the celestial gods and goddesses, then the smoke should rise; if to a chthonic deity, then the smoke should seep to the ground. Other omens such as the calls of birds or the sound of lightning are also taken into consideration.

D) Next the sacrifice is to be sanctified to the deity. Over the sacrifice some mola salsa should be sprinkled. In ancient times the mola salsa was specifically used in sanctifying a blood sacrifice. Yet its components, salt and spelt, go back to an earlier period, before blood sacrifices were used (Fasti 1.37-38). A sacrifice of bread, or grain, fruit or herbs, or even some inanimate objects may be sanctified with a sprinkling of pure salt, or mola salsa which has been specially prepared for ritual use. The sacrifice should also be sprinkled with either wine or milk (salted water may be substituted) depending upon the deity invoked. Over the sacrifice is then murmured a formula invoking the deity by His or Her secret names. Here an ancient formula of invocation is made, making use of alliteration and assonance in an enumeration of attributes, made with parallels of paired terms, the second term expanded from the first, and the parallels linked together in a chiasmus relation. Also to be enumerated are the reasons the sacrifice is being made. A slit is then made into the sacrifice. Sacrificial knives were usually made of chipped flint or bronze, iron and steel should not be used anywhere in the area of a sacrifice. The sacrifice is now sanctified and may no longer be touched by human hands. Instruments are used to cut the sacrifice into small pieces, stack them into a pile, and feed them into a flame. In the case where votives are being offered, they are held with one instrument and struck by a hammer to bend or break them, before being deposited into the ground. Prayers said while making an offering are usually made with the right hand extended over the fire, palm down, and striking the chest over the heart whenever the name of the deity is said. The chest is also struck at the name of the deity while bending over the sacrifice in sanctifying it.

E) If the sacrifice is to involve a shared meal (daps), a portion offered to the deity and the rest to be eaten by the celebrants, then the latter must be profaned. The entire sacrifice was first sanctified to the deity and is thus sacred. That which is offered to the deity is therefore not to be touched by human hands. In contrast, what is then to be served to the celebrants is touched by the priest, profaning it so that humans may eat of it. In De Agricultura 132, Cato refers to the sanctified sacrifice itself as being Jove, which is "piously profaned," Jove caste profanato sua contagione. If the sacrifice were several loaves of bread, one loaf might be offered into the fire, the rest would each have to be touched by the popa before distributing them to the celebrants. These must all be consumed immediately, within the sacred place that was made for the sacrifice (Cato's Ubi res divina facta erit, statim ibidem consumito ~De Agricultura 83.) Sacrifices made to the Dii Inferni may not be shared in this manner, but must be completely consumed by fire, or otherwise buried in a manner that will not be disturbed. A sacrifice offered to the Dii Inferni becomes one with them as with all sanctified sacrifices, and as they are deities of putrefaction, among other things, the sanctified sacrifice is no longer suitable for human consumption.

F) A final consideration is that a sacrifice offered to the deity may be found unacceptable. In that case an additional sacrifice is made. Here again reference is made to Cato, as in De Agricultura 141. "If less than all of the sacrifice is successfully made," then make an additional sacrifice with the formula "if something of this sacrifice was not pleasing to you, this sacrifice (I make) to you in atonement."

4) Finally the ceremony is concluded with additional offerings of wine (or milk) and incense. These may include offerings to the deities invited in the first part of the ceremony to witness it, and to the deity invoked in the sacrifice, and properly should conclude with an offering to Vesta. Use of this guide

The above description of sacrificial rites is to serve as a general guide for modern practitioners of the religio Romana. Any ceremony developed for your own rites should be carefully researched. Ancient texts will provide guidance on different aspects of a ceremony, but rarely provide guidance on a complete ceremony.

Praefatio

A more solemn sacrifice (namely a sacrifice of a living victim) starts with a *praefatio*, which consists on offerings of incense and wine where some deities are invited to witness the sacrifice. Small offerings like the offering to Iuppiter Dapalis [Cato, *De Agricultura*, 132] do not include a *praefatio*. Others like [Cato, *De Agricultura* 134] seem to present two *praefationes*, one of incense and wine and another of cakes and wine. In temple sacrifices, the *praefatio* was performed before the temple entrance using a portable hearth, the *foculus*.

The *praefatio* starts with the invocation of Ianus [Cicero, *De Natura Deorum*, II.67], the god of beginnings. Cato adds Iuppiter [Cato, *De Agricultura* 141] and Iuno [Cato, *De Agricultura* 134]. According to [Ovidius, Fasti, 6.303 seq.], Vesta can also be among the deities invoked in the *praefatio*, as she governs the fire of the hearth through which the offerings reach the gods (see [Servius, ad

Aen., 1.292]). In [ILS154] the deity in whose honor the sacrifice is performed is addressed in the *praefatio*.

The following procedures illustrate a *praefatio* where the deities invoked are Ianus and Iuppiter. The prayers are based on [Cato, *De Agricultura* 134].

1) The sacrificer will normally be wearing a toga (the *toga praetexta* is used by magistrates in public sacrifices). The sacrificer veils his head with the toga (called *capite velato* or *cinctu Gabinu*) as the deities invoked in the praefatio are to be honored *romano ritu* (according to the roman rite). [CIL 32329] shows that this is true even if the main sacrifice is performed *graeco ritu*.

2) The sacrificer offers incense to Ianus as follows:

"Iano pater, te hoc ture ommovendo bonas preces precor, uti sies volens propitius mihi liberisque meis domo familiaeque meae."

"Father Ianus, in offering this incense to you I pray good prayers, so that you may be propitious to me and my children, to my house and to my household."

The sacrificer places the incense on the *focus*.

3) Then incense is offered to Iuppiter in the same way:

"Iuppiter, te hoc ture ommovendo bonas preces precor, uti sies volens propitius mihi liberisque meis domo familiaeque meae."

"Iuppiter, in offering this incense to you I pray good prayers, so that you may be propitious to me and my children, to my house and to my household."

The sacrificer places the incense on the *focus*.

4) Then an offering dish (*patera*) of wine is offered to Ianus:

"Iano pater, uti te ture ommovendo bonas preces bene precatus sum, eiusdem rei ergo macte vino inferio esto."

"Father Janus, as in offering to you the incense virtuous prayers were well prayed, for the sake of this be honored by this wine offered in libation."

The sacrificer pours the wine on the *focus*.

5) Then the same to Iuppiter:

"Iuppiter macte isto ture esto, macte vino inferio esto."

"Iuppiter, be honored by that incense, be honored by this wine below."

The sacrificer pours the wine on the *focus*.

Precatio

The main sacrifice starts with a prayer directed to the deity in whose honor the sacrifice is performed. In this prayer, the sacrificer states the reason for the sacrifice, the goods that he will sacrifice, and the blessings he wants to receive in return. In [Horatius, Carmina, 3.23] it is suggested that the altar or Lararium should be touched while the prayers are being said, which is confirmed by [Virgilius, Aeneis, 4.219]. According to Servius Honoratus, Varro wrote that this gesture is necessary to grant the good will of the deity [Servius, Aeneidos Commentarius, 4.219].

The following procedures illustrate the *precatio*. The prayer is taken from [Cato, *De Agricultura*, 132], where the deity to be honored in the sacrifice is Iuppiter Dapalis:

1) If the sacrifice is to be performed *graeco ritu*, the sacrificer uncovers his head, adorns his head with a laurel crown and takes off his *toga*, becoming dressed with his tunic only (usually a fringed

tunic).

2) The sacrificer washes his hands on a vessel placed beside him, or carried by one of the assistants. Although this is the usual place for this observance, [Cato, *De Agricultura*, 132] places the washing of the hands after the prayer in step 3.

3) The sacrificer touches the altar or Lararium and addresses the deity with a prayer where the purpose and nature of the sacrifice are described:

"Iuppiter dapalis, quod tibi fieri oportet in domo familia mea culignam vini dapi, eius rei ergo macte hac illace dape pollucenda esto."

"Iuppiter Dapalis, because it is proper for a cup of wine to be given to you in the house of my family for the sacred feast, for the sake of this thing may you be honored by this feast offering."

When the sacrifice was performed Graeco Ritu, some Greek words could be interspersed in the Latin text.

Immolatio

This part only applies to blood sacrifices, i.e. when the offering is a living creature. As the Collegium Pontificum of Nova Roma has many reserves towards this type of sacrifice, the information in this section should be regarded as informative only with no intentions of motivating its practice. Although blood sacrifices were common in classical Rome, it must be said that the Religio Romana has also an ancient tradition for the absence of that practice as stated in [Ovid, *Fasti*, I.337]:

"Of old the means to win the goodwill of gods for man were spelt and the sparkling grains of pure salt. As yet no foreign ship had brought across the ocean waves the black-distilled myrrh; the Euphrates had sent no incense, India no balm, and the red saffron's

filaments were still unknown. The altar was content to smoke with savine, and the laurel burned with crackling loud. To garlands woven of meadow flowers he who could violets add was rich indeed. The knife that now lays bare the bowels of the slaughtered bull had in sacred rites no work to do. (...)"

The immolation procedures are better known in the public context than in the domestic context. Nevertheless it is very likely that domestic sacrifices followed at least a subset (probably variable according to the habits and possibilities of each household) of the public sacrifices.

The sacrificed victims were always domestic animals carefully selected according to species, sex, color and size, in order to match the nature of the deity to which they were offered. Male deities received male victims (some received castrated victims, others complete victims), while female deities received female victims. White victims were offered to the Celestial gods, black victims to the Underworld gods (*Dii Inferi* such as Dis, Proserpina, the Manes) or of the night, red victims were offered to Vulcanus and Robigo. Pregnant sows were offered to Ceres and Tellus in some expiatory rites. Swine and rams were usually offered in funerary sacrifices.

Blood sacrifices required special preparation. The animals were washed and adorned with ribbons and strips of white or scarlet wool. The horns of the bovines were usually gilded and/or adorned with disk. The back of the porcines and bovines was covered with a richly decorated fringed coverture (*dorsuale*). The phases of the immolation were the following:

1) The first act was the consecration of the victim, which was different depending on the rite (*Ritus Romanus* or *Ritus Graecus*). According to the *Ritus Romanus*, the sacrificer consecrated the victim by the *mola salsa* (roasted wheat flour with added salt originally made by the Vestales and thus associated with the fire of Vesta; the *mola salsa* is origin for the word *immolatio* or *inmolatio*), wine and the knife (*mola, vino cultroque*). In order to do this he powdered the back of the victim with the *mola salsa*, poured a little wine on its forehead with a *patera*, and finally passed the sacrificial knife along the back of the animal.

In the *Ritus Graecus*, the sacrificer consecrated the victim by dropping a few grains of corn and some drops of water on the head of the victim. He then cut some hair from the head of the victim and offered it on the fire.

2) After the consecration, the sacrificer or the butchers (*victimarii*) proceeded to kill the victim (if butchers were available, the sacrificer would give the sign). The victim should show no sign of panic, otherwise that would be considered a bad omen and the sacrifice would be polluted. On the contrary, the victim should show its consent by lowering its head helped by the sacrificer. Bigger victims (e.g. bovines) were firstly stunned with a poleaxe and then bled to death. Smaller victims had their throat cut.

3) The victim was then laid on its back, and its belly was opened. With the help of its assistants (namely the *haruspex*), the sacrificer verified if the victim had been well accepted through the examination of the entrails: the liver, the lungs, the biliary blister, peritoneum and heart. If entrails did not present any anomalies it was considered that the sacrifice had been accepted (*litatio*) and it could proceed. Otherwise the sacrifice was aborted and had to restart with new victims. This was repeated until the *litatio* was achieved. Sometimes the entrails could be examined in Etruscan fashion with the purpose of divination (*haruspicatio*).

4) The victim was then divided. The entrails (*exta*) were destined to the deity. The rest would normally be destined to the humans, being eaten in a banquet (*epulum*) after the sacrifice. With the exception of some deities of more savage nature (e.g. Mars - see [Suetonius, *Vita Divi Augusti*, 1] and [Arnobius, *Adversus Nationes*, 2.68]), the entrails were cooked before being offered. Those of bovines were boiled, while those of porcines and ovines were grilled on skewers. The entrails were then powdered with *mola salsa* and wine before being offered to the deity (see below).

Redditio

In this phase the offerings are actually given to the deity. Usually, only a part of the offerings is actually given to the deity, the rest being profanated and consumed by the humans after the sacrifice. An exception is when the sacrifice is performed in honor of the Underworld gods (e.g. Dis and Proserpina, etc.), as no one can sit at the same table with the gods that govern Death and the Dead.

If the sacrifice is performed in honor of a water divinity, it is usually thrown to the water (a river, sea, spring, etc.). If the sacrifice is performed in honor of a chtonic deity (e.g. Lar/Genius Loci, Ceres, etc.) the offering is simply thrown to the ground or burned inside a ditch previously excavated for the effect. The latter also applies to the Underworld gods, in which case the offering is completely burned on the ditch.

For other deities, including the domestic deities (Genii, Lares and Penates, etc.), the offerings are normally given through the fire of the *focus*. Of course there were some variations depending of the specific deity or the specific offering (e.g. flowers were usually to be offered as a decoration and not to be burned; the same was true regarding the ears of grain offered to Ceres).

While giving each offering, the act is confirmed with words. The following example is again taken from [Cato, *De Agricultura*, 132]. Like many other public and private sacrifices it takes the form of "[Deity (voc.)], macte [offerings (abl.)] esto":

"Iuppiter dapalis, macte istace dape pollucenda esto, macte vino inferio esto."

"Iuppiter Dapalis, may you be honored by this feast offering, may you be honored by the wine offered below."

Meat offerings are usually sprinkled with wine and salt or *mola salsa* (roasted wheat flour with added salt) before being served to the deities.

Besides the main deity of the sacrifice, other deities may receive offerings as well during this phase. This happens for example in [Cato, *De Agricultura* 134], where Ianus and Iuppiter receive cakes and wine in the style of a *postfatio* after the entrails of the sow are cut, but before the entrails are actually given to Ceres.

On the other hand, [Cicero, *De Natura Deorum*, II.67] says that Vesta is the last deity to receive offerings during sacrifices for she governs the sacrificial fire. This is confirmed by [Cato, *De Agricultura*, 132], where the reader is given the option to offer to Vesta after Iuppiter Dapalis has received his share of the feast.

Profanatio

Usually, if the sacrifice is not in honor of the gods of Hades, only a small fraction of it is actually offered to the deity, the rest being eaten by the humans, as if the humans were now guests of the deity to whom the offerings were given. In order to make this possible, the sacrificer must profanate the offerings (i.e. make the given offerings become again human property) with his touch, a procedure explicitly instructed in [Cato, *De Agricultura*, 132].

Epulum

After the profanation, the remaining offerings are eaten by the sacrificer and sometimes the other officiants, family and guests in a banquet. During the banquet, people sometimes address the deities, making additional offerings and asking for favors and blessings in return.

Table of Traditional Offerings and Sacrifices

The table below provides some general guidelines for the offerings and sacrificial procedures that are most propitious to specific deities. It is by no means an exhaustive reference and it will be expanded in the future. Moreover, some of the data (namely in what concerns blood sacrifice) is based on the public cult, which means that in a domestic context there could be some variations and offerings would be typically more modest. Variations related to specific rites/celebrations and/or specific aspects of the deities are also not reflected in the table:

Deity	Character	Rite	Known Inanimate Offerings	Known Living Offerings	Comments	Sources
Penates (domestic gods) in general	Domestic	Ritus Romanus	incense, wine, cakes, food, etc.	ewe-lamb (see below on the Lares Familiares), cow	The Penates were the set of gods worshiped in a household. This row presents default guidelines for their worship. The specificities of some gods are presented below.	[Cicero, De Divinatione, II.39] [Dionysius of Halicarnassus, Roman Antiquities, 2.23] [Festus-Paul, On the meaning of the words, Lindsay ed. p.298] [CIL 6.2042]

Lar Familiaris / Lares Familiares	Domestic	Ritus Romanus	incense, wine, food (namely fruits and roasted meat with *mola salsa*), garlands of flowers	ewe-lamb, pig, ram (funeral)	Flowers are to adorn the Lararium and not to be burnt.	[Plautus, Aulularia] [Plinius, Naturalis Historia, 21.11] [Plinius, Naturalis Historia, 28.27] [Varro in Nonius Marcellus, De Compendiosa Doctrina, Lindsay ed. p.554 1-2] [Deutero-Servius, Aeneidos, 1.730] [Ovidius, Fasti, 2.633] [Ovidius, Fasti, 2.631-634] [Valerius Maximus, Memorable deeds and sayings, 2.5.5] [Horatius, Satries, 2.5.14] [Horatius, Odes, 3.23.4] [Tibullus, Elegies, 1.3.33 seq.] [Tibullus, Elegies, 1.1.23] [Virgilius, Bucolics, 1.43]

personal Genius or Iuno	Domestic	Ritus Romanus	incense, wine, cakes of boiled salted wheat (*liba*)	two-month old piglet (on the Saturnalia)	Blood sacrifice was not recommended on one's birthday	[Persius, Satires, 2.1-3] [Tibullus, Elegies, 2.6.8] [Ovidius, Tristia, 5.5.12] [Tibullus, Elegies, 4.6.14] [Plinius, Naturalis Historia, 18.84] [Varro in Censorinus, De Die Natali, 2.2] [Horatius, Odes, 3.17.14-16]
Manes	Underworld	Ritus Romanus	unmixed wine, fresh milk, blood of sacrificial victims, roses, violets, black beans, salted corn, wheat mixed with wine	ewe, pig, black bull-calves	Inanimate offerings are dropped/poured to the ground in libation without burning. Banquet can take place in the presence of the deceased.	[Virgilius, Aeneidos, 5.55-103] [Plinius, Naturalis Historia, 21.11] [Ovidius, Fasti, 2.535-540]
Mania / Mater Larum (mother of the Lares)	Underworld	Ritus Romanus	garlic, poppy heads	sheep	The poppy heads seem to have replaced primitive human sacrifices of children.	[Macrobius, Saturnalia, 1.7.35 seq.] [ILS 5047]

Deity	Type	Rite	Offerings	Animal	Notes	Sources
Lar/Genius Loci	Domestic/Chtonic	Ritus Romanus	fruits of the Earth (namely first samplings), wine, garlands of flowers	pig, heifer, ewe-lamb	Inanimate offerings should be dropped/poured to the ground or natural altar in libation	[Cato, De Agricultura 139 - 140] [Apuleius, Apologia, 56.5-6] [Apuleius, Florides, 1.3-4] [Tibullus, Elegies, 1.1.19-24]
Lares Compitales	Chtonic	Ritus Romanus	?	pig shining with grease		[Propertius, Elegies, 4.1.23]
Vesta	Domestic	Ritus Romanus	incense, meat	sheep		[Cato, De Agricultura, 132] [Ovidius, Fasti, 3.418] [ILS 5047]
Ceres	Chtonic	Ritus Romanus (a part of the cult celebrated on the Aventine Hill corresponded to the Mysteries of Eleusis and was considered Graeca Sacra and thus not included in the Roman public cult)	spelt cakes, incense, salt, bread, first samplings of ears of wheat, oak leaves, wine, honeycombs mixed with milk	sow (sometimes pregnant)		[Cato, De Agricultura 134] [Tibullus, Elegies, 1.1.11-18] [Virgilius, Georgics, 1.338-349] [Ovidius, Fasti, 2.520] [Ovidius, Fasti, 1.657-704] [Ovidius, Fasti, 4.393-416] [Ovid, Metamorphoses, 10.433] [Macrobius, Saturnalia, 3.11.10]
Tellus	Chtonic	Ritus Romanus	spelt cakes	sow (sometime	Ceres and Tellus were	[Ovid, Fasti, 1.657-704]

						usually identified and normally the offerings that suited Ceres also suited Tellus.	[Ovid, Fasti, 629-636]
Ianus		Domestic (doors, passages) / Celestial (beginnings and ends)	Ritus Romanus	incense, wine, cakes (*strues*)	ram		[Cato, De Agricultura 141] [Cato, De Agricultura 134] [Varro, De Lingua Latina, 6.12] [ILS 5047]
Iuppiter		Celestial	Ritus Romanus	incense, wine (namely first samplings), cakes (*fertum*), meat, spelt cake (*far*), fruits	white heifer, ox, ewe-lamb, whether, *suovetaurilia* (sheep, pig and ox), bull?, ram?	According to the ancient books, only castrated victims should be offered to Iuppiter.	[Cato, De Agricultura 141] [Cato, De Agricultura 134] [Festus-Paul, On the meaning of the words, Lindsay ed., p.40.27 and 57.16-18] [Ovidius, Fasti, 1.55-57] [Ovidius, Fasti, 1.83 seq.] [Ovidius, Fasti, 2.67-70] [Ovidius, Fasti, 3.730] [Ovidius, Fasti, 4.863-900] [Servius, ad Virg. Eclog., 8.82] [Macrobius, Saturnalia,

						3.10.3] [CIL 6.2065] [ILS 5047]
Iuno	Celestial	Ritus Romanus	incense, wine	bull, ram, cow, sheep, *suovetaurilia* (sheep, pig and bull),		[Cato, De Agricultura 134] [ILS 5047] [Feriale Duranum]
Mars	Celestial	Ritus Romanus	spelt, bacon fat, meat, wine, cakes (*strues* and *fertum*)	*suovetaurilia* (sheep, pig and bull), bull, ram	Entrails were offered raw	[Suetonius, Vita Divi Augusti, 1] [Macrobius, Saturnalia, 3.10.4] [ILS 5047]
Saturnus	Chtonic	Ritus Graecus	?	pig?	Saturnus is worshiped according to the *Ritus Graecus* although he is a very ancient Roman deity.	[Festus-Paul, On the meaning of the words, Lindsay ed., p.274.29-32]
Salus	Celestial	Ritus Romanus	?	cow		[CIL 6.2065]
Minerva	Celestial	Ritus Romanus	?	cow, *suovetaurilia* (sheep, pig and bull),		[CIL 6.2065]
Victoria	Celestial	Ritus Romanus	Incense	cow		[Ambrosius, Epistles 18.31] [Feriale Duranum]
Dis	Underworld	Ritus Romanus	?	black sheep and other black victims		[Valerius Maximus, Factorum et Dictorum Memorabilium, 2.4.5] [Macrobius, Saturnalia, 3.9.10-12]

Proserpina	Underworld	Ritus Romanus	?	black victims		[Valerius Maximus, Factorum et Dictorum Memorabilium, 2.4.5]
Liber Pater	Chtonic	Ritus Romanus (the Bachannalia are considered Graeca Sacra, i.e. a foreign rite not included in the Roman public cult)	cakes (*liba*), libations of must (namely first samplings)	?		[Ovid, Fasti, 3.713-740] [Plinius, Naturalis Historia, 18.8] [Festus-Paul, On the meaning of the words, Lindsay ed., p.423.1 seq.]
Neptunus	Waterly	Ritus Romanus	?	bull		[Macrobius, Saturnalia, 3.10.4]
Diana	Celestial	Ritus Romanus (although at the Ludi Saeculares she was honored - like any other deity - Graeco Ritu)	cakes of cheese, cakes of honey, cakes of parsley	hind, white she-goat?, cow		[Livius, Ab Urbe Condita, 1.45] [Livius, Ab Urbe Condita, 25.12, 27, 23.5] [Ovidius, Fasti, 1.387-388] [CIL 6.32323] [Valerius Maximus, Factorum et Dictorum Memorabilium, 7.3.1]
Carna	Domestic	Ritus Romanus	beans mixed with hot spelt, bacon	-		[Ovid, Fasti, 6.169-170]
Robigo	Chtonic	Ritus Romanus	incense, wine	red (?) dog, ewe, unweaned		[Columella, De Re Rustica, 342 seq.]

				puppy		[Festus-Paul, On the meaning of the words, Lindsay ed., p.358.27-30]
Vulcanus	Fiery (destructive)	Ritus Romanus		fish, red (?) animals	Victims were burned alive	[Varro, De Lingua Latina, 6.20] [Festus-Paul, On the meaning of the words, Lindsay ed., p.276.3]
Genius Augusti	Celestial	Ritus Romanus	incense, wine	bull, bull-calf		[Petronius, Satiricon, 60.7] [Horatius, Odes, 4.5.30 seq.] [CIL 6.32352]
Iuno Augustae	Celestial	Ritus Romanus	incense, wine	cow		[CIL VI.2043]
Numen Augusti	Celestial	Ritus Romanus	incense, wine	bull-calf		[ILS 154], [CIL 12.4333]
Lares Augusti	Domestic	Ritus Romanus	same as Lares Familiares	same as Lares Familiares, wether		[ILS 5047]
Divus	Celestial	Ritus Romanus	?	ox, sheep	Probably the same as Iuppiter	[ILS 5047] [Feriale Duranum]
Diva	Celestial	Ritus Romanus	?	cow	Probably the same as Iuno	[CIL 6.32349]
Apollo	Celestial	Ritus Graecus	cakes of cheese, cakes of honey, cakes of parsley, crowns of laurel	bull		[Macrobius, Saturnalia, 3.10.4] [CIL 6.32323] [Livius, Ab Urbe Condita, 25.12, 27, 23.5]
Ilithyia	Domestic	Ritus Graecus (at least at the	cakes of cheese, cakes of	-		[CIL 6.32323]

		Ludi Saeculares. Anyway she is a Greek deity)	honey, cakes of parsley				
Priapus	Domestic/Fertility	Ritus Romanus	milk, cakes (*liba*)	-			[Virgilius, Eclogae, 7.33-34]

15 POSTURE AND GESTURE IN ROMAN PRAYER

Both textual and pictorial testimonies show that prayer and gesture complement themselves. It is known that some rare sacrifices involved no prayer [Livius, Ab Urbe Condita, XLI.16.1], though this was rare according to Pliny [Plinius, Historia Naturalis, 28.3.10]. The equivalence of meaning between prayer and gesture is also attested by several descriptions of sacrifices (namely taken from the *Comentarii Fratrum Arvalium*) which describe the consecration of the victim by the *mola salsa*, wine and the knife, while usually they omit the corresponding prayer.

Written sources

Some books like the Dictionary of Roman Religion by Lesley and Roy Adkins (1996) oversimplify the problem of ritual attitude claiming that the Romans prayed with the arms outstretched. In fact there are some Roman descriptions and depictions of rites being performed with outstretched arms. The following picture is a relief, in which the cultor is attending prayer. His arms are not outstretched; however, he may be in between prayers.

This ritual is the *supplicatio* (supplication), and is textually described in the surviving *Acta Ludorum Saeculariorum*. The following was taken from the description of the *Ludi Saeculares* of 17 BC in CIL VI 32323:

"DEINDE CX MATRIBVS FAMILIAS NVPTIS QVIBVS DENVINTIATVM ERAT .... M AGRIPPA] / PRAEIT IN HAEC VERBA / IVNO REGINA AST QVID EST QVOD MELI[VS SIET P R QVIRITIBVS .... MATRES FAMILIAE / NVPTAE GENIBVS NIXAE TE VTI .... / MAIESTATEMQVE P R QVIRITI[VM DVELLI DOMIQVE AVXIS VTIQVE SEMPER LATINVM NOMEN TVEARE INCOLVMITATEM] / SEMPITERNAM VICTORIAM [VALETVDINEM POPVLO ROMANO QVIRITIBVS TRIBVAS FAVEASQVE POPVLO ROMANO QVIRITIBVS LEGIONIBVSQVE P R] / QVIRITIVM REMQVE PVBLI[CAM P R QVIRITIVM SALVAM SERVES VTI SIES VOLENS PROPITIA POPVLO ROMANO] / QVIRITIBVS XVVIR S F NO[BIS .... HAEC MATRES FAMILIAS CX POPVLI ROMANI] / QVIRITIVM NVPTAE GENI[BVS NIXAE QVAESVMVS PRECAMVRQVE]"

"After that, to/by 110 married matresfamilias to whom was announced ...[this part is lost] M. Agrippa precedes/dictates with the following words: ' Iuno Regina, yet this is as far as any better may fall on the roman people of the quirites ...[this part is lost] married matresfamilias kneeling to you may you ... [this part is lost] majesty of the roman people of the quirites both in the war and at the homeland, and also that you may always watch over the Latin name. May you provide to the roman people of the quirites the eternal safety victory and good health and may you also favour the roman people of the quirites as well as its legions. May you preserve the public affairs ["res publica" = Republic] of the roman people of the quirites unarmed. May you be willing to be propitious to the roman people of the quirites, to the Quindecemviri Sacris Faciundis and to us... [We,] 110 married matresfamilias of the roman people of the quirites on our knees beg and pray ... [this part is lost]'"

To extend the hand or hands to heaven seems to be used also when addressing deities of the sky [Horatius, Odes, III.XXIII]:

Caelo supinas si tuleris manus Nascente luna, [O pie erga divem], Si ture placaris et horna Fruge Lares [sacrificares]: Nec pestilentem sentiet Africum Fecunda vitis nec sterilem seges Robiginem aut dulces alumni Pomifero grave tempus anno...

This is confirmed by the description of a *devotio*, which was vowed before the walls of Carthage. The *devotio* was a ritual performed with the objective of vowing someone to the gods of the underworld (*Dii Inferi*), the gods of death. Its use was more common in a military context, where an enemy army and/or city were vowed to destruction. Sometimes this act involved the self-sacrifice of the commander or a soldier chosen for the effect. According to Macrobius the ritual was the following [Macrobius, Saturnalia, 3.9.10-12]:

"DIS PATER VEIOVIS MANES, SIVE QUO ALIO NOMINE FAS EST NOMINARE, UT OMNES ILLAM URBEM CARTHAGINEM EXERCITUMQUE QUEM EGO ME SENTIO DICERE FUGA FORMIDINE TERRORE CONPLEATIS, QUIQUE ADVERSUM LEGIONES EXERCITUMQUE NOSTRUM ARMA TELAQUE FERENT, UTI VOS EUM EXERCITUM EOS HOSTES EOSQUE HOMINES URBES AGROSQUE EORUM ET QUI IN HIS LOCIS REGIONIBUSQUE AGRIS URBIBUSVE HABITANT ABDUCATIS LUMINE SUPERO PRIVETIS EXERCITUMQUE HOSTIUM URBES AGROSQUE EORUM QUOS ME, SENTIO DICERE, UTI VOS EAS URBES AGROSQUE CAPITA AETATESQUE EORUM DEVOTAS CONSECRATASQUE HABEATIS OLLIS LEGIBUS QUIBUS QUANDOQUE SUNT MAXIME HOSTES DEVOTI. EOSQUE EGO VICARIOS PRO ME FIDE MAGISTRATUQUE MEO PRO POPULO ROMANO EXERCITIBUS LEGIONIBUSQUE NOSTRIS DO DEVOVEO, UT ME MEAMQUE FIDEM IMPERIUMQUE LEGIONES EXERCITUMQUE NOSTRUM QUI IN HIS REBUS GERUNDIS SUNT BENE SALVOS SIRITIS ESSE. SI HAEC ITA FAXITIS UT EGO SCIAM SENTIAM INTELLEGAMQUE, TUNC QUISQUIS HOC VOTUM FAXIT UBI FAXIT RECTE FACTUM ESTO OVIBUS ATRIS TRIBUS. TELLUS MATER TEQUE IUPPITER OBTESTOR. Cum Tellurem dicit, manibus terram tangit: cum Iovem dicit, manus ad caelum tollit: cum votum recipere dicit, manibus pectus tangit."

"DIS PATER, VEIOVIS, MANES, OR WHOM WHOSE NAME IS LAWFUL TO NAME, MAY YOU FULFILL TO PUT TO FLIGHT IN PANIC AND TERROR ALL THOSE INHABITANTS OF THAT CITY OF CARTHAGE AND ARMY, WHICH I INTEND TO DESIGNATE, AS WELL AS THOSE WHO OPPOSE OUR

LEGIONS AND ARMY WITH ARMS AND SPEARS. MAY YOU DRIVE AWAY THAT ENEMY ARMY AND MEN, CITIES AND FIELDS, AND THOSE WHO INHABIT THIS PLACE AND REGIONS, FIELDS AND CITIES. DEPRIVE THE ENEMY ARMY, THEIR CITIES AND FIELDS, WHICH I INTEND TO DESIGNATE FROM THE LIGHT OF THE SKY. MAY YOU HAVE THOSE CITIES AND FIELDS, THOSE HEADS AND PEOPLE OF ALL AGES DEVOTED AND CONSECRATED, ACCORDING TO THOSE PRINCIPLES BY WHICH AND AT WHICH TIME THE ENEMIES ARE ESPECIALLY DEVOTED. THEM I CONSECRATE AS SUBSTITUTES FOR MYSELF, FOR MY CREDIT AND MAGISTRACY, FOR THE ROMAN PEOPLE, FOR OUR ARMIES AND LEGIONS. MAY YOU ALLOW MY CREDIT AND AUTHORITY, OUR LEGIONS AND ARMY THAT ARE CARRIED ON IN THIS AFFAIR TO BE WELL SAFE. IF YOU LET ME KNOW, FEEL AND UNDERSTAND THAT YOU WILL ACT IN THIS WAY, WHOEVER HAS PROMISED TO SACRIFICE THREE BLACK EWES TO YOU, WHEREVER HE HAS DONE SO, LET IT BE UNDERSTOOD THAT HE HAS ACTED WITHIN THE RULES. I CALL ON YOU TO WITNESS, MOTHE EARTH, AND YOU, IUPPITER. **Touches the ground with the hands while saying 'Tellus', directs the hands to the sky while saying 'Iuppiter' and touches his chest with the hands while saying the vow to be received.**"

The important part is the last sentence in which it is said that while pronouncing the formula, the vower "touches the ground while saying 'Tellus', directs the hands to the sky while saying 'Iuppiter' and touches his chest with the hands while saying the vow to be received". Again, the arms are extended to heaven when a deity of the sky (Iuppiter) is invoked, but the ground is touched when chtonic deities are invoked.

This is very important when compared with other information. In [Horatius, Carmina, 3.23] it is suggested that the altar should be touched while the prayers are being said, which is confirmed by [Virgilius, Aeneis, 4.219].

According to Servius Honoratus, Varro wrote that this gesture is necessary to grant the good will of the deity [Servius, Aeneidos

Commentarius, 4.219]. These examples suggest that it was a norm to direct the hands (or hand) towards the deity (or alternately touching the altar when one was present) when saying the prayer.

The posture of the officiant is also referred, for example, in another description of the *devotio* ritual provided by Livy. He describes the *devotio* performed by Consul Decius under the direction of a *Pontifex*, during a battle against the Latin League [Livius, Ab Urbe Condita, 8.9.4-8]:

"(...) pontifex eum togam praetextam sumere iussit et uelato capite, manu subter togam ad mentum exserta, super telum subiectum pedibus stantem sic dicere: 'Iane, Iuppiter, Mars pater, Quirine, Bellona, Lares, Diui Nouensiles, Di Indigetes, Diui, quorum est potestas nostrorum hostiumque, Dique Manes, uos precor ueneror, ueniam peto feroque, uti populo Romano Quiritium uim uictoriam prosperetis hostesque populi Romani Quiritium terrore formidine morteque adficiatis. sicut uerbis nuncupaui, ita pro re publica [populi Romani] Quiritium, exercitu, legionibus, auxiliis populi Romani Quiritium, legiones auxiliaque hostium mecum Deis Manibus Tellurique deuoueo.' (...)"

"(...) the Pontifex ordered him [i.e. Decius] to take the 'toga praetexta' and with the head covered, a hand protruding from beneath the toga touching the chin, standing with his feet over a spear said the following: "Janus, Jupiter, Father Mars, Quirinus, Bellona, Lares, ye Novensiles and Indigetes, deities to whom belongs the power over us and over our foes, and ye, too, Divine Manes, I pray to you, I do you reverence, I crave your grace and favor that you will bless the Roman People, the Quirites, with power and victory, and visit the enemies of the Roman People, the Quirites, with fear and dread and death. In like manner as I have uttered this prayer so do I now on behalf of the commonwealth of the Quirites, on behalf of the army, the legions, the auxiliaries of the Roman People, the Quirites, devote the legions and auxiliaries of the enemy, together with myself to the Divine Manes and to Earth. (...)"

Important information can be extracted from this description.

Here we see that before saying the formula, Decius is instructed to dress the *toga praetexta* and to cover his head, which, as we have already seen, are usual procedures of a standard sacrifice *Romano Ritu*. The only elements not found elsewhere are the use of a spear laid on the ground and the act of touching the chin.

While the detail of the spear is surely specific of the *devotio* (for Livy says later that the spear could not be captured by the enemy), the act of touching the chin may or may not be specific of the *devotio*. In fact it resembles the *adoratio* (kissing of one's right hand used to salute a deity [Plinius, Historia Naturalis, 28.25]), and it might well be a variant. But it can also be a symbol that Decius was also an offering to the gods as he was about to give his life in the sacrifice.

Let's see another example, which is the yearly announcement of the sacrifice to Dea Dia by the *Fratres Arvales* before the temple of Concordia, extracted from the *Comentarii Fratrum Arvalium* [CIL VI, 32340.0-20]:

"ille mag. manibus lautis capite velato sub divo contra orientem sacrificium indixit deae Diae sic Quod bonum faustum felix fortunatumque sit populo Romano Quiritibus, fratribusque arvalibus, Tiberio Caesar Augusto, Iuliae Augustae et liberis nepotibus totique domui eorum, sacrificium deae Diae hoc anno erit a.d. VI Kalendas Iunias"

"The *magister* [of the *Fratres Arvales*], with washed hands, head covered, below the open sky and turned to East proclaimed the sacrifice to Dea Dia in the following way: 'In order that it may be auspicious, prosperous and happy to the Roman people of the Quirites, to the *Fratres Arvales*, to Tiberius Caesar Augustus, to Iulia Augusta and to all grandchildren of their household, the sacrifice to Dea Dia this year will be on the 6th day before the Kalends of June.'"

The description refers to the act of covering the head (*capite velato*), the direction of the officiant and details like the washing of hands, but it does not mention anything about the gestures made while prayer is being said. This may be due to the fact that special gestures were not required in this ritual. But it mentions that the prayer should be directed to the East, which is the preferred direction to offer prayer according to [Vitruvius, De Architectura, IV.5], which was a guideline for the construction of temples. Nevertheless, temples were built with a variety or orientations according to the possibilities, and Vitruvius implies that the sacrificer should in any case be looking at the deity during the sacrifice. In case of the announcement of the sacrifice to Dea Dia, the ceremony is done before the temple of Concordia and so the *magister* addresses Dea Dia towards the East. This may indicate that if there is no altar or image of the deity the prayers should be addressed to the East. Varro indicates an association of Ceres with the East [Varro, De Lingua Latina, 7.9], which can be related with this.

Depictions

Although there is a large number of bas-reliefs and paintings representing traditional Roman sacrifices both private and public, these depictions usually obey to rigid artistic conventions, which limit the information we can extract from them. Yet, they are a valuable source of information.

The available depictions of traditional Roman sacrifice invariably depict the sacrificer during the act of offering at the burning altar or hearth, usually during the *praefatio* or preliminary offering of incense and wine (for a detailed study about Roman sacrifice see [Scheid, J., Romulus et ses Freres - Le College des Freres Arvales, modele du culte public dans la Rome des Empereurs, Ecole frangaise de Rome, 1990, ISBN 2-7283-0203-7]). An example of this is the bas-relief that decorates the temple of Vespasian in Pompey:

The sacrificer is standing *cinctu Gabino* (with the head covered - *capite velato* - by a fold of the *toga praetexta*), placing the offerings on the fire with one hand, while the other hand is free holding the *toga*.

A similar scene is depicted in the following relief in which Marcus Aurelius sacrifices before the temple of Iuppiter Capitolinus. In this case the emperor seems to be imposing his right hand over the fire (a *foculus*, usually used for the *praefatio*), which may be equivalent to touching the altar. But it can also be the simple gesture of the orator who is saying a prayer:

Similar scenes are also depicted in private *lararia*, such as the following:

In this case the sacrificer is holding a *rhytium* (drinking horn) with the right hand while placing the offering on the sacred fire with the other hand.

16 FOREIGN PRIESTS IN ANCIENT ROME

The "foreign" cults include religions that came to Rome from other countries and were never completely adopted as part of the official Religio Romana, as well as the cults of deities that were specific to the various Provinciae. Most cults were not "officially" recognized, but did maintain a presence and operated under the guise of the private cultus or, in some cases, clandestinely. Generally such priesthoods are referred to as a Sacerdos (pl. Sacerdotes), unless there is another specific historical title.

Greco-Roman Cults

Apollo

- Apollinis Templi Sacerdotes *(priests who tend the temple of Apollo)*

Dionysian or Bacchic Mysteries (Rome)

- Hierophant (*Chief Priest*) and Matrona (*High Priestess*)
- Dominus and Domina (*Priest and Priestess*)
- Mystagogos *(Priest who leads others in initiation)*

Eleusinian Mysteries

- Archon Basileus (*Chief Priest*)
- Hierophant (*High Priest*)

- Dadoukhos (*Torch Bearer for Initiations*)
- Mystagogos (*Priest who leads others in initiation*)
- Epoptes (*Grade II Initiate*)
- Mystes (*Grade I Initiate*)

Roman-Persian Cults

Mithraic Mysteries

- Grade VII Initiate: Pater (*Father*)
- Grade VI Initiate: Heliodromus (*Courier of the Sun*)
- Grade V Initiate: Perses (*Persian*)
- Grade IV Initiate: Leo (*Lion*)
- Grade III Initiate: Miles (*Soldier*)
- Grade II Initiate: Nymphus (*Bride*)
- Grade I Initiate: Corax (*Raven*)

Orphic Mysteries

- Archiboukoloi (*Chief Priests*)
- Boukoloi hieroi (*Holy Priests*)
- Boukoloi (*Priests*)
- Hymnodidaskaloi (*Hymn Teachers*)

Mysteries of Magna Mater (Cybele)

- Archigalli *(senior priests who are responsible for performing the Taurobolium sacrifice)*
- Galii *(eunuch-priests-- cannot be Citizens of Rome)*
- Sacerdotes Magnae Matris *(ordinary priests and priestesses)*

Roman-Egyptian Cults

Mysteries of Isis and Serapis

- Sacerdotes *(ordinary priests and priestesses)*

17 GODS AND GODDESSES OF ROME

Introduction

At the founding of Rome, the gods were numina, divine manifestations, faceless, formless, but no less powerful. The idea of gods as anthropomorphized beings came later, with the influence from Etruscans and Greeks, which had human form. Some of the Roman Gods are at least as old as the founding of Rome.

The concept of numen continued to exist and it was related to any manifestation of the divine. For the Romans, everything in Nature is thought to be inhabited by numina, which explains the big number of deities in the Roman pantheon, as will be shown. Numina manifest the divine will by means of natural phenomena, which the pious Roman constantly seeks to interpret. That's why great attention is paid to omens and portents in every aspect of Roman daily life.

A group of twelve Gods called Dii Consentes is especially honored by the Romans:

- **Iuppiter**
- **Iuno**
- **Minerva**
- **Vesta**
- **Ceres**

- **Diana**
- **Venus**
- **Mars**
- **Mercurius**
- **Neptunus**
- **Vulcanus**
- **Apollo**

These are the ones listed by the Poet Ennius about the 3rd Century, B.C.E.. Their gilt statues stood in the Forum, later apparently in the Porticus Deorum Consentium. As there were six male and six female, they may well have been the twelve worshipped at the lectisternium of 217 BC.

A lectisternium is a banquet of the gods, where the statues of the gods were put upon cushions, and where these statues were offered meals. The number 12 was taken from the Etruscans, which also worshipped a main pantheon of 12 Gods. Nevertheless, the Dii Consentes were not identified with Etruscan deities but rather with the Greek Olympian Gods (though the original character of the Roman Gods was different from the Greek, having no myths traditionally associated). The twelve Dii Consentes are led by the first three, which for the Capitoline Triad. These are the three cornerstones of Roman religion, whose rites were conducted in the Capitoleum Vetus on the Capitoline Hill.

But what better characterizes the traditional Roman Religion is the household or family cult of the Dii Familiaris. In this cult, the Lar Familiaris (guardian spirit - Genius - of the family), the Lares Loci (guardian spirits of the place where the house is built), the Genius of the paterfamilias (House-Father), the Dii Penates (patron gods of the storeroom), the Dii Manes (spirits of the deceased) and a multitude of other domestic deities are daily worshipped by the members of the family. The household cult is so important that it even serves as the model for several practices of the state cult (e.g. there were the Lar Praestites, Penates Publici, etc.. Even during the Empire, the Imperial cult came to be based on the household cult, now interpreted as the cult of the Genius of the Emperor, paterfamilias of the family of all the Romans).

Other important Gods are

- **Ianus**
- **Saturnus**
- **Quirinus**
- **Volturnus**
- **Pales**
- **Furrina**
- **Flora**
- **Carmenta**
- **Pomona**
- **Portunus**
- **Fontanus**

There is also a group of mysterious deities formed by native tutelary deities, river Gods or deified heroes from Latium which are collectively called Dii Indigites (e.g. deified Aeneas, Faunus, Sol Indiges, Iuppiter Indiges, Numicus). A multitude of other deities is also traditionally worshipped, which includes tutelary deities (e.g. Roma, Tiberinus), native Latin deities (e.g. Bellus, Bellona, Liber, Libera), abstract deities such as Fortuna (Fate), Concordia (Concord), Pax (Peace), Iustitia (Justice), etc.. Pre-Roman native Italian deities mainly adopted from the Sabines and Etruscans are also worshipped: Nerio (Sabine deity and the consort of Mars), Dius Fidius (Sabine as well), etc. In fact, Quirinus and Vertumnus were also adopted respectively from the Sabines and Etruscans. The Dii Inferi, Gods of the Underworld (Inferus) are Dis/Orcus and Proserpina, equated to the Greek Gods Hades/Plouton (Pluto in Latin) and Persephone. These Gods symbolize the creative power of the Earth which provide human beings the means for subsistence (Dis = wealth = Plouton in Greek). The Inferus is also traditionally regarded as the home for the spirits of the dead, though the concept of afterlife was quite varied.

The pious spirit of the Romans consists of a constant wish to bring the favor of the divine upon him, the family and the state. As such, the Roman is naturally willing to pay the deserved homage and sacrifice to foreign deities, especially if he is in their land. In order to achieve victory in war, the Romans often asked the favor of the Gods of their enemies, paying them sacrifices even greater than those offered by their own people. This spirit joined by the affluence of foreigners which resulted either from trade or conquest, brought new cults to Rome. These were, as expected, democratically adopted by permitting the priests of these Gods to establish temples in Rome. Among the foreign deities, the Dii Novensiles, are Apollo, Ceres (these were adopted as early as to allow them to become part of the Dii Consentes), Bacchus/Dionysus, Sol Invictus Elagabalus, Isis, Serapis, Cybele, Attis, Mithras and many others.

Dii Consentes

Iuppiter is the God of the sky, moon, winds, rain and thunder, who became king of the Gods after overthrowing his father Saturnus. The ancient name of Iuppiter was Diespiter, whose root is Dios (= Zeus, God) + Pater (= Father). As Iuppiter Optimus Maximus, he is the tutelary God of Rome. As a warrior, he is Iuppiter Stator, protector of the City and State who exhorts soldiers to be steadfast in battle. But Iuppiter has many aspects, attributes, names and epithets...

Iuno is Iuppiter's sister, wife and queen of the Gods, is the protectress of the Roman State. Her festival, the Matronalia, is celebrated in March on the Kalends. She is also honored as Iuno Lucetia, celestial light; Iuno Lucina, childbirth, in which the child is brought into light; Iuno Sospita, who protects labor and delivery of children; Iuno Moneta, whose sacred geese warned Rome of an impending invasion. Iuno Moneta's temple was near the mint, thus her name was the root for "money". But Iuno has many aspects, attributes, names and epithets...

Minerva, Goddess of wisdom and learning, meditation, inventiveness, accomplishments, the arts, spinning and weaving, and commerce. Minerva was identified with Pallas Athene, bestower of victory, when Pompey the Great built her temple with the proceeds from his eastern campaigns. Minerva and Mars are honored Quinquatras, five days at the Spring equinox. But Minerva has many aspects, attributes, names and epithets...

Vesta is the Goddess of hearth and home, of domestic and religious fire. Her festival is the Vestalia, held on June 7, when Her temple is open to all mothers who bring plates of food. Vesta's temple was the hearth of Rome, where the sacred fire burned. The fire was tended by six Vestal Virgins, priestesses who were dedicated to the Goddess' service for thirty years, and who were headed by the Virgo Maxima, the eldest Vestal. Vestals were always preceded by lictors, the only women in Rome allowed the privilege. If a condemned man met a Vestal, he was reprieved. When a Roman made his will, he entrusted it to the Vestal Virgins. But Vesta has many aspects, attributes, names and epithets...

Ceres is the Goddess of agriculture. During a drought in 496 BCE, the Sibylline Books ordered the institution of the worship of Demeter, Dionysus and Persephone, called by the Latin names Ceres, Liber and Libera. Ceres was the Goddess of the plebeians: the Ædiles Plebis cared for her temple and had their official residences in it, and were responsible for the games at the Cerealia, her original festival on April 12-19. There was a women's 9-day fast and festival when women offered the first corn harvest to Ceres, originally celebrated every five years, but later - by the time of Augustus - held every October 4.

Diana, Goddess of the Moon and of wild places, the Divine Huntress, protectress of women and virgin Goddess. In earlier times, She was the mother Goddess of Nature. Her temple at Lake Nemi was in a sacred grove and was guarded by her priest, the Rex Nemorensis, the King of the Wood. He was always an escaped slave who was entitled to food, sanctuary and honor - until he was slain by the next candidate. But Diana has many aspects, attributes, names and epithets...

Venus was originally a Goddess of Spring, flowers and vines. By order of the Sibylline Books a temple on Mt. Eryx was dedicated to Venus as the Goddess of love and beauty. She was also Venus Genetrix, mother of the Roman people through Her son Aeneas, Who was also an ancestor of the Julii. Both Julius Caesar and Hadrian dedicated temples to Venus Genetrix. Hadrian's still stands near the Flavian Amphitheatre. She has darker aspects too, such as Venus Libitina, an aspect of Venus associated with the extinction of life force. But Venus has many aspects, attributes, names and epithets...

Mars, God of war, was originally an agricultural God whose character changed with that of His people. For this reason, he is the most Roman of the Gods, representing the abundance of the fields, and the battles that must be won to keep and enlarge the provinces that kept Rome fed and thriving. His priests were dancing warriors, the Salii, who sang their war-songs in the streets during his festivals. His sacred spears and 12 shields were kept in his temple on the Palatine Hill. But Mars has many aspects, attributes, names and epithets...

Mercurius is the God of commerce. The guild of merchants honored Mercurius at his temple near the Circus Maximus on his festival on May 15. They also sprinkled themselves and their merchandise with sacred water in a ceremony at the Capena Gate. When Mercurius became identified with Hermes, he took on the duties of messenger of the Gods, Psychopompus who guides the souls of the dead through the Underworld, and God of sleep and dreams. He also became God of thieves and trickery, owing to a trick he had played on Apollo by stealing and hiding the Sun God's cattle. His serpent-twined staff, the caduceus, was originally a magician's wand for wealth (which may be why it is the symbol of the medical profession) but became identified later as a herald's staff. But Mercurius has many aspects, attributes, names and epithets...

Neptunus, God of all the fresh water (from rivers, springs, etc.) and of equestrian accomplishments. Equated to the Greek Poseidon, He is also the God of the sea. He had temples in the Circus Flaminius and later on the Campus Martius. His festival, the Neptunalia is celebrated on July 23. But Neptunus has many aspects, attributes, names and epithets...

Vulcanus, the God of the fire of the sky, the lightning and the fires caused by it, he is the raging fire (opposed to the domestic fire, Vesta). He was equated to the Greek Haephestus, God of the fire, forge and volcanos. As a Nature God, he was married to Maia, Goddess of Spring. Equated to Haephestus, he made Iuppiter's thunderbolts and married to Venus. At his festival, the Volcanalia on August 23, fishes were thrown into the hearth fires. The eruption of mount Vesuvius in 79 AD took place in the day of His festival. As God of metal workers, He also has a festival on May 23. As God of conflagration, His temples were built outside the pomerium, on the Campus Martius. But Vulcanus has many aspects, attributes, names and epithets...

Apollo, Greek God of the Sun, prophecy, archery, music, poetry, inspiration and healing, perfection of male beauty, twin brother of Diana. Apollo came to prominence in the 5th century BCE, when the Sibylline Books of Apollo's prophecy (which had been offered to King Tarquinius Superbus by the Sibyl of Cumae) dictated the introduction of His cult in Rome following a plague. Besides Cumae, His oracles were also in other places such as Ionia, Delos, Delphi, Erithrea. It was Apollo who gave the gift of prophecy to His lover Cassandra, who was doomed to speak the truth, but never to be believed. Apollo is father of the God Aesculapius. But Apollo has many aspects, attributes, names and epithets...

Dii Familiaris

The **Lar Familiaris** is the guardian spirit of a family and symbolizes the household. He was honored on all family occasions: a new bride offered a coin and a sacrifice on entering her new house. Rams are sacrificed to the Lar Familiaris after funerals as a purification rite. During the 1st century AD, the Romans came to honor two Lares instead of one, becoming strongly connected with the Penates. In the lararium, the Lares are usually represented in dancing poses, carrying Greek rhytones of wine.

The **Lares Loci** are the guardian spirits of a place. In the lararium, the Lares Loci of the place where the house is built are also honored, being represented by one or more serpents.

Each man has a **Genius**, each woman a **Iuno**. This is the creative force that engenders the individual and imbues him/her with growth, learning and morality. This spirit stays with the person until death. The Genius of the paterfamilias deserves special honor, and is represented in the lararium by a man dressed in white with the head covered by the toga.

The **Penates** are connected with each family. If the family moves, the Penates go with it. They are the spirits of the larder, of food and drink, and they share the hearth as an altar with the Goddess Vesta.

The **Manes** are the spirits of the dead ancestors. When the deceased receives the due honors and rites, he is allowed to ascend from the Underworld to protect his family. This is in contrast with the Lemures or Larvae, evil ghosts which are the souls of the dead who the Dii Inferi refused to receive in the Underworld.

Each corner of the house is under the influence of a protector God. **Forculus** protects the door, **Limentinus** the threshold, **Cardea** the hinges. **Vesta** protects the hearth. Each tool has also its protector spirit: **Deverra** protects the broom, **Pilumnus** the rammer, **Intercidona** the axe.

The generation of a human being is also ruled by protector Gods. **Iuno** and **Mena** assure the menstrual flux of the future mother. **Jugatinus** presides to the union of man and woman. **Cinxia** or **Virginensis** uncover the woman's girdle. **Subigus** delivers her to the man. **Prema** commands the penetration. **Inuus** (**Tutunus** or **Mutunus**) and **Pertunda** put an end to virginity. **Ianus**, God of passage, opens the way for the generating seed emanated from **Saturnus**, but it is Liber who allows the ejaculation. Once **concepted**, the new human being needs **Fluonia** or **Fluvionia**, Who retains the nourishing blood. But the nourishing itself is presided by **Alemona**. To avoid the dangers of upside-down pregnancy, **Postverta** and **Prosa** are invoked. **Diana Nemorensis** is also invoked to allow a good pregnancy. Three deities protect the mother from the violence of **Silvanus**: **Intercidona**, **Deverra** and **Pilumnus**. In the atrium, a bet is setup for **Pilumnus** and **Picumnus** or **Iuno**, and a table is setup for **Hercules**. **Nona** and **Decima** allow the birth between the ninth and tenth month. But it is **Egeria** who makes the baby come out (egerere). **Parca** or **Partula** preside to the birth, but it is **Vitumnus** Who gives life, **Sentinus** the senses. After the birth, **Lucina**, bringer of light, must be invoked. **Lucina** is also the Goddess to whom sterile (or with pregnancy disease) women direct their prayer. After the birth, the pregnant women must be purified, and it is **Iuno Februa** (**Februalis** or **Februlis**) Who frees them from the placental membrane. With the aid of **Levana**, the sage-woman raises and presents the child to the mother. The father then raises the child with the aid of **Statina** (**Statilina**, **Statinus** or **Statilinus**).

Dii Indigetes

There is also a group of mysterious deities formed by native tutelary deities, river gods or deified heroes from Latium which are collectively called **Dii Indigetes** (e.g. deified **Aeneas**, **Faunus**, **Sol Indiges**, **Iuppiter Indiges**, **Numicus**). A multitude of other deities is also traditionally worshipped, which includes tutelary deities (e.g. **Roma**, **Tiberinus**), native Latin deities (e.g. **Bellus**, **Bellona**, **Liber**, **Libera**), abstract deities such as **Fortuna** (Fortune), **Concordia** (Concord), **Pax** (Peace), **Iustitia** (Justice), etc.

Pre-Roman native Italian deities mainly adopted from the Sabines and Etruscans are also worshipped: **Nerio** (Sabine deity and the consort of Mars), **Dius Fidius** (Sabine as well), etc. In fact, **Quirinus** and **Vertumnus** were also adopted respectively from the Sabines and Etruscans.

Other important gods are **Ianus**, **Saturnus**, **Quirinus**, **Volturnus**, **Pales**, **Furrina**, **Flora**, **Carmenta**, **Pomona**, **Portunus** and **Fontanus**.

Dii Novensiles

The pious spirit of the Romans consists of a constant wish to bring the favor of the divine upon him, the family and the state. As such, the Roman is naturally willing to pay the deserved homage and sacrifice to foreign deities, especially if he is in their land. In order to achieve victory in war, the Romans often asked the favor of the gods of their enemies, paying them sacrifices even greater than those offered by their own people. This spirit joined by the affluence of foreigners which resulted either from trade or conquest, brought new cults to Rome. These were as expected democratically adopted by permitting the priests of these gods to establish temples in Rome. Among the foreign deities, the Dii Novensiles, are **Apollo**, **Ceres** (these were adopted as early as to allow them to become part of the Dii Consentes), **Bacchus** (Dionysus), **Sol Invictus**, **Isis**, **Serapis**, **Magna Mater (Cybele)**, **Attis**, **Mithras** and many others.

Dii Inferi

The Dii Inferi, gods of the Underworld (Inferus) are **Dis (Orcus)** and **Proserpina**, equated to the Greek gods Hades/Pluton (Pluto in Latin) and Persephone. These gods symbolize the creative power of the Earth which provide human beings the means for subsistence (Dis = wealth = Pluton in Greek). The Inferus is also traditionally regarded as the home for the spirits of the dead, though the concept of afterlife was quite varied.

The Roman Pantheon & Associated Deities

This is a directory of Roman gods and goddesses, their offspring and consorts, and other minor deities:[1]

Abundantia
A minor Roman goddess of abundance, prosperity and good fortune. Her attribute is a cornucopia ("horn of plenty") with which she distributes grain and money. After the Roman occupation of France, she remained in French folklore as Lady Hobunde.

Acca Larentia

In Roman myth a loose woman and a mistress of Hercules. She married the wealthy Tarutius and after his death she donated his money to the Roman people. In return, Rome celebrated the festival of the Larentalia (possible a feast of the dead in honor of the goddess Larentia) on December 23. In another version, Acca Larentia is the wife of the shepherd Faustulus who raised the twins Romulus and Remus. Italic Goddess of cornfields.

According to a late legend dating to the Augustan era, she was the wife of Faustulus who together raised Romulus and Remus. She was said to have had twelve sons, with whom she made sacrifices once a year for the fertility of the fields. When one of her sons died, Romulus took his place and instituted the collegium Fratres Arvales. She is therefore identified with the Dea Dia of that collegium. On 23 Dec. a parentatio was performed for her by the flamen Quirinalis. The flamen Quirinalis acted in the role of Romulus (deified as Quirinus) performs funerary rites for his foster mother. Larentia, or Larentina, is also identified with Larunda, Mana Genita, and Muta.

Acestes

A hero of Trojan origin, who founded Segesta on Sicily. In a trial of skill Acested shot his arrow with such force that it took fire. He helped Aeneas when the latter arrived on Sicily after his wanderings.[2]

Achates

A loyal friend and companion of Aeneas.

Acmon

A companion of Aeneas.

Adeona

Italic Goddess of journeys, She is a protrectress of travelers. The Roman goddess who guides the child back home, after it has left the parental house for the first time.

Adonis (Etruscan Atunis)

Mortal lover of Venus and Proserpina in later myth. Like Proserpina he spent part of the year in the Underworld with Her, and the other part of the year with Venus.

Aeclanuii (Oscan Vertumnus)
The God of internal warmth, and ripener of fruits.

Aequitas
The Roman god of fair dealing.

Aera Cura
The Roman goddess of the infernal regions.

Aesai
The Oscan "Holy Ones," like the Etruscan Aiseras, or "The Shrouded Gods," a general name for the Gods, or the Hidden Sanctuary.

Aesculapius
God of healing adopted from the Greeks, His festival held on 1 Jan. to commemorate His temple being built on an isle in the Tiber, 293 BCE

Aeternitas
The Roman personification of eternity. He is symbolized a worm or serpent biting its own tail (similar to the Ouroboros) and by a phoenix rising from its ashes.

Africus
The Roman personification of the south-western wind.

Agenoria
See Angerona.

Aita
Etruscan God of the Underworld, in Rome called Pluto.

Aius Locutus
A divine voice that shouted a warning to the Romans at the approach of the Gauls in 390 BCE.

Albunea
A Roman nymph of the sulfuric spring near Tibur (the current Tivoli). The White Sybil, associated with the sulphurous River Albula.

Alemonia
The Roman goddess who feeds the unborn child.

Alernus
An unknown deity, mentioned by Ovid (Fasti VI. 105-106) who had a sacred grove at Rome near the Tiber River.

Alpan
Etruscan Goddess of love and of the Underworld, associated with a Lasa.

Anchises
Anchises was the son of Capys, and a cousin of King Priam of Troy. He was loved by Venus, who bore him a son, Aeneas. Anchises was the owner of six remarkable horses, which he acquired by secretly mating his own mares with the divinely-bred stallions of Laomedon. But he was chiefly remembered because of the career of his son. After the fall of Troy, Aeneas escaped from the burning ruins of the city, carrying his father and the household gods (see Lares and Penates) on his shoulders. Anchises then accompanied Aeneas and the band of Trojan refugees who set sail for Italy, where it was prophesied that they would found the city of Rome. Anchises died before the trip was over, and was buried in Sicily. After his death, Anchisessaw his son once more, when Aeneas visited the underworld to learn more about his own destiny.

Angerona (or Agenoria)
The protecting deity of ancient Rome and a goddess of secrecy and of the winter solstice. Angerona is shown with a bandaged mouth, her hand cupping her chin with a crooked index finger to her lips commanding silence. Her feast -- the Divalia or Angeronalia -- was celebrated at sunset on December 21.

Angita
An early Roman goddess of healing and witchcraft.

Angitia (or Anguitina)
A Roman snake-goddess who was especially worshipped by the Marsi, a tribe in central Italy. Oscan Goddess of healing, especially from poison. A sister of Circe, Her sacred grove was at Lake Fuscinus where both sacred snakes and healing herbs were found, like the Bona Dea at Rome. A Procession of the Serpents is still held in Her honor on 1 May in Lanciano, Abruzzia.

Anna
The daughter of Belus, and sister of Dido. After Dido's death she fled from Africa to Latium, where she was welcomed by Aeneas. Dido's shade warned her for the jealousy of Lavinia, the wife of Aeneas. After hearing this, she threw herself into the river Numicius and drowned. As a river nymph she was later venerated as Anna Perenna. According to some sources, this name has no connection with Dido's sister.

Anna Perenna
The Roman goddess of the new year. Her festival was celebrated on March 15. The Romans gave various explanations to the origin or her name, amnis perennis ("eternal stream"): she was a river nymph; her name was derived from annis ("year"); she was a moon-goddess of the running year; also, she was equated with Anna, the sister of Dido, who was received in Latium by Aeneas, but drowned herself in a river. In the class-struggle between the patricians and plebeians she chose the side of the plebeians.

Italian Goddess of the moon, long life, and rejuvenation. She is associated with the New Year. At the first full moon of March (originally the Ides, 15 March, when the calendar was fixed to the lunar cycle) a feast was held in her honor in a grove of fruits trees at the first mile of the Via Flaminia. The Romans wished each other as many years of life as they could drink cups of wine at Her feast.

Annonaria
An alternative name of Fortuna as protector of the corn supplies.

Anterus
Numen of mutual love.

Antevorte
The Roman goddess of the future.

Appiades
The five Roman goddesses who had a temple near the Appian aqueducts. They are Concordia, Minerva, Pax, Venus, and Vesta.

Appias
A Roman nymph. Two fountains dedicated to her flanked the entrance to the temple of Venus Genitrix on the Forum of Caesar in Rome.

Apollo (Etruscan Apula, Greek Apollon)
Among the Italians and Gauls, Apollo was mostly known as a god of healing, music, poetry, prophecy and hunting. He was 217 BCE made one of the Di consentes under Greek influence, when He also became identified as a solar deity. His main festival was held at the Ludi Apollini, 6-13 July, and on 23 September together with Diana.

Apula
See Apollo.

Atargatis
Known as the Dea Syria, consort of Hadad, or Derketo at Ascalon, Her worship was centered in the East, Roman citizens composing most of Her worshipers at Delos, where a statue of Her was consecrated for the wellbeing of Rome in 118/117 BCE. At Eryx in Sicily She was identified with Punic Astarte, who among the Etruscans was called Astres, identified with Ishtar/Inanna. At Rome She was assimilated as the Celestial Venus of the Aeneid legend. Her temple at Eryx, with its sacred prostitutes playing the role of Dido, became popular with Roman consuls and generals who assumed the role of Aeneas. At Rome She is Venus Erycina, Her temple on the Capitoline dedicated 23 April, after the Roman defeat by Hannibal at Lake Trasimene, 217 BCE. Lucian's Ode 43 is dedicated to Dea Syria.

She was the main deity of Arabia, known as Allath, Her main temple known today as the Ka'abah.

Aquilo
The Roman personification of the North Wind. His Greek counterpart is Boreas.

Aurora
Aurora is the Roman personification of the dawn. She is also the Roman equivalent of the Greek goddess Eos. Aurora is seen as a lovely woman who flies across the sky announcing the arrival of the sun. Aurora has two siblings: a brother, the sun, and a sister, the moon. She has had quite a number of husbands and sons. Four of her sons are the four winds (north, south, east, and west). According to one myth, her tears cause the dew as she flies across the sky weeping for one of her sons, who was killed. Aurora is certainly not the most brilliant goddess as she asked Zeus to grant one of her husbands immortality, but forgot to ask for everlasting youth. As a result, her husband soon became aged. Aurora is not one of the better-known goddesses. However, Shakespeare refers to her in his famous play Romeo and Juliet.

Ascanius
Ascanius was the son of Aeneas and Creusa, and the grandson of Venus; he was also called Iulus. He accompanied his father to Italy after the fall of Troy, and fought briefly in the Italian wars. The Julian gens claimed descent from him.

Atunis
See Adonis.

Auster
The personification of the south wind which brought fogs and rain or sultry heat. He is equivalent with the Greek Notus. It is the modern sirocco.

Averna
The Roman queen of the dead

Bacchus
The Roman god of wine and intoxication, equated with the Greek Dionysus. His festival was celebrated on March 16 and 17. The Bacchanalia, orgies in honor of Dionysus, were introduced in Rome

around 200 BCE. These infamous celebrations, notorious for their sexual and criminal character, got so out of hand that they were forbidden by the Roman Senate in 186 BCE. Bacchus is also identified with the old-Italian god Liber. Oscan Patir Libero and Pupluna, the Etruscan Fulfuns, and identified with the Roman God of the Vine, Pater Liber, only after 186 BCE.

Bellona
The Roman goddess of war, popular among the Roman soldiers. She accompanied Mars in battle, and was variously given as his wife, sister or daughter. She had a temple on the Capitolinus (inaugurated in 296 BCE and burned down in 48 BCE), where, as an act of war, a spear was cast against the distant enemy. Her festival was celebrated on June 3. Bellona's attribute is a sword and she is depicted wearing a helmet and armed with a spear and a torch. She could be of Etruscan origin, and is identified with the Greek Enyo.

Bibesia
Numen of drink.

Bona Dea
Bona Dea ("the Good Goddess") is a Roman fertility goddess, especially worshipped by the Roman matrons. She presided over both virginity and fertility in women. She is the daughter of the god Faunus and she herself is often called Fauna. She had a temple on the Aventine Hill, but her secret rites (on December 3) were not held there but in the house of a prominent Roman magistrate. Only women were admitted and even representations of men and beasts were removed. At these secret meetings it was forbidden to speak the words 'wine' and 'myrtle' because Faunus had once made her drunk and beaten her with a myrtle stick.

Her festival was observed on May 1. Similarly, no men were allowed to be present here either. She was also a healing goddess and the sick were tended in her temple garden with medicinal herbs. Bona Dea was portrayed sitting on a throne, holding a cornucopia. The snake is her attribute, a symbol of healing, and consecrated snakes were kept in her temple at Rome, indicating her phallic nature. Her image could often be found on coins. She is associated with Fauna, Ops, Maia, and other earth goddesses. She is a goddess of chastity, fruitfulness, and the earth's bounty, especially with healing herbs. Her festivals are on 1 May, 3-4 May; and 3 Dec. In Her Aventine temple was kept a supply of healing herbs guarded by snakes.

Bubona
The Roman goddess of horses, cattle and cattl breeding. She is equal to the Gaulish goddess Epona, whose cult was later adopted by the Roman army.

Caca
The Roman goddess of the hearth and the sister of the fire-breathing giant Cacus. When Heracles returned with the cattle of Geryon, Cacus stole some of the animals and hid them in his cave. According to some sources, out of sympathy for the hero, Caca told Heracles the location of that cave and he killed the giant. Caca was later succeeded by Vesta. Supposed numen of excrement, her name is derived as a female form of Cacus, and there is considerable doubt that any such numen was recognized at Rome.

Cacus (Oscan Cacuui)
Originally a pre-Roman god of fire, who gradually became a fire-breathing demon. Cacus lived in a cave in the Aventine Hill from where he terrorized the countryside. When Heracles returned with the cattle of Geryon, he passed Cacus' cave and lay down to sleep in the vicinity. At night Cacus dragged some of the cattle to his cave backward by their tails, so that their tracks would point in the opposite direction. However, the lowing of the animals betrayed their presence in the cave to Heracles and he retrieved them and slew Cacus. Other sources claim that Cacus' sister told Heracles the location of his cave. On the place were Heracles slew Cacus he erected an altar, where later the Forum Boarium, the cattle market, was held. He is associated with Orion.

Cacuui
See Cacus.

Caeculus
An ancient Italian hero, son of Vulcan. He is regarded as the founder of Praeneste (the current Palestrina).

Caia Caecilia
The deified mortal princess, Tanaquil, She is a Goddess of Healing.

Camenae
The Camenae were originally ancient Roman goddesses of wells and springs. Later they were identified with the Greek Muses. In Rome, they were worshipped in a sacred forest at the Porta Capena.

Candelifera
The Roman goddess of birth. She is identified with Carmenta and the goddess Lucina.

Canens
A nymph from Latium and the personification of song. She was the wife of king Picus, who was loved by Circe but when he rejected her, Circe transformed him into a woodpecker. After she had wandered for six days without finding him, Canens threw herself from a rock into the Tiber. After one final song she evaporated. She is the mother of Faunus, She called for Her husband until She wasted away to a disembodied voice. She is the Voice of the Woods.

Cardea
The goddess of thresholds and especially door-pivots (cardo "door-pivot"). Just as Carna she is also a goddess of health. Cardea is the protectress of little children against the attacks of vampire-witches. She obtained the office from Janus in exchange for her personal favors. Ovid says of Cardea, apparently quoting a religious formula: 'Her power is to open what is shut; to shut what is open. Indigimentum or wife of Janus for hinges, who protects the house from evil spirits. She was given a twig of Hawthorn by Her husband Janus as a wedding gift, and such a twig is struck against the door hinges and hung over the door in an annual rite to protect the house.

Seaa also Clererca.

Carmenae
Fourteen nymphs of childbirth, associated with the Muses, whose festival is held on 13 Aug.

Carmenta
Carmenta is the Roman goddess of childbirth and prophecy, one of the Camenae. Her temple (where it was forbidden to wear leather), was in Rome, next to the Porta Carmentalis. She had a flamen Carmentalis at Rome. Associated with Porrima and Postuorta (past and future). Also a Goddess of Springs. Her festival, the Carmentalia, took place on 11 and 15 January, commemorated at the Porta Carmentalis, and was mostly celebrated by women. She is the mother of Euander (Evander).

Carnea or Carneis (Oscan)
Protective goddess of a healthy body and especially of the large organs – heart, lungs, and liver, whose shrine was on the Caelian. On 1 June beans and bacon were eaten in Her honor and offered to Her in sacrifice.

Castor and Pollux
Popular twins, their temple dedication of 484 BCE is commemorated on 15 July, their main festivals held on 27 Jan. and 13 Aug. They were commonly sworn by, like Hercules, in the forms of mecastor, or edepol.

Castores
The Roman name of the Dioscuri; from Castor, who seems to have been the first of the twins to be worshipped by the Romans.

Catha (or Cautha)
Etruscan solar god, comparable to Greek Helios.

Catillus
The brother of the river-deity Tibertus, and co-founder of the city of Tibur (current Tivoli).

Cautha
See Catha.

Celscan

Etruscan giant, literally "Son of Cel." Associated with the highest Apennine peak, Monte Corno, ("the Horn"), where he is also the consort of Ceres. Men wear a talisman of Celscan for virility in the form of a golden horn or red pepper.

Cenetai
Oscan numen of childbirth, comparable to Greek Eileithyia

Ceres
The old-Italian goddess of agriculture, grain, and the love a mother bears for her child. The cult of Ceres was originally closely connected with that of Tellus, the goddess earth. In later mythology, Ceres is identified with the Greek Demeter. She is the daughter of Saturn and the mother of Proserpina. Ceres had a temple on the Aventine Hill, were she was worshipped together with Liber and Libera. Ceres is portrayed with a scepter, a basket with flowers or fruits, and a garland made of the ears of corn. Another festival was the Ambarvalia, held in May. Oscan Kerri, and Etruscan Cels: Goddess of grain, agriculture and law giving. With Her daughter Libitania (Proserpina), She is the Goddess of the renewal of the earth and all regeneration. She is the daughter of Ops, and closely identified with or as Tellus. She has been associated with the central Apennines since the Neolithic period, symbolized by the Three Sacred Mountains and the mons venere within. Her main festivals are the Ceralia on 12-19 April and on 4 October a fast is held in Her honor.

Cerfu
An Umbrian God found at Iguvium in a triad with Jupiter and Mars, each associated with Grabovius, God of the Oaks, invoked to protect that city from barbarian invaders. He is the Oscan Cerus, consort of Ceres, protector of the boundaries of fields and of the plants within, from disease and intemperate weather.

Cerreri
The individual souls of men and women, called Genius for men and Juno for women in Rome.

Charun
Etruscan demon, leader of the Charonte demons who torment the dead. He is portrayed as winged, with a vulture's beak and pointed ears, carrying a large hammer after the manner of Orcus.

Chnubis
A Roman syncretic god with Greek and Egyptian associations, portrayed as a snake with a lion's head.

Cinxia
The Roman goddess of marriage. Indigimentum of Juno who loosens the girdle of brides.

Clementia
The Roman goddess of mercy and clemency.

Clererca
Italian goddess of hinges, family life and protection from strigae, She was at Rome called Cardea.

Clitumnus
An Umbrian river god of healing and prophecy.

Clitunno
A Roman river deity.

Cloacina
Numen of sewers, She is an indigimentum of Venus, "The Purifier." The goddess who presides of the system of sewers (from the Latin cloaca, "sewer") which drained the refuse of the city of Rome. The main sewer was called Cloaca Maxima.

Coelus
"Sky". The Roman personified god of the heavens who is identified with the Greek Uranus. His wife is Terra.

Collatina
Indigimentum of Tellus for hills and downs.

Cominuii
Oscan Manes.

Comus
Numen of night life and nighttime revelry.

Concordia

The Roman goddess of concord, whose festival is July 22. She was worshipped in many temples, but the oldest was on the Forum Romanum and dates back to 367 BCE and was built by Camilus. The temple also served as a meeting-place for the Roman senate. Concordia is portrayed sitting, wearing a long cloak and holding a sacrificial bowl in her left hand and a cornucopia in her right. Sometimes she can be seen standing between two members of the Royal House who clasp hands.

Conditor

Indigimentum of Ceres for the storing of grain in barns. The Roman god of harvesting the crops.

Consentes, Dii

The twelve major gods of the Roman pantheon, identified by the Roman with the Greek Olympians. Six male and six female gods and goddesses. They are: Jupiter and Juno, Neptune and Minerva, Apollo and Diana, Mars and Venus, Vulcan and Vesta, and Mercury and Ceres. Their statues could be found in the hall of the Consentes Dii at the Forum Romanum.

Consiva

Indigimentum of Ceres for sowing and reaping.

Consus

The Roman god who presides over the storing of grain. Since the grain was stored in holes underneath the earth, Consus' altar was also placed beneath the earth (near the Circus Maximus). The Consualia falls on 21 Aug after harvest, the traditional date of the Rape of the Sabine women. His other festivals are on 12 and 15 Dec after sowing. His altar lies below ground and is uncovered three times a year for sacrifices. It was uncovered only during the Consualia. At Rome He was also a god of horses. One of the main events during this festival was a mule race (the mule was his sacred animal). Also on this day, farm and dray horses were not permitted to work and attended the festivities. He is closely connected with the fertility goddess Ops (Ops Consiva). Later he was also regarded as god of secret counsels.

Convector
Indigimentum of Ceres for the harvest home. The Roman god of bringing in the crops.

Copia
The Roman goddess of wealth and plenty, who carried a cornucopia ("horn of plenty"). She belongs to the retinue of Fortuna.

Corus
The Roman god representing the north/north-west wind.

Cuba
The Roman goddess who protects the infants in their cribs and sends them to sleep.

Culsu
Etruscan demoness who guards Gates of the Underworld with scissors and a torch.

Cumaean Sibyl
The earliest of the Sibyls. She was believed to have come from the rest, and resided at Cumae. She owned, according to tradition, nine books of prophecies. When the Roman king Targuin (Tarquinius Priscus) wanted to buy those books he thought the price she asked far too high. The Sibyl threw three books into the fire and doubled the price; this she did again with the next three books, and the king was forced the buy the remaining three books for a price four times as high as the original nine. makes the victim fall in love.

He is also portrayed as a young man with his beloved Psyche, with Venus or with a small group of winged infants (the Amoretti or Amorini). Some traditions say that he was born from a silver egg. His Greek equivalent is Eros. The name is derived from the Latin cupido, "desire".

Cupid
God of love, son of Venus, and husband of Psyche.

Cura
A goddess who first fashioned humans from clay.

Curis

A Sabine God, the Oscan Kurrenui, in Rome He was Quirinus. His name derives from the Oscan word for spear and He was seen as a god of defensive war, protecting the homeland, and also of protecting farmlands. In this last aspect He protects plants from disease and intemperate weather like Cerus.

Curtius

Marcus Curtius, a Roman hero. When one day a gap suddenly appeared on the Forum in Rome, an oracle said that it could only be closed by the most precious thing Rome possessed. The wellbeing of the town depended on it. Curtius sacrificed himself by jumping fully armed and mounted on the finest horse into the gap, which then closed itself. The gap, called the Lacus Curtius is situated at the Forum Romanum. According to other sources, the gap was created when lightning struck, which was then consecrated by the consul Caius Curtius in 445 BCE.[4]

Dea Dia

A Roman goddess of growth, identified with Ceres. Her priests were the Fratres Arvales who honored her in the feast of the Ambarvalia, held in May. During these days, the priests blessed the fields and made offerings to the powers of the underworld. She is at times identified with Acca Larentia as goddess of corn and wheat fields, otherwise as Mana Genita, Mother of the Lares (Larunda).

Dea Tacita

The 'silent goddess'. A Roman goddess of dead.

Decima

A Roman goddess of childbirth. Together with Nona and Morta she forms the Parcae (the Roman goddesses of Fate).

Dei Lucrii

The Roman gods of profit. In time they were superseded by Mercury.

Deiuai

Oscan for "the Goddesses," dual mothers of a God of Crops.

Deuerra

Deuerra is the Roman goddess that rules the brooms used to purify ritual sites. One of three numina who protect newborns from Silvanus. A house ceremony is held by three men knocking on the thresholds:

1. Intercidona, numina of hewing timbers knocks with axhead,
2. Picumnus knocks with a pestle,
3. Deuerra sweeps with a broom.

Ceremony performed while the mother is in bed with her child.

Devera

See Deuerra.

Di Inferi

The Roman deities of the underworld. They were honored with the Ludi Tauri quinquennales, games which took place every five years on June 25 and 26 and which was held at the Circus Flaminius in Rome. The games were, according to legend, instituted to placate the gods of the underworld who were held responsible for sending a plague during the reign of Tarquinius Superbus (534-510 BCE).

Dia

Her name shows that she was one of Italy's original goddesses, but there is little information about her today.

Diana

Etruscan Artumes: Italic counterpart to Janus, She is the Moon Goddess, bringer of light. As Diana Lucina, like Juno, she is a Goddess of Childbirth. Diana as a huntress, sister of Apollo, a bringer/protector from disease, is a later Greek form. She shared a festival with Her brother Apollo on 13 August.

The Roman goddess of nature, fertility and childbirth. She is closely identified with the Greek goddess Artemis. Diana is also a moon-goddess and was originally worshipped on the mountain Tifata near Capua and in sacred forests (such as Aricia in Latium). Her priest lived in Aricia and if a man was able to kill him with a bough broken from a tree in this forest, he would become priest himself 1.

Also torch bearing processions were held in her honor here.

Later she was given a temple in the working-class area on the Aventine Hill where she was mainly worshipped by the lower class (plebeians) and the slaves, of whom she was the patroness. Slaves could also ask for asylum in her temple. Her festival coincided with the idus (13th) of August. Diana was originally a goddess of fertility and, just as Bona Dea, she was worshipped mainly by women as the giver of fertility and easy births. Under Greek influence she was equated with Artemis and assumed many of her aspects. Her name is possibly derived from 'diviana' ("the shining one"). She is portrayed as a huntress accompanied by a deer. Diana was also the goddess of the Latin commonwealth.

Dii consentes
In 217 BCE the Senate ordered a special festival called a lecistratum to be held in honor of the Dii consentes. Six gods and six goddesses were honored in the ceremony, in which Their images were set out on couches upon the Capitoline, to share a sacred meal with the people of Rome. The Dii consentes were then regarded as the celestial deities who headed the Roman pantheon. These particular deities – Juno and Juppiter, Apollo and Diana, Ceres and Neptune, Mars and Venus, Vesta and Volconus - were selected as the Dii consentes because of Their close identity with the Olympian gods of Greek myth.

Dii inferi
As a counterpoint to the Dii consentes were the gods and goddesses of the Earth. While other gods and goddesses such as Faunus and Fauna might be included among the Di Inferi those most closely identified as such were Dis and Proserpina, Februus, Hecate, and Nemesis.

Dii Mauri
The 'Moorish gods' mentioned in Latin inscriptions in North Africa, who are almost never named. They were supposed to be 'salutares' (redemptory), 'immortales' (immortal), and 'augusti' (exalted).

Dioue patir
See Diuuei.

Dirae
Literally "the terrible"; a Latin name for the Furies. The name was mainly used in poetry.

Dis Pater
The Roman ruler of the underworld and fortune, similar to the Greek Hades. Every hundred years, the Ludi Tarentini were celebrated in his honor. The Gauls regarded Dis Pater as their ancestor. The name is a contraction of the Latin Dives, "the wealthy", Dives Pater, "the wealthy father", or "Fater Wealth". It refers to the wealth of precious stone below the earth.

Disciplina
Disciplina is the Roman goddess of discipline.

Discordia
The personified Roman goddess of strife and discord. She belonged to the retinue of Mars and Bellona. She is the Greek Eris.

Dius Fidus
The Roman god of oaths. Dius Fidus is of Sabine origin.

Diuuei
Oscan Jove, literally "the God," He is also called Dioue patir.

Domiduca
The Roman goddess who escorts the child safely back home.

Domiducus
The Roman god who guides a bride to her new home.

Domitius
The Roman god who kept a woman in the house of her husband.

Duellona
A Roman goddess.

Edesia
Numen of food.

Egeria

The Roman goddess who inspired and guided Numa Pompilius, the successor of Romulus in the kingship of Rome. She is also regarded as his wife. They used to meet in a sacred grove in the midst of which a spring gushed forth and there she taught him wise legislation and the forms of public worship. After his death in 673 BCE she changed into a well in the forest of Aricia in Latium, which was dedicated to Diana. Egeria is one of the Camenae and was also worshipped as a goddess of birth. At Aricia she was recognized as a goddess, forming a triad with Diana and Virbius.

Egestes

The Roman personification of poverty. Virgil mentioned her later as a demon in the underworld.

Empanda

This goddess personified the idea of openness and generosity.

Endovelicus

Endovelicus is a native god of the pre-Roman communities (Iron Age) in Lusitania (south west of Iberia) later adopted by the Romans themselves. As a god he was concerned with the good health and welfare of the people. There are hundreds of inscriptions of him in Portugal and Spain.

Epona

Originally a Celtic goddess of horses, She was accepted into the Roman pantheon and had a festival on 18 Dec.

Erycina

An epithet of Venus because of her worship on mount Eryx on Sicily.

Euan

Etruscan for an individual's immortal soul, like the Roman genius and juno or Oscan cereri.

Euander (Evander)

A minor Roman deity who was believed to have introduced the Greek pantheon, laws, the alphabet, and other arts and skills in

Rome.

Evander
See Euander.

Eventus Bonus
Eventus Bonus ("good ending") is the Roman god of success in business, but who also ensured a good harvest. His statue stood on the Capitol in Rome, near the temple of Jupiter Optimus Maximus.

Fabulinus
A minor Roman god of infants. Mentioned by Varro, Fabulinus taught Roman children to utter their first word. He received an offering when the child spoke its first words. (From fabulari, to speak.)

Facunditas
The Roman personification of fertility.

Falacer
A deified Italic hero, served by a flamen Falaceris, nothing is really known about Him. May have had some relationhip to the defense of city walls and/or the Pomerium.

Fama
The Roman personified goddess of fame, and the personification of popular rumor. What she heard she repeated first in a whisper to few, then louder and louder until she communicated it to all heaven and earth. Mentioned as a daughter of Tellus. Not truly a goddess, she was more a literary conceit. She had as many eyes, ears, and tongues as she had feathers. Virgil mentions Fama ("rumor") as a horrible creature with multiple tongues and tattling mouths. The Greek version is Pheme.[5]

Fames
The Roman personification of hunger. Virgil mentioned that Fames lived in the underworld, next to Poverty. Ovid wrote that she lived in the inhospitable Scythia.

Fascinus

Italic phallic numen, associated with Liber, and who has the power to ward off the evil eye. The phallus hung over a doorway for good luck, much like a horseshoe is today, with the epithet, "Hic habitat Felicitas," or "Here dwells Happiness." Large phallics were also placed in Roman gardens to ensure fertility.

Fatuai

The Oscan Goddess called Fauna by the Romans, Daughter of Faunus, She is identified as the Bona Dea. Her Temple of Bona Dea on the Aventine, stored medicinal herbs, guarded by snakes. Her festivals are held on 13 Feb. and the Faunalia on 5 Dec. Another name for Her at Tarentum is Damia.

Fauna

A Roman earth-mother and fertility goddess, usually termed the Bona Dea. She is thought to be the wife, sister or daughter of Faunus. Fauna is identified with Terra, Tellus or Ops.

Fauns

Among the Romans, fauns were wild forest deities with little horns, the hooves of a goat, and a short tail. They accompanied the god Faunus. Fauns are analogous to the Greek satyrs.

Faunus

The god of wild nature and fertility, also regarded as the giver of oracles. He was later identified with the Greek Pan and also assumed some of Pan's characteristics such as the horns and hooves. As the protector of cattle he is also referred to as Lupercus ("he who wards off the wolf"). One particular tradition tells that Faunus was the king of Latium, and the son of Picus. After his death he was deified as Fatuus, and a small cult formed around his person in the sacred forest of Tibur (Tivoli). On February 15 (the founding date of his temple) his feast, the Lupercalia, was celebrated. Priests (called the Luperci) wearing goat skins walked through the streets of Rome and hit the spectators with belts made from goat skin. Another festival was the Faunalia, observed on December 5. He is accompanied by the fauns, analogous to the Greek satyrs. His feminine counterpart is Fauna. The wolf skin, wreath, and a goblet are his attributes.

Faustitas
The goddess who protects the herds.

Faustulus
In Roman myth, the shepherd who found the twins Romulus and Remus on the Palatine Hill where they were reared by a she-wolf. He took them with him and gave them to his wife Acca Larentia to rear.

Favonius
The Roman god of the gentle western wind, the herald of spring. Favonius ("favorable") is equal to the Greek Zephyrus.

Febris
Numen to ward off fevers. The goddess who protects against fever. Febris ("fever") had three temples in ancient Rome, of which one was located between the Palatine and Velabrum.

Felicitas
The Roman personification of success and good fortune. Her temples were closely associated with the person of the emperor and one was located on the Forum Romanum. She is depicted with cornucopia and herald's staff, celebrated on 9 Oct.

Ferentina
Oscan form of Libitina, combining Flora, Venus, and Ceres, She is the Earth Goddess of the Latin League and one of the secret names of Roma. Her main sanctuaries were at Aricia, and Ferentium of the Hernicii.

Ferentina
The goddess of the mountain city of Ferentinum in Latium. She was protector of the Latin commonwealth.

Feronia
The Roman goddess who was invoked to secure a bountiful harvest. Italic Goddess of fire and fertility flowers, blossoms, and ripe fruit of fields and trees, also the goddess of the flower of youth and its pleasures. She is an Italic goddess combining attributes of Flora, Venus and Libera, and is sometimes identified with Vesta. She

tames wild areas with orchards, and is also a goddess of woods and all trees.

She was worshipped in Capena, located at the base of Mount Soracte, and Terracina, and had a temple on the Campus Martius in Rome. She was worshipped as the goddess of freedom by slaves, for it was believed that those who sat on a holy stone in her sanctuary were set free. Her festival took place on November 15.

Fessonia
Goddess who aids the weary.

Fides (Fides Publica)
The Roman goddess of good faith and faithfulness. She was worshipped as Fides Publica Populi Romani (loyalty towards the Roman state). In her temple on the Capitol the Roman Senate confirmed state treaties with foreign powers, which were kept there under her protection. The goddess of verbal contracts; on 1 Oct the flamines Dialis, Martialis, and Quirinitalis made sacrifices to them on the Capitol, arriving in two-horse drawn chariots.

Flora
The goddess of blossoming flowers of spring. She had a minor temple on the Quirinalis and was given a sanctuary near the Circus Maximus in 238 BCE. The festival of the Floralia, celebrated on April 28 -May 1, existed until the 4th century CE. The Ludi Florales held in Her honor became annual games in 173 BCE, and under the empire were extended until May 3 for the Floralia. They began with theatrical performances, followed by races, and ending with sacrifices to Flora. Hares and goats were set loose, and vetches, beans, and lupines were distributed to the spectators. Flora is identified with the Greek Chloris.

Florus
Oscan god of first fruits, husband of Flora; not found at Rome.

Fluonia
Numen of menstruation.

Fons
God of Springs, son of Janus and Juturna, His altar on the Janiculum, was honored at the Fontinalia on 13 October.

Forculus
Numen of doorways.

Fontus
The Roman god of wells and springs, son of Janus and Juturna. The festival of Fontus took place on October 13. He is also called Fons.

Fontanus
See Fontus.

Fornax
Fornax ("oven") is the personified Roman goddess of the baking of bread. Oscan Purasia: Goddess of the ovens used to roast grain, honored in the Fornacalia during first part of February. Her festival involved roasting grain in an ancient fashion, the ovens set up in the Forum. The festival was conducted by the Curiae under the supervision of the Curio Maximus. Those who missed sacrificing on the date it was held were called stulti (fools) and had to make a special sacrifice on the Quirinalia.

Fortuna
The Roman personification of good fortune, originally a goddess of blessing and fertility and in that capacity she was especially worshipped by mothers. Her cult is thought to be introduced by Servius Tullius. She had a temple on the Forum Boarium and a sanctuary, the Fortuna Populi Romani, stood on the Quirinalis. In Praeneste she had an oracle where a small boy randomly choose a little oak rod (sors), upon which a fate was inscribed.

Some of Fortuna's names include: Primigenia, Virilis, Respiciens, Muliebris, and Annonaria. She is portrayed standing, wearing a rich dress. The cornucopia, rudder, ball, and blindfold are her attributes. Her Greek counterpart is Tyche.

Perhaps the most important goddess, Pliny says, "Fortuna alone is invoked, alone commended, alone accused and subjected to reproaches; deemed volatile and indeed, by most men, blind as well, wayward, capricious, fickle in Her favors and favoring the unworthy. Her many names include:

F. Primigenia sets the destiny of children at their birth, 13 Nov.
F. Privata of family life.
F. Publica of the state, 5 April.
F. Liberum of children.
F. Virginalis of virgins, 11 June.
F. Muliebris of women.
F. Virilis of boys, youths, and the happiness of women in marriage.
F. Barbata to whom boys dedicated the first shaving of their beards.
F. Victrix who gave victories.
F. Redux who brought people home safely.
F. Tranquilla for prosperous voyages.
F. Comes or Dux for the fortune of leaders
F. Caesaris and F. Augusta for the fortune of emperors
F. Patricia of the Patrician Order
F. Plebis of the Plebeian Order
F. Bona for good fortune
F. Mala to ward off bad luck
F. Blanda for flattering
F. Obsequens for yielding
F. Viscata for enticing
F. Dubia for doubtful luck
F.. Brevis for fickle fortune
F. Manens for constant luck.
F. Equestris for horses, 13 August.
Fors Fortuna for games of chance, 25 May and 24 June.
F. Huiusque for luck of the day, 30 July.

Her main temple in Rome was in the Forum Boarum, Her largest temple, and an oracle was at Praeneste,

Fraus
The Roman personification of treachery. Daughter of Orcus and Nox, with a snake's tail and hidden deformities, She is a goddess of fraud and deception.

Frutesca
Numen of fruit.

Fulfuns
See Bacchus.

Fulgora
Numen of lightning. The Roman goddess of lightning.

Furies
The Roman goddess of vengeance. They are equivalent to the Greek Erinyes. The Furies, who are usually characterized as three sisters (Alecto, Tisiphone, and Magaera) are the children of Gaia and Uranus. They resulted from a drop of Uranus' blood falling onto the earth. They were placed in the Underworld by Virgil and it is there that they reside, tormenting evildoers and sinners. However, Greek poets saw them as pursuing sinners on Earth. The Furies are cruel, but are also renowned for being very fair.

Furina
The Roman goddess of thieves and highway bandits.

Furrina
An ancient Roman goddess, who was perhaps a spirit of darkness. Her festival, the Furrinalia, continued to be observed on July 25 in later Roman times, despite the fact that her nature had been forgotten. Her priest was called the flamen Furrinalis. It was in the grove of Furrina that Gaius Sempronius Gracchus ordered his slave to kill him.

Galli
The hierodules or priests of Cybele, who castrated themselves in identification with the goddess. The Roman name for the Corybantes.

Garanos
Italic hero, slayer of Cacus, he was later identified as Hercules.

Geminus
"Double". An epithet of Janus, referring to his two faces.

Genii Cucllati
Hooded figures, usually singular, except in Britannia where three hooded figures were depicted, representing fertility, prosperity and regeneration. See Suleviae Junones.

Genius / Juno
In Roman mythology, the genius was originally the family ancestor who lived in the underworld. Through the male members he secured the existence of the family. Later, the genius became more a protecting or guardian spirit for persons. These spirits guided and protected that person throughout his life. Every man had a genius, to whom he sacrificed on birthdays. It was believed that the genius would bestow success and intellectual powers on its devotees. Women had their own genius, which was called a juno.

The juno was the protector of women, marriage and birth. It was worshipped under many names: Virginalis (juno of the virgin), Matronalis (of the married woman), Pronuba (of the bride), Iugalis (of marriage), etc. Juno was also the name for the queen of the gods. However, not only individuals had guardian spirits: families, households, and cities had their own. Even the Roman people as a whole had a genius. The genius was usually depicted as a winged, naked youth, while the genius of a place was depicted as a serpent. (See also: Lares.)

Genius Publicus
Numen of public spirit, honored on 9 October.

Gods of Early Childhood
The indigimenta of Juno, Potina and Educa teach children to eat and drink after being weaned. Cuba protects child while being transferred from cradle to bed. Ossipaga protects a child's bones, Carna the flesh and major organs. Levana guides a child to raise self from ground. Statilinus or Dea Statina aids child to stand. Abeona and Adeona for first steps. Farinus teaches the child to talk.

Gods of Marriage
Different indigimenta of Juno are associated with marriage ceremonies. In addition there is mention of indigimenta of the first wedding night. The only source for these latter indigimenta is

however Augustine of Hippo, writing against the pagan gods, so it cannot be certain that the indigimenta of the wedding night were ever part of the Roman pantheon. These indigimenta then are Pronuba or Jugatinus and Juga of marriage, Domiduca who leads the bride to her husband's house and Domitius who keeps the bride at her new home, Unxia who anoints the doorposts of the bride's new home, Cinxia who ties and loosens the bride's girdle, Virginiensis of the bride's virginity, Subigus to tame the bride, Prema the mother goddess who overpowers the husband by holding the bride, Pertunda along with Venus and Priapus to ensure penetration in coitus of the first night, Perficia for coitus, and Maturna who sees that the bride and groom remain together.

Grabovius
Umbrian Krapuvi: Italic God of Oaks, the original Capitoline deity, later identified with Jupiter.

Hecate
One of the Dii Inferi, a goddess of revenge, and a protectress. Goddess of the crossroads, and of abandoned infants, She may be identified with Laverna. Her title in Oscan as Mother of the Manes is Maauissa and thus She is the Genita Manuana. Otherwise She is the sister of Latona and often identified with Diana.

Hercules
Oscan Herekleis and Etruscan Hercle: Unlike the Heracles of Greek myth, he married Minerva and fathered Maris. A guardian of vows as Sancus, or Dius Fidius, he is also called Victor, Invictus on 12-13 August, Custos on 4 June, and Defensor. At Silchester in Britannia he was Hercules Saegon, in northeast Gaul. H. Magusanus and in Narbonensis, H. Ilunnus. At Rome his Ara Maxima was in the Forum Boarum. A semidivine hero in early myths, later he became a solar savior deity.

Hercules, the Latin equivalent of Heracles, was the son of Jupiter and Alcmene. His jealous stepmother, Juno, tried to murder the infant Hercules by putting a serpent in his cradle. Luckily for Hercules, he was born with great strength and killed the serpent. By the time Hercules was an adult, he had already killed a lion. Eventually, Juno drove Hercules insane. Due to his insanity,

Hercules killed his wife, Megara, and their three children. Hercules exiled himself because of the shame that he had brought on himself through his lack of sanity. Hercules decided to ask the Delphic Oracle what he should do to regain his honor. The Oracle told Hercules to go to Eurystheus, king of Mycenae, and serve him for twelve years. King Eurystheus couldn't think of any tasks that might prove difficult for the mighty son of Jupiter, so Juno came down from her palace on Olympus to help him.

Together, the twosome came up with twelve tasks for Juno's mortal stepson to complete. These tasks are now known as the twelve labors of Hercules.

Hercules' first labor was to kill the menacing Nemean Lion; Hercules strangled the creature and carried it back to Mycenae.

The second task was to overcome the nine-headed snake known as the Hydra; Hercules' cousin Ioloas helped him out by burning the stumps of the heads after Hercules cut off the heads; since the ninth head was immortal, Hercules rolled a rock over it.

The third task was to find the golden-horned stag and bring it back alive; Hercules followed the stag around for one full year; he finally captured the stag and took it back alive.

The fourth labor was to capture a wild boar that terrorized Mycenae's people; Hercules chased the boar up a mountain where the boar fell in to a snow drift, where Hercules subdued it.

The fifth task of Hercules was to clean the Augean stables, where thousands of cattle were housed, in a single day; Hercules diverted two rivers so that they would flow into the Augean stables.

The sixth labor was to destroy the man-eating Stymphalian birds; Hercules drove them out of their hiding places with a rattle and shot them with poison-tipped arrows.
The seventh task was for Hercules to capture a Cretean savage bull; Hercules wrestled it to the ground and took it back to King Eurystheus.

The eighth labor was to capture the four man-eating mares of Thrace; Hercules threw the master of the mares to them; the horses became very tame, so Hercules safely led them back to Mycenae.

Hercules' ninth labor was to obtain the girdle of the fierce Amazon warrior queen, Hippolyta; Hippolyta willingly gave her girdle to Hercules, but Juno convinced the Amazons that Hercules was trying to take Hippolyta from them, so Hercules fought them off and returned to his master with the girdle.
The tenth labor was to capture the cattle of the monster, Geryon; Hercules killed Geryon, claimed the cattle, and took them back to the king.

The eleventh task was to get the golden-apples of the Hesperides; Hercules told Atlas that if he would get the apples for him, he (Hercules) would hold the heavens for him; when Atlas returned from his task, Hercules tricked him into taking back the heavens.

The final labor of Hercules was to bring the three-headed watchdog of the underworld, Cerberus, to the surface without using any weapons; Hercules seized two of Cerberus' heads and the dog gave in. Hercules took the dog to his master, who ordered him to take it back.

Finally, after twelve years and twelve tasks, Hercules was a free man. Hercules went to the town of Thebes and married Deianira. She bore him many children. Later on in their life, the male centaur, Nessus, abducted Deianira, but Hercules came to her rescue by shooting Nessus with a poison tipped arrow. The dying Nessus told Deianira to keep a portion of his blood to use as a love potion on Hercules if she felt that she was losing him to another woman. A couple of a months later, Deianira thought that another woman was coming between her and her husband, so Deianira washed one of Hercules' shirts in Nessus' blood and gave it to him to wear. Nessus had lied to her, for the blood really acted as a poison and almost killed Hercules. On his funeral pyre, the dying Hercules ascended to Olympus, where he was granted immortality and lived among the gods.

Herentai
Oscan Venus, Goddess of Beauty and Love. She is also a Goddess of Gardens and garden flowers.

Hersilia
The Sabine wife of Romulus. She was, just as her husband, deified after his death by Iuno and became Hora.

Herulus
The son of the goddess Feronia. He had three lives and was killed by Evander.

Hinthial
Etruscan for ghost, shade, or reflection.

Hippona
The Roman goddess of horses. Her image is derived from the Gallic goddess Epona, whose cult was adopted by the Roman soldiers.

Honos (Honor)
The numen of honor whose festival was on 17 July. The Roman deity of morality and military honor. There were several temples devoted to him in Rome. Honos is depicted as a young warrior bearing a lance and a Cornucopia ("horn of plenty").

Horatus Cocles
A legendary hero from the earliest history of Rome. When the Etruscans lay siege to Rome and occupied the Ianiculus Hill, Cocles defended the bridge that led to the city all by himself, against overwhelming odds. Meanwhile the Romans demolished the bridge behind his back and when they were done, he dove into the water and swam to safety.

Imporcitor
The Roman god of the third ploughing. See also Redarator and Vervactor.

Indigites, Dii
The group of original, native Roman gods, in contrast to the Novensiles Dii, gods imported from elsewhere. The Indigites Dii

were only invoked in special situations. They are the protectors of homes, stables, barns, fields, meadows, et cetera.

Indigetes
A class of lesser deities, like the heroes Aeneas and Evander.

Indivia
The Roman goddess of jealousy.

Inferi, Dii
The Roman gods of the underworld.

Intercidona
A goddess who protects the household and family from the evil wishes of others. See Deuerra.

Inuus
The Roman gods of herds. Oscan Faunus, god of fertility and sexual intercourse, who Livy claimed was the deity originally honored at Lupercalia on 15 February.

Iris
See Mercurius.

Italus
An ancient Italian hero, the son of Penelope and Telegonus. He was king of the Oenotrians or of the Siculi, who are regarded as the first inhabitants of Italy.

Iuppiter
See Jupiter below.

Jana
A minor Roman goddess. She is the wife of the god Janus.

Janus
Etruscan Ani: Pater Matutinus, "breaker of the day," the oldest God, the God of gods, the Good Creator, the beginner of all things. Light, the sun, opener of the heavenly gates. As Consiuius (The Sower) He is the spouse of Juturna, goddess of springs, and father of

Fontus. Janus is also spouse of Venila, a Goddess of shallow seas who is sometimes considered the wife of Neptune. As Janus Quirinus he is a god of peace, that is, peace won by the vigilant Quirites. Janus Pater the creator of 1 January and 17 August. He is called Janus Bifrons (two-faced), Janus Patulcius (the opened door during wartime), and Janus Clusivus (the closed door during peace). A minor deity of same name is a guardian of doorways.

Janus is the Roman god of gates and doors (ianua), beginnings and endings, and hence represented with a double-faced head, each looking in opposite directions. He was worshipped at the beginning of the harvest time, planting, marriage, birth, and other types of beginnings, especially the beginnings of important events in a person's life. Janus also represents the transition between primitive life and civilization, between the countryside and the city, peace and war, and the growing-up of young people. One tradition states that he came from Thessaly and that he was welcomed by Camese in Latium, where they shared a kingdom. They married and had several children, among which the river god Tiberinus (after whom the river Tiber is named). When his wife died, Janus became the sole ruler of Latium. He sheltered Saturn when he was fleeing from Jupiter. Janus, as the first king of Latium, brought the people a time of peace and welfare; the Golden Age. He introduced money, cultivation of the fields, and the laws. After his death he was deified and became the protector of Rome. When Romulus and his associates stole the Sabine Virgins, the Sabines attacked the city. The daughter of one of the guards on the Capitoline Hill betrayed her fellow countrymen and guided the enemy into the city. They attempted to climb the hill but Janus made a hot spring erupt from the ground, and the would-be attackers fled from the city.

Ever since, the gates of his temple were kept open in times of war so the god would be ready to intervene when necessary. In times of peace the gates were closed. His most famous sanctuary was a portal on the Forum Romanum through which the Roman legionaries went to war. He also had a temple on the Forum Olitorium, and in the first century another temple was built on the Forum of Nerva. This one had four portals, called Janus Quadrifons. When Rome became a republic, only one of the royal functions survived, namely that of rex sacrorum or rex sacrificulus. His priests regularly sacrificed to him. The month of January (the eleventh Roman month) is named after him. Janus was represented with two faces, originally one face was bearded while the other was not (probably a symbol of the sun and the moon). Later both faces were bearded. In his right hand he holds a key. The double-faced head appears on many Roman coins, and around the 2nd century BCE even with four faces.

Jove
The genitive form of the name, and specifically in this form, of the sky god Jupiter.

Juga
An Italic Goddess of Courtship, who at Rome became an indigimentum of Juno.

Jugatina
Numen of mountain ridges; diminuative form of Juga.

Juno
Protector and special counselor of the Roman state and queen of the gods. She is a daughter of Saturn and sister (but also the wife) of the chief god Jupiter and the mother of Juventus, Mars, and Vulcan. As the patron goddess of Rome and the Roman empire she was called Regina ("queen") and, together with Jupiter and Minerva, was worshipped as a triad on the Capitol (Juno Capitolina) in Rome. As the Juno Moneta (she who warns) she guarded over the finances of the empire and had a temple on the Arx (one of two Capitoline hills), close to the Royal Mint. She was also worshipped in many other cities, where temples were built in her honor. The primary feast of Juno Lucina, called the Matronalia, was celebrated on March 1. On this day, lambs and other cattle were sacrificed to her. Another festival took place on July 7 and was called Nonae Caprotinae ("The Nones of the Wild Fig"). The month of June was named after her. She can be identified with the Greek goddess Hera and, like Hera, Juno was a majestical figure, wearing a diadem on the head. The peacock is her symbolic animal. A juno is also the protecting and guardian spirit of females. Her many names are:

I. Sospita Mater Regina is the Savior, regenerator of the dead on 1

Feb.
I. Curitis or I. Quiritis, is the Sabine war goddess, 7 Oct..
I. Sororia of girls at puberty on 1 Oct.
I. Domiduca leads the bride to her husband's house
I. Unxia anoints the doorstep.
I. Cinxia unties and loosens the bride's girdle
Iunoa Pronuba and I. Iuga is the foundress of marriage
I. Moneta is "the Advisor," on 1 June and 10 Oct.
I. Caprotina, "of the goat," on 7 July, and celebrated by slave girls and ancillae.
I. Lucina and I. Opigena of childbirth.
I. Regina, Queen of Heaven, 1 Sept.
I. Populonia and I. Sispes, she is honored together with Jupiter, Her brother and husband, on 1 July and 13 Sept. on the anniversary of the dedication of the Capitoline temple in 507 BCE.

Her other temple on the Aventine was dedicated in 392 BCE.

Juno
Numen of the female power of bearing; also the individual spirit in females.

Juno Iovino
Oscan Cerna, and Etruscan Uni: the Bringer of Light, Goddess of Birth and of beginnings.

Jupiter
Jupiter is the supreme god of the Roman pantheon, called dies pater, "shining father". He is a god of light and sky, and protector of the state and its laws. He is a son of Saturn and brother of Neptune and Juno (who is also his wife). The Romans worshipped him especially as Jupiter Optimus Maximus (all-good, all-powerful). This name refers not only to his rulership over the universe, but also to his function as the god of the state who distributes laws, controls the realm and makes his will known through oracles. His English name is Jove. He had a temple on the Capitol, together with Juno and Minerva, but he was the most prominent of this Capitoline triad.

His temple was not only the most important sanctuary in Rome; it was also the center of political life. Here official offerings were made, treaties were signed and wars were declared, and the triumphant generals of the Roman army came here to give their thanks. Other titles of Jupiter include: Caelestis (heavenly), Lucetius (of the light), Totans (thunderer), Fulgurator (of the lightning). As Jupiter Victor he led the Roman army to victory. Jupiter is also the protector of the ancient league of Latin cities. His attribute is the lightning bolt and the eagle is both his symbol and his messenger. Jupiter is completely identical with the Greek Zeus.

Justitia
The Roman goddess of justice, portrayed as a woman holding a cornucopia and scales. Later she is portrayed with a blindfold, holding scales and a sword (or scepter).

Juturna
The Roman goddess of wells, foundations, rivers and springs, sister of Turnus (the king of Rutuli) whom she supported in his battle against Aeneas. Jupiter turned her into a nymph and gave her a well near Lavinium in Latium. She also gave her name to a well near the Vesta-temple of the Forum Romanum, called the Lacus Juturnae. The water from this well was used for the state-offerings. Also, the Dioscuri were thought to have watered their horses here. She is the mother of Fontus (Fons) and wife of Janus. She had a temple in the Campus Martius and a shrine at a sacred spring where on 11 January the Juturnalia was celebrated.

Juventas (Juenta)
Numen of youth celebrated on 19 December. An early Roman goddess of youth, equal to the Greek goddess Hebe. Boys offered a coin to her when they wore a man's toga for the first time. The temple of Juventas on the Capitol was more ancient than that of Jupiter. She also had a second temple in the Circus Maximus.

Kerri
Oscan form of Ceres, an Earth Mother who is both a Goddess of Grain, and a Goddess of Regeneration.

Krapuvi
See Grabovius.

Kurueii
See Kurrenui.

Kurrenui (or Kurreii)
He is the Samnite version of Roman Quirinus and Sabine Curis. See Curis.

Lactans
The Roman god of agriculture of whom it was said that he made the crops 'yield milk' (thrive).

Lara
Lara is a nymph who betrayed the love affair of Jupiter and Juturna. As punishment, the chief god struck her with dumbness. She is regarded as the mother of the Lares.

Laran
Etruscan war god, depicted with cape and spear.

Larenta
The Roman earth-goddess, also called Dea Tacita, the silent goddess. Her festival, called the Larentalia, was observed on December 23. On this day offerings were brought to her in a mundus, a opened groove.

Larentina
A Goddess of Death, also called Acca Larentia, Larunda, Mania, and Lara, Mother of the Lares. Also called Muta after Jupiter tore out Her tongue for revealing one of His indiscretions.. She is the mother of the Manes sacrificed to by the flamen Quirinalis at Larentalia on 23 December.

Lares
Roman guardian spirits of house and fields. The cult of the Lares is probably derived from the worshipping of the deceased master of the family. It was believed that he blessed the house and brought fertility to the fields. Just like the Penates, the Lares were worshipped in small sanctuaries or shrines, called Lararium, which could be found in every Roman house. They were placed in the atrium (the main room) or in the peristylium (a small open court)

of the house. Here people sacrificed food to the Lares on holidays. In contrast to their malignant counterparts the Larvae (Lemures), the Lares are beneficent and friendly spirits. There were many different types of guardians.

The most important are the Lares Familiares (guardians of the family), Lares Domestici (guardians of the house), Lares Patrii and Lares Privati. Other guardians were the Lares Permarini (guardians of the sea), Lares Rurales (guardians of the land), Lares Compitales (guardians of crossroads), Lares Viales (guardians of travelers) and Lares Praestitis (guardians of the state). The Lares are usually depicted as dancing youths, with a horn cup in one hand and a bowl in the other. As progenitors of the family, they were accompanied by symbolic phallic serpents.

Larvae (or Lemurae)
The Larvae are Roman spirits of deceased family members. These malignant spirits dwell throughout the house and frighten the inhabitants. People tried to reconcile or avert the Larvae with strange ceremonies which took place on May 9, 11, and 13; this was called the "Feast of the Lemures". The master of the house usually performed these ceremonies, either by offering black beans to the spirits or chasing them away by making a lot of noise. Their counterparts are the Lares, friendly and beneficent house spirits.

Lasa
Etruscan female guardian of graves, often depicted with mirrors, wreaths, sometimes winged. Unlike the Manes, Lares, or Lemurae, the Lasae were guardian angels in one's lifetime, and remained at a gravesite after death. In the Carim Fratrum Arvalum the Lasae are identified with the Lares Praestites.

Latarius
"God of Latium", an epithet of Jupiter.

Latinus
The son of Faunus and the nymph Marica. He was the king of Laurentum in Latium and ancestor of the Latini. According to Roman myth he had welcomed Aeneas, who returned from exile, and offered the hero the hand of his daughter Lavinia.[6]

Latona

The Roman name of Leto. Leto, the daughter of the Titans Phoebe and Coeus. Known as the hidden one and bright one, her name came to be used for the moon Selene. Hera was jealous of Leto because Zeus, the husband of Hera, had fallen in love with her. From their union Leto bore the divine twins, Artemis and Apollo. Leto found this to be an arduous task, as Hera had refused Leto to give birth on either terra firma or on an island out at sea. The only place safe enough to give birth was Delos because Delos was a floating island. Therefore, Leto did not refute the wishes of Hera. In some versions, Leto was refused by other vicinities because they feared the great power of the god she would bear. To show her gratitude, Leto anchored Delos to the bottom of the Aegean with four columns, to aid its stability. A conflict of legends arises when in one version it says that Artemis was born one day before Apollo, and the birth took place on the island of Ortygia. Then the next day, Artemis helped Leto to cross to the island of Delos, and aided Leto with the delivery of Apollo. Leto, being the mother of Artemis and Apollo, figured as the motive for the slaughter was Niobe's children was that Niobe had been bragging to Leto about bearing fourteen children (in some versions six or seven). Leto had only born two, and to make matters worse, Niobe then had the audacity to say, it must make her more significant than Leto. When the divine twins were told of this insult, they killed all Niobe's children with their deadly arrows. After which Niobe wept for her dead children so much that she turned into a pillar of stone. From one version of how Apollo slew the monster Python, it was said that while Leto was still pregnant with the divine twins, Python tried to molest her. As punishment, Apollo killed him and then took control of the oracle of Delphi. Leto was worshiped throughout Greece, but principally in Lycia (Asia Minor).

In Delos and Athens, there were temples dedicated to her, although in most regions she was worshiped in conjunction with her children, Artemis and Apollo. In Egypt there is the Temple of Leto (Wadjet) at Buto, which was described by Herodotus as being connected to an island which floated. On this island (Khemmis) stood a temple to Apollo, but Herodotus dismissed the claim that it floated as merely the legend of Delos brought to Egypt from Greek tradition. The Romans called Leto "Latona".

Laverna
The Roman goddess of unlawfully obtained profits and therefore a goddess of thieves, imposters and frauds. Her sanctuary in Rome was near the Porta Lavernalis. She was also the goddess of lost children.

Lavinia
The daughter of Latinus and Amata. Although she was engaged to Turnus, king of the Rutuli, she was given by her father to Aeneas as his bride. This resulted in a grim battle between Turnus and Aeneas, which is described by Virgil in one of his last books of the epic 'Aeneas', and which ended with the death of Turnus. Aeneas married Lavinia and she gave birth to Silvius. The city Aeneas founded in Latium, called Lavinium, was named after her.

Lemurae
See Larvae.

Letum (Letus)
Roman equivalent of Thanatos, the Greek God of Death.
A monster which lives in the underworld. The name means 'death'.

Letus
See Letum.

Levana
Levana ("lifter") is the protector of newborn babes. The father recognized his child by lifting it from the ground, where it was placed by the mother.

Liber
The old-Italian god of fertility and growth in nature. In later times Liber ("the free one") was equated with Dionysus and became thus a god of viniculture. His feminine counterpart is Libera. Their festival, the Liberia, was observed on March 17.

Liber Pater
The Roman god of fertility, both human and agricultural. He is closely connected with Dionysus. Liber was later as Pater Liber identified with Bacchus (after 186 BCE) and African Shadrapa.

Libera
A Roman goddess. Wife of Liber and Daughter of Ceres, most often associated with Proserpina but more properly as Libitina. Also She may be seen as a younger form of Ceres. She is a star goddess Astera (Virgo) of the underworld, that is, the portion of the zodiac lying beneath the celestial equator.

Liberalitas
The Roman god of generosity.

Libertas
The Roman goddess of freedom. Originally as goddess of personal freedom, she later became the goddess of the Roman commonwealth. She had temples on the Aventine Hill and the Forum. Libertas was depicted on many Roman coins as a female figure with a pileus (a felt cap, worn by slaves when they were set free), a wreath of laurels and a spear.

Libitina
Italic Goddess of voluptuous delight, gardens, vineyards, and also of death and the departed, She combines attributes of Venus and Proserpina.

The Roman goddess of corpses and the funeral, her name often being a synonym for death itself. In her temple all the necessary equipment for burials were kept. Here, people could rent these attributes as well as grave diggers. Later she was equated with Proserpina. In Her temple was kept the register of the dead.

Lima (Limentina)
The Roman goddess of thresholds.

Limentinus
The Roman god of thresholds.

Lina
A Goddess of weaving.

Losna
Etruscan moon goddess.

Lua
Wife of Saturn who protected all things purified by and for rituals. The goddess to whom the Romans offered captured weapons by ritually burning them.

Lucina
The Roman goddess of childbirth, who eased the pain and made sure all went well. Lucina became later an epithet of Juno, as "she who brings children into the light" (Latin: lux). At Rome adopted as an indigimenta of both Diana and Juno, She is an Italic goddess "bringing things to light," a moon goddess ruling over women and birth.

Luna
The personified goddess of the moon. Later she is identified with Diana and Hecate. Her temple, on the Aventine Hill, was erected in the 6th century BCE but was destroyed by the great fire under Nero's regime. She is equivalent to the Greek Selene. Her festivals are celebrated 31 March, 24 & 28 August. festivals are celebrated 31 March, 24 & 28 August.

Lupercus
The Roman god of agriculture and shepherds, also an epithet of Faunus. The Luperci sacrificed two goats and a dog on the festival of the Lupercalia, celebrated on February 15. This took place in the Lupercal, a cave were, according to tradition, the twins Romulus and Remus were reared by a wolf. This cave is located at the base of the Palatine Hill. Goats were used since Lupercus was a god of shepherds, and the dog as protector of the flock.

Maatreis Maauissa
Oscan Mother goddess similar to Hecate, She is a form of Ceres as a Goddess of the dead, and as Mater Matuta and Mania Genita. See Manes.

Mafitei
Oscan Ceres and Libitina, Mother and Daughter as manifestations of one another. The Bona Dea who at Rome is otherwise identified with Fauna.

Magna Mater

The Roman name for the Phrygian goddess Cybele, but also an appellation of Rhea. The full name was Magna Mater deorum Idaea: Great Mother of the gods, who was worshipped on Mount Ida. The cult spread through Greece from the 6th to 4th century, and was introduced in Rome in 205 BCE.

Maia
The goddess of whom the month of May is probably named after. Offerings were made to her in this month. She is associated with Vulcan and sometimes equated with Fauna and Ops.

Maiesta
The Roman goddess of honor and reverence, and the wife of the god Vulcan. Some sources say that the month of May is named after her. Others say she is the goddess Maia or Ops. The Oscan Earth Mother. She is also a goddess of Spring, identified at Rome with Fauna and the Bona Dea, She is the wife of Vulcan, mother of Mercury. In Greek myth she was regarded as one of the Pleiades and is so found in Latin literature as well.

Mamerurius Venturius
The "Old Man of March" who is driven out of the city each year to ward off disease.

Manes
Spirits of the dead. Manes or Di Manes ("good ones") is the euphemistic description of the souls of the deceased, worshipped as divinities. The formula D.M. (= Dis Manibus; "dedicated to the Manes-gods") can often be found on tombstones. Manes also means metaphorically 'underworld' or 'realm of death'. Three times each year (24 Aug, 5 Oct, 8 Nov) the stone was lifted from the mundus, to allow the Manes to arise. They were led by Mania Genita, also called Lara or Larunda, and by Ovid, Muta (the Mute).

In earliest times they were sacrificed young boys, later with poppies and garlic, woolen dolls, called maniae, that were hung over doorways for protection. On the Night of the Dead, at new moon around 1 Nov, houses are sealed, the windows shuttered and mirrors turned to the wall, for if the Manes see a child they steal her away. The father of the household performs a rite of propitiation to keep the Manes away from his children at Lemuralia. Festivals in honor of the dead were the Parentalia and the Feralia, celebrated in February. Offer beans, egg, wine, bread, roses, violets, milk and honey, oil, blood of sheep on 13 Feb. at Feralia.

Mania
Mania was known as the Roman goddess of the dead. She is also the guardian of the underworld, together with Mantus. Mania -- the name -- is the Greek personification of madness. In addition, she is called the mother or grandmother of ghosts. She is also considered the mother of the Lares and Nanes, the gods of the household. Etruscan God and Goddess of the Underworld, they are the Oscan Mantua and Mantoua.

Mantus
See Mania.

Marica
An Italian nymph, the consort of Faunus and mother of Latinus[7] According to others, she was the mother of Faunus. She possessed a sacred forest near Minturnae (Minturno) on the border of Latium and Campania[8] . A lake near Minturnae was named after her.

Mars
The god of war, and one of the most prominent and worshipped gods. In early Roman history he was a god of spring, growth in nature, and fertility, and the protector of cattle. Mars is also mentioned as a chthonic god (earth-god) and this could explain why he became a god of death and finally a god of war. He is the son of Jupiter and Juno. According to some sources, Mars is the father of Romulus and Remus by the Vestal Ilia (Rhea Silvia). Because he was the father of these legendary founders of Rome, and thus of the Roman people, the Romans styled themselves 'sons of Mars'. His main sanctuaries where the temple on the Capitol, which he shared with Jupiter and Quirinus, the temple of Mars Gradivus ("he who precedes the army in battle") where the Roman army gathered before they went to war, and the temple of Mars Ultor ("the avenger"), located on the Forum Augustus. The Campus Martius ("field of Mars"), situated beyond the city walls, was also

dedicated to him. Here the army was drilled and athletes were trained. In the Regia on the Forum Romanum, the 'hastae Martiae' ("lances of Mars") were kept. When these lances 'moved', it was seen as a portent of war. The warlord who was to lead the army into battle had to move the lances while saying 'Mars vigila' ("Mars awaken").

As Mars Gradivus, the god preceded the army and led them to victory. He had several festivals in his honor. On March 1, the Feriae Marti was celebrated. The Armilustrium was held on October 19, and on this day the weapons of the soldiers were ritually purified and stored for winter. Every five years the Suovetaurilia was held.

During these fertility and cleansing rites, a pig (sus), a sheep (ovis) and bull (taurus) were sacrificed. The Equirria were on February 27 and March 14, on which horse races were held. The Quinquatrus was on March 19 and the Tubilustrium on March 23, on which weapons and war-trumpets were cleansed. The priests of Mars, who also served Quirinus, were called the Salii ("jumpers"), derived from the procession through the streets of the city which they completed by jumping the entire way and singing the Carmen Saliare. Mars' own priest was called the flamen Martialis.

Mars is portrayed as a warrior in full battle armor, wearing a crested helmet and bearing a shield. His sacred animals are the wolf and the woodpecker, and he is accompanied by Fuga and Timor, the personifications of flight and fear. The month March (Martius) is named after him (wars were often started or renewed in spring). His Greek equivalent is the god Ares.

Mars, Mavors, Mamers, Oscan Bellante and Maris Tiusta not to be confused with Maris below): One of the Dii Consentes, he is the son of Juno by virgin birth (She having conceived Him from a lily), brother of Bellona, and husband of Nerio. God who defends herds, boundaries, fields, and agriculture, later to become the Roman God of War. Originally, He may have been identified as a Latin Cerus or Quirinus, warding off disease from fields and animals, or else He later took those roles at Rome. At Iguvium He is invoked alongside Jupiter and Cerus, all associated with Grabovius. As God of War He became Mars Gradivus (the Strider), awakened to battle by generals striking His sacred shield (ancilla) and spear (hasta) with the cry, "Mars viliga!" He is accompanied by Pavor and Pallor who instill fear and confusion in His enemies. His altar was in the Campus Martius, His temple on the Via Appia outside Rome. Later, August built a Temple of Mars Ultor (Mars the Avenger) in the Forum Augusti in 2 BCE, commemorated on 1 June. The entire month of March is dedicated to Him, the Salii performing a dancing procession with the ancillae throughout Rome. His festivals are the Equirria celebrated with contests for war steeds on 27 Feb., as Mars Pater, the father of Romulus and Remus, on 1 March, the Tubilustrium of 23 March, as Mars Invictus on 14 May, October Equus on 15 Oct. and at the Armilustrium on 19 October.

Maris
Italic thrice-born god who lived 130 years, he is the son of Minerva and Hercules. He is called Maris Husrnana when a child of Minerva, Maris Halna, as an adult with (possibly his wife) Amamtunia, and Maris Isminthianus in death with Leinth.

Matres Suleviae
See Suleviae Iunones.

Matronae
The three mother-goddess of Roman mythology who oversee fertility. They are lovers of peace, tranquility and children.

Maturna
Numen who keeps couples together.

Matuta
The Roman goddess of the dawn. Later she was known as Mater Matuta, the patroness of newborn babes, but also of the sea and harbors. Her temple was situated on the Forum Boarium (the cattle market). Every June 11, the Matralia was celebrated here, and mothers prayed to her for their nieces and nephews. This festival was only open to women who were still in their first marriage. She was associated with Aurora and identified with the Greek Eos.

Mavors
An ancient and poetic name for Mars.[9]

Meditrina

A Roman goddess of wine and health whose name means "healer". Her festival, the Meditrinalia, was observed on October 11. Daughter of Aesculapis, She is the Goddess of Healing, unlike Her sister Hygenia who preserves health.

Mefitis

Numen of the stench of sewers and swamps that produce disease. The Roman goddess who was especially worshipped in volcanic areas and swamps. She is the personification of the poisonous vapors of the earth.

Melite

A Roman sea nymph.

Mellona

Goddess of honey. The Roman divinity who protects the bees. Her name is derived from mel ("honey").

Mena

Prudence and intelligence celebrated on 8 July, this was also a term for an individual's (mind) spirit. The Roman goddess of menstruation.

Mens

The Roman goddess of mind and consciousness. Her festival was observed on May 8.

Mephitis

A Roman goddess who was particularly worshipped regions with volcanoes or solfataras (volcanic vents emitting hot gases and vapors). She was called upon to protect against damages and poisonous gases).

Mercia

Numen of laziness.

Mercurius (Mercury)

Son of Maia and Volcalnus, Mercury is god of trade, commerce and profit, merchants and travelers, but originally of the trade in corn.

In later times he was equated with the Greek Hermes. He had a temple in Rome near the Circus Maximus on the Aventine Hill which dates back to 495 BCE. This temple was connected to some kind of trade fair. His main festival, the Mercuralia, was celebrated on May 15 and on this day the merchants sprinkled their heads and their merchandise with water from his well near the Porta Capena. During the time of the Roman Empire the cult of Mercury was widely spread, especially among the Celtic and Germanic peoples.

The Celts have their Gaulish Mercury, and the Germans identified him with their Wodan. The attributes of Mercury are the caduceus (a staff with two intertwined snakes) and a purse (a symbol of his connection with commerce). He is portrayed similarly to Hermes: dressed in a wide cloak, wearing talaria (winged sandals) and petasus (winged hat). Mercury is also known as Alipes ("with the winged feet"). He leads male spirits into incarnation, and in death leads them back to the stars. (Iris for female spirits).

Mercury
See Mercurius.

Messia
Messia as a goddess of reaping, was an indigimenta of Ceres.

Messor
Messor ("mower") is the Roman god agriculture, and especially of mowing. Messor was the indigimenta of Consus as a god of reaping.

Minerva
The Roman goddess of wisdom, medicine, the arts, dyeing, weaving, science and trade, but also of war. As Minerva Medica she is the patroness of physicians. She is the daughter of Jupiter. In the temple on the Capitoline Hill she was worshipped together with Jupiter and Juno, with whom she formed a powerful triad of gods. Another temple of her was located on the Aventine Hill. The church of Santa Maria sopra Minerva is built on one of her temples. Every year from March 19 - 23 the Quinquatria was held, the primary Minerva-festival. This festival was mainly celebrated by artisans but also by students. On June 13 the minor Quinquatrus was observed. Minerva is believed to be the inventor of numbers

and musical instruments. She is thought to be of Etruscan origin, as the goddess Menrva or Menerva. Later she was equated with the Greek Athena.

Etruscan Menrva, in Oscan Catanai or Ciistai: Goddess of good wisdom, weaving, arts, and written laws. Under Greek influence, identified with their war goddesses, Athene, Minerva became identified as a goddess of stratagems in warfare, unlike Mars or Bellona who were deities of the fury of battle. She is unlike the Greek virginal Athena in that She was married to Hercules and bore him a mortal son, Maris, by drawing him from an urn. Her festivals are held on 19 March, 19 June, and 13 September. Together with Jupiter and Juno: She had a temple on the Capitoline, dedicated in 507 BCE. Another temple was located on the Aventine. Minerva Capta whose temple was on the Caelia, was brought to Rome from the Falscii. The Esquiline Nympheum was also a Temple of Minerva Medica. Another important temple and cult center for Minerva was at Praeneste.

Molae
Daughter of Mars, goddess of the grindstones, and patroness of millers.

Moneta
A Roman goddess of prosperity.

Mors
The personified Roman god of death. It is a translation of Thanatos.

Morta
The Roman goddess of death. She is one of the Parcae.

Mulciber
"The softener". A surname of the smith-god Vulcan and alluding to the softening of metals in his fiery forge.

Murcia
A Roman goddess of indistinct origin and of whom is little known. As Murtia she was sometimes equated with Venus. She had a

temple in the vale between the Aventine and the Palatine Hill.

Muta
The Roman personification of silence, and its goddess.

Mutinus Mutunus
A Roman fertility god who was invoked by women seeking to bear children. He was depicted as ithyphallic or as a phallus. Also the Roman form (Mutinus) of the Greek Priapus.

Naenia
Naenia is the Roman goddess of funerals and dirges (naeniae).

Nascio
One of the many Roman goddesses of birth.

Necessitas
Necessitas ("necessity") is a Roman goddess of destiny. She is similar to the Greek Ananke.

Nemesis
One of the Dii Inferi, She chastises the prideful, wreaks vengeance on the unjust, and punishes the impious. She maintains and restores the natural balance of nature. Her attributes are the measuring rod, bridle and yoke, a sword and scourge, wings and wheel, and She rides a chariot drawn by griffins. She was especially worshipped at Rome by generals, less She punish them for having extraordinary good fortune in battle or for their boastfulness. Her power extends over both gods and men, and She is not under the authority of Jupiter.

Nemestrinus
A Roman god of the woods and groves. In Gaul, he was identified as Mars.

Neptune
The god of the sea among the Romans, one of the Dii Consentes, God of the Seas, and husband of Salacia. He was not a very powerful god, and little is known of his origin. When he was first introduced in Rome, he already had all the characteristics of the Greek

Poseidon. Despite the fact that his cult grew after his equation with Poseidon, Neptune was far less popular among sailors than Poseidon was among the Greek mariners. Neptune was held in much higher regard as Neptune Equester, the god and patron of horse-racing and horses. One of temples was located near the Circus Flaminius, one of the larger chariot racetracks, and a festival for Him was held there on December 1. Another sanctuary was in the Campus Martius (25 BCE) were the Neptunalia was celebrated on July 23. The trident is Neptune's attribute.

Nerio
A minor Roman goddess of fertility, and the consort of Mars.

Neverita
A wife of Neptune.

Nixi
Roman divinities who were invoked by women in labor and who assisted in giving birth (from the Latin nitor, "give birth to").

Noduterensi
An indigimentum of Ceres for the threshing-floor.

Nodutus
The Roman god who was held responsible for making the knots in the stalks of corn and on the stems of grain plants; indigimentum of Ceres.

Nona
The Roman goddess of pregnancy. Nona ("ninth") was called upon by a pregnant mother in the ninth month when the child was due to be born. In later times she became associated with the goddesses Morta and Decima and formed the Parcae, the Roman Fates.

Nortia
Etruscan Fortuna.

Novensilus
The Roman appellation of the nine great gods of the Etruscans.

Nox
"Night". The Roman goddess and personification of the night.

Nundina
The Roman goddess of the ninth day, on which the newborn child received its name.

Obarator
The Roman god of ploughing. An indigimentum of Ceres for topdressing of fields (such as with manure).

Occator
The Roman god of harrowing. An indigimentum of Ceres for harrowing.

Ops
The Roman (Sabine) goddess of the earth as a source of fertility, and a goddess of abundance and wealth in general (her name means "plenty"). As goddess of harvest she is closely associated with the god Consus. She is the sister and wife of Saturn. One of her temples was located near Saturn's temple, and on August 10 a festival took place there. Another festival was the Opalia, which was observed on December 9.

On the Forum Romanum she shared a sanctuary with the goddess Ceres as the protectors of the harvest. The major temple was of Ops Capitolina, on the Capitoline Hill, where Caesar had located the Treasury. Another sanctuary was located in the Regia on the Forum Romanun, where also the Opiconsivia was observed on August 25. At the Opiconsiva, Ops was invoked with one hand touching earth. She is the mother of Jupiter, and also called Maia, Tellus, or Mater (Tellus). Only the official priests and the Vestal Virgins had access to this altar.

Orbona
Numen invoked by childless couples to assist in pregnancy. The Roman goddess invoked by parents who became childless, and begged her to grant them children again.

Orcus

The Roman god of death and the underworld, either a terrible god or a gentle one. He is the god of oaths and punisher of perjurers. Orcus is identical to the Greek Hades, both the god and his domains. Originally, an Italic demon that carried the dead off to the Underworld, he carried a large mallet to first stun the dead.

Pales

The Roman patron goddess of shepherds and flocks. Pales also presides over the health and fertility of the domestic animals. Her festival is the Palilia (also called the Parilia) and was celebrated by shepherds on April 21, the legendary founding date of Rome. On that day large fires were made through which they drove the cattle. Pales was originally a single deity, variously male or female, with the same characteristics. The name is believed by some to be related to the Greek and Latin word phallus.

An ancient Goddess of Shepherds. 21 April Parilia. Another festival on 7 July. Purification rite of sacred groves and fountains, also of houses and of herds. With a mixture of sulfur, incense and sheep's blood, spread on three bundles of the herb beanstraw, then set on fire; they are then leaped over three times. In Rome there was another Pales of alleyways.

Palici

Protectors of pasturelands. The twin sons of Jupiter and the nymph Thalia. They were chthonic deities worshipped at the Palica, near Mount Etna. In early times humans were sacrificed to them and oaths were verified through divine judgment.

Parcae

The Parcae are the Roman goddess of fate, similar to the Greek Moirae (Fates). Originally there was only one of them, Parca, a goddess of birth. Her name is derived from parere ("create, give birth") but later it was associated with pars (Greek: moira, "part") and thus analogous with the three Greek Moirae. The three Parcae are also called Tria Fata.

Partula

A minor Roman goddess of birth. She is concerned with the

parturition.

Patalena
The Roman deity who protects the blossoms. Indigimentum of Ceres, being the husks of corn when they first open to allow the ears to emerge.

Patir Libero
See Bacchus.

Patir Maatutinui
The Oscan title for Janus as "Opener of the Ways". See Janus.

Paventia
The Roman goddess who protects children against sudden fright.

Pax
Pax ("peace") is the personified Roman goddess of peace, corresponding with the Greek Eirene. Under the rule of Augustus, she was recognized as a goddess proper. She had a minor sanctuary, the Ara Pacis, on the Campus Martius, and a temple on the Forum Pacis. A festival in her honor was celebrated on January 3. Her attributes are the olive branch, a cornucopia, and a scepter. She carries a cornucopia in her left hand and an olive branch in her right.

Pellonia
Numen that drives away enemies.

Penates
Numina of the storeroom or pantry, closely identified with the Lares. In Roman mythology, the Penates ("the inner ones") are the patron gods of the storeroom. Later they gradually changed into patron gods for the entire household. Their cult is closely related to that of Vesta and the Lares. They were worshipped at the hearth and were given their part of the daily meals. The Roman state had its own Penates, called Penates Publici. They were rescued by Aeneas from burning Troy and via Lavinium and Longa brought to Rome. Upon their arrival, the Penates were housed in the Temple of Vesta, on the Forum Romanum.

Perficia
Numen of coitus.

Pertunda
An Italic goddess of female virginity, modesty and chastity, She was in Rome Pudicitia.

Peta
Numen of prayer.

Picumnus
Picumnus is a minor Roman god of growth and the fertility of the fields. He is the patron of matrimony and infants at birth and stimulated their growth. He is also worshipped as Sterquilinus (or Stercutus) because he invented the manuring of the fields. Italic God of Agriculture, inventor of the use of manure, at Rome he became Saturnus. Husband of Canens, brother of Pilumnus. Both brothers are guardians of newborn infants and women in childbirth.

Picus
The ancient Roman deity of agriculture. He also possessed the powers of prophecy. He was changed into a woodpecker by Circe when he did not requite her passion. Son of Saturnus, father of Faunus by Canens, He is an old Italian God of Agriculture, also a forest deity of prophecy. In a diminutive form He became a warlike hero, king of Latium, turned into a woodpecker (picus) for spurning Circe. Picumnus is reborn as His own son in Picus.

Pietas
Numen of domestic affection. The Roman personification of feelings of duty towards the gods, the state and one's family. Her temple at the foot of the Capitoline Hill dates from the beginning of the second century BCE.

Pilumnus
Pilumnus is a minor Roman god, the brother of Picumnus and together they stimulated the growth of little children and avert sickness. To ensure to help of these gods, people made an extra bed right after the birth of a child. Pilumnus is also believed to have

taught mankind how to grind corn. An old Italic god of bakers, He is the inventor of the mortar and pestle.

Pluto
Pluto is the Roman god of the underworld and the judge of the dead. Pluto was the son of Saturn. Pluto's wife was Proserpina (Greek name, Persephone) whom he had kidnapped and dragged into the underworld. His brothers were Jupiter and Neptune. People referred to Pluto as the rich one because he owned all the wealth in the ground. People were afraid to say his real name because they were afraid it might attract his attention. Black sheep were offered to him as sacrifices. Pluto was known as a pitiless god because if a mortal entered his Underworld they could never hope to return. Pluto's Greek name is Hades.

As Plutus, He was the Roman god of the wealth of the earth. He has more to do with minerals than vegetation. His name was sometimes used in place of Dis Pater as a kind of Hades although He was not originally a god of the Underworld.

Pluvius
Literally, "sender of rain", an epithet of the Roman god Jupiter. During long droughts the ancient Romans called upon Jupiter using that name. It is also an epithet of the Hyades.

Poena
The Roman goddess of punishment.

Pomona
The goddess presiding over fruit and fruit trees. She was the beloved of many ancient Roman rustic deities such as Silvanus and Picus until Vertumnus, disguised as an old woman, goaded her into marrying him. Her special priest is the flamen Pomonalis. The pruning knife is her attribute.

Portunus (Portunes)
The Roman god of ports and harbors, identified with the Greek Palaemon or Melicertes. Originally he was an Italic god of keys and doors, thus a doorman with the attribute of a key and of domestic animals. He protects the warehouses where grain is stored, and is as

such a god of the harbors. His temple was located near the Forum Boarium. The Portunalia were observed on August 17, and on this festival keys were thrown into the fire to safeguard them against misfortune. His attribute is a key.

Porus
The Roman god of plenty.

Postverta
The Roman goddess of the past.

Potina
The Roman goddess associated with the first drink of children or children's potions.

Priapus
The Roman patron god of gardens, viniculture, sailors and fishermen. A Hellenistic ithyphallic god, a son of Bacchus and Venus, He was especially popular in southern Italy. He is portrayed wearing a long dress that leaves the genitals uncovered. The Romans placed a satyr-like statue of him, painted red and with an enormous phallus, in gardens as some kind of scarecrow, but also to ensure fruitfulness, fertility, prosperity, and good luck.. The fruits of the fields, honey and milk were offered to him, and occasionally donkeys. He was very popular and in his honor the Priapea was written--a collection of 85 perfectly written poems, sometimes funny but usually obscene.

Originally, Priapus was a fertility god from Asia Minor, especially in Lampsacus on the Hellespont, and was the most important god of the local pantheon (see: the Greek Priapus). He was introduced in Greece around 400 BCE but never was very popular. Priapus' attribute is the pruning knife.

Promitor
The Roman god associated with the bringing out of the harvest from the barns. An indigimentum of Ceres of when grain is moved to kitchens. Also a god of sheep and goatherds.

Prorsa Postverta

The Roman double-goddess who was called upon by women in labor. She guarded over the position of the child in the womb (forwards or backwards). Some sources mention her as another aspect of Carmenta.

Proserpina
Oscan Libitina: "Germinator of the Seed," Her name is derived from the Greek Persephone, daughter of Demeter, and therefore, a goddess of the dead. Originally She was more a daughter of Ceres in the sense of an agricultural goddess (see Libitina). Special festivals to honor Her and Dis were ordered by the Senate in 249 and 207 BCE.

The Roman name for the Greek Persephone. The name is possibly derived from proserpere ("to emerge"), meaning the growing of the grain. Gradually, Libera was equated with her.

Providentia
The Roman goddess of forethought.

Pudicitia
A numen of modesty and chastity. Literally, "modesty". The personified Roman goddess of modesty and chastity.

Pupluna
See Bacchus.

Purasia
See Fornax.

Puta
A Roman goddesses who watched over the pruning of vines and trees.

Quirinus
An old Roman deity whose origin is uncertain, and there is also little known about his cult. He was worshipped by the Sabines, an old Italian people who lived north-east of Rome. They had a fortified settlement near Rome, the Quirinal, which was named after their god. Later, when Rome expanded, this settlement was

absorbed by the city, and Quirinus became, together with Jupiter and Mars, the god of the state. The Quirinalis, one of the Roman hills, was named after him. His consort is Hora. He was usually depicted as a bearded man who wears clothing that is part clerical and part military. His sacred plant is the myrtle. His festival, the Quirinalia, was celebrated on February 17. Romulus was also identified with Quirinus, especially in the late-Roman era.

The Roman name for the Sabine Curis who founded the Sabine capital of Cures. He is the Oscan Kurrenui, identified at Rome as the apotheotic Romulus, and regarded by some as another form of Mars as Romulus is His son. He was likely a war god, protector, and defender of cities among the Sabines, later becoming a kind of God of War in times of peace, vigilant defense. Mars was originally more an agricultural God, only later becoming warlike. Since the armies of both Rome and the Sabines were originally composed of gentry, both Mars and Quirinus are connected to war and agriculture.

See also Curis.

Quiritis
Quiritis is a Sabine protective goddess of motherhood.

Rederator (Reparator)
The Roman god of the second ploughing. See also Imporcitor and Vervactor.

Rederator
The Roman god of the second ploughing. Indigimentum of Ceres of the second plowing, Aratio secundus. See also Imporcitor and Vervactor.

Remus
The twin brother of Romulus. He was killed by his brother during a quarrel.

Reparator
See Rederator.

Rhea
The wife of Saturnus.

Rhea Silvia
The Vestal virgin who became, by Mars, the mother of the twins Romulus and Remus. She is the daughter of king Numitor of Alba Longa, who was dethroned by his brother Amulius. Her uncle gave her to the goddess Vesta so she would remain a virgin for the rest of her life. Amulius had learned from an oracle that her children would become a threat to his power. However, because she had violated her sacred vow, she and her children were cast in the Tiber. The god Tiberinus rescued her and made her his wife. Based on a very early earth mother goddess.

Robigo
A Roman goddess of corn. She is probably the feminine form of Robigus. Protective deities of crops against blight. Also deities of ecstatic prophecy resulting from the use of ergot infected rye and similar infections of other grains. 25 April, Robigalia, where the flamen Quirinalis made offerings of dog and sheep to Robigo. In the Fasti Ovid used a feminine form of Robigo as the deity worshipped at Robigalia. Columella and Augustine agreed with Ovid, while Varro (L.L. 6.16) and Verius Flaccus (CIL 1:236, 316) use the male form Robigus. Ovid says the sacrifice made to Robigo on the Robigalia was a dog; Columella has the sacrum canarium as a suckling puppy (Rustica 10. 343-3). But this latter sacrifice was made at the Porta Catularia when the Dog Star Sirius was rising, which Ovid says at Fasti 4. 904. However the rising of Sirius would have been setting at this time of year, rising only in early August.

Pliny mentions instead an augurium canarium being made in late spring before the ears of grain emerged from their husks (N.H. 18. 14). A dog was also sacrificed at the Lupercalia, along with goats, and a feast was then held. Ovid's mention of only the exta being brought to the grove of Robigo indicates that the dog meat was included in the sacrificial meal, as would be normal with any sacrifice. See Robigus.

Robigus
The Roman god who protected the corn against diseases. Robigus

("wheat rust", "mildew") was worshipped together with Flora. His festival, the Robigalia, took place on April 25. His functions were also attributed to the female goddess Robigo. See Robigo.

Roma
The personification of the city of Rome. She is portrayed as a helmed woman sitting on a throne, holding a spear and a sword. Resting against her throne is a shield. Her head was commonly depicted on coins, symbolizing the Roman state. Her temple and the temple of Venus were situated on the Velian Hill in Rome. Hadrianus started building it in 121 CE and the temple was inaugurated around 140 CE by Antonius Pius. The numen of Rome projected over the empire, She is not the same as the genius loci of the city itself, nor the protective goddess of Rome, whose name was held secret (Pliny, N.H. III.65)

Romulus
Romulus and Remus were the twin sons of Rhea Silvia and Mars. They were, together with their mother, cast into the Tiber. The god Tiberinus saved Rhea Silvia from drowning, and the brothers were miraculously rescued by a she-wolf. The wolf reared the twins together with her cubs underneath a fig tree (the 'ruminalus ficus'). After a few years they were found by the shepherd Faustulus, who took the brothers home and gave them to his wife Acca Larentia to rear. When they reached maturity they killed Amelius, the brother of their grandfather, and built a settlement on the Palatine Hill. During a quarrel where Remus mocked the height of the walls, Romulus slew Remus and became the sole ruler of the new Rome, which he had named after himself. He took Hersilia as his wife. To enlarge his empire, he allowed exiles and refugees, homicides and runaway slaves to populate the area. The shortage of women he solved by stealing Sabine women whom he invited to a festival. After a few wars, the Sabines agreed to accept Romulus as their king. Upon his death he was taken to the heavens by his father Mars. He is later revered as the god Quirinus.

Rumina (and Rumino)
The Roman protector of nursing mothers and suckling infants, both human and animal. She had a temple near the Ficus Ruminales, the fig tree on the Palatine Hill were Romulus and Remus were reared

by a she-wolf. When the tree started to droop in 58 CE this was seen as a bad portent.

Rumina and Rumino are the protective deities of suckling cattle specifically, and of mothers suckling infants. They are connected to the Rumina ficus, or the suckling tree in the legend of Romulus and Remus.. Ancient deities who received offerings of milk, They are symbolized by two fig trees in a grotto. A sanctuary of Rumina was located at the foot of the Palatine Hill.

Rumino
See Rumina.

Runcina
A Roman deity associated with reaping.

Rusina (Rusor)
A Roman divinity who protects the fields (also known as Rusor). An indigimetum of Ceres, being the personification of wheat fields and farmlands.

Rusor
See Rusina.

Sabazios
Originally a Thracio-Phrygian god of fermented juice, at Rome He became closely identified with Juppiter and Bacchus. As a syncretic savior god, Conservator, of the Imperial period, He was closely associated the Carthaginian Tanit, called Venus Caelistis at Rome, and with Mithraism, also with Castor and Pollux, Mercury, and as Attis with Cybele.

Sabus
The son of Sancus, the oldest king of the Sabines, who worshipped him as a god.

Salacia
A Roman sea goddess. The god Neptune wanted to marry her but she ran off and hid from him in the Atlantic ocean. Neptune sent a dolphin to look for her and when the animal found her it brought

her back to him. Salacia agreed to marry Neptune and the dolphin was awarded a place in the heavens. Salacia bore Neptune three children. She is identified with the Greek god, Amphitrite, and the goddess of the salty ocean depths.

Salus

Salus ("salvation") is the personified Roman goddess of health, healing and prosperity, both of the individual and the state. As Salus Publica Populi Romani ("goddess of the public welfare of the Roman people") she had a temple on the Quirinal, inaugurated in 302 BCE[15]. Later she became more a protector of personal health.

Around 180 BCE sacrificial rites in honor of Apollo, Aesculapius, and Salus took place there. Her attribute was a snake or a bowl and her festival was celebrated on March 30. Salus is identified with the Greek Hygieia.

Sancus

An ancient Roman deity who presides over oaths and good faith. He is also called Semo Sancus Dius Fidus.

Saritor

The Roman god of weeding and hoeing. An indigimentum of Ceres for hoeing.

Saturnus (Saturn or Semino)

The Roman god of agriculture concerned with the sowing of the seeds. Titan father of the Di consentes, God of the Abundant Earth and consort of Ops. Representing the father of the gods of the pre-Italic peoples, the Ausones, He brought an earlier form of agriculture to Italy, prior to Ceres instituting grain cultivation, and ruled the earth during the Golden Age.

His main festival is the Saturnalia on 17-23 Dec. At the foot of the Capitoline His temple served as the state treasury, the aerarium Saturni. He was later identified at Rome with the Greek Cronus. Many of the Neolithic megaliths and stone walls of Italy are attributed to the "Sons of Saturnus" who were giants. He is regarded as the father of Jupiter, Ceres, Juno and many others. His wife is the goddess Ops. Jupiter supposedly chased him away and he was taken in by the god Janus in Latium where he introduced agriculture and viniculture. This event heralded a period of peace, happiness and prosperity, the Golden Age. In memory of this Golden Age, each year the Saturnalia was observed on December 17 at his temple on the Forum Romanum. This temple, below the Capitoline Hill, contained the Royal Treasury and is one of the oldest in Rome.

The Saturnalia was one of the major events of the year. Originally only one day, it was later extended to seven days. During this festival, business was suspended, the roles of master and slaves were reversed, moral restrictions were loosened and gifts were exchanged. Offerings made in his honor were done with uncovered heads, contrary to the Roman tradition. In contrast to his festival, Saturn himself was never very popular. From the 3rd century on, he was identified with the Greek Cronus, and his cult became only marginally more popular. That he ruled over the Golden Age is an extension to the Greek myth. Saturday is named after him.

Scabies
Numen of itching and skin diseases.

Segetia
An indigimentum of Consus as grain ripens above ground.

Seia
Indigimentum of Consus for sown grain seeds.

Semino
See Saturnus.

Semonia
The Roman goddess of sowing.

Sentia
The Roman goddess who brought about a young child's first awareness.

Sergestus
One of the companions of Aeneas. He was the ancestor of the gens

Sergia, a renowned Patrician family of Rome, to whom also Catilina belonged[17].

Sethlans
An Etruscan Vulcanus from the Punic Sethlos.

Silvanus
The Roman god of forests, groves and wild fields. As fertility god he is the protector of herds and cattle and is associated with Faunus. He shows many similarities with the Greek Pan (Silvanus also liked to scare lonely travelers). The first fruits of the fields were offered to him, as well as meat and wine--a ritual women were not allowed to witness. His attributes are a pruning knife and a bough from a pine tree.

Etruscan Selvans was the ancient God of boundaries between woodlands and meadows, of farms, fields and gardens, His sacred grove is always on the border of an estate. As Silvanus Domesticus He is guardian of the house. Silvanus Agrestis watches over flocks. Silvanus Orientalis is the guardian of boundaries. Silvanus Callirius is King of the Woodland or God of the Hazel Wood at Colchester. Silvanus Cocidius was a god of hunting along Hadrian's Wall. As Silvanus Nodens together with Mars Nodens at Lydney, or as Mars Silvanus, He is a god of healing, warding off disease.

Silenus
Depicted as an intoxicated, jolly old man, fat and balding, with large ears and a pug nose, He was renown for His wisdom and was the teacher of Bacchus. Originally maybe a sylvan, He began to appear at Rome in the 5th century with His own characteristic features.

Silvius
The son of Aeneas and Lavinia. He was the successor of Ascanius as the king of Alba Longa.

Sima
A snub-nosed satyr of Etruscan myth.

Sol
The personified Roman god of the sun, completely identical to the Greek Helios. He was possibly worshipped as Sol Indiges in his temple on the Quirinalis. A second temple was located at the Circus Maximus, near the race-tracks, where he was considered to be the protector of the four-in-hands which joined the races. The emperor Heliogabalus imported the cult of Sol Invictus ("the invincible sun") from Syria and Sol was made god of the state. Sol, the sun; as Sol Indiges on 9 Aug., identified with Apollo on 28 Aug., and as Sol Invictus on 25 December.

Somnus
The Roman god of sleep, a translation of the Greek Hypnos. Somnus caused the death of Palunurus, the helmsman of Aeneas, who fell asleep at the coast of Lucania[19]

Soranus
A Sabine sun-god, often identified with Apollo, who was venerated at Mount Soracte (north of Rome). His priests were called the Hirpini Sorani ("wolfs of Soranus") who celebrated a rite in which they carried offerings to Him by walking barefoot on burning coals. Virgil identified Soranus with Apollo (as Apollo Soranus)[20]. At the foot of the Soracte was the precinct of Feronia. He was a mediator between the gods and men, who oversees health and purification through savage, ecstatic rites. Soranus is also known as the wolf god Sancus at Rome, as Hirpus among the Samnite Hirpini. His female counterpoint is Hirpa, sometimes called Feronia, also known in Rome as Angeronia who was regarded as the protective goddess of Rome and was silenced to prevent Her from revealing Her secret name, thought to be Sorania.

Sors
A Roman god of luck.

Spes
Numen of hope, her festival was held on 1 August. The personified Roman goddess of hope. She had a sanctuary on the vegetable market. Spes is portrayed as a young woman holding a cornucopia and a flower.

Spiniensis
Numen for uprooting thorn bushes. The Roman god who was called upon when people removed thorns from the fields. The name is derived from spina ("spine").

Stata Mater
Numen protectress against fires. The Roman goddess who guards against fires, and was thus associated with Vulcan. She was at times equated with Vesta. A statue of Stata Mater was located on the Forum.

Statanus
The Roman god who, together with his wife Statina, watched over the first time a child went away and returned.

Stator
An alternative name of Jupiter as the god who halted retreat or flight (stare - standing). In Rome there were two temples of Jupiter Stator. The oldest (on the Velia Hill) was, according to legend, built by Romulus himself during the war against the Sabeans, when the Romans where forced to retreat[21]. The simple sanctuary of Romulus was replaced by a proper temple in 294 BCE [22] .

Sterculinius
See Stercutus.

Stercutus (Sterculinius)
A Roman god who took care of the fertilization of farmland (stercus, manure). An alternative name of Saturn or, according to others, Picumnus. An indigimentum of Ceres for fertilizing fields with manure, Fecundus.

Stimula
The Roman goddess who incites passion in women (especially in the Bacchae). She is equated with the Greek Semele.

Strenua
The Roman goddess of strength and vigor, of Sabine origin. She was worshipped in Rome at the beginning of the new year. Her sanctuary was in the Via Sacra. Also a Goddess of Prosperity, She oversees gift giving at New Years, and is made offerings for

prosperity in the coming year. A Roman version of Her as Goddess of Health is Salus, She resided in Rome under both names. On 1 Jan. good luck charms called strenae, composed of twigs of the "Sabine tree", juniper, were brought from Her grove and exchanged as gifts.

Suadela
Numen of persuasion. The goddess of persuasion, and especially in love. She is a follower of Venus.

Subigus
Numen of the wedding night.

Subruncinator
The Roman god of weeding.

Suleviae Iunones (or Matres Suleviae)
A triad of goddesses for fertility, health, and regeneration.

Summanus
The Roman god of nightly thunder (Jupiter is the god of thunder during daytime). He was the protective God of the Night, whoroared with thunder and cast lightining about. Sammunas' temple stood at the Circus Maximus and on June 20 cakes were offered to him. Probably of Etruscan or Sabean origin. A Roman or Etruscan marital demon who was called upon when the bride was taken to the house of the groom. He is supposed to have been a friend of Romulus and played a part in the stealing of Sabine women. The term 'Talassio' was used when the bride entered her new house.

Sylvani
Semidivine woodland creatures, similar to satyrs with whom they began to be identified in the 6th century BCE, but with equine features and large pointed ears, they are lecherous males associated with nymphs.

Tages
Indigetis of Etruscan myth, he arose from a furrow in the form of a infant on a cloud of smoke, and became the giver of sacred books on prophecy, haruspicini, and the rites of the Aiseras.

Tainai
The Oscan form of Diana, or Etruscan Tana, a Goddess of the Moon.

Talassio
Numen of marriage, her name was called out as a bride was carried through the streets to the house of the groom's family.

Taraxippus
A demon that makes horses shy.

Tarchon (and Tyrrhenus)
Indigites founders of the Etruscan League.

Tarpeia
Goddess of Death and disease. At Rome on the Capitoline Hill, criminals were cast of the Tarpeian Rock to their deaths.

Tellus
Mother Earth, invoked during earthquakes. Associated with Ops, Ceres, and Maia. Her festivals are on 24 Jan., 15 April, and 13 Dec.

Tellumui
Oscan form of Plutoun, spouse of Tellus, He is associated with the mineral bounty of the earth, rather than vegetation, and does not have any association with an Underworld of the dead.

Tempestates
A Goddess of Weather, who had a temple at Rome, especially concerned with storms at sea, to Whom sacrifices were made in propitiation.

Terminus
God of Boundaries, especially stone walls. His festival is held on 23 Feb., Terminalia. May be associated with Monte Termino as a guardian of the mountain sanctuary of Ceres.

Terra
"Earth". The personified Roman goddess of the earth. She is also a fertility goddess, known as Bona Dea.

Terra Mater
The Roman 'mother earth', the goddess of fertility and growth. Her most prominent festival was the Fordicidia on April 15 where cows being with young were sacrificed. Another festival was the Feriae Sementivae ("the sowing feast in January") where offering where made to her and Ceres before harvesting.

Thalna
Etruscan goddess of childbirth, consort of Tinia.

Tiberinus
The Roman god and Genius loci of the river Tiber. On 15 May the Pontiff Maximus and Vestal Virgins, accompanied by the praetors, walk in procession to the Pons Sublicius and cast the argei, 24 straw puppets substituted for old men that were believed to once have been sacrificed. With Gaia He is honored on 8 December. When Aeneas and his Trojan exiles arrived in Latium, the god assisted them. Later Tiberinus also appeared to Aeneas to give him advise. The Volturnia was his festival. His is the father of Ocnus with Manto. There existed a cult of Tiberinus in the early days of Rome, but practically nothing is known about it now.

Tibertus
The god of the river Anio, a tributary of the Tiber. Legend has it that he founded the Italian city Tibur (Tivoli).

Tin (Tinia)
Etruscan Jupiter, more specifically a sky god of the North.

Tinia
See Tin.

Tiv
Etruscan goddess of night and the moon.

Trivia
In Roman mythology, Trivia is the personified deity of crossroads, derived from the Latin trivium ("meeting of three roads"). She was represented with three faces, and sometimes identified with the Greek Hecate.

Tuchulucha
Etruscan Underworld demon with snake hair, a vulture's beak and wings.

Turan
Etruscan goddess of love, health, and fertility, often shown as a winged young woman. She is closely identified with Venus, but also has aspects where she is a protectress of marriage, or a goddess of love in marriage. She is very uncharacteristic of the Roman Venus.

Turms
Etruscan form of Hermes as a psychopomp.

Tutanus (and Tutilina)
Numina of grain resting in barn, invoked in times of trouble. Tutilina was also an indigimentum of Consus as a goddess of stored grain.

Tutilina
See Tutanus.

Tyrrhenus (and Tarchon)
Indigites founders of the Etruscan League.

Ultor
A title given to Mars when, after defeating the murderers of Julius Caesar at Philippi, Augustus built a temple to him in the Forum at Rome.

Ulysses
Ulysses, the Latin equivalent of the Greek Odysseus, was the king of Ithaca, a Greek island. He was married to Penelope and they had a son named Telemachus. He was one of the Greek leaders in the Trojan War. The Greeks fought the Trojans for ten years, but Ulysses came up with a plan to burn down Troy and save Helen, the wife of Melanos, the Spartan king. He had the Greek army build a wooden horse that he and nineteen other soldiers could fit in. All of the Greek warships left the shores of Troy and left the horse behind.

The Trojans thought that it was a gift from the Greeks, so the people of Troy brought it through the gates of the city. Late that night, Ulysses and the nineteen soldiers snuck out of the wooden horse and let the newly arrived Greek army through the gates. The Greeks burned down Troy and saved Helen, but Ulysses still had a long journey ahead of him. Ulysses and his men set sail for Ithaca. After a few weeks of sailing, Ulysses and his men ran out of food. They landed on an island, to look for food and water. They found a whole cave full of food, but they soon found out that the food belonged to a one-eyed giant called a cyclops. Ulysses and his men tricked the cyclops and escaped with the food.

Unfortunately for Ulysses, the cyclops was a son of Neptune, the God of the Sea. Once again, Ulysses' men ran out of food, so they landed on another island. The sailors divided into two groups, Ulysses and some of the crew stayed with the ship, while the others went to look for food. The next morning, one of the "food-searchers" came running back to the boat. The sailor told Ulysses of a sorceress named Circe who had turned the other crew members into hogs. At once, Ulysses ran with the sailor to Circe's palace, but on the way, Mercury came with a gift from one of the gods.
It was a magical flower that would act a shield on Ulysses from Circe's magic. Ulysses met with Circe. Circe tried to use her magic on him, but it didn't work, so she gave in and turned the back into humans. Plus, she warned Ulysses of the dangers to come. With lots of food, Ulysses and his men left the island. Thanks to Circe, Ulysses overcame the next dangers. He overcame the dooming song of the Sirens by plugging the ears of he and his crew.

The sailors came upon the six-headed monster called Scylla. Though all of his crew were eaten by Scylla, Ulysses escaped, only to be washed ashore by a storm where a princess found him and took him to her father. The king gave Ulysses his fastest ship to use to sail home with. When, Ulysses reached Ithaca, he deceived the men that wanted to marry his wife, and killed them. Ulysses finally reclaimed his throne.

Uni (Uniel)
Etruscan form of Juno, but also Astarte, so that she became a goddess of the cosmos, Perugia.

Uniel
See Uni.

Vacuna
A Sabean goddess of agriculture and victory. She was worshipped in a sacred forest near Reate (the current Reati). She is also identified with Bellona. Also recognized as a God of leisure and repose, His festival in Rome is held in December.

Valentina
Umbrian Goddess of Healing, Her sanctuary was at Oriculum.

Vallonia
Numen of valleys.

Vanth
An Etruscan demon of death, with all seeing eyes on his wings, he assists the ill on their deathbeds. His attributes include the snake, torch and key.

Veiovis (Vediovis)
Veiovis is one of the oldest of the Roman gods. He is a god of healing, and was later associated with the Greek Asclepius. He was mostly worshipped in Rome and Bovillae in Latium. On the Capitoline Hill and on the Tiber Island temples were erected in his honor. In spring, goats were sacrificed to avert plagues. Veiovis is portrayed as a young man, holding a bunch of arrows (or lightning bolts) in his hand, and is accompanied by a goat. He may be based on the Etruscan god Veive. Also, an Italic God of expiation and protector of runaway criminals. He is a God of the underworld, but unlike Pluto. Rather, He is "the opposite of Jupiter," called upon against enemy cities as Jupiter is called upon to defend Rome and its cities. His festivals are on 1 Jan., 7 March, 21 May.

Veive
An Etruscan god of revenge, whose attributes are the goat, laurel wreath, and arrows.

Venelia
Wife of Neptune who oversees shallows seas.

Venus
The Roman goddess of love and beauty, but originally a vegetation goddess and patroness of gardens and vineyards. Later, under Greek influence, she was equated with Aphrodite and assumed many of her aspects. Her cult originated from Ardea and Lavinium in Latium. The oldest temple known of Venus dates back to 293 BCE, and was inaugurated on August 18. Later, on this date the Vinalia Rustica was observed. A second festival, that of the Veneralia, was celebrated on April 1 in honor of Venus Verticordia, who later became the protector against vice. Her temple was built in 114 BCE.

After the Roman defeat near Lake Trasum in 215 BCE, a temple was built on the Capitol for Venus Erycina. This temple was officially opened on April 23, and a festival, the Vinalia Priora, was instituted to celebrate the occasion. Venus is the daughter of Jupiter, and some of her lovers include Mars and Vulcan, modeled on the affairs of Aphrodite. Venus' importance rose, and that of her cult, through the influence of several Roman political leaders. The dictator Sulla made her his patroness, and both Julius Caesar and the emperor Augustus named her the ancestor of their (Julian) family: the 'gens Julia' was Aeneas, son of Venus and the mortal Anchises.

Ceasar introduced the cult of Venus Genetrix, the goddess of motherhood and marriage, and built a temple for her in 46 BCE. She was also honored in the temple of Mars Ultor. The last great temple of Venus was built by the emperor Hadrianus near the Coliseum in 135 CE. Roman statues and portraits of Venus are usually identical to the Greek representations of Aphrodite.

Oscan Herentina and Libitina: Goddess of Love, also considered a goddess of flowers and of gardens. Her earliest Roman name appears to have been Murcia as a goddess of gardens and spring flowers, later interpreted as Myrtea, Goddess of Myrtles. She may then have been a goddess of spring flowers and gardens, with which She was closely identified at Rome. First mention of Venus is in 217 BCE when Venus Erycina was brought to Rome from Sicily, by order of the Sibylline Books following the Roman defeat at Lake Trasieme (see Atargatis). That same year was held the Lecistratum introducing the Dii Consentes as Rome's counterpart to the Greek

Olympians, and Venus became identified with Aphrodite.

Venus Genetrix was the mother of Aeneas, and therefore regarded as the mother of the Roman people, and especially of gens Iulii through Aeneas' son Julus. Julius Caesar built a temple to Her in the Forum in 46 BCE. The Templum Urbis built by Hadrian in 135 CE was dedicated to Roma and Venus Genetrix. Her festival on 1 April, Veneralia, was shared with Fortuna Virilis, and Verticordia (Concordia as a goddess who turns the hearts of women towards chastity and modesty).

The Vinalia of 23 April was dedicated to Venus Erycina and Jupiter. The Vinalia of 19 Aug. was dedicated to Jupiter and Venus Libitina, where She was also recognized as a goddess of prostitution. She was closely identified with Flora, Herentina, and Libitina, yet She was unlike Etruscan Turan who was a Goddess of Love in marriage and chastity.

Identified with Aphrodite She became the wife of Vulcanus (Greek Hephaestus). As Venus Victorix She charmed Mars, a popular motif in Roman art. The mother of Cupid and also the mother of Priapus by Bacchus, most if not all of Her myths were derived from Greek myth.

Vercvactor (Vervator, Vervactor)
The Roman god of the first ploughing. See also Imporcitor and Redarator.

Veritas
Veritas ("truth") is the Roman goddess of truth. She is a daughter of Saturn.

Verminus
Verminus ("worm-god") is the Roman god of the worms in cattle. He is also a Roman god of the dead and of disease. His name means "wormy".

Vertumnus (or Vortumnus)
The Roman divinity of seasons, changes and ripening of plant life. "The Turner," "the Changer," an Italic God of fruit, changer of

seasons, protector of gardeners. He was also a shape-shifter who won Pomona as his wife after She had vowed to remain virgin. He is the patron of gardens and fruit trees. He has the power to change himself into various forms, and used this to gain the favor of the goddess Pomona. Vertumnus' cult was introduced in Rome around 300 BCE and a temple was built on the Aventine Hill in 264 BCE. The Vertumnalias, observed on August 13, is his festival. A statue of Vertumnus stood at the Vicus Tuscus. See also, Aeclanuii.

Vervactor
See Vercvactor.

Vervator
See Vercvactor.

Vesta
One of the most popular and mysterious goddesses of the Roman pantheon. Vesta is the goddess of the hearth, equated with the Greek Hestia. There is not much known of her origin, except that she was at first only worshipped in Roman homes, a personal cult. Her cult eventually evolved to a state cult. One myth tells that her service was set up by king Numa Pompilius (715-673 BCE). In her temple on the Palatine Hill, the sacred fire of the Roman state burned, which was maintained by the Vestal Virgins.

At the start of the new Roman year, March 1, the fire was renewed. The sacred fire burned until 394 CE. Vesta's temple was situated on the Forum Romanum and was built in the third century BCE. None of her temples, however, contained a statue of the goddess. Her festival is the Vestalia, which was observed from June 7 - 15. On the first day of this festival, the 'penus Vestae', the inner sanctum of the Vesta temple which was kept closed the entire year, was opened for women who came to bring offerings bare-footed. The temple was ritually cleansed on the last day.

The ass is Vesta's sacred animal, whose braying supposedly kept the lascivious Priapus away. Vesta is portrayed as a stern woman, wearing a long dress and with her head covered. Her right hand rests against her side and in her left hand she holds a scepter.

Vestius Alonieus
A god who was revered in north-west Hispania. He had a military function and was associated with the bull.

Vica Pota
An ancient Roman goddess of victory. She had a temple at the base of the Velia, Rome.[24]

Victoria
The Roman personification of Victory, worshipped as a goddess, especially by triumphant generals returning from battle. She was held in higher regard by the Romans then her counterpart Nike by the Greeks and when in 382 CE her statue was removed by the emperor Gratianus there was much resistance in the heathen reactionary circles.

Viduus
Viduus ("divider") is the Roman deity who separates soul from the dead body.

Virbius
A minor Roman deity who is mainly mentioned as the consort of Diana. He was worshipped in the sacred forest of Egeria, near Aricia in Latium, and identified with the resurrected Hippolytus. An Italic God, with Diana, of the wood and the chase, in later legend raised to life by Asclepius. He is the spirit of the Diana nemus at Aricia who is instilled in the Rex Nemorensis

Viriplaca
The Roman goddess to whom spouses made offering when they had domestic problems.

Virtus
The Roman god of courage and military prowess.

Vitalia
Numen of Italy

Vitumnus
The Roman god who gave life to the child in the mother's womb.

Volturnus
A river deity associated with the river Volturnus in Campania (Italy), but it could also be an ancient name for the Tiber. The Volturnalia was observed on August 27.

Volumna
The Roman protective goddess of the nursery.

Volcanus (Vulcan, Vulcanus)
The Roman god of fire, especially destructive fire, and craftsmanship. His forge is located beneath Mount Etna. It is here that he, together with his helpers, forges weapons for gods and heroes. Vulcanus is closely associated with Bona Dea with whom he shared the Volcanalia, observed on August 23. This festival took place during the height of the Mediterranean drought and the period of highest risk of fire. On the banks of the river Tiber, fires were lighted on which living fish were sacrificed. His temples were usually located outside the cities, due to the dangerous nature of fire.

In 215 BCE his temple on the Circus Flaminius was inaugurated. In Ostia he was the chief god as the protector against fire in the grain storages. He is identified with the Greek Hephaestus. Italic husband of Maiesta (Maia), who ripens fruit through his inner warmth, at Rome he became one of the Dii consentes in 217 BCE, identified with the Greek Hephaestus and husband to Venus. The Volcanalia was held on 23 August. Also as Mulciber, "The Smelter," His festival is on 23 May.

Volta
A wolf-headed monster.

Voltumna
The Etruscan chthonic God, Veltha, later the supreme deity of the Volsini, sometimes identified with Vertumnus in Rome.

Volturnus
A god of wind and water. The Roman god of the East Wind, equal to the Greek Eurus. A river deity associated with the river Volturnus in Campania (Italy), but it could also be an ancient name for the

Tiber. The Volturnalia was observed on August 27.

Voluptes
Numen of sensuality.

Volumna
The Roman protective goddess of the nursery.

Volutina
An indigimentum of Ceres for husks of corn while folded over ears of grain.

Vulcan (Vulcanus)
See Volcanus.

Vulturnus
See Volturnus.

References

1. Micha F. Lindemans, Micha F., Ryan Tuccinardi, Risa Gordon, Mitchell Mendis, James Hunter, and Liz Gunner. Encyclopediae Mythica: Roman Mythology. M.F. Lindemans, Ed. www.pantheon.org. 1995.
2. Virgil I, 550; V, 36, 61, 73. Aeneid V, 525.
3. Virgil I, 188, 312; VI, 34, 158.
4. Livius VII, 6.
5. Thebaid 2.205, 4.32, 9.32
6. Virgil VII, 45, 52, 69, 96.
7. Virgil VII, 47.
8. Livius XXVII, 37,2
9. Virgil VIII, 630.
10. Virgil V, 825.
11. Virgil V, 721.
12. Virgil I, 292
13. Livius I, 5
14. Livius I, 3
15. Livius X, 1, 9

16. *Livius XL, 19*
17. *Virgil IV, 288*
18. *Virgil VI, 763*
19. *Virgil V, 838*
20. *Aeneid XI, 785*
21. *Livius I, 12*
22. *Livius X, 36*
23. *Livius I, 9,12[25]*
24. *pantheon.org*
25. *Societas via Romana.*

18 ROMAN FESTIVALS AND LUDI (GAMES)

Festivals in ancient Rome were an important part of Roman religious life during both the Republican and Imperial eras, and one of the primary features of the Roman calendar. Feriae ("holidays" in the sense of "holy days"; singular also feriae or dies ferialis) were either public (publicae) or private (privatae). State holidays were celebrated by the Roman people and received public funding. Games (ludi), such as the Ludi Apollinares, were not technically feriae, but the days on which they were celebrated were dies festi, holidays in the modern sense of days off work. Although feriae were paid for by the state, ludi were often funded by wealthy individuals. Feriae privatae were holidays celebrated in honor of private individuals or by families.[1] This article deals only with public holidays, including rites celebrated by the state priests of Rome at temples, as well as celebrations by neighborhoods or families held simultaneously throughout Rome.

Feriae were of three kinds:

• ***Stativae*** were annual holidays that held a fixed or stable date on the calendar.

• ***Conceptivae*** were annual holidays that were moveable feasts (like Easter on the Christian calendar, or Thanksgiving in North America); the date was announced by the magistrates or priests who were responsible for them.

- *Imperativae* were holidays held "on demand" (from the verb impero, imperare, "to order, command") when special celebrations or expiations were called for.[2]

One of the most important sources for Roman holidays is Ovid's Fasti, an incomplete poem that describes and provides origins for festivals from January to June at the time of Augustus.

Keeping the feriae

Varro defined feriae as "days instituted for the sake of the gods."[3] Religious rites were performed on the feriae, and public business was suspended. Even slaves were supposed to be given some form of rest. Cicero says specifically that people who were free should not engage in lawsuits and quarrels, and slaves should get a break from their labors.[4]

Agricultural writers recognized that some jobs on a farm might still need to be performed, and specified what these were. Some agricultural tasks not otherwise permitted could be carried out if an expiation were made in advance (piaculum), usually the sacrifice of a puppy.[5]

Within the city of Rome, the flamens and the priest known as the Rex sacrorum were not allowed even to see work done.

On a practical level, those who "inadvertently" worked could pay a fine or offer up a piaculum, usually a pig. Work considered vital either to the gods or preserving human life was excusable, according to some experts on religious law. Although Romans were required not to work, they were not required to take any religious action unless they were priests or had family rites (sacra gentilicia) to maintain.[6]

List of festivals by month

Following is a month-by-month list of Roman festivals and games that had a fixed place on the calendar. For some, the date on which they were first established is recorded. A deity's festival often marked the anniversary (dies natalis, "birthday") of the founding of a temple, or a rededication after a major renovation.

Festivals not named for deities are thought to be among the oldest on the calendar.[7]

Some religious observances were monthly. The first day of the month was the Kalends (or Calends, from which the English word "calendar" derives). Each Kalends was sacred to Juno, and the Regina sacrorum ("Queen of the Rites," a public priestess) marked the day by presiding over a sacrifice to the goddess. A pontiff and the Rex sacrorum reported the sighting of the new moon, and the pontiff announced whether the Nones occurred on the 5th or 7th of that month.

On the Nones, announcements were made regarding events to take place that month; with the exception of the Poplifugia, no major festivals were held before the Nones, though other ceremonies, such as anniversaries of temple dedications, might be carried out.

The Ides (usually the 13th, or in a few months the 15th) were sacred to Jupiter. On each Ides, a white lamb was led along the Via Sacra to the Capitolium for sacrifice to Jupiter.

The list also includes other notable public religious events such as sacrifices and processions that were observed annually but are neither feriae nor dies natales. Unless otherwise noted, the calendar is that of H.H. Scullard, Festivals and Ceremonies of the Roman Republic.

Ianuarius (January)

1 (Kalends): From 153 BC onward, consuls entered office on this date, accompanied by vota publica (public vows for the wellbeing of the republic and later of the emperor) and the taking of auspices. Festivals were also held for the imported cult of Aesculapius and for the obscure god Vediovis.[8]
3-5: most common dates for Compitalia, a moveable feast (feriae conceptivae)
5 (Nones): Dies natalis (founding day) of the shrine of Vica Pota on the Velian Hill[9]
9: Agonalia in honor of Janus, after whom the month January is named; first of at least four festivals named Agonalia throughout the year
11 and 15: Carmentalia, with Juturna celebrated also on the 11th
13 (Ides)
24-26: most common dates for the Sementivae, a feriae conceptivae of sowing, perhaps also known as the Paganalia as celebrated by the pagi
27: Dies natalis of the Temple of Castor and Pollux, or perhaps marking its rededication (see also July 15); Ludi Castores ("Games of the Castors") celebrated at Ostia during the Imperial period

Februarius (February)

In the archaic Roman calendar, February was the last month of the year. The name derives from februa, "the means of purification, expiatory offerings." It marked a turn of season, with February 5 the official first day of spring bringing the renewal of agricultural activities after winter.[10]
1 (Kalends): Dies natalis for the Temple of Juno Sospita, Mother and Queen; sacra at the Grove of Alernus, near the Tiber at the foot of the Palatine Hill
5: Dies natalis for the Temple of Concordia on the Capitoline Hill
13 (Ides): minor festival of Faunus on the Tiber Island
13-22: Parentalia, a commemoration of ancestors and the dead among families 13: Parentatio, with appeasement of the Manes beginning at the 6th hour and ceremonies performed by the chief Vestal; temples were closed, no fires burned on altars, marriages

were forbidden, magistrates took off their insignia, until the 21st
15: Lupercalia
17: last day of the feriae conceptivae Fornacalia, the Oven Festival; Quirinalia, in honor of Quirinus
21: Feralia, the only public observation of the Parentalia, marked F (dies festus) in some calendars and FP (a designation of uncertain meaning) in others, with dark rites aimed at the gods below (di Inferi)
22: Caristia (or Cara Cognatio, "Dear Kindred"), a family pot luck in a spirit of love and forgiveness
23: Terminalia, in honor of Terminus
24: Regifugium
27: Equirria, first of two horse-racing festivals to Mars

Martius (March)

In the old Roman calendar (until perhaps as late as 153 BC), the mensis Martius ("Mars' Month") was the first month of the year. It is one of the few months to be named for a god, Mars, whose festivals dominate the month.
1 (Kalends): the original New Year's Day when the sacred fire of Rome was renewed; the dancing armed priesthood of the Salii celebrated the Feriae Marti (holiday for Mars), which was also the dies natalis ("birthday") of Mars; also the Matronalia, in honor of Juno Lucina, Mars' mother
7: a second festival for Vediovis
9: a dies religiosus when the Salii carried the sacred shields (ancilia) around the city again
14: the second Equirria, a Feriae Marti also called the Mamuralia or sacrum Mamurio
15 (Ides): Feriae Iovi, sacred to Jove, and also the feast of the year goddess Anna Perenna
16–17: the procession of the Argei
17: Liberalia, in honor of Liber; also an Agonalia for Mars
19: Quinquatrus, later expanded into a five-day holiday as Quinquatria, a Feriae Marti, but also a feast day for Minerva, possibly because her temple on the Aventine Hill was dedicated on this day
23: Tubilustrium, purification of the trumpets

24: a day marked QRFC, when the Comitia Calata met to sanction wills
31: anniversary of the Temple of Luna on the Aventine

Aprilis (April)

A major feriae conceptivae in April was the Latin Festival.
1 (Kalends): Veneralia in honor of Venus
4–10: Ludi Megalenses or Megalesia, in honor of the Magna Mater or Cybele, whose temple was dedicated April 10, 191 BC
5: anniversary of the Temple of Fortuna Publica
12–19: Cerialia or Ludi Cereri, festival and games for Ceres, established by 202 BC
13 (Ides): anniversary of the Temple of Jupiter Victor
15: Fordicidia, offering of a pregnant cow to Tellus ("Earth")
21: Parilia, rustic festival in honor of Pales, and the dies natalis of Rome
23: the first of two wine festivals (Vinalia), the Vinalia Priora for the previous year's wine, held originally for Jupiter and later Venus
25: Robigalia, an agricultural festival involving dog sacrifice
27 (28 in the Julian calendar) to May 1: Ludi Florales in honor of Flora, extended to May 3 under the Empire

Maius (May)

The feriae conceptivae of this month was the Ambarvalia.
1 (Kalends): Games of Flora continue; sacrifice to Maia; anniversary of the Temple of Bona Dea on the Aventine; rites for the Lares Praestites, tutelaries of the city of Rome
3: in the Imperial period, a last celebration for Flora, or the anniversary of one of her temples
9, 11, 13: Lemuria, a festival of the dead with both public and household rites, possibly with a sacrifice to Mania on the 11th
14: anniversary of the Temple of Mars Invictus (Mars the Unconquered); a second procession of the Argei[11]
15 (Ides): Mercuralia, in honor of Mercury; Feriae of Jove
21: one of four Agonalia, probably a third festival for Vediovis
23: a second Tubilustrium; Feriae for Vulcanus (Vulcan)

24: QRCF, following Tubilustrium as in March
25: anniversary of the Temple of Fortuna Primigenia

Iunius (June)

Scullard places the Taurian Games on June 25-26,[12] but other scholars doubt these ludi had a fixed date or recurred on a regular basis.[13]
1 (Kalends): anniversaries of the Temple of Juno Moneta; of the Temple of Mars on the clivus (slope, street) outside the Porta Capena; and possibly of the Temple of the Tempestates (storm goddesses); also a festival of the complex goddess Cardea or Carna
3: anniversary of the Temple of Bellona
4: anniversary of the restoration of the Temple of Hercules Custos
5: anniversary of the Temple of Dius Fidius
7: Ludi Piscatorii, "Fishermen's Games"
7–15: Vestalia, in honor of Vesta; June 9 was a dies religiosus to her
8: anniversary of the Temple of Mens
11: Matralia in honor of Mater Matuta; also the anniversary of the Temple of Fortuna in the Forum Boarium
13 (Ides): Feriae of Jove
13–15: Quinquatrus minusculae, the lesser Quinquatrus celebrated by tibicines, flute-players in their role as accompanists to religious ceremonies
19: a commemoration involving the Temple of Minerva on the Aventine, which had its anniversary March 19
20: anniversary of the Temple of Summanus
24: festival of Fors Fortuna, which "seems to have been a rowdy affair"[14]
27: poorly attested observance in honor of the Lares; anniversary of the Temple of Jupiter Stator
29: anniversary of the Temple of Hercules Musarum, Hercules of the Muses

Iulius (Quinctilis) (July)

Until renamed for Julius Caesar, this month was called Quinctilis or Quintilis, originally the fifth month (quint-) when the year began in

March. From this point in the calendar forward, the months had numerical designations.
1 (Kalends): a scarcely attested anniversary of a temple to Juno Felicitas
5: Poplifugia
6–13: Ludi Apollinares, games in honor of Apollo, first held in 212 BC as a one-day event (July 13) and established as annual in 208 BC.
6: anniversary of the Temple of Fortuna Muliebris
7 (Nones): Nonae Caprotinae; Ancillarum Feriae (Festival of the Serving Women);[15] sacrifice to Consus by unspecified public priests (sacerdotes publici); also a minor festival to the two Pales
8: Vitulatio
14–19: a series of markets or fairs (mercatus) following the Ludi Apollinares; not religious holidays
15 (Ides): Transvectio equitum, a procession of cavalry
17: anniversary of the Temple of Honos and Virtus; sacrifice to Victory
18: a dies ater ("black day," meaning a day of ill omen) marking the defeat of the Romans by the Gauls at the Battle of the Allia in 390 BC, leading to the sack of Rome by the Gauls
19, 21: Lucaria
20–30: Ludi Victoriae Caesaris, "Games of the Victorious Caesar", held annually from 45 BC [16]
22: anniversary of the Temple of Concordia at the foot of the Capitol
23: Neptunalia held in honor of Neptune
25: Furrinalia, feriae publicae in honor of Furrina
30: anniversary of the Temple of the Fortune of This Day (Fortunae Huiusque Diei)

Augustus (Sextilis) (August)

1 (Kalends): anniversary of the Temple of Spes (Hope) in the Forum Holitorium, with commemorations also for the "two Victories" on the Palatine
3: Supplicia canum ("punishment of the dogs") an unusual dog sacrifice and procession at the temples of Iuventas ("Youth") and Summanus, connected to the Gallic siege
5: public sacrifice (sacrificium publicum) at the Temple of Salus on

the Quirinal
9: public sacrifice to Sol Indiges
12: sacrifice of a heifer to Hercules Invictus, with a libation from the skyphos of Hercules
13 (Ides): festival of Diana on the Aventine (Nemoralia), with slaves given the day off to attend; other deities honored at their temples include Vortumnus, Fortuna Equestris, Hercules Victor (or Invictus at the Porta Trigemina), Castor and Pollux, the Camenae, and Flora
17: Portunalia in honor of Portunes; anniversary of the Temple of Janus
19: Vinalia Rustica, originally in honor of Jupiter, but later Venus
21: Consualia, with a sacrifice on the Aventine
23: Vulcanalia or Feriae Volcano in honor of Vulcan, along with sacrifices to Maia, the Nymphs in campo ("in the field", perhaps the Campus Martius), Ops Opifera, and a Hora
24: sacrifices to Luna on the Graecostasis; and the first of three days when the mysterious ritual pit called the mundus was opened
25: Opiconsivia or Feriae Opi in honor of Ops Consivae at the Regia
27: Volturnalia, when the Flamen Volturnalis made a sacrifice to Volturnus
28: Games at the Circus Maximus (circenses) for Sol and Luna

September

1 (Kalends): ceremonies for Jupiter Tonans ("the Thunderer") on the Capitolium, and Juno Regina on the Aventine
5: anniversary of one of the temples to Jupiter Stator
5-19, Ludi Romani or Ludi Magni, "the oldest and most famous" of the ludi[17]
13 (Ides): anniversary of the Temple to Jupiter Optimus Maximus; an Epulum Iovis; an epulum to the Capitoline Triad
14: Equorum probatio ("Approval of the Horses"), a cavalry parade of the Imperial period
20-23: days set aside for markets and fairs (mercatus) immediately following the Ludi Romani
23: anniversary of the rededication of the Temple of Apollo in the Campus Martius; Latona was also honored
26: anniversary of the Temple of Venus Genetrix vowed by Julius

Caesar

October

1 (Kalends): ceremonies for Fides and the Tigillum Sororium
3-12: Ludi Augustales, established 14 AD after the death of Augustus, based on the Augustalia[18]
4: Ieiunium Cereris, a day of fasting in honor of Ceres, instituted in 191 BC as a quinquennial observance, made annual by Augustus
5: second of the three days when the mundus was opened
6: dies ater ("black day") to mark the anniversary of the battle of Arausio (105 BC)
7 (Nones): rites for Jupiter Fulgur (Jupiter of daytime lightning) and Juno Curitis
9: rites at shrines for the Genius Publicus, Fausta Felicitas, and Venus Victrix on the Capitolium
10: ceremonies to mark a rededication of the Temple of Juno Moneta
11: Meditrinalia
12: Augustalia, celebrated from 14 AD in honor of the divinized Augustus, established in 19 BC with a new altar and sacrifice to Fortuna Redux[19]
13: Fontinalia in honor of Fons
14: ceremonies to mark a restoration of the Temple of the Penates Dei on the Velian Hill
15 (Ides): October Horse sacrifice to Mars in the Campus Martius; also Feriae of Jupiter
19: Armilustrium, a dies religiosus in honor of Mars
26 to November 1: Ludi Victoriae Sullanae, "Victory Games of Sulla", established as an annual event in 81 BC

November

1 (Kalends): Ludi circenses to close the Sullan Victory Games
4-17: Plebeian Games
8: third of the three days when the mundus ritual pit was opened
13 (Ides): Epulum Jovis; also ceremonies for Feronia and Fortuna Primigeniae

14: a second Equorum probatio (cavalry parade), as on July 15	
18–20: markets and fairs (mercatus)	

December

1 (Kalends): ceremonies at temples for Neptune and for Pietas
3: Bona Dea rites for women only
5 (Nones): a country festival for Faunus held by the pagi
8: festival for Tiberinus Pater and Gaia
11: Agonalia for Indiges; also the (probably unrelated) Septimontium
12: ceremonies at the Temple of Consus on the Aventine
13 (Ides): dies natalis of the Temple of Tellus, and associated lectisternium for Ceres
15: Consualia or Feriae for Consus, the second of the year
17–23: Saturnalia in honor of Saturn, with the public ritual on the 17th
19: Opalia in honor of Ops
21: Divalia in honor of Angerona; Hercules and Ceres also received a sacrifice
22: anniversary of the Temple of the Lares Permarini in the Porticus Minucia
23: Larentalia; commemorations for the temples of Diana and Juno Regina in the Circus Flaminius, and for the Tempestates; Sigillaria, the last day of the Saturnalia, devoted to gift-giving
25: Dies Natalis Solis Invicti ("Birthday of the Unconquered Sun"); Brumalia (both Imperial)

Feriae conceptivae

The following "moveable feasts" are listed roughly in chronological order.

- **Compitalia**, held sometime between December 17 (the Saturnalia) and January 5; in the later Empire, they were regularly held January 3–5, but Macrobius (5th century AD) still categorized them as conceptivae.[20]

- **Sementivae**, a festival of sowing honoring Tellus and Ceres, placed on January 24–26 by Ovid, who regards these feriae as the same as Paganalia; Varro may indicate that the two were separate festivals.[21]

- **Fornacalia**, a mid-February baking festival celebrated by the curiae, the 30 archaic divisions of the Roman people; the date was announced by the curio maximus and set for each curia individually, with a general Fornacalia on February 17 for those who had missed their own or who were uncertain to which curia they belonged.

- **Amburbium**, a ceremony to purify the city (urbs) as a whole, perhaps held sometime in February.

- **Feriae Latinae (Latin Festival)**, a major and very old conceptivae in April.

- **Ambarvalia**, purification of the fields in May.

The **Rosalia** or "Festival of Roses" also had no fixed date, but was technically not one of the feriae conceptivae with a date announced by public priests based on archaic practice.

Feriae imperativae

Festivals were also held in ancient Rome in response to particular events, or for a particular purpose such as to propitiate or show gratitude toward the gods. For example, Livy reports that following the Roman destruction of Alba Longa in the 7th century BC, and the removal of the Alban populace to Rome, it was reported to have rained stones on the Mons Albanus.

A Roman deputation was sent to investigate the report, and a further shower of stones was witnessed. The Romans took this to be a sign of the displeasure of the Alban gods, the worship of whom had been abandoned with the evacuation of Alba Longa. Livy goes on to say that the Romans instituted a public festival of nine days, at the instigation either of a 'heavenly voice' heard on the Mons Albanus, or of the haruspices. Livy also says that it became the longstanding practice in Rome that whenever a shower of stones was reported, a festival of nine days would be ordered in response.[22]

Mercatus

The noun mercatus (plural mercatūs) means "commerce" or "the market" generally, but it also refers to fairs or markets held immediately after certain ludi. Cicero said[23] that Numa Pompilius, the semi-legendary second king of Rome, established mercatus in conjunction with religious festivals to facilitate trade, since people had already gathered in great numbers.

In early times, these mercatus may have played a role in wholesale trade, but as commerce in Rome became more sophisticated, by the late Republic they seem to have become retail fairs specialized for the holiday market. The Sigillaria attached to the Saturnalia may have been a mercatus in this sense. Surviving fasti[24] record Mercatus Apollinares, July 14–19; Mercatus Romani, September 20–23; and Mercatus Plebeii, November 18–20. Others may have existed. The English word "fair" derives from Latin feria.[25]

References

1. H.H. Scullard, *Festivals and Ceremonies of the Roman Republic* (Cornell University Press, 1981), pp. 38–39.
2. Scullard, *Festivals and Ceremonies of the Roman Republic*, p. 39.
3. Varro, *De lingua latina* 6.12 (*dies deorum causa instituti*, as cited by Scullard, p. 39, noting also the phrase *dis dedicati*, "dedicated to the gods," in Macrobius, *Saturnalia* 1.16.2.

4. Cicero, *De legibus* 2.29, as cited by Scullard, p. 39.
5. Cato the Elder, *De agricultura* 138; Columella 2.21.2; Scullard, *Festivals and Ceremonies of the Roman Republic*, p. 39.
6. Scullard, *Festivals and Ceremonies of the Roman Republic*, pp. 39–40.
7. Hendrik Wagenvoort, "Initia Cereris," in *Studies in Roman Literature, Culture and Religion* (Brill, 1956), pp. 163–164.
8. Scullard, *Festivals and Ceremonies of the Roman Republic*, pp. 52–58.
9. Recorded only in the Fasti Antiates.
10. Scullard, *Festivals and Ceremonies of the Roman Republic*, pp. 70–71.
11. Alternatively dated to May 15.
12. Scullard, *Festivals and Ceremonies of the Roman Republic*, p. 156.
13. John H. Humphrey, *Roman Circuses: Arenas for Chariot Racing* (University of California Press, 1986), p. 543; Robert Turcan, *The Gods of Ancient Rome* (Edinburgh University Press, 2000), p. 82.
14. Scullard, *Festivals and Ceremonies of the Roman Republic*, p. 155.
15. Recorded only by Polemius Silvius.
16. http://bmcr.brynmawr.edu/1997/97.08.07.html
17. Scullard, *Festivals and Ceremonies of the Roman Republic*, p. 183.
18. Matthew Bunson, *A Dictionary of the Roman Empire* (Oxford University Press, 1995), pp. 246–247; Roland Auguet, *Cruelty and Civilization: The Roman Games* (Routledge, 1972, 1994) pp. 212–213.
19. John Scheid, "To Honour the Princeps and Venerate the Gods: Public Cult, Neighbourhood Cults, and Imperial Cult in Augustan Rome," translated by Jonathan Edmondson, in *Augustus* (Edinburgh University Press, 2009), pp. 288–290.
20. Scullard, *Festivals and Ceremonies of the Roman Republic*, p. 58.
21. Scullard, *Festivals and Ceremonies of the Roman Republic*, p. 68.
22. Livy, *Ab urbe condita*, 1:31
23. Cicero, *Republic* 2.27.
24. Fasti Antiates Ministrorum, Fasti Fratrum Arvalium, and the "so-called" Fasti Maffeani = Inscriptiones Italiae XIII.2.377.
25. Claire Holleran, *Shopping in Ancient Rome: The Retail Trade in the Late Republic and the Principate* (Oxford University Press, 2012), pp. 189–190, 193.
26. "Cruelty". *The Oxford Dictionary of Phrase, Saying, and Quotation*, 2nd edition. Susan Ratcliffe, ed. New York: Oxford University Press, 2002,109-110.

19 ROMAN BELIEFS ABOUT THE AFTERLIFE

Preparation

This essay was posted to the Nova Roma mailing list by Flavia Claudia, Founder, Vestal Order of Nova Roma, in response to a question about what Romans believed happened after death.

When you die ("you" being a good Roman of the Religio persuasion), you are escorted to the River Styx by spirits. There, you and the other recently life-challenged are met by Charon, the ferryman. A coin, an obolus, will have been placed in your former body's mouth to pay Charon (although an aurus gets you a better seat in the boat, some believed). This payment is not representative of money so much as of the relationship between god and man, acknowledging your debt to the gods and their protection and guidance to you.

On the other side of Styx, you will pass Cerberus, the three-headed watchdog belonging to Father Dis, god of the Underworld. Cerberus will be friendly — he only becomes unfriendly when shades try to get OUT of the Underworld unauthorized.

You will go before the three judges, Minos, Rhadamanthos and Aeacus, who will ask you to account for your life. After you've made your accounting, you will be given the water of the River Lethe, the river of forgetfulness and one of five Rivers in the Underworld, which makes you forget your past life. You will be sent to the

Elysian Fields (a version of paradise) if you've been a warrior or hero; The Plain of Asphodel, if you've been a good citizen, where you will continue to live a good life as a shade; or — if you've really offended the gods — to Tartarus, where you'll be punished by the Furies until your debt to society is paid. (There's no "eternal damnation" in the Roman underworld, although you can be there a pretty long time, depending on what you've done.) Your punishment depends on your crime.

Every once in a while, Dis or Persephone, the Queen of the Underworld, will reprieve a candidate for the entire process and send him or her back to live again, especially if the deceased was unjustly murdered. He is given the Water of Forgetfulness and sent back across the Styx, presumably with a treat for Cerberus! (This is where the old phrase, " a sop for Cerberus" comes from — a bribe.)

Dis, while he is God of the Underworld, is NOT the God of Death. He does not decide who lives and dies. Instead, this is determined by the Three Fates. However, Dis does dispatch the god of death, Mors or Thanatos, to do his duty. He also has some connection with Morpheus, god of dreams. Interestingly, Dis Pater is the only god with no name. He is known by the name of his kingdom: Hades, Pluto, or Dis, all of which refer to the secret riches of the earth.

20 THE ROMAN VIRTUES

Personal virtues

These are the qualities of life to which every citizen (and, ideally, everyone else) should aspire. They are the heart of the Via Romana — the Roman Way — and are thought to be those qualities which gave the Roman Republic the moral strength to conquer and civilize the world. Today, they are the rods against which we can measure our own behavior and character, and we can strive to better understand and practice them in our everyday lives.

Auctoritas
"Spiritual Authority" The sense of one's social standing, built up through experience, Pietas, and Industria.

Comitas
"Humour" Ease of manner, courtesy, openness, and friendliness.

Clementia
"Mercy" Mildness and gentleness.

Dignitas
"Dignity" A sense of self-worth, personal pride.

Firmitas
"Tenacity" Strength of mind, the ability to stick to one's purpose.

Frugalitas
"Frugalness" Economy and simplicity of style, without being miserly.

Gravitas
"Gravity" A sense of the importance of the matter at hand, responsibility and earnestness.

Honestas
"Respectibility" The image that one presents as a respectable member of society.

Humanitas
"Humanity" Refinement, civilization, learning, and being cultured.

Industria
"Industriousness" Hard work.

Pietas
"Dutifulness" More than religious piety; a respect for the natural order socially, politically, and religiously. Includes the ideas of patriotism and devotion to others.

Prudentia
"Prudence" Foresight, wisdom, and personal discretion.

Salubritas
"Wholesomeness" Health and cleanliness.

Severitas
"Sternness" Gravity, self-control.

Veritas
"Truthfulness" Honesty in dealing with others.

Public virtues

In addition to the private virtues which were aspired to by individuals, Roman culture also strove to uphold virtues which were shared by all of society in common. Note that some of the virtues to which individuals were expected to aspire are also public virtues to be sought by society as a whole. These virtues were often expressed by minting them on coinage; in this way, their message would be shared by all the classical world. In many cases, these virtues were personified as deities.

Abundantia
"Abundance, Plenty" The ideal of there being enough food and prosperity for all segments of society.

Aequitas
"Equity" Fair dealing both within government and among the people.

Bonus Eventus
"Good fortune" Rememberance of important positive events.

Clementia
"Clemency" Mercy, shown to other nations.

Concordia
"Concord" Harmony among the Roman people, and also between Rome and other nations.

Felicitas
"Happiness, prosperity" A celebration of the best aspects of Roman society.

Fides
"Confidence" Good faith in all commercial and governmental dealings.

Fortuna
"Fortune" An acknowledgement of positive events.

Genius
"Spirit of Rome" Acknowledgement of the combined spirit of Rome, and its people.

Hilaritas
"Mirth, rejoicing" An expression of happy times.

Iustitia
"Justice" As expressed by sensible laws and governance.

Laetitia
"Joy, Gladness" The celebration of thanksgiving, often of the resolution of crisis.

Liberalitas
"Liberality" Generous giving.

Libertas
"Freedom" A virtue which has been subsequently aspired to by all cultures.

Nobilitas
"Noblility" Noble action within the public sphere.

Ops
"Wealth" Acknowledgement of the prosperity of the Roman world.

Patientia
"Endurance, Patience" The ability to weather storms and crisis.

Pax
"Peace" A celebration of peace among society and between nations.

Pietas
"Piety, Dutifulness" People paying honor to the gods.

Providentia
"Providence, Fortethought" The ability of Roman society to survive trials and manifest a greater destiny.

Pudicita
"Modesty, Chastity." A public expression which belies the accusation of "moral corruptness" in ancient Rome.

Salus
"Safety" Concern for public health and wellfare.

Securitas
"Confidence, Security" Brought by peace and efficient governance.

Spes
"Hope" Especially during times of difficulty.

Uberitas
"Fertility" Particularly concerning agriculture.

Virtus
"Courage" Especially of leaders within society and government.

21 GLOSSARY OF ROMAN RELIGIOUS TERMS

abominari
The verb abominari ("to avert an omen", from ab-, "away, off," + ominari, "to pronounce on an omen") was a term of augury for an action that rejects or averts an unfavorable omen indicated by a signum, "sign". The noun is abominatio, from which English "abomination" derives. At the taking of formally solicited auspices (auspicia impetrativa), the observer was required to acknowledge any potentially bad sign occurring within the templum he was observing, regardless of the interpretation.[2] He might, however, take certain actions in order to ignore the signa, including avoiding the sight of them, and interpreting them as favourable. The latter tactic required promptness, wit and skill based on discipline and learning.[3] Thus the omen had no validity apart from the observation of it.[4]

aedes
The aedes was the dwelling place of a god.[5] It was thus a structure that housed the deity's image, distinguished from the templum or sacred district.[6] Aedes is one of several Latin words that can be translated as "shrine" or "temple"; see also delubrum and fanum. For instance, the Temple of Vesta, as it is called in English, was in Latin an aedes.[7] See also the diminutive aedicula, a small shrine.

In his work On Architecture, Vitruvius always uses the word templum in the technical sense of a space defined through augury, with aedes the usual word for the building itself.[8] The design of a deity's aedes, he writes, should be appropriate to the characteristics of the deity.

For a celestial deity such as Jupiter, Coelus, Sol or Luna, the building should be open to the sky; an aedes for a god embodying virtus (valor), such as Minerva, Mars, or Hercules, should be Doric and without frills; the Corinthian order is suited for goddesses such as Venus, Flora, Proserpina and the Lymphae; and the Ionic is a middle ground between the two for Juno, Diana, and Father Liber. Thus in theory, though not always in practice, architectural aesthetics had a theological dimension.[9]

The word aedilis (aedile), a public official, is related by etymology; among the duties of the aediles was the overseeing of public works, including the building and maintenance of temples.[10] The temple (aedes) of Flora, for instance, was built in 241 BC by two aediles acting on Sibylline oracles. The plebeian aediles had their headquarters at the aedes of Ceres.[11]

ager
In religious usage, ager (territory, country, land, region) was terrestrial space defined for the purposes of augury in relation to auspicia. There were five kinds of ager: Romanus, Gabinus, peregrinus, hosticus and incertus. The ager Romanus originally included the urban space outside the pomerium and the surrounding countryside.[12] According to Varro, the ager Gabinus pertained to the special circumstances of the oppidum of Gabii, which was the first to sign a sacred treaty (pax) with Rome.[13] The ager peregrinus[14] was other territory that had been brought under treaty (pacatus).

Ager hosticus meant foreign territory; incertus, "uncertain" or "undetermined," that is, not falling into one of the four defined categories.[15] The powers and actions of magistrates were based on and constrained by the nature of the ager on which they stood, and ager in more general usage meant a territory as defined legally or politically. The ager Romanus could not be extended outside Italy (terra Italia).[16]

ara

The focal point of sacrifice was the altar (ara, plural arae). Most altars throughout the city of Rome and in the countryside would have been simple, open-air structures; they may have been located within a sacred precinct (templum), but often without an aedes housing a cult image.[17] An altar that received food offerings might also be called a mensa, "table."[18]

Perhaps the best-known Roman altar is the elaborate and Greek-influenced Ara Pacis, which has been called "the most representative work of Augustan art."[19] Other major public altars included the Ara Maxima.

arbor felix
See also: Ficus Ruminalis

A tree (arbor) was categorized as felix if it was under the protection of the heavenly gods (di superi). The adjective felix here means not only literally "fruitful" but more broadly "auspicious".

Macrobius[20] lists arbores felices (plural) as the oak (four species thereof), the birch, the hazelnut, the sorbus, the white fig, the pear, the apple, the grape, the plum, the cornus and the lotus. The oak was sacred to Jupiter, and twigs of oak were used by the Vestals to ignite the sacred fire in March every year. Also among the felices were the olive tree, a twig of which was affixed to the hat of the Flamen Dialis, and the laurel and the poplar, which crowned the Salian priests.[21]

Arbores infelices were those under the protection of chthonic gods or those gods who had the power of turning away misfortune (avertentium). As listed by Tarquitius Priscus in his lost ostentarium on trees,[22] these were buckthorn, red cornel, fern, black fig, "those that bear a black berry and black fruit," holly, woodland pear, butcher's broom, briar, and brambles."[23]

attrectare
The verb attrectare ("to touch, handle, lay hands on") referred in specialized religious usage to touching sacred objects while performing cultic actions. Attrectare had a positive meaning only in reference to the actions of the sacerdotes populi Romani ("priests of the Roman people"). It had the negative meaning of "contaminate"

(= contaminare) or pollute when referring to the handling of sacred objects by those not authorized, ordained, or ritually purified.[24]

augur

An augur (Latin plural augures) was an official and priest who solicited and interpreted the will of the gods regarding a proposed action. The augur ritually defined a templum, or sacred space, declared the purpose of his consultation, offered sacrifice, and observed the signs that were sent in return, particularly the actions and flight of birds. If the augur received unfavorable signs, he could suspend, postpone or cancel the undertaking (obnuntiatio). "Taking the auspices" was an important part of all major official business, including inaugurations, senatorial debates, legislation, elections and war, and was held to be an ancient prerogative of Regal and patrician magistrates. Under the Republic, this right was extended to other magistrates. After 300 BC, plebeians could become augurs.

auguraculum

The solicitation of formal auspices required the marking out of ritual space (auguraculum) from within which the augurs observed the templum, including the construction of an augural tent or hut (tabernaculum). There were three such sites in Rome: on the citadel (arx), on the Quirinal Hill, and on the Palatine Hill. Festus said that originally the auguraculum was in fact the arx. It faced east, situating the north on the augur's left or lucky side.[25] A magistrate who was serving as a military commander also took daily auspices, and thus a part of camp-building while on campaign was the creation of a tabernaculum augurale. This augural tent was the center of religious and legal proceedings within the camp.[26]

augurium

Augurium (plural auguria) is an abstract noun that pertains to the augur. It seems to mean variously: the "sacral investiture" of the augur;[27] the ritual acts and actions of the augurs;[28] augural law (ius augurale);[29] and recorded signs whose meaning had already been established.[30] The word is rooted in the IE stem *aug-, "to increase," and possibly an archaic Latin neuter noun *augus, meaning "that which is full of mystic force." As the sign that manifests the divine will,[31] the augurium for a magistrate was valid for a year; a priest's, for his lifetime; for a temple, it was perpetual.[32]

The distinction between augurium and auspicium is often unclear. Auspicia is the observation of birds as signs of divine will, a practice held to have been established by Romulus, first king of Rome, while the institution of augury was attributed to his successor Numa.[33] For Servius, an augurium is the same thing as auspicia impetrativa, a body of signs sought through prescribed ritual means.[34] Some scholars think auspicia would belong more broadly to the magistracies and the patres[35] while the augurium would be limited to the rex sacrorum and the major priesthoods.[36]

Ancient sources record three auguria: the augurium salutis in which every year the gods were asked whether it was fas (permissible, right) to ask for the safety of the Roman people (August 5); the augurium canarium, a dog sacrifice to promote the maturation of grain crops, held in the presence of the pontiffs as well as the augurs;[37] and the vernisera auguria mentioned by Festus, which should have been a springtime propitiary rite held at the time of the harvest (auguria messalia).

auspex

The auspex, plural auspices, is a diviner who reads omens from the observed flight of birds (avi-, from avis, "bird", with -spex, "observer", from spicere). See auspicia following and auspice.

auspicia

The auspicia (au- = avis, "bird"; -spic-, "watch") were originally signs derived from observing the flight of birds within the templum of the sky. Auspices are taken by an augur. Originally they were the prerogative of the patricians,[38] but the college of augurs was opened to plebeians in 300 BC.[39] Only magistrates were in possession of the auspicia publica, with the right and duty to take the auspices pertaining to the Roman state.[40] Favorable auspices marked a time or location as auspicious, and were required for important ceremonies or events, including elections, military campaigns and pitched battles.

According to Festus, there were five kinds of auspicia to which augurs paid heed: ex caelo, celestial signs such as thunder and lightning; ex avibus, signs offered by birds; ex tripudiis, signs produced by the actions of certain sacred chickens; ex quadrupedibus, signs from the behavior of four-legged animals; and ex diris, threatening portents.[41] In official state augury at Rome, only the auspicia ex caelo and ex avibus were employed.

The taking of the auspices required ritual silence (silentium). Watching for auspices was called spectio or servare de caelo. The appearance of expected signs resulted in nuntiatio, or if they were unfavorable obnuntiatio. If unfavorable auspices were observed, the business at hand was stopped by the official observer, who declared alio die ("on another day").[42]

The practice of observing bird omens was common to many ancient peoples predating and contemporaneous with Rome, including the Greeks,[citation needed] Celts,[43] and Germans.[citation needed]

auspicia impetrativa
Auspicia impetrativa were signs that were solicited under highly regulated ritual conditions (see spectio and servare de caelo) within the templum.[44] The type of auspices required for convening public assemblies were impetrativa,[45] and magistrates had the "right and duty" to seek these omens actively.[46] These auspices could only be sought from an auguraculum, a ritually constructed augural tent or "tabernacle" (tabernaculum).[47] Contrast auspicia oblativa.

auspicia maiora
The right of observing the "greater auspices" was conferred on a Roman magistrate holding imperium, perhaps by a Lex curiata de imperio, although scholars are not agreed on the finer points of law.[48] A censor had auspicia maxima.[49] It is also thought that the flamines maiores were distinguished from the minores by their right to take the auspicia maiora; see Flamen.

auspicia oblativa
Signs that occurred without deliberately being sought through formal augural procedure were auspicia oblativa. These unsolicited signs were regarded as sent by a deity or deities to express either

approval or disapproval for a particular undertaking. The prodigy (prodigium) was one form of unfavorable oblativa.[50] Contrast auspicia impetrativa.

auspicia privata
Private and domestic religion was linked to divine signs as state religion was. It was customary in patrician families to take the auspices for any matter of consequence such as marriages, travel, and important business.[51] The scant information about auspicia privata in ancient authors[52] suggests that the taking of private auspices was not different in essence from that of public auspices: absolute silence was required,[53] and the person taking the auspices could ignore unfavorable or disruptive events by feigning not to have perceived them.[54] In matters pertaining to the family or individual, both lightning[55] and exta (entrails)[56] might yield signs for privati, private citizens not authorized to take official auspices. Among his other duties, the Pontifex Maximus advised privati as well as the official priests about prodigies and their forestalling.[57]

averruncare
In pontifical usage, the verb averruncare, "to avert," denotes a ritual action aimed at averting a misfortune intimated by an omen. Bad omens (portentaque prodigiaque mala) are to be burnt, using trees that are in the tutelage of underworld or "averting" gods (see arbores infelices above).[58] Varro says that the god who presides over the action of averting is Averruncus.[59]

bellum iustum
A "just war" was a war considered justifiable by the principles of fetial law (ius fetiale).[60] Because war could bring about religious pollution, it was in itself nefas, "wrong," and could incur the wrath of gods unless iustum, "just".[61] The requirements for a just war were both formal and substantive. As a formal matter, the war had to be declared according to the procedures of the ius fetiale. On substantive grounds, a war required a "just cause," which might include rerum repetitio, retaliation against another people for pillaging, or a breach of or unilateral recession from a treaty; or necessity, as in the case of repelling an invasion.[62] See also Jus ad bellum.

caerimonia

The English word "ceremony" derives from the Latin caerimonia or caeremonia, a word of obscure etymology first found in literature and inscriptions from the time of Cicero (mid-1st century BC), but thought to be of much greater antiquity. Its meaning varied over time. Cicero used caerimonia at least 40 times, in three or four different senses: "inviolability" or "sanctity", a usage also of Tacitus; "punctilious veneration", in company with cura (carefulness, concern); more commonly in the plural caerimoniae, to mean "ritual prescriptions" or "ritual acts." The plural form is endorsed by Roman grammarians.

Hendrik Wagenvoort maintained that caerimoniae were originally the secret ritual instructions laid down by Numa, which are described as statae et sollemnes, "established and solemn."[63] These were interpreted and supervised by the College of Pontiffs, flamens, rex sacrorum and the Vestals. Later, caerimoniae might refer also to other rituals, including foreign cults.[64] These prescribed rites "unite the inner subject with the external religious object", binding human and divine realms. The historian Valerius Maximus makes clear that the caerimoniae require those performing them to attain a particular mental-spiritual state (animus, "intention"), and emphasizes the importance of caerimoniae in the dedication and first sentence of his work. In Valerius' version of the Gallic siege of Rome, the Vestals and the Flamen Quirinalis rescue Rome's sacred objects (sacra) by taking them to Caere; thus preserved, the rites take their name from the place.[65] Although this etymology makes a meaningful narrative connection for Valerius,[66] it is unlikely to be correct in terms of modern scientific linguistics. An Etruscan origin has sometimes been proposed. Wagenvoort thought that caerimonia derived from caerus, "dark" in the sense of "hidden", hence meaning "darknesses, secrets."[67]

In his Etymologiae, Isidore of Seville says that the Greek equivalent is orgia, but derives the word from carendo, "lacking", and says that some think caerimoniae should be used of Jewish observances, specifically the dietary law that requires abstaining from or "lacking" certain foods.[68]

calator (kalator)
The calatores were assistants who carried out day-to-day business on behalf of the senior priests of the state such as the flamines maiores. A calator was a public slave.[69] Festus derives the word from the Greek verb kalein, "to call."

capite velato
At the traditional public rituals of ancient Rome, officiants prayed, sacrificed, offered libations, and practiced augury capite velato,[70] "with the head covered" by a fold of the toga drawn up from the back. This covering of the head is a distinctive feature of Roman rite in contrast with Etruscan practice[71] or ritus graecus, "Greek rite."[72] In Roman art, the covered head is a symbol of pietas and the individual's status as a pontifex, augur or other priest.[73]
It has been argued that the Roman expression of piety capite velato influenced Paul's prohibition against Christians praying with covered heads: "Any man who prays or prophesies with his head covered dishonors his head."[74]

carmen
In classical Latin, carmen usually means "song, poem, ode." In magico-religious usage, a carmen (plural carmina) is a chant, hymn, spell, or charm. In essence "a verbal utterance sung for ritualistic purposes", the carmen is characterized by formulaic expression, redundancy, and rhythm.[75] Fragments from two archaic priestly hymns are preserved, the Carmen Arvale of the Arval Brethren and the Carmina Saliaria of the Salii. The Carmen Saeculare of Horace, though self-consciously literary in technique, was also a hymn, performed by a chorus at the Saecular Games of 17 BC and expressing the Apollonian ideology of Augustus.[76]

A carmen malum or maleficum is a potentially harmful magic spell; a carmen sepulchrale is a spell that evokes the dead from their tombs; a carmen veneficum, a "poisonous" charm.[77] In magic, the word carmen comes to mean also the object on which a spell is inscribed, hence a charm in the physical sense.[78]

castus, castitas
Castus is an adjective meaning morally pure or guiltless (English "chaste"), hence pious or ritually pure in a religious sense. Castitas

is the abstract noun. Various etymologies have been proposed, among them two IE stems: *k'(e)stos[79] meaning "he who conforms to the prescriptions of rite"; or *kas-, from which derives the verb careo, "I defice, am deprived of, have none..." i.e. vitia.[80] In Roman religion, the purity of ritual and those who perform it is paramount: one who is correctly cleansed and castus in religious preparation and performance is likely to please the gods. Ritual error is a pollutant; it vitiates the performance and risks the gods' anger. Castus and castitas are attributes of the sacerdos (priest),[81] but substances and objects can also be ritually castus.[82]

cinctus gabinus

A priest or officiant who was cinctus Gabinus wore his toga bound around the waist in a "Gabinian cincture", a particular belting for a vestment that was derived from the practice of Gabii.[83] This style of fastening left both hands free to perform ritual tasks, as the wearing of the toga usually did not.[84] The cincture accompanied the veiling or covering of the head (capite velato) with a cowl-like fold of the toga.[85] Like the conical, helmet-like headgear worn by priests such as the Salii, the Gabinian cincture was originally associated with warriors, and was worn for a solemn declaration of war. It was also part of Etruscan priestly dress.[86]

clavum fingere

Clavum fingere ("to nail in, to fasten or fix the nail") was an expression that referred to the fixing or "sealing" of fate.[87] A nail was one of the attributes of the goddess Necessitas[88] and of the Etruscan goddess Athrpa (Greek Atropos). According to Livy, every year in the temple of Nortia, the Etruscan counterpart of Fortuna, a nail was driven in to mark the time. In Rome, the senior magistrate[89] on the Ides of September drove a nail called the clavus annalis ("year-nail")[90] into the wall of the Temple of Jupiter Optimus Maximus. The ceremony occurred on the dies natalis ("birthday" or anniversary of dedication) of the temple, when a banquet for Jove (Epulum Jovis) was also held. The nail-driving ceremony, however, took place in a templum devoted to Minerva, on the right side of the aedes of Jupiter, because the concept of "number" was invented by Minerva and the ritual predated the common use of written letters.[91]

The importance of this ritual is lost in obscurity, but in the early Republic it is associated with the appointment of a dictator clavi figendi causa, "dictator for the purpose of driving the nail,"[92] one of whom was appointed for the years 363, 331, 313, and 263 BC.[93] Livy attributes this practice to religio, religious scruple or obligation. It may be that in addition to an annual ritual, there was a "fixing" during times of pestilence or civil discord that served as a piaculum.[94] Livy says that in 363, a plague had been ravaging Rome for two years. It was recalled that a plague had once been broken when a dictator drove a ritual nail, and the senate appointed one for that purpose.[95] The ritual of "driving the nail" was among those revived and reformed by Augustus, who in 1 AD transferred it to the new Temple of Mars Ultor. Henceforth a censor fixed the nail at the end of his term.[96]

collegium

A collegium ("joined by law"), plural collegia, was any association with a legal personality. The priestly colleges oversaw religious traditions, and until 300 BC only patricians were eligible for membership. When plebeians began to be admitted, the size of the colleges was expanded. By the Late Republic, three collegia wielded greater authority than the others, with a fourth coming to prominence during the reign of Augustus. The four great religious corporations (quattuor amplissima collegia) were:

Pontifices, the College of Pontiffs headed by the Pontifex Maximus;
Augures;
Quindecimviri sacris faciundis, the fifteen priests in charge of the Sibylline Books;
Septemviri epulonum, the board of seven priests who organized public banquets for religious holidays.

Augustus was a member of all four collegia, but limited membership for any other senator to one.[97]

In Roman society, a collegium might also be a trade guild or neighborhood association; see Collegium (ancient Rome).

comitia calata

The comitia calata ("calate assemblies") were non-voting assemblies (comitia) called for religious purposes. The verb calare, originally meaning "to call," was a technical term of pontifical usage, found also in calendae (Calends) and calator. According to Aulus Gellius,[98] these comitia were held in the presence of the college of pontiffs in order to inaugurate the rex (the king in the Regal Period or the rex sacrorum in the Republic)[99] or the flamines. The pontifex maximus auspiciated and presided; assemblies over which annually elected magistrates presided are never calata, nor are meetings for secular purposes or other elections even with a pontiff presiding.[100]

The comitia calata were organized by curiae or centuriae.[101] The people were summoned to comitia calata to witness the reading of wills, or the oath by which sacra were renounced (detestatio sacrorum).[102] They took no active role and were only present to observe as witnesses.[103]

Mommsen thought the calendar abbreviation QRCF, given once as Q. Rex C. F.[104] and taken as Quando Rex Comitiavit Fas, designated a day when it was religiously permissible for the rex to "call" for a comitium, hence the comitia calata.[105]

commentarii augurales

The Commentaries of the Augurs were written collections probably of the decreta and responsa of the college of augurs. Some scholarship, however, maintains that the commentarii were precisely not the decreta and responsa.[106] The commentaries are to be distinguished from the augurs' libri reconditi, texts not for public use.[107] The books are mentioned by Cicero,[108] Festus,[109] and Servius Danielis.[110] Livy includes several examples of the augurs' decreta and responsa in his history, presumably taken from the commentarii.[111]

commentarii pontificum

The Commentaries of the Pontiffs contained a record of decrees and official proceedings of the College of Pontiffs. Priestly literature was one of the earliest written forms of Latin prose, and included rosters, acts (acta), and chronicles kept by the various collegia,[112] as well as religious procedure.[113] It was often occultum genus litterarum,[114] an arcane form of literature to which by definition only priests had access. The commentarii, however, may have been

available for public consultation, at least by senators,[115] because the rulings on points of law might be cited as precedent.[116] The public nature of the commentarii is asserted by Jerzy Linderski in contrast to libri reconditi, the secret priestly books.[117]
The commentarii survive only through quotation or references in ancient authors.[118] These records are not readily distinguishable from the libri pontificales; some scholars maintain that the terms commentarii and libri for the pontifical writings are interchangeable. Those who make a distinction hold that the libri were the secret archive containing rules and precepts of the ius sacrum (holy law), texts of spoken formulae, and instructions on how to perform ritual acts, while the commentarii were the responsa (opinions and arguments) and decreta (binding explications of doctrine) that were available for consultation.

Whether or not the terms can be used to distinguish two types of material, the priestly documents would have been divided into those reserved for internal use by the priests themselves, and those that served as reference works on matters external to the college.[119] Collectively, these titles would have comprised all matters of pontifical law, ritual, and cult maintenance, along with prayer formularies[120] and temple statutes.[121] See also libri pontificales and libri augurales.

coniectura
Coniectura is the reasoned but speculative interpretation of signs presented unexpectedly, that is, of novae res, "novel information." These "new signs" are omens or portents not previously observed, or not observed under the particular set of circumstances at hand. Coniectura is thus the kind of interpretation used for ostenta and portenta as constituting one branch of the "Etruscan discipline"; contrast observatio as applied to the interpretation of fulgura (thunder and lightning) and exta (entrails). It was considered an ars, a "method" or "art" as distinguished from disciplina, a formal body of teachings which required study or training.[122]

The origin of the Latin word coniectura suggests the process of making connections, from the verb conicio, participle coniectum (con-, "with, together", and iacio, "throw, put"). Coniectura was also a rhetorical term applied to forms of argumentation, including court cases.[123] The English word "conjecture" derives from coniectura.

Consecration

Consecratio was the ritual act that resulted in the creation of an aedes, a shrine that housed a cult image, or an ara, an altar. Jerzy Linderski insists that the consecratio should be distinguished from the inauguratio, that is, the ritual by which the augurs established a sacred place (locus) or templum (sacred precinct).[124] The consecration was performed by a pontiff reciting a formula from the libri pontificales, the pontifical books.[125] One component of consecration was the dedicatio, or dedication, a form of ius publicum (public law) carried out by a magistrate representing the will of the Roman people.[126] The pontiff was responsible for the consecration proper.[127]

cultus

Cicero defined religio as cultus deorum, "the cultivation of the gods."[128] The "cultivation" necessary to maintain a specific deity was that god's cultus, "cult," and required "the knowledge of giving the gods their due" (scientia colendorum deorum).[129] The noun cultus originates from the past participle of the verb colo, colere, colui, cultus, "to tend, take care of, cultivate," originally meaning "to dwell in, inhabit" and thus "to tend, cultivate land (ager); to practice agriculture," an activity fundamental to Roman identity even when Rome as a political center had become fully urbanized. Cultus is often translated as "cult", without the negative connotations the word may have in English, or with the Anglo-Saxon word "worship", but it implies the necessity of active maintenance beyond passive adoration. Cultus was expected to matter to the gods as a demonstration of respect, honor, and reverence; it was an aspect of the contractual nature of Roman religion (see do ut des).[130] St. Augustine echoes Cicero's formulation when he declares that "religio is nothing other than the cultus of God."[131]

decretum

Decreta (plural) were the binding explications of doctrine issued by the official priests on questions of religious practice and interpretation. They were preserved in written form and archived.[132] Compare responsum.

delubrum
A delubrum was a shrine. Varro says it was a building that housed the image of a deus, "god",[133] and emphasizes the human role in dedicating the statue.[134] According to Varro,[135] the delubrum was the oldest form of an aedes, a structure that housed a god. It is an ambiguous term for both the building and the surrounding area ubi aqua currit ("where water runs"), according to the etymology of the antiquarian Cincius.[136] Festus gives the etymology of delubrum as fustem delibratum, "stripped stake," that is, a tree deprived of its bark (liber) by a lightning bolt, as such trees in archaic times were venerated as gods. The meaning of the term later extended to denote the shrine built to house the stake.[137] Compare aedes, fanum, and templum.

Isidore connected the delubrum with the verb diluere, "to wash", describing it as a "spring-shrine", sometimes with annexed pool, where people would wash before entering, thus comparable to a Christian baptismal font.[138]

detestatio sacrorum
When a person passed from one gens to another, as for instance by adoption, he renounced the religious duties (sacra) he had previously held in order to assume those of the family he was entering.[139] The ritual procedure of detestatio sacrorum was enacted before a calate assembly.[140]

deus, dea, di, dii
Deus, "god"; dea, "goddess", plural deae; di or dii, "gods", plural, or "deities", of mixed gender. The Greek equivalent is theos, which the Romans translated with deus. Servius says[141] that deus or dea is a "generic term" (generale nomen) for all gods.[142] In his lost work Antiquitates rerum divinarum, assumed to have been based on pontifical doctrine,[143] Varro classified dii as certi, incerti, praecipui or selecti, i.e. "deities whose function could be ascertained",[144] those whose function was unknown or indeterminate, main or selected gods.[145] Compare divus. For etymological discussion, see Deus and Dyeus. See also List of Roman deities.

devotio

The devotio was an extreme form of votum in which a Roman general vowed to sacrifice his own life in battle along with the enemy to chthonic deities in exchange for a victory. The most extended description of the ritual is given by Livy, regarding the self-sacrifice of Decius Mus.[146] The English word "devotion" derives from the Latin. For another votum that might be made in the field by a general, see evocatio.

dies imperii

A Roman emperor's dies imperii was the date on which he assumed imperium, that is, the anniversary of his accession as emperor. The date was observed annually with renewed oaths of loyalty and vota pro salute imperatoris, vows and offerings for the wellbeing (salus) of the emperor. Observances resembled those on January 3, which had replaced the traditional vows made for the salus of the republic after the transition to one-man rule under Augustus. The dies imperii was a recognition that succession during the Empire might take place irregularly through the death or overthrow of an emperor, in contrast to the annual magistracies of the Republic when the year was designated by the names of consuls serving their one-year term.[147]

The dies Augusti or dies Augustus was more generally any anniversary pertaining to the imperial family, such as birthdays or weddings, appearing on official calendars as part of Imperial cult.[148] References to a dies Caesaris are also found, but it is unclear whether or how it differed from the dies Augusti.[149]

dies lustricus

The dies lustricus ("day of purification") was a rite carried out for the newborn on the eighth day of life for girls and the ninth day for boys. Little is known of the ritual procedure, but the child must have received its name on that day; funerary inscriptions for infants who died before their dies lustricus are nameless.[150] The youngest person found commemorated on a Roman tombstone by name was a male infant nine days old (or 10 days in Roman inclusive counting).[151] Because of the rate of infant mortality, perhaps as high as 40 percent,[152] the newborn in its first few days of life was held as in a liminal phase, vulnerable to malignant forces (see List of Roman birth and childhood deities). Socially, the child did not exist.[153] The dies lustricus may have been when the child received the bulla, the protective amulet that was put aside when a boy passed into adulthood.[154]

dies natalis
Page listing imperial natales by month from the 17th-century Codex Vaticanus Barberini latinus, based on the Calendar of Filocalus (354 AD)

A dies natalis was a birthday ("natal day"; see also dies lustricus above) or more generally the anniversary of a founding event. The Romans celebrated an individual's birthday annually, in contrast to the Greek practice of marking the date each month with a simple libation.[155] The Roman dies natalis was connected with the cult owed to the Genius.[156] A public figure might schedule a major event on his birthday: Pompeius Magnus ("Pompey the Great") waited seven months after he returned from his military campaigns in the East before he staged his triumph, so he could celebrate it on his birthday.[157] The coincidence of birthdays and anniversaries could have a positive or negative significance: news of Decimus Brutus's victory at Mutina was announced at Rome on his birthday, while Caesar's assassin Cassius suffered defeat at Philippi on his birthday and committed suicide.[158] Birthdays were one of the dates on which the dead were commemorated.[159]

The date when a temple was founded, or when it was rededicated after a major renovation or rebuilding, was also a dies natalis, and might be felt as the "birthday" of the deity it housed as well. The date of such ceremonies was therefore chosen by the pontiffs with regard to its position on the religious calendar. The "birthday" or foundation date of Rome was celebrated April 21, the day of the Parilia, an archaic pastoral festival.[160] As part of a flurry of religious reforms and restorations in the period from 38 BC to 17 AD, no fewer than fourteen temples had their dies natalis moved to another date, sometimes with the clear purpose of aligning them with new Imperial theology after the collapse of the Republic.[161]

The birthdays of emperors were observed with public ceremonies as an aspect of Imperial cult. The Feriale Duranum, a military calendar of religious observances, features a large number of imperial birthdays. Augustus shared his birthday (September 23) with the anniversary of the Temple of Apollo in the Campus Martius, and elaborated on his connection with Apollo in developing his special religious status.[158]

A birthday commemoration was also called a natalicium, which could take the form of a poem. Early Christian poets such as Paulinus of Nola adopted the natalicium poem for commemorating saints.[162] The day on which Christian martyrs died is regarded as their dies natalis; see Calendar of saints.

dies religiosus
According to Festus, it was wrong (nefas) to undertake any action beyond attending to basic necessities on a day that was religiosus on the calendar. On these days, there were to be no marriages, political assemblies, or battles. Soldiers were not to be enlisted, nor journeys started. Nothing new was to be started, and no religious acts (res divinae) performed. Aulus Gellius said that dies religiosi were to be distinguished from those that were nefasti.[163]

dies vitiosus
The phrase diem vitiare ("to vitiate a day") in augural practice meant that the normal activities of public business were prohibited on a given day, presumably by obnuntiatio, because of observed signs that indicated defect (morbus; see vitium).[164] Unlike a dies religiosus or a dies ater ("black day," typically the anniversary of a calamity), a particular date did not become permanently vitiosus, with one exception. Some Roman calendars (fasti) produced under Augustus and up to the time of Claudius[165] mark January 14 as a dies vitiosus, a day that was inherently "vitiated". January 14 is the only day to be marked annually and officially by decree of the Roman senate (senatus consultum) as vitiosus. LInderski calls this "a very remarkable innovation."[166] One calendar, the Fasti Verulani (c. 17–37 AD), explains the designation by noting it was the dies natalis of Mark Antony, which the Greek historian and Roman senator Cassius Dio says had been declared ἡμέρα μιαρά (hēmera miara) (= dies vitiosus) by Augustus.[167] The emperor Claudius, who was the grandson of Antony, rehabilitated the day.[168]

dirae
The adjective dirus as applied to an omen meant "dire, awful." It often appears in the feminine plural as a substantive meaning "evil omens." Dirae were the worst of the five kinds of signs recognized by the augurs, and were a type of oblative or unsought sign that foretold disastrous consequences. The ill-fated departure of Marcus Crassus for the invasion of Parthia was notably attended by dirae (see Ateius Capito). In the interpretive etymology of ancient writers,[169] dirae was thought to derive from dei irae, the grudges or anger of a god, that is, divine wrath. Dirae is an epithet for the Furies, and can also mean curses or imprecations,[170] particularly in the context of magic and related to defixiones (curse tablets).[171] In explaining why Claudius felt compelled to ban the religion of the druids, Suetonius[172] speaks of it as dirus, alluding to the practice of human sacrifice.[173]

disciplina Etrusca
The collective body of knowledge pertaining to the doctrine, ritual practices, laws, and science of Etruscan religion and cosmology was known as the disciplina Etrusca.[174] Divination was a particular feature of the disciplina. The Etruscan texts on the disciplina that were known to the Romans are of three kinds: the libri haruspicini (on haruspicy), the libri fulgurales (lightning), and the libri rituales (ritual).[175] Nigidius Figulus, the Late Republican scholar and praetor of 58 BC, was noted for his expertise in the disciplina.[176] Extant ancient sources on the Etrusca disciplina include Pliny the Elder, Seneca, Cicero, Johannes Lydus, Macrobius and Festus.

divus
The adjective divus, feminine diva, is usually translated as "divine." As a substantive, divus refers to a "deified" or divinized mortal. Both deus and divus derive from Indo-European *deywos, Old Latin deivos. Servius confirms[177] that deus is used for "perpetual deities" (deos perpetuos), but divus for people who become divine (divos ex hominibus factos). While this distinction is useful in considering the theological foundations of Imperial cult, it sometimes vanishes in practice, particularly in Latin poetry; Vergil, for instance, mostly uses deus and divus interchangeably. Varro and Ateius,[178] however, maintained that the definitions should be reversed.[179] See also Imperial cult: Divus, deus and the numen.

do ut des

The formula do ut des ("I give that you might give") expresses the reciprocity of exchange between human being and deity, reflecting the importance of gift-giving as a mutual obligation in ancient society and the contractual nature of Roman religion. The gifts offered by the human being take the form of sacrifice, with the expectation that the god will return something of value, prompting gratitude and further sacrifices in a perpetuating cycle.[180] The do ut des principle is particularly active in magic and private ritual.[181] Do ut des was also a judicial concept of contract law.[182]

In Pauline theology, do ut des was viewed as a reductive form of piety, merely a "business transaction", in contrast to the Christian God's unilateral grace (χάρις, charis).[183] Max Weber, in The Sociology of Religion, saw it as "a purely formalistic ethic."[184] In The Elementary Forms of Religious Life, however, Émile Durkheim regarded the concept as not merely utilitarian, but an expression of "the mechanism of the sacrificial system itself" as "an exchange of mutually invigorating good deeds between the divinity and his faithful."[185]

effatio

The verb effari, past participle effatus, means "to create boundaries (fines) by means of fixed verbal formulas."[186] Effatio is the abstract noun. It was one of the three parts of the ceremony inaugurating a templum (sacred space), preceded by the consulting of signs and the liberatio which "freed" the space from malign or competing spiritual influences and human effects.[187] A site liberatus et effatus was thus "exorcized and available."[188] The result was a locus inauguratus ("inaugurated site"), the most common form of which was the templum.[189] The boundaries had permanent markers (cippi or termini), and when these were damaged or removed, their effatio had to be renewed.[190]

evocatio

The "calling forth" or "summoning away" of a deity was an evocatio, from evoco, evocare, "summon." The ritual was conducted in a military setting either as a threat during a siege or as a result of surrender, and aimed at diverting the favor of a tutelary deity from the opposing city to the Roman side, customarily with a promise of better-endowed cult or a more lavish temple.[191] As a tactic of psychological warfare, evocatio undermined the enemy's sense of security by threatening the sanctity of its city walls (see pomerium) and other forms of divine protection. In practice, evocatio was a way to mitigate otherwise sacrilegious looting of religious images from shrines.[192]

Recorded examples of evocations include the transferral of Juno Regina ("Juno the Queen", originally Etruscan Uni) from Veii in 396 BC;[193] the ritual performed by Scipio Aemilianus in 146 BC at the defeat of Carthage, involving Tanit (Juno Caelestis);[194] and the dedication of a temple to an unnamed, gender-indeterminate deity at Isaura Vetus in Asia Minor in 75 BC.[195] Some scholars think that Vortumnus (Etruscan Voltumna) was brought by evocation to Rome in 264 BC as a result of M. Fulvius Flaccus's defeat of the Volsinii.[196] In Roman myth, a similar concept motivates the transferral of the Palladium from Troy to Rome, where it served as one of the pignora imperii, sacred tokens of Roman sovereignty.[197] Compare invocatio, the "calling on" of a deity.

Formal evocations are known only during the Republic.[198] Other forms of religious assimilation appear from the time of Augustus, often in connection with the establishment of the Imperial cult in the provinces.[199]

Evocatio, "summons", was also a term of Roman law without evident reference to its magico-religious sense.[200]

exauguratio

A site that had been inaugurated (locus inauguratus), that is, marked out through augural procedure, could not have its purpose changed without a ceremony of reversal.[201] Removing a god from the premises required the correct ceremonial invocations.[202] When Tarquin rebuilt the temple district on the Capitoline, a number of deities were dislodged by exauguratio, though Terminus and Juventas "refused" and were incorporated into the new structure.[203] A distinction between the exauguratio of a deity and an evocatio can be unclear.[204] The procedure was in either case rare, and was required only when a deity had to yield place to another, or when the site was secularized. It was not required when a site was upgraded, for instance, if an open-air altar were to be replaced with a temple building to the same god.[205]

The term could also be used for removing someone from a priestly office (sacerdotium).[206] Compare inauguratio.

eximius

An adjective, "choice, select," used to denote the high quality required of sacrificial victims: "Victims (hostiae) are called 'select' (eximiae) because they are selected (eximantur) from the herd and designated for sacrifice, or because they are chosen on account of their choice (eximia) appearance as offerings to divine entities (numinibus)."[207] The adjective here is synonymous with egregius, "chosen from the herd (grex, gregis)."[208] Macrobius says it is specifically a sacerdotal term and not a "poetic epithet" (poeticum ἐπίθετον).

exta

The exta were the entrails of a sacrificed animal, comprising in Cicero's enumeration the gall bladder (fel), liver (iecur), heart (cor), and lungs (pulmones).[209] The exta were exposed for litation (divine approval) as part of Roman liturgy, but were "read" in the context of the disciplina Etrusca. As a product of Roman sacrifice, the exta and blood are reserved for the gods, while the meat (viscera) is shared among human beings in a communal meal. The exta of bovine victims were usually stewed in a pot (olla or aula), while those of sheep or pigs were grilled on skewers. When the deity's portion was cooked, it was sprinkled with mola salsa (ritually prepared salted flour) and wine, then placed in the fire on the altar for the offering; the technical verb for this action was porricere.[210]

fanaticus

Fanaticus means "belonging to a fanum," a shrine or sacred precinct.[211] Fanatici as applied to people refers to temple attendants or devotees of a cult, usually one of the ecstatic or orgiastic religions such as that of Cybele (in reference to the Galli),[212] Bellona-Ma,[213] or perhaps Silvanus.[214] Inscriptions indicate that a person making a dedication might label himself fanaticus, in the neutral sense of "devotee".[215] Tacitus uses fanaticus to describe the troop of druids who attended on the Icenian queen Boudicca.[216] The word was often used disparagingly by ancient Romans in contrasting these more emotive rites to the highly scripted procedures of public religion,[217] and later by early Christians to deprecate religions other than their own; hence the negative connotation of "fanatic" in English.

Festus says that a tree struck by lightning is called fanaticus,[218] a reference to the Romano-Etruscan belief in lightning as a form of divine sign.[219] The Gallic bishop Caesarius of Arles, writing in the 5th century, indicates that such trees retained their sanctity even up to his own time,[220] and urged the Christian faithful to burn down the arbores fanatici. These trees either were located in and marked a fanum or were themselves considered a fanum. Caesarius is somewhat unclear as to whether the devotees regarded the tree itself as divine or whether they thought its destruction would kill the numen housed within it. Either way, even scarcity of firewood would not persuade them to use the sacred wood for fuel, a scruple for which he mocked them.[221]

fanum
A fanum is a plot of consecrated ground, a sanctuary,[222] and from that a temple or shrine built there.[223] A fanum may be a traditional sacred space such as the grove (lucus) of Diana Nemorensis, or a sacred space or structure for non-Roman religions, such as an Iseum or Mithraeum. Cognates such as Oscan fíisnú,[224] Umbrian fesnaf-e,[225] and Paelignian fesn indicate that the concept is shared by Italic peoples.[226] By the Augustan period, fanum, aedes, templum, and delubrum are scarcely distinguishable in usage,[227] but fanum was a more inclusive and general term.[228]

The fanum or ambulatory temple of Roman Gaul was often built over an originally Celtic religious site, and its plan was influenced by the ritual architecture of earlier Celtic sanctuaries. The masonry temple building of the Gallo-Roman period had a central space (cella) and a peripheral gallery structure, both square.[229] Romano-Celtic fana of this type are found also in Roman Britain.[230][better source needed]

The English word "profane" ultimately derives from Latin pro fano,[231] "before, i.e. outside, the temple", "In front of the sanctuary," hence not within sacred ground.

fata deorum

Fata deorum or the contracted form fata deum are the utterances of the gods; that is, prophecies.[232] These were recorded in written form, and conserved by the state priests of Rome for consultation. The fata are both "fate" as known and determined by the gods, or the expression of the divine will in the form of verbal oracles.[233] Fata deum is a theme of the Aeneid, Vergil's national epic of Rome.[234]

The Sibylline books (Fata Sibyllina or Libri Fatales), composed in Greek hexameters, are an example of written fata. These were not Roman in origin, but were believed to have been acquired in only partial form by Tarquin. They were guarded by the priesthood of the decemviri sacris faciundis ("ten men for carrying out sacred rites"), later fifteen in number (quindecimviri). No one read the books in their entirety; they were consulted only when needed. A passage was selected at random, and its relevance to the current situation was a matter of expert interpretation.[235] They were thought to contain fata rei publicae aeterna, "prophecies eternally valid for Rome".[236] They continued to be consulted throughout the Imperial period until the time of Christian hegemony. Augustus installed the Sibylline books in a special golden storage case under the statue of Apollo on the Palatine Hill.[237] The emperor Aurelian chastised the senate for succumbing to Christian influence and not consulting the books.[238] Julian consulted the books regarding his campaign against Persia, but departed before he received the unfavorable response of the college; Julian was killed, and the Palatine Temple of Apollo burned.[239]

fas

Fas is a central concept in Roman religion. Although translated in some contexts as "divine law,"[240] fas is more precisely that which is "religiously legitimate,"[241] or an action that is lawful in the eyes of the gods.[242] In public religion, fas est is declared before announcing an action required or allowed by Roman religious custom and by divine law.[243] Fas is thus both distinguished from and linked to ius (plural iura), "law, lawfulness, justice," as indicated by Vergil's often-cited phrase fas et iura sinunt, "fas and iura allow (it)," which Servius explains as "divine and human laws permit (it), for fas pertains to religion, iura to the human being."[244]

The Fasti Antiates Maiores, a pre-Julian calendar in a reconstructed drawing

In Roman calendars, days marked F are dies fasti, when it is fas to attend to the concerns of everyday life.[245] In non-specialized usage, fas est may mean generally "it is permissible, it is right."

The etymology of fas is debated. It is more commonly associated with the semantic field of the verb for, fari, "to speak,"[246] an origin pressed by Varro.[247] In other sources, both ancient and modern, fas is thought to have its origin in an Indo-European root meaning "to establish," along with fanum and feriae.[248] See also Fasti and nefas.

fasti
A record or plan of official and religiously sanctioned events. All state and societal business must be transacted on dies fasti, "allowed days". The fasti were the records of all details pertaining to these events. The word was used alone in a general sense or qualified by an adjective to mean a specific type of record. Closely associated with the fasti and used to mark time in them were the divisions of the Roman calendar.

The Fasti is also the title of a six-book poem by Ovid based on the Roman religious calendar. It is a major source for Roman religious practice, and was translated into English by J.G. Frazer.

felix
In its religious sense, felix means "blessed, under the protection or favor of the gods; happy." That which is felix has achieved the pax divom, a state of harmony or peace with the divine world.[249] It is rooted in Indo-European *dhe(i)l, meaning "happy, fruitful, productive, full of nourishment." Related Latin words include femina, "woman" (a person who provides nourishment or suckles);

felo, "to suckle"; and filius, "son" (a person suckled).[250] See also Felicitas, both an abstraction that expressed the quality of being felix and a deity of Roman state religion.

feria

A feria on the Roman calendar is a "free day", that is, a day in which no work was done. No court sessions were held, nor was any public business conducted. Employees were entitled to a day off, and even slaves were not obliged to work. These days were codified into a system of legal public holidays, the feriae publicae, which could be

- stativae, "stationary, fixed", holidays which recurred on the same date each year;

- conceptivae, recurring holidays for which the date depended on some other factor, usually the agrarian cycle. They included Compitalia, Paganalia, Sementivae and Latinae (compare the moveable Christian holiday of Easter);

- imperativae, one-off holidays ordered to mark a special occasion, established with an act of auctority of a magistrate.

In the Roman Rite a feria is a weekday on which the faithful are required to attend Mass, such as Ash Wednesday. The custom throughout Europe of holding markets on the same day gave rise to the word "fair" (Spanish Feria, Italian Fiera), from feria.

festus

In the Roman calendar, a dies festus is a festive or holy day, that is, a day dedicated to a deity or deities. On such days it was forbidden to undertake any profane activity, especially official or public business. All dies festi were thus nefasti. Some days, however, were not festi and yet might not be permissible as business days (fasti) for other reasons. The days on which profane activities were permitted are profesti.[251]

fetial

The fetiales, or fetial priests, formed a college whose main responsibilities pertained to Rome's international affairs. They made formal proclamations of peace and of war, and confirmed treaties. They also served as traveling diplomats or ambassadors. They were said to have been first created by the Aequian king Ferter Resius and introduced to Rome by Ancus Martius.[252]

finis
The finis (limit, border, boundary), plural fines, was an essential concept in augural practice, which was concerned with the definition of the templum. Establishing fines was an important part of a magistrate's duties.[253] Most scholars regard the finis as having been defined physically by ropes, trees, stones, or other markers, as were fields and property boundaries in general. It was connected with the god Terminus and his cult.[254]

flamen
The fifteen flamines formed part of the College of Pontiffs. Each flamen served as the high priest to one of the official deities of Roman religion, and led the rituals relating to that deity. The flamines were regarded as the most ancient among the sacerdotes, as many of them were assigned to deities who dated back to the prehistory of Latium and whose significance had already become obscure by classical times.

The archaic nature of the flamens is indicated by their presence among Latin tribes. They officiated at ceremonies with their head covered by a velum and always wore a filamen, thread, in contrast to public rituals conducted by Greek rite (ritus graecus) which were established later. Ancient authors derive the word flamen from the custom of covering the head with the filamen, but it may be cognate to Vedic Brahman. The distinctive headgear of the flamen was the apex.

focus
The circular bowl in the capital (top) of an ara (altar), where hot coals are placed during sacrifices. Correctly done, a slab of turf is placed on the capital of the focus, the center pushed down into the focus, and the coals are lit on top of the turf in the turf indention.

Fratres Arvales
The "Brothers of the Field" were a college of 12 priests and one flamen whose duties were concerned with agriculture and farming.

They were the most ancient religious sodalitas: according to tradition they were created by Romulus, but probably predated the foundation of Rome.

Gabinus
The adjective gabinus describes an element of religion that the Romans attributed to practices from Gabii, a town of Latium with municipal status about 12 miles from Rome. The incorporation of Gabinian traditions indicates their special status under treaty with Rome. See cinctus gabinus and ager gabinus.[83]

hostia
The hostia was the offering, usually an animal, in a sacrifice. The word is used interchangeably with victima by Ovid and others, but some ancient authors attempt to distinguish between the two.[255] Servius says[256] that the hostia is sacrificed before battle, the victima afterward, which accords with Ovid's etymology in relating the "host" to the "hostiles" or enemy (hostis), and the "victim" to the "victor."[257]

The difference between the victima and hostia is elsewhere said to be a matter of size, with the hostia smaller (minor).[258] Hostiae were also classified by age: lactentes were young enough to be still taking milk, but had reached the age to be purae; bidentes had reached two years of age[259] or had the two longer (bi-) incisor teeth (dentes) that are an indication of age.[260]

Hostiae could be classified in various ways. A hostia consultatoria was an offering for the purpose of consulting with a deity, that is, in order to know the will of a deity; the hostia animalis, to increase the force (mactare) of the deity.[261]

The victim might also be classified by occasion and timing. The hostia praecidanea was an "anticipatory offering" made the day before a sacrifice.[262] It was an advance atonement "to implore divine indulgence" should an error be committed on the day of the formal sacrifice.[263] A preliminary pig was offered as a praecidanea the day before the harvest began.[264] The hostia praecidanea was offered to Ceres a day in advance of a religious festival (sacrum, before the beginning of the harvest) in expiation for negligences in the duties of piety towards the deceased.[clarification needed] The hostia praesentanaea was a pig offered to Ceres during a part of the funeral rites conducted within sight of the deceased, whose family was thereby ritually absolved.[265] A hostia succidanea was offered at any rite after the first sacrifice had failed owing to a ritual impropriety (vitium).[266] Compare piaculum, an expiatory offering.

Hostia is the origin of the word "host" for the Eucharistic sacrament of the Western Church; see Sacramental bread: Catholic Church. See also votum, a dedication or a vow of an offering to a deity as well as that which fulfilled the vow.

inauguratio
A rite performed by augurs by which the concerned person received the approval of the gods for his appointment or their investiture. The augur would ask for the appearance of certain signs (auspicia impetrativa) while standing beside the appointee on the auguraculum. In the Regal period, inauguratio concerned the king and the major sacerdotes.[267] After the establishment of the Republic, the rex sacrorum,[268] the three flamines maiores,[269] the augurs, and the pontiffs[270] all had to be inaugurated.

The term may also refer to the ritual establishing of the augural templum and the tracing of the wall of a new city.[citation needed]

indigitamenta
The indigitamenta were lists of gods maintained by the College of Pontiffs to assure that the correct divine names were invoked for public prayers. It is sometimes unclear whether these names represent distinct minor entities, or epithets pertaining to an aspect of a major deity's sphere of influence, that is, an indigitation, or name intended to "fix" or focalize the local action of the god so invoked.[271] Varro is assumed to have drawn on direct knowledge of the lists in writing his theological books, as evidenced by the catalogues of minor deities mocked by the Church Fathers who used his work[272] as a reference.[273] Another source is likely to have been the non-extant work De indigitamentis of Granius Flaccus, Varro's contemporary.[274] Not to be confused with the di indigetes.

invocatio

The addressing of a deity in a prayer or magic spell is the invocatio, from invoco, invocare, "to call upon" the gods or spirits of the dead.[275] The efficacy of the invocatio depends on the correct naming of the deity, which may include epithets, descriptive phrases, honorifics or titles, and arcane names. The list of names (nomina) is often extensive, particularly in magic spells; many prayers and hymns are composed largely of invocations.[276] The name is invoked in either the vocative[277] or the accusative case.[278] In specialized usage pertaining to augural procedure, invocatio is a synonym for precatio, but specifically aimed at averting mala, evil occurrences.[279] Compare evocatio.

The equivalent term in ancient Greek religion is epiklesis.[280] Pausanias distinguished among the categories of theonym proper, poetic epithet, the epiclesis of local cult, and an epiclesis that might be used universally among the Greeks.[281] Epiclesis remains in use by some Christian churches for the invocation of the Holy Spirit during the Eucharistic prayer.

ius

Ius is the Latin word for justice, right, equity, fairness and all which came to be understood as the sphere of law. It is defined in the opening words of the Digesta with the words of Celsus as "the art of that which is good and fair" and similarly by Paulus as "that which is always just and fair".[282] The polymath Varro and the jurist Gaius[283] consider the distinction between divine and human ius essential[284] but divine order is the source of all laws, whether natural or human, so the pontifex is considered the final judge (iudex) and arbiter.[285] The jurist Ulpian defines jurisprudence as "the knowledge of human and divine affairs, of what is just and unjust".[286]

ius divinum

"Sacred law"[287] or "divine law," particularly in regard to the gods' rights pertaining to their "property," that which is rightfully theirs.[288] Recognition of the ius divinum was fundamental to maintaining right relations between human beings and their deities. The concern for law and legal procedure that was characteristic of ancient Roman society was also inherent in Roman religion.[289] See also pax deorum.

lectisternium
The lectisternium was a ceremonial meal offered to deities represented by clothed statues or figures. The word derives from lectum sternere, "to spread (or "drape") a couch."

lex
The word lex (plural leges) derives from the Indo-European root *leg, as do the Latin verbs lego, legare, ligo, ligare ("to appoint, bequeath") and lego, legere (" to gather, choose, select, discern, read": cf. also Greek verb legein "to collect, tell, speak"), and the abstract noun religio.[290] Parties to legal proceedings and contracts bound themselves to observance by the offer of sacrifice to witnessing deities.[291]

Even though the word lex underwent the frequent semantic shift in Latin towards the legal area, its original meaning of set, formulaic words was preserved in some instances. Some cult formulae are leges: an augur's request for particular signs that would betoken divine approval in an augural rite (augurium), or in the inauguration of magistrates and some sacerdotes is named legum dictio.[292] The formula quaqua lege volet ("by whatever lex, i.e. wording he wishes") allowed a cult performer discretion in his choice of ritual words.[293] The leges templi regulated cult actions at various temples.[294][295]

In civil law, ritualized sets of words and gestures known as legis actiones were in use as a legal procedure in civil cases; they were regulated by custom and tradition (mos maiorum) and were thought to involve protection of the performers from malign or occult influences.[296]

libatio
Libation (Latin libatio, Greek spondai) was one of the simplest religious acts, regularly performed in daily life. At home, a Roman who was about to drink wine would pour the first few drops onto the household altar.[297] The drink offering might also be poured on the ground or at a public altar. Milk and honey, water, and oil were also used.[298]

liberatio

The liberatio (from the verb liberare, "to free") was the "liberating" of a place (locus) from "all unwanted or hostile spirits and of all human influences," as part of the ceremony inaugurating the templum (sacred space). It was preceded by the consulting of signs and followed by the effatio, the creation of boundaries (fines).[299] A site liberatus et effatus was "exorcized and available" for its sacred purpose.[300]

libri augurales

The augural books (libri augurales) represented the collective, core knowledge of the augural college. Some scholars[301] consider them distinct from the commentarii augurum (commentaries of the augurs) which recorded the collegial acts of the augurs, including the decreta and responsa.[302] The books were central to the practice of augury. They have not survived, but Cicero, who was an augur himself, offers a summary in De Legibus[303] that represents "precise dispositions based certainly on an official collection edited in a professional fashion."[304]

libri pontificales

The libri pontificales (pontifical books) are core texts in Roman religion, which survive as fragmentary transcripts and commentaries. They may have been partly annalistic, part priestly; different Roman authors refer to them as libri and commentarii (commentaries), described by Livy as incomplete "owing to the long time elapsed and the rare use of writing" and by Quintillian as unintelligibly archaic and obscure. The earliest were credited to Numa, second king of Rome, who was thought to have codified the core texts and principles of Rome's religious and civil law (ius divinum and ius civile).[305] See also commentarii pontificum.

litatio

In animal sacrifice, the litatio followed on the opening up of the body cavity for the inspection of the entrails (inspicere exta). Litatio was not a part of divinatory practice as derived from the Etruscans (see extispicy and Liver of Piacenza), but a certification according to Roman liturgy of the gods' approval. If the organs were diseased or defective, the procedure had to be restarted with a new victim (hostia). The importance of litatio is illustrated by an incident in

176 BC[306] when the presiding consuls attempted to sacrifice an ox, only to find that its liver had been inexplicably consumed by a wasting disease. After three more oxen failed to pass the test, the senate's instructions were to keep sacrificing bigger victims until litatio could be obtained.[307] The point was not that those sacrificing had to make sure that the victim was perfect inside and out; rather, the good internal condition of the animal was evidence of divine acceptance of the offering. The need for the deity to approve and accept (litare) underscores that the reciprocity of sacrifice (do ut des) was not to be taken for granted.[308]

lituus
The distinctively curved staff of an augur, or a similarly curved war trumpet. On Roman coins, the lituus is frequently accompanied by a ritual jug or pitcher to indicate that either the moneyer or person honored on the obverse was an augur.

lucus
In religious usage, a lucus was a grove or small wooded area considered sacred to a divinity. Entrance might be severely restricted: Paulus[309] explains that a capitalis lucus was protected from human access under penalty of death. Leges sacratae (laws for the violation of which the offender is outlawed)[310] concerning sacred groves have been found on cippi at Spoleto in Umbria and Lucera in Apulia.[311] See also nemus.

ludi
Ludi were games held as part of religious festivals, and some were originally sacral in nature. These included chariot racing and the venatio, or staged animal-human blood sport that may have had a sacrificial element.

Luperci
The "wolf priests", organized into two colleges and later three, who participated in the Lupercalia. The most famous Lupercus was Mark Antony.

lustratio
A ritual of purification which was held every five years under the jurisdiction of censors in Rome. Its original meaning was purifying

by washing in water (Lat. lustrum from verb luo, "I wash in water"). The time elapsing between two subsequent lustrations being of five years the term lustrum took up the meaning of a period of five year.[312]

manubia

Manubia is a technical term of the Etruscan discipline, and refers to the power of a deity to wield lightning, represented in divine icons by a lightning bolt in the hand. It may be either a Latinized word from Etruscan or less likely a formation from manus, "hand," and habere, "to have, hold."[313] It is not apparently related to the more common Latin word manubiae meaning "booty (taken by a general in war)."[314] Seneca uses the term in an extended discussion of lightning.[315] Jupiter, as identified with Etruscan Tinia,[316] held three types of manubiae[317] sent from three different celestial regions.[318] Stefan Weinstock describes these as:

1. mild, or "perforating" lightning;

2. harmful or "crushing" lightning, which is sent on the advice of the twelve Di Consentes and occasionally does some good;

3. destructive or "burning" lightning, which is sent on the advice of the di superiores et involuti (hidden gods of the "higher" sphere) and changes the state of public and private affairs.[319]

Jupiter makes use of the first type of beneficial lightning to persuade or dissuade.[320] Books on how to read lightning were one of the three main forms of Etruscan learning on the subject of divination.[321]

miraculum

One of several words for portent or sign, miraculum is a non-technical term that places emphasis on the observer's response (mirum, "a wonder, marvel").[322] Livy uses the word miraculum, for instance, to describe the sign visited upon Servius Tullius as a child, when divine flames burst forth from his head and the royal household witnessed the event.[323] Compare monstrum, ostentum, portentum, and prodigium.

Miraculum is the origin of the English word "miracle." Christian writers later developed a distinction between miracula, the true forms of which were evidence of divine power in the world, and mere mirabilia, things to be marveled at but not resulting from God's intervention. "Pagan" marvels were relegated to the category of mirabilia and attributed to the work of demons.[324]

mola salsa
Flour mixed with salt was sprinkled on the forehead and between the horns of sacrificial victims, as well as on the altar and in the sacred fire. This mola salsa (salted flour) was prepared ritually from toasted wheat or emmer, spelt, or barley by the Vestals, who thus contributed to every official sacrifice in Rome.[325] Servius uses the words pius and castus to describe the product.[326] The mola was so fundamental to sacrifice that "to put on the mola" (Latin immolare) came to mean "to sacrifice." Its use was one of the numerous religious traditions ascribed to Numa, the Sabine second king of Rome.[327]

monstrum
A monstrum is a sign or portent that disrupts the natural order as evidence of divine displeasure.[328] The word monstrum is usually assumed to derive, as Cicero says, from the verb monstro, "show" (compare English "demonstrate"), but according to Varro it comes from moneo, "warn."[329] Because a sign must be startling or deviant to have an impact, monstrum came to mean "unnatural event"[330] or "a malfunctioning of nature."[331] Suetonius said that "a monstrum is contrary to nature <or exceeds the nature> we are familiar with, like a snake with feet or a bird with four wings."[332] The Greek equivalent was teras.[333] The English word "monster" derived from the negative sense of the word. Compare miraculum, ostentum, portentum, and prodigium.

In one of the most famous uses of the word in Latin literature, the Augustan poet Horace calls Cleopatra a fatale monstrum, something deadly and outside normal human bounds.[334] Cicero calls Catiline monstrum atque prodigium[335] and uses the phrase several times to insult various objects of his attacks as depraved and beyond the human pale. For Seneca, the monstrum is, like tragedy, "a visual and horrific revelation of the truth."[336]

mundus

Literally "the world", also a pit supposedly dug and sealed by Romulus as part of Rome's foundation rites. Its interpretation is problematic; it was normally sealed, and was ritually opened only on three occasions during the year. Still, in the most ancient Fasti, these days were marked C(omitiales)[337] (days when the Comitia met) suggesting the idea that the whole ritual was a later Greek import.[338] However Cato[disambiguation needed] and Varro as quoted by Macrobius considered them religiosi.[339] When opened, the pit served as a cache for offerings to underworld deities, particularly Ceres, goddess of the fruitful earth. It offered a portal between the upper and lower worlds; its shape was said to be an inversion of the dome of the upper heavens.[340]

nefandum

An adjective derived from nefas (following). The gerund of verb fari, to speak, is commonly used to form derivate or inflected forms of fas. See Vergil's fandi as genitive of fas. This use has been invoked to support the derivation of fas from IE root *bha, Latin fari.

nefas

Anything or action contrary to divine law and will is nefas (in archaic legalese, ne (not) ... fas).[341] Nefas forbids a thing as religiously and morally offensive, or indicates a failure to fulfill a religious duty.[342] It might be nuanced as "a religious duty not to", as in Festus' statement that "a man condemned by the people for a heinous action is sacer" — that is, given over to the gods for judgment and disposal — "it is not a religious duty to execute him, but whoever kills him will not be prosecuted".[343]

Livy records that the patricians opposed legislation that would allow a plebeian to hold the office of consul on the grounds that it was nefas: a plebeian, they claimed, would lack the arcane knowledge of religious matters that by tradition was a patrician prerogative. The plebeian tribune Gaius Canuleius, whose lex it was, retorted that it was arcane because the patricians kept it secret.[344]

nefastus
Usually found with dies (singular or plural), as dies nefasti, days on which official transactions were forbidden on religious grounds. See also nefas, fasti and fas.

nemus
Nemus, plural nemora, was one of four Latin words that meant "forest, woodland, woods." Lucus is more strictly a sacred grove,[345] as defined by Servius as "a large number of trees with a religious significance",[346] and distinguished from the silva, a natural forest; saltus, territory that is wilderness; and a nemus, an arboretum that is not consecrated.[347] In Latin poetry, a nemus is often a place conducive to poetic inspiration, and particularly in the Augustan period takes on a sacral aura.[348]

Named nemora include:
The nemus of Anna Perenna.[349]
Nemus Caesarum, dedicated to the memory of Augustus's grandsons Gaius and Lucius.[350]
The nemus Aricinum sacred to Diana, Egeria and Virbius.

nuntiatio
The chief responsibility of an augur was to observe signs (observatio) and to report the results (nuntiatio).[351] The announcement was made before an assembly. A passage in Cicero states that the augur was entitled to report on the signs observed before or during an assembly and that the magistrates had the right to watch for signs (spectio) as well as make the announcement (nuntiatio) prior to the conducting of public business, but the exact significance of Cicero's distinction is a matter of scholarly debate.[352]

obnuntiatio
Obnuntiatio was a declaration of unfavorable signs by an augur in order to suspend, cancel or postpone a proposed course of action. The procedure could be carried out only by an official who had the right to observe omens (spectio).[353] The only source for the term is Cicero, a conservative politician and himself an augur, who refers to it in several speeches as a religious bulwark against popularist politicians and tribunes. Its details and workings are unknown; it

may have derived from a radical intervention into traditional augural law of a civil Lex Aelia Fufia,[clarification needed] proposed by dominant traditionalists in an attempt to block the passing of popular laws and used from around the 130s BC. Legislation by Clodius as Tribune of the plebs in 58 BC was aimed at ending the practice,[354] or at least curtailing its potential for abuse; obnuntiatio had been exploited the previous year as an obstructionist tactic by Julius Caesar's consular colleague Bibulus. That the Clodian law had not deprived all augurs or magistrates of the privilege is indicated by Mark Antony's use of obnuntatio in early 44 BC to halt the consular election.[355]

observatio
Observatio was the interpretation of signs according to the tradition of the "Etruscan discipline", or as preserved in books such as the libri augurales. A haruspex interpreted fulgura (thunder and lightning) and exta (entrails) by observatio. The word has three closely related meanings in augury: the observing of signs by an augur or other diviner; the process of observing, recording, and establishing the meaning of signs over time; and the codified body of knowledge accumulated by systematic observation, that is, "unbending rules" regarded as objective, or external to an individual's observation on a given occasion. Impetrative signs, or those sought by standard augural procedure, were interpreted according to observatio; the observer had little or no latitude in how they might be interpreted. Observatio might also be applicable to many oblative or unexpected signs. Observatio was considered a kind of scientia, or "scientific" knowledge, in contrast to coniectura, a more speculative "art" or "method" (ars) as required by novel signs.[356]

omen
An omen, plural omina, was a sign intimating the future, considered less important to the community than a prodigium but of great importance to the person who heard or saw it.[357]

Omens could be good or bad. Unlike prodigies, bad omens were never expiated by public rites but could be reinterpreted, redirected or otherwise averted. Sometime around 282 BC, a diplomatic insult formally "accepted as omen" was turned against Tarentum and helped justify its conquest. After a thunderclap cost Marcellus his very brief consulship (215 BC) he took care to avoid sight of possible bad omens that might affect his plans.[358] Bad omens could be more actively dealt with, by countersigns or spoken formulae. Before his campaign against Perseus of Macedon, the consul L Aemilius Paullus was said to have heard of the death of Perseus, his daughter's puppy. He accepted the omen and defeated King Perseus at the Battle of Pydna (168 BC).[359]

In 217 BC the consul Flaminius "disregarded his horse's collapse, the chickens, and yet other omens, before his disaster at Lake Trasimene".[360] Licinius Crassus took ship for Syria despite an ominous call of "Cauneas!" ("Caunean figs!"), which might be heard as "Cave ne eas!" ("Beware, don't go!")'. He was killed on campaign. Cicero saw these events as merely coincidental; only the credulous could think them ominous.[361] though by his time, politicians, military magnates and their supporters actively circulated tales of excellent omens that attended their births and careers.

See also abominari and signum.

ostentarium
One form of arcane literature was the ostentarium, a written collection describing and interpreting signs (ostenta).[362] Tarquitius Priscus wrote an Ostentarium arborarium, a book on signs pertaining to trees, and an Ostentarium Tuscum, presumably translations of Etruscan works.[363] Pliny cites his contemporary Umbricius Melior for an ostentarium aviarium, concerning birds.[364] They were consulted until late antiquity; in the 4th century, for instance, the haruspices consulted the books of Tarquitius before the battle that proved fatal to the emperor Julian — according to Ammianus Marcellinus, because he failed to heed them.[365] Fragments of ostentaria survive as quotations in other literary works.[366]

ostentum
According to Varro, an ostentum is a sign so called because it shows (ostendit) something to a person.[367] Suetonius specified that "an ostentum shows itself to us without possessing a solid body and affects both our eyes and ears, like darkness or a light at

night."[368] In his classic work on Roman divination, Auguste Bouché-Leclercq thus tried to distinguish theoretical usage of ostenta and portenta as applying to inanimate objects, monstra to biological signs, and prodigia for human acts or movements, but in non-technical writing the words tend to be used more loosely as synonyms.[369]

The theory of ostenta, portenta and monstra constituted one of the three branches of interpretation within the disciplina Etrusca, the other two being the more specific fulgura (thunder and lightning) and exta (entrails). Ostenta and portenta are not the signs that augurs are trained to solicit and interpret, but rather "new signs", the meaning of which had to be figured out through ratio (the application of analytical principles) and coniectura (more speculative reasoning, in contrast to augural observatio).[370]

ordo sacerdotum

A religious hierarchy implied by the seating arrangements of priests (sacerdotes) at sacrificial banquets. As "the most powerful", the rex sacrorum was positioned next to the gods, followed by the Flamen Dialis, then the Flamen Martialis, then the Flamen Quirinalis and lastly, the Pontifex Maximus.[371] The ordo sacerdotum observed and preserved ritual distinctions between divine and human power. In the human world, the Pontifex Maximus was the most influential and powerful of all sacerdotes.

paludatus

Paludatus (masculine singular, plural paludati) is an adjective meaning "wearing the paludamentum,"[372] the distinctive attire of the Roman military commander. Varro[373] and Festus say that any military ornament could be called a paludamentum, but other sources indicate that the cloak was primarily meant. According to Festus, paludati in the augural books meant "armed and adorned" (armati, ornati).[374] As the commander crossed from the sacred boundary of Rome (pomerium), he was paludatus, adorned with the attire he would wear to lead a battle and for official business.[375] This adornment was thus part of the commander's ritual investiture with imperium.[376] It followed upon the sacrifices and vows the commander offered up on the Capitol, and was concomitant with his possession of the auspices for war.[377]

Festus notes elsewhere that the "Salian virgins", whose relation to the Salian priests is unclear, performed their rituals paludatae,[378] dressed in military garb.[379]

pax deorum
Pax, though usually translated into English as "peace," was a compact, bargain or agreement.[380] In religious usage, the harmony or accord between the divine and human was the pax deorum or pax divom ("the peace of the gods" or "divine peace").[381] Pax deorum was only given in return for correct religious practice. Religious error (vitium) and negligence led to divine disharmony and ira deorum (the anger of the gods).

piaculum
A piaculum is an expiatory sacrifice, or the victim used in the sacrifice; also, an act requiring expiation.[382]

Because Roman religion was contractual (do ut des), a piaculum might be offered as a sort of advance payment; the Arval Brethren, for instance, offered a piaculum before entering their sacred grove with an iron implement, which was forbidden, as well as after.[383] The pig was a common victim for a piaculum.[384] The Augustan historian Livy says P. Decius Mus is "like" a piaculum when he makes his vow to sacrifice himself in battle (see devotio).[385]

pius
The origin of the English word "pious", pius is found in Volscian as pihom estu, Umbrian as pihaz (a past participle equivalent to Latin piatum) and Oscan as pehed, from the Proto-Indo-European root *q(u)ei-.[386] In Latin and other Italic languages, the word seems to have meant "that which is in accord with divine law." Later it was used to designate actions respectful of divine law and even people who acted with respect towards gods and godly rules. The pius person "strictly conforms his life to the ius divinum.[387] "Dutiful" is often a better translation of the adjective than "pious."[388] Pius is a regular epithet of the Roman founding hero Aeneas in Vergil's Aeneid.[389] See also pietas, the related abstract noun.

pietas
Pietas, from which English "piety" derives, was the devotion that

bound a person to the gods, to the Roman state, and to his family. It was the outstanding quality of the Roman hero Aeneas, to whom the epithet pius is applied regularly throughout the Aeneid.

pollucere
A verb of unknown etymology meaning "to consecrate."[390]

pontifex
The pontifex was a priest of the highest-ranking college. The chief among the pontifices was the Pontifex Maximus. The word has been considered as related to pons, bridge, either because of the religious meaning of the pons Sublicius and its ritual use[391] (which has a parallel in Thebae and in its gephiarioi) or in the original IE meaning of way.[392] Pontifex in this case would be the opener of the way corresponding to the Vedic adharvayu, the only active and moving sacerdos in the sacrificial group who takes his title from the figurative designation of lithurgy as a way. Another hypothesis[393] considers the word as a loan from Sabine, language in which it would mean member of a college of five people, from Osco-Umbrian ponte, five. This explanation takes into account the fact that the college was established by Sabine king Numa Pompilius and the institution is Italic: the expressions pontis and pomperias found in the Iguvine Tablets may denote a group or division of five or by five. The pontifex would thence be a member of a sacrificial college known as pomperia (Latin quinio).[394]

popa
The popa was one of the lesser-rank officiants at a sacrifice. In depictions of sacrificial processions, he carries a mallet or axe with which to strike the animal victim. Literary sources in late antiquity say that the popa was a public slave.[395] See also victimarius.

porricere
The verb porricere had the specialized religious meaning "to offer as a sacrifice," especially to offer the sacrificial entrails (exta) to the gods.[396] Both exta porricere and exta dare referred to the process by which the entrails were cooked, cut into pieces, and burnt on the altar. The Arval Brethren used the term exta reddere, "to return the entrails," that is, to render unto the deity what has already been given as due.[397]

portentum
A portentum is a kind of sign interpreted by a haruspex, not an augur, and by means of coniectura rather than observatio. Portentum is a close but not always exact synonym of ostentum, prodigium, and monstrum.[398] Cicero uses portentum frequently in his treatise De divinatione, where it seems to be a generic word for prodigies.[399] The word could also refer in non-technical usage to an unnatural occurrence without specific religious significance; for instance, Pliny calls an Egyptian with a pair of non-functional eyes on the back of his head a portentum.[400] Varro derives portentum from the verb portendit because it portends something that is going to happen.[401]

In the schema of A. Bouché-Leclercq, portenta and ostenta are the two types of signs that appear in inanimate nature, as distinguished from the monstrum (a biological singularity), prodigia (the unique acts or movements of living beings), and a miraculum, a non-technical term that emphasizes the viewer's reaction.[402] The sense of portentum has also been distinguished from that of ostentum by relative duration of time, with the ostentum of briefer manifestation.[403]

Although the English word "portent" derives from portentum and may be used to translate it, other Latin terms such as ostentum and prodigium will also be found translated as "portent."[404] Portentum offers an example of an ancient Roman religious term modified for Christian usage; in the Christian theology of miracles, a portentum occurring by the will of the Christian God could not be regarded as contrary to nature (contra naturam), thus Augustine specified that if such a sign appeared to be unnatural, it was only because it was contrary to nature as known (nota) by human beings.[405]

precatio
The precatio was the formal addressing of the deity or deities in a ritual. The word is related by etymology to prex, "prayer" (plural preces), and usually translated as if synonymous. Pliny says that the slaughter of a sacrificial victim is ineffectual without precatio, the recitation of the prayer formula.[406] Priestly texts that were collections of prayers were sometimes called precationes.[407]

Two late examples of the precatio are the Precatio Terrae Matris ("The Prayer of Mother Earth") and the Precatio omnium herbarum ("Prayer of All the Herbs"), which are charms or carmina written metrically,[408] the latter attached to the medical writings attributed to Antonius Musa.[409] Dirae precationes were "dire" prayers, that is, imprecations or curses.[410]

In augural procedure, precatio is not a prayer proper, but a form of invocation (invocatio) recited at the beginning of a ceremony or after accepting an oblative sign. The precatio maxima was recited for the augurium salutis, the ritual conducted by the augurs to obtain divine permission to pray for Rome's security (salus).[411]

In legal and rhetorical usage, precatio was a plea or request.[412]

prex
Prex, "prayer", usually appears in the plural, preces. Within the tripartite structure that was often characteristic of formal ancient prayer, preces would be the final expression of what is sought from the deity, following the invocation and a narrative middle.[413] A legitimate request is an example of bonae preces, "good prayer."[414] Tacitae preces are silent or sotto voce prayers as might be used in private ritual or magic; preces with a negative intent are described with adjectives such as Thyesteae ("Thyestean"), funestae ("deadly"), infelices (aimed at causing unhappiness), nefariae,[415] or dirae.[416]

In general usage, preces could refer to any request or entreaty. The verbal form is precor, precari, "pray, entreat." The Umbrian cognate is persklu, "supplication." The meaning may be "I try and obtain by uttering appropriate words what is my right to obtain." It is used often in association with quaeso in expressions such as te precor quaesoque, "I pray and beseech you", or prece quaesit, "he seeks by means of prayer."[417] In Roman law of the Imperial era, preces referred to a petition addressed to the emperor by a private person.[418]

prodigium
Prodigia (plural) were unnatural deviations from the predictable order of the cosmos. A prodigium signaled divine displeasure at a

religious offense and must be expiated to avert more destructive expressions of divine wrath. Compare ostentum and portentum, signs denoting an extraordinary inanimate phenomenon, and monstrum and miraculum, an unnatural feature in humans.

Prodigies were a type of auspicia oblativa; that is, they were "thrust upon" observers, not deliberately sought.[419] Suspected prodigies were reported as a civic duty. A system of official referrals filtered out those that seemed patently insignificant or false before the rest were reported to the senate, who held further inquiry; this procedure was the procuratio prodigiorum. Prodigies confirmed as genuine were referred to the pontiffs and augurs for ritual expiation.[420] For particularly serious or difficult cases, the decemviri sacris faciundis could seek guidance and suggestions from the Sibylline Books.[421]

The number of confirmed prodigies rose in troubled times. In 207 BC, during one of the worst crises of the Punic Wars, the senate dealt with an unprecedented number, the expiation of which would have involved "at least twenty days" of dedicated rites.[422] Major prodigies that year included the spontaneous combustion of weapons, the apparent shrinking of the sun's disc, two moons in a daylit sky, a cosmic battle between sun and moon, a rain of red-hot stones, a bloody sweat on statues, and blood in fountains and on ears of corn. These were expiated by the sacrifice of "greater victims".

The minor prodigies were less warlike but equally unnatural; sheep became goats; a hen become a cock, and vice-versa. The minor prodigies were duly expiated with "lesser victims". The discovery of a hermaphroditic four-year-old child was expiated by its drowning[423] and a holy procession of 27 virgins to the temple of Juno Regina, singing a hymn to avert disaster; a lightning strike during the hymn rehearsals required further expiation.[424] Religious restitution was proved only by Rome's victory.[425]
The expiatory burial of living human victims in the Forum Boarium followed Rome's defeat at Cannae in the same wars. In Livy's account, Rome's victory follows its discharge of religious duties to the gods.[426] Livy remarked the scarcity of prodigies in his own day as a loss of communication between gods and men. In the later

Republic and thereafter, the reporting of public prodigies was increasingly displaced by a "new interest in signs and omens associated with the charismatic individual."[427]

profanum
Literally, "in front of the shrine", therefore not within a sacred precinct; not belonging to the gods but to humankind.

propitius; praepetes (aves)
An adjective of augural terminology meaning favourable. From pro- before and petere seek, but originally fly. It implies a kind of favourable pattern in the flight of birds, i.e. flying before the person who is taking the auspices. Synonym secundus.[428]

pulvinar
The pulvinar (plural pulvinaria) was a special couch used for displaying images of the gods, that they might receive offerings at ceremonies such as the lectisternium or supplicatio.[429] In the famous lectisternium of 217 BC, on orders of the Sibylline books, six pulvinaria were arranged, each for a divine male-female pair.[430] By extension, pulvinar can also mean the shrine or platform housing several of these couches and their images. At the Circus Maximus, the couches and images of the gods were placed on an elevated pulvinar to "watch" the games.

regina sacrorum
The wife of the rex sacrorum, who served as a high priestess with her own specific religious duties.

religio
The word religio originally meant an obligation to the gods, something expected by them from human beings or a matter of particular care or concern as related to the gods.[431] In this sense, religio might be translated better as "religious scruple" than with the English word "religion".[432] One definition of religio offered by Cicero is cultus deorum, "the proper performance of rites in veneration of the gods."[433]

Religio among the Romans was not based on "faith", but on knowledge, including and especially correct practice.[434] Religio (plural religiones) was the pious practice of Rome's traditional cults, and was a cornerstone of the mos maiorum,[435] the traditional social norms that regulated public, private, and military life. To the Romans, their success was self-evidently due to their practice of proper, respectful religio, which gave the gods what was owed them and which was rewarded with social harmony, peace and prosperity.

religiosus

Religiosus was something pertaining to the gods or marked out by them as theirs, as distinct from sacer, which was something or someone given to them by humans. Hence, a graveyard was not primarily defined as sacer but a locus religiosus, because those who lay within its boundaries were considered belonging to the di Manes.[440] Places struck by lightning were taboo[441] because they had been marked as religiosus by Jupiter himself.[442] See also sacer and sanctus.

res divinae

Res divinae were "divine affairs," that is, the matters that pertained to the gods and the sphere of the divine in contrast to res humanae, "human affairs."[443] Rem divinam facere, "to do a divine thing," simply meant to do something that pertained to the divine sphere, such as perform a ceremony or rite. The equivalent Etruscan term is ais(u)na.[444]

The distinction between human and divine res was explored in the multivolume Antiquitates rerum humanarum et divinarum, one of the chief works of Varro (1st century BC). It survives only in fragments but was a major source of traditional Roman theology for the Church Fathers. Varro devoted 25 books of the Antiquitates to res humanae and 16 to res divinae. His proportional emphasis is deliberate, as he treats cult and ritual as human constructs.[445] Varro divides res divinae into three kinds:

the mythic theology of the poets, or narrative elaboration;

the natural theology of the philosophers, or theorizing on divinity among the intellectual elite;

the civil theology concerned with the relation of the state to the divine.

The schema is Stoic in origin, though Varro has adapted it for his own purposes.[446]

Res divinae is an example of ancient Roman religious terminology that was appropriated for Christian usage; for St. Augustine, res divina is a "divine reality" as represented by a sacrum signum ("sacred sign") such as a sacrament.[447]

responsum
Responsa (plural) were the "responses," that is, the opinions and arguments, of the official priests on questions of religious practice and interpretation. These were preserved in written form and archived.[448] Compare decretum.

rex sacrorum
The rex sacrorum was a senatorial priesthood[449] reserved for patricians. Although in the historical era the Pontifex Maximus was the head of Roman state religion, Festus says[450] that in the ranking of priests, the rex sacrorum was of highest prestige, followed by the flamines maiores.[451]

ritus
Although ritus is the origin of the English word "rite" via ecclesiastical Latin, in classical usage ritus meant the traditional and correct manner (of performance), that is, "way, custom". Festus defines it as a specific form of mos: "Ritus is the proven way (mos) in the performance of sacrifices." The adverb rite means "in good form, correctly."[452] This original meaning of ritus may be compared to the concept of ṛtá ("visible order", in contrast to dhāman, dhārman) in Vedic religion, a conceptual pairing analogous to Latin fas and ius.[453]

For Latin words meaning "ritual" or "rite", see sacra, caerimoniae, and religiones.[454]

ritus graecus
A small number of Roman religious practices and cult innovations

were carried out according to "Greek rite" (ritus graecus), which the Romans characterized as Greek in origin or manner. A priest who conducted ritu graeco wore a Greek-style fringed tunic, with his head bare (capite aperto) or laurel-wreathed. By contrast, in most rites of Roman public religion, an officiant wore the distinctively Roman toga, specially folded to cover his head (see capite velato). Otherwise, "Greek rite" seems to have been a somewhat indefinite category, used for prayers uttered in Greek, and Greek methods of sacrifice within otherwise conventionally Roman cult.

Roman writers record elements of ritus graecus in the cult to Hercules at Rome's Ara Maxima, which according to tradition was established by the Greek king Evander even before the city of Rome was founded at the site. It thus represented one of the most ancient Roman cults. "Greek" elements were also found in the Saturnalia held in honor of the Golden Age deity Saturn, and in certain ceremonies of the Ludi saeculares. A Greek rite to Ceres (ritus graecus cereris) was imported from Magna Graecia and added to her existing Aventine cult in accordance with the Sibylline books, ancient oracles written in Greek. Official rites to Apollo are perhaps "the best illustration of the Graecus ritus in Rome."

The Romans regarded ritus graecus as part of their own mos maiorum (ancestral tradition), and not as novus aut externus ritus, novel or foreign rite. The thorough integration and reception of rite labeled "Greek" attests to the complex, multi-ethnic origins of Rome's people and religious life.[455]

sacellum
Sacellum, a diminutive from sacer ("belonging to a god"),[456] is a shrine. Varro and Verrius Flaccus give explanations that seem contradictory, the former defining a sacellum in its entirety as equivalent to a cella,[457] which is specifically an enclosed space, and the latter insisting that a sacellum had no roof.[458] "The sacellum," notes Jörg Rüpke, "was both less complex and less elaborately defined than a temple proper."[459] Each curia had its own sacellum.[460]

sacer
See also: homo sacer

Sacer describes a thing or person given to the gods, thus "sacred" to them. Human beings had no legal or moral claims on anything sacer. Sacer could be highly nuanced; Varro associates it with "perfection".[461] Through association with ritual purity, sacer could also mean "sacred, untouchable, inviolable".

Anything not sacer was profanum: literally, "in front of (or outside) the shrine", therefore not belonging to it or the gods. A thing or person could be made sacer (consecrated), or could revert from sacer to profanum (deconsecrated), only through lawful rites (resecratio) performed by a pontiff on behalf of the state.[462] Part of the ver sacrum sacrificial vow of 217 BC stipulated that animals dedicated as sacer would revert to the condition of profanum if they died through natural cause or were stolen before the due sacrificial date. Similar conditions attached to sacrifices in archaic Rome.[463] A thing already owned by the gods or actively marked out by them as divine property was distinguished as religiosus, and hence could not be given to them or made sacer.[464][465]

Persons judged sacer under Roman law were placed beyond further civil judgment, sentence and protection; their lives, families and properties were forfeit to the gods. A person could be declared sacer who harmed a plebeian tribune, failed to bear legal witness,[466] failed to meet his obligations to clients, or illicitly moved the boundary markers of fields.[467] It was not a religious duty (fas) to execute a homo sacer, but he could be killed with impunity.[468][469]

Dies sacri ("sacred days") were nefasti, meaning that the ordinary human affairs permitted on dies profani (or fasti) were forbidden.

Sacer was a fundamental principle in Roman and Italic religions. In Oscan, related forms are sakoro, "sacred," and sakrim, "sacrificial victim". Oscan sakaraklum is cognate with Latin sacellum, a small shrine, as Oscan sakarater is with Latin sacratur, consecrare, "consecrated". The sacerdos is "one who performs a sacred action" or "renders a thing sacred", that is, a priest.[470]

A sacerdos (plural sacerdotes, a word of either masculine or feminine gender) was any priest or priestess, from *sakro-dho-ts, "the one who does the sacred act."[471] There was no priestly caste in ancient Rome, and in some sense every citizen was a priest in that he presided over the domestic cult of his household. Senators, magistrates, and the decurions of towns performed ritual acts, though they were not sacerdotes per se.[472] The sacerdos was one who held the title usually in relation to a specific deity or temple.[473] See also collegium and flamen.

sacra
Sacra (neuter plural of sacer) are the traditional cults, either publica or privata, both of which were overseen by the College of Pontiffs.

The sacra publica were those performed on behalf of the whole Roman people or its major subdivisions, the tribes and curiae. They included the sacra pro populo, "rites on behalf of the Roman people," i.e., all the feriae publicae of the Roman calendar year and the other feasts that were regarded of public interest, including those pertaining to the hills of Rome,[474] to the pagi and curiae, and to the sacella, "shrines".[475] The establishment of the sacra publica is ascribed to king Numa Pompilius, but many are thought to be of earlier origin, even predating the founding of Rome. Thus Numa may be seen as carrying out a reform and a reorganization of the sacra in accord with his own views and his education.[476] Sacra publica were performed at the expense of the state, according to the dispositions left by Numa, and were attended by all the senators and magistrates.[477]

Sacra privata were particular to a gens, to a family, or to an individual, and were carried out at the expense of those concerned. Individuals had sacra on dates peculiar to them, such as birthdays, the dies lustricus, and at other times of their life such as funerals and expiations, for instance of fulgurations.[478] Families had their own sacra in the home or at the tombs of their ancestors, such as those pertaining to the Lares, Manes and Penates of the family, and the Parentalia. These were regarded as necessary and imperishable, and the desire to perpetuate the family's sacra was among the reasons for adoption in adulthood.[479] In some cases, the state assumed the expenses even of sacra privata, if they were regarded as important to the maintenance of the Roman religious system as a whole; see sacra gentilicia following.

sacra gentilicia

Sacra gentilicia were the private rites (see sacra above) that were particular to a gens ("clan"). These rites are related to a belief in the shared ancestry of the members of a gens, since the Romans placed a high value on both family identity and commemorating the dead.[480] During the Gallic siege of Rome, a member of the gens Fabia risked his life to carry out the sacra of his clan on the Quirinal Hill; the Gauls were so impressed by his courageous piety that they allowed him to pass through their lines.[481] The Fabian sacra were performed in Gabine dress by a member of the gens who was possibly named a flamen.[482] There were sacra of Minerva in the care of the Nautii, and rites of Apollo that the Iulii oversaw.[483] The Claudii had recourse to a distinctive "propudial pig" sacrifice (propudialis porcus, "pig of shame") by way of expiation when they neglected any of their religious obligations.[484]

Roman practices of adoption, including so-called "testamentary adoption" when an adult heir was declared in a will, were aimed at perpetuating the sacra gentilicia as well as preserving the family name and property.[485] A person adopted into another family usually renounced the sacra of his birth (see detestatio sacrorum) in order to devote himself to those of his new family.[486]

Sacra gentilicia sometimes acquired public importance, and if the gens were in danger of dying out, the state might take over their maintenance. One of the myths attached to Hercules' time in Italy explained why his cult at the Ara Maxima was in the care of the patrician gens Potitia and the gens Pinaria; the diminution of these families by 312 BC caused the sacra to be transferred to the keeping of public slaves and supported with public funding.[487]

sacra municipalia

The sacra of an Italian town or community (municipium) might be perpetuated under the supervision of the Roman pontiffs when the locality was brought under Roman rule. Festus defined municipalia sacra as "those owned originally, before the granting of Roman citizenship; the pontiffs desired that the people continue to observe them and to practice them in the way (mos) they had been accustomed to from ancient times."[488] These sacra were regarded as preserving the core religious identity of a particular people.[489]

sacramentum
Sacramentum is an oath or vow that rendered the swearer sacer, "given to the gods," in the negative sense if he violated it.[490] Sacramentum also referred to a thing that was pledged as a sacred bond, and consequently forfeit if the oath were violated.[491] Both instances imply an underlying sacratio, act of consecration.

In Roman law, a thing given as a pledge or bond was a sacramentum. The sacramentum legis actio was a sum of money deposited in a legal procedure[492] to affirm that both parties to the litigation were acting in good faith.[493] If correct law and procedures had been followed, it could be assumed that the outcome was iustum, right or valid. The losing side had thus in effect committed perjury, and forfeited his sacramentum as a form of piaculum; the winner got his deposit back. The forfeited sacramentum was normally allotted by the state to the funding of sacra publica.[494]

The sacramentum militare (also as militum or militiae) was the oath taken by soldiers in pledging their loyalty to the consul or emperor. The sacramentum that renders the soldier sacer helps explain why he was subjected to harsher penalties, such as execution and corporal punishment, that were considered inappropriate for civilian citizens, at least under the Republic.[495] In effect, he had put his life on deposit, a condition also of the fearsome sacramentum sworn by gladiators.[496] In the later empire, the oath of loyalty created conflict for Christians serving in the military, and produced a number of soldier-martyrs.[497] Sacramentum is the origin of the English word "sacrament", a transition in meaning pointed to by Apuleius's use of the word to refer to religious initiation.[498]

The sacramentum as pertaining to both the military and the law indicates the religious basis for these institutions. The term differs from iusiurandum, which is more common in legal application, as for instance swearing an oath in court. A sacramentum establishes a direct relation between the person swearing (or the thing pledged in the swearing of the oath) and the gods; the iusiurandum is an oath of good faith within the human community that is in accordance with ius as witnessed by the gods.[499]

sacrarium

A sacrarium was a place where sacred objects (sacra) were stored or deposited for safekeeping.[500] The word can overlap in meaning with sacellum, a small enclosed shrine; the sacella of the Argei are also called sacraria.[501] In Greek writers, the word is hierophylakion (hiero-, "sacred" + phylakion, something that safeguards).[502] See sacellum for a list of sacraria.

The sacrarium of a private home lent itself to Christian transformation, as a 4th-century poem by Ausonius demonstrates;[503] in contemporary Christian usage, the sacrarium is a "special sink used for the reverent disposal of sacred substances" (see piscina).[504]

sacrificium

An event or thing dedicated to the gods for their disposal. The offer of sacrifice is fundamental to religio. See also Sacer and Religion in ancient Rome: Sacrifice.

sacrosanctus

An adjective first introduced to define the inviolability of the function (potestas) of the tribunes of the plebs and of other magistrates sanctioned by law leges Valeriae Horatiae in 449 BC, mentioned by Livy III 55, 1. It seems the sacrality of the function the tribune had already been established in earlier times through a religio and a sacramentum,[505] however it obliged only the contracting parties. In order to become a rule that obliged everybody it had to be sanctioned through a sanctio that was not only civil but religious as well: the trespasser was to be declared sacer, his family and property sold.[506] Sacer would thus design the religious compact, sanctus the law. According to other passages in Livy, the law was not approved by some jurists of the time who maintained that only those who infringed the commonly recognized divine laws (id (or Iovi corr. Mueller) sacrum sanciti) could fall into the category of those to be declared sacri. In fact in other places Livy states that only the potestas and not the person of the tribune was defined as sacrosancta.[507] The word is used in Livy III 19, 10 by the critics of the law in this way: "These people postulate they themselves should be sacrosancti, they who do not hold even gods for sacred and saint?"[508]

The meaning of the word is given as guaranteed by an oath by H. Fugier, however Morani thinks it would be more appropriate to understand the first part of the compound as a consequence of the second: sanxit tribunum sacrum the tribune is sanctioned by the law as sacer. This kind of word composition based on an etymological figure has parallels in other IE languages in archaic constructions.

Salii
The Salii were the "leaping" priests of Mars, so called because of the ritual dance they performed with sacred shields (ancilia).

sancio
A verb meaning to ratify a compact and put it under the protection of a sanctio, penalty, sanction. The formation and original meaning of the verb are debated. Some scholars think it is derived by the IE stem root *sak (the same of sacer) through a more recent way of word formation, i.e. by the insertion of a nasal n infix and the suffix -yo, such as Lithuanian iung-iu from IE stem *yug. Thence sancio would mean to render something sacer, i.e. belonging to the gods in the sense of having their guarantee and protection.[509] Some think it is a derivation from the theonym Sancus, the god of the ratification of foedera and protection of good faith, from the root sancu- plus suffix -io as inquio>incio.[510] In such case the verb would mean an act that reflects or conforms to the function of this god, i.e. the ratifying and guaranteeing compacts.

sanctus
Sanctus, an adjective formed on the past participle of verb sancio, describes that which is "established as inviolable" or "sacred", most times in a sense different to that of sacer and religiosus. In fact its original meaning would be that which is protected by a sanction (sanctio). It is connected to the name of the Umbrian or Sabine founder-deity Sancus (in Umbrian Sancius) whose most noted function was the ratifying and protecting of compacts (foedera).[511] The Roman jurist Ulpian distinguishes sanctus as "neither sacred (sacer) nor profane (profanum) ... nor religiosus."[512] Gaius writes that a building dedicated to a god is sacrum, a town's wall and gate are res sanctae because they belong "in some way" to divine law, and a graveyard is religiosus because it

is relinquished to the di Manes. Thus some scholars think that it should originally be a concept related to space i.e. concerning inaugurated places, because they enjoyed the armed protection (sanctio) of the gods.[513][514] Various deities, objects, places and people – especially senators and magistrates – can be sanctus. Claudia Quinta is described as a sanctissima femina (most virtuous woman) and Cato the Younger as a sanctus civis (a morally upright citizen).[515][516] See also sanctuary.

Later the epithet sanctus is given to many gods including Apollo Pythius by Naevius, Venus and Tiberinus by Ennius and Livy: Ennius renders the Homeric dia theaoon as sancta dearum; in the early Imperial era, Ovid describes Terminus, the god who sanctifies land boundaries, as sanctus[517] and equates sancta with augusta (august).[518] The original spacial connotation of the word is still reflected in its use as an epithet of the river Tiber and of god Terminus that was certainly ancient: borders are sancti by definition and rivers used to mark borders. Sanctus as referred to people thus over time came to share some of the sense of Latin castus (morally pure or guiltless), pius (pious), and none of the ambiguous usages attached to sacer and religiosus.

In ecclesiastical Latin, sanctus is the word for saint, but even in the Christian era it continues to appear in epitaphs for people who had not converted to Christianity.[519]

servare de caelo
Literally, "to watch (for something) from the sky"; that is, to observe the templum of the sky for signs that might be interpreted as auspices. Bad omens resulted in a report of obnuntiatio.[520]

signum
A signum is a "sign, token or indication".[521] In religious use, signum provides a collective term for events or things (including signs and symbols) that designate divine identity, activity or communication, including prodigia, auspicia, omina, portenta and ostenta.

silentium
Silence was generally required in the performance of every religious ritual.[522] The ritual injunction favete linguis, "be favourable with

your tongues," meant "keep silent." In particular, silence assured the ritual correctness and the absence of vitia, "faults," in the taking of the auspices.[523] It was also required in the nomination (dictio) of the dictator.[524]

sodalitas
A sodalitas was a form of voluntary association or society. Its meaning is not necessarily distinct from collegium in ancient sources, and is found also in sodalicium, "fraternity."[525] The sodalis is a member of a sodalitas, which describes the relationship among sodales rather than an institution. Examples of priestly sodalitates are the Luperci, fetiales, Arval brothers and Titii; these are also called collegia, but that they were a kind of confraternity is suggested by the distinctive convivial song associated with some.[526] An association of sodales might also form a burial society, or make religious dedications as a group; inscriptions record donations made by women for the benefit of sodales.[527] Roman Pythagoreans such as Nigidius Figulus formed sodalicia,[528] with which Ammianus Marcellinus compared the fellowship (sodalicia consortia) of the druids in Gallo-Roman culture.[529] When the cult of Cybele was imported to Rome, the eunuchism of her priests the galli discouraged Roman men from forming an official priesthood; instead, they joined sodalitates to hold banquets and other forms of traditional Roman cultus in her honor.[530]

The sodalitates are thought to originate as aristocratic brotherhoods with cultic duties, and their existence is attested as early as the late 6th or early 5th century BC. The Twelve Tables regulated their potential influence by forbidding them to come in conflict with public law (ius publicum).[531] During the 60s BC, certain forms of associations were disbanded by law as politically disruptive, and in Ciceronian usage sodalitates may refer either to these subversive organizations or in a religious context to the priestly fraternities.[532] See also Sodales Augustales. For the Catholic concept, see sodality.

spectio
Spectio ("watching, sighting, observation") was the seeking of omens through observing the sky, the flight of birds, or the feeding

of birds. Originally only patrician magistrates and augurs were entitled to practice spectio, which carried with it the power to regulate assemblies and other aspects of public life, depending on whether the omens were good or bad.[533] See also obnuntiatio.

sponsio
Sponsio is a formal, religiously guaranteed obligation. It can mean both betrothal as pledged by a woman's family, and a magistrate's solemn promise in international treaties on behalf of the Roman people.[534]

The Latin word derives from a Proto-Indo-European root meaning a libation of wine offered to the gods, as does the Greek verb spendoo and the noun spondai, spondas, and Hittite spant-.[535] In Greek it also acquired the meaning "compact, convention, treaty" (compare Latin foedus), as these were sanctioned with a libation to the gods on an altar. In Latin, sponsio becomes a legal contract between two parties, or sometimes a foedus between two nations.

In legal Latin the sponsio implied the existence of a person who acted as a sponsor, a guarantor for the obligation undertaken by somebody else. The verb is spondeo, sponsus. Related words are sponsalia, the ceremony of betrothal; sponsa, fiancée; and sponsus, both the second-declension noun meaning a husband-to-be and the fourth declension abstract meaning suretyship.[536] The ceremonial character of sponsio suggests[537] that Latin archaic forms of marriage were, like the confarreatio of Roman patricians, religiously sanctioned. Dumézil proposed that the oldest extant Latin document, the Duenos inscription, could be interpreted in light of sponsio.[538]

superstitio
Superstitio was excessive devotion and enthusiasm in religious observance, in the sense of "doing or believing more than was necessary",[539] or "irregular" religious practice that conflicted with Roman custom. "Religiosity" in its pejorative sense may be a better translation than "superstition", the English word derived from the Latin.[540] Cicero defined superstitio as the "empty fear of the gods" (timor inanis deorum) in contrast to the properly pious cultivation of the gods that constituted lawful religio,[541] a view

that Seneca expressed as "religio honors the gods, superstitio wrongs them."[542] Seneca wrote an entire treatise on superstitio, known to St. Augustine but no longer extant.[543] Lucretius's famous condemnation of what is often translated as "Superstition" in his Epicurean didactic epic De rerum natura is actually directed at Religio.[544]

Before the Christian era, superstitio was seen as a vice of individuals. Practices characterized as "magic" could be a form of superstitio as an excessive and dangerous quest for personal knowledge.[545] By the early 2nd century AD, religions of other peoples that were perceived as resistant to religious assimilation began to be labeled by some Latin authors as superstitio, including druidism, Judaism, and Christianity.[546] Under Christian hegemony, religio and superstitio were redefined as a dichotomy between Christianity, viewed as true religio, and the superstitiones or false religions of those who declined to convert.[547]

supplicatio
Supplicationes are days of public prayer when the men, women, and children of Rome traveled in procession to religious sites around the city praying for divine aid in times of crisis. A suplicatio can also be a thanksgiving after the receipt of aid.[548] Supplications might also be ordered in response to prodigies; again, the population as a whole wore wreaths, carried laurel twigs, and attended sacrifices at temple precincts throughout the city.[549]

tabernaculum
See auguraculum. The origin of the English word "tabernacle."

templum
A templum was the sacred space defined by an augur for ritual purposes, most importantly the taking of the auspices, a place "cut off" as sacred: compare Greek temenos, from temnein to cut.[550] It could be created as temporary or permanent, depending on the lawful purpose of the inauguration. Auspices and senate meetings were unlawful unless held in a templum; if the senate house (Curia) was unavailable, an augur could apply the appropriate religious formulae to provide a lawful alternative.[551]

To create a templum, the augur aligned his zone of observation (auguraculum, a square, portable surround) with the cardinal points of heaven and earth. The altar and entrance were sited on the east-west axis: the sacrificer faced east. The precinct was thus "defined and freed" (effatum et liberatum).[552] In most cases, signs to the augur's left (north) showed divine approval and signs to his right (south), disapproval.[553] Temple buildings of stone followed this ground-plan and were sacred in perpetuity.[554]

Rome itself was a kind of templum, with the pomerium as sacred boundary and the arx (citadel), and Quirinal and Palatine hills as reference points whenever a specially dedicated templum was created within. Augurs had authority to establish multiple templa beyond the pomerium, using the same augural principles.

verba certa
Verba certa (also found nearly as often with the word order certa verba) are the "exact words" of a legal or religious formula, that is, the words as "set once and for ever, immutable and unchangeable." Compare certae precationes, fixed prayers of invocation, and verba concepta, which in both Roman civil law and augural law described a verbal formula that could be "conceived" flexibly to suit the circumstances.[555] With their emphasis on exact adherence, the archaic verba certa[556] are a magico-religious form of prayer.[557] In a ritual context, prayer (prex) was not a form of personal spontaneous expression, but a demonstration that the speaker knew the correct thing to say. Words were regarded as having power; in order to be efficacious, the formula had to be recited accurately, in full, and with the correct pronunciation. To reduce the risk of error (vitium), the magistrate or priest who spoke was prompted from the text by an assistant.[558]

verba concepta
In both religious and legal usage, verba concepta ("preconceived words") were verbal formulas that could be adapted for particular circumstances. Compare verba certa, "fixed words." Collections of verba concepta would have been part of the augural archives. Varro preserves an example, albeit textually vexed, of a formula for founding a templum.[559]

In the legal sense, concepta verba (the phrase is found with either word order) were the statements crafted by a presiding praetor for the particulars of a case.[560] Earlier in the Roman legal system, the plaintiff had to state his claim within a narrowly defined set of fixed phrases (certa verba); in the Mid Republic, more flexible formulas allowed a more accurate description of the particulars of the issue under consideration. But the practice may have originated as a kind of "dodge," since a praetor was liable to religious penalties if he used certa verba for legal actions on days marked nefastus on the calendar.[561]

St. Augustine removed the phrase verba concepta from its religious and legal context to describe the cognitive process of memory: "When a true narrative of the past is related, the memory produces not the actual events which have passed away but words conceived (verba concepta) from images of them, which they fixed in the mind like imprints as they passed through the senses."[562] Augustine's conceptualizing of memory as verbal has been used to elucidate the Western tradition of poetry and its shared origins with sacred song and magical incantation (see also carmen), and is less a departure from Roman usage than a recognition of the original relation between formula and memory in a pre-literate world.[563] Some scholars see the tradition of stylized, formulaic language as the verbal tradition from which Latin literature develops, with concepta verba appearing in poems such as Carmen 34 of Catullus.[564]

ver sacrum
The "sacred spring" was a ritual migration.

victima
The victima was the animal offering in a sacrifice, or very rarely a human. The victim was subject to an examination (probatio victimae) by a lower-rank priest (pontifex minor) to determine whether it met the criteria for a particular offering.[565] With some exceptions, male deities received castrated animals. Goddesses were usually offered female victims, though from around the 160s AD the goddess Cybele was given a bull, along with its blood and testicles, in the Taurobolium. Color was also a criterion: white for the upper deities, dark for chthonic, red for Vulcan and at the Robigalia. A

sacred fiction of sacrifice was that the victim had to consent, usually by a nod of the head perhaps induced by the victimarius holding the halter. Fear, panic, and agitation in the animal were bad omens.[566][567]

The word victima is used interchangeably with hostia by Ovid and others, but some ancient authors attempt to distinguish between the two.[568] Servius says[569] that the hostia is sacrificed before battle, the victima afterward, which accords with Ovid's etymology of "victim" as that which has been killed by the right hand of the "victor" (with hostia related to hostis, "enemy").[570]

The difference between the victima and hostia is elsewhere said to be a matter of size, with the victima larger (maior).[258] See also piaculum and votum.

victimarius

The victimarius was an attendant or assistant at a sacrifice who handled the animal.[571] Using a rope, he led the pig, sheep, or bovine that was to serve as the victim to the altar. In depictions of sacrifice, a victimarius called the popa carries a mallet or axe with which to strike the victima. Multiple victimarii are sometimes in attendance; one may hold down the victim's head while the other lands the blow.[572] The victimarius severed the animal's carotid with a ritual knife (culter), and according to depictions was offered a hand towel afterwards by another attendant. He is sometimes shown dressed in an apron (limus). Inscriptions show that most victimarii were freedmen, but literary sources in late antiquity say that the popa was a public slave.[573]

vitium

A mistake made while performing a ritual, or a disruption of augural procedure, including disregarding the auspices, was a vitium ("defect, imperfection, impediment"). Vitia, plural, could taint the outcome of elections, the validity of laws, and the conducting of military operations. The augurs issued an opinion on a given vitium, but these were not necessarily binding. In 215 BC the newly elected plebeian consul M. Claudius Marcellus resigned when the augurs and the senate decided that a thunderclap expressed divine disapproval of his election.[574] The original meaning of the semantic root in vitium may have been "hindrance", related to the verb vito, vitare, "to go out of the way"; the adjective form vitiosus can mean "hindering", that is, "vitiating, faulty."[575]

vitulari
A verb meaning chanting or reciting a formula with a joyful intonation and rhythm.[576] The related noun Vitulatio was an annual thanksgiving offering carried out by the pontiffs on 8 July, the day after the Nonae Caprotinae. These were commemorations of Roman victory in the wake of the Gallic invasion. Macrobius says vitulari is the equivalent of Greek paianizein (παιανίζειν), "to sing a paean", a song expressing triumph or thanksgiving.[577]

votum
In a religious context, votum, plural vota, is a vow or promise made to a deity. The word comes from the past participle of voveo, vovere; as the result of the verbal action "vow, promise", it may refer also to the fulfillment of this vow, that is, the thing promised. The votum is thus an aspect of the contractual nature of Roman religion, a bargaining expressed by do ut des, "I give that you might give."[578]

References

1. Robert Schilling, "The Decline and Survival of Roman Religion", Roman and European Mythologies (University of Chicago Press, 1992, from the French edition of 1981), p. 110 online.
2. Jerzy Linderski, "The Augural Law", Aufstieg und Niedergang der römischen Welt II.16 (1986), p. 2266, note 472.
3. J. Bayet Histoire politique et psychologique de la religion romaine Paris, 1969, p. 55.
4. Synonyms for abominari include improbare, execrari, and refutare, with instances noted by Cicero, De divinatione 1.46; Livy, 1.7, 5.55, 9.14, and 29.29; and Servius, note to Aeneid 5.530; Auguste Bouché-Leclercq, Histoire de la divination dans l'antiquité (Jérôme

Millon, 2003 reprint, originally published 1883), pp. 136–137.
5. Robert Schilling, "Roman Gods", *Roman and European Mythologies* (University of Chicago Press, 1992, from the French edition of 1981), p. 72.
6. John W. Stamper, *The Architecture of Roman Temples: The Republic to the Middle Empire* (Cambridge University Press, 2005), p. 10.
7. Mary Beard, Simon Price, John North, *Religions of Rome: Volume 1, a History*, illustrated, Cambridge University Press, 1998. p. 22.
8. Morris H. Morgan, *Notes on Vitruvius* Harvard Studies in Classical Philology 17 (1906, pp. 12–14).
9. Vitruvius, *De architectura* 1.2.5; John E. Stambaugh, "The Functions of Roman Temples," *Aufstieg und Niedergang der römischen Welt* II.16.1 (1978), p. 561.
10. Andrew Lintott, *The Constitution of the Roman Republic* (Oxford: Clarendon Press, 1999, reprinted 2002), pp. 129–130; Karl Loewenstein, *The Governance of Rome* (Martinus Nijhoff, 1973), p. 62.
11. Lawrence Richardson, *A New Topographical Dictionary of Ancient Rome* (Johns Hopkins University Press, 1992), pp. 80–81 on Ceres, p. 151 on Flora; see also Barbette Stanley Spaeth, *The Roman Goddess Ceres* (University of Texas Press, 1996), p. 86ff.
12. J. Linderski Augural law in ANRW pp.[citation needed]
13. Varro, *De lingua latina* 5.33. See also Roger D. Woodard, *Indo-European Sacred Space: Vedic and Roman Cult* (Chicago 2006), pp. 236-238. The treaty was preserved in the temple of Semo Sancus.
14. For usage of the term peregrinus, compare also the status of a person who was peregrinus.
15. Varro, *De lingua latina* 5.33.
16. Livy 27.5.15 and 29.5; P. Catalano, Aspetti spaziali del sistema giuridico-religioso romano, *Aufstieg und Niedergang der römischen Welt* II.16.1 (1978), pp. 529 ff.
17. Mary Beard, J.A. North, and S.R.F. Price, *Religions of Rome: A Sourcebook* (Cambridge University Press, 1998), p. 83.
18. Ulrike Egelhaaf-Gaiser, "Roman Cult Sites: A Pragmatic Approach," in *A Companion to Roman Religion* (Blackwell, 2007), p. 206.
19. Karl Galinsky, *Augustan Culture: An Interpretive Introduction* (Princeton University Press, 1996), p. 141.
20. Macrobius III 20, 2, quoting Veranius in his lost work *De verbis*

pontificalibus.
21. Macrobius III 12
22. Quoted by Macrobius, Saturnalia 3.20.
23. These are the modern English identifications of Robert A. Kaster in his translation of the Saturnalia for the Loeb Classical Library; in Latin, alternum sanguinem filicem, ficum atram, quaeque bacam nigram nigrosque fructus ferunt, itemque acrifolium, pirum silvaticum, pruscum rubum sentesque. On the textual issues raised by the passage, see Kaster, Studies on the Text of Macrobius' Saturnalia (Oxford University Press, 2010), p. 48.
24. Vergil Aeneid II 717-720; Macrobius III 1, 1; E. Paratore Virgilio, Eneide I, Milano, 1978, p. 360 and n. 52; Livy V 22, 5; R. G. Austin P. Vergili Maronis Aeneidos liber secundus Oxford 1964, p. 264
25. William Warde Fowler, The Religious Experience of the Roman People (London, 1922), p. 209.
26. John Scheid, An Introduction to Roman Religion (Indiana University Press, 2003), pp. 113-114; Jerzy Linderski, "The Augural Law", Aufstieg und Niedergang der römischen Welt II.16 (1986), pp. 2164-2288, especially p. 2174 on the military auguraculum.
27. Robert Schilling, Roman and European Mythologies (University of Chicago Press, 1992), p. 95.
28. In the view of Wissowa, as cited by Jerzy Linderski, "The Augural Law", Aufstieg und Niedergang der römischen Welt II.16 (1986), p. 2150.
29. Linderski, "The Augural Law," pp. 2241 et passim.
30. Linderski, "The Augural Law," p. 2237.
31. Schilling, "Augurs and Augury," Roman and European Mythologies, p. 115.
32. Veit Rosenberger, "Republican nobiles: Controlling the res publica," in A Companion to Roman Religion (Blackwell, 2007), p. 299.
33. Schilling, p. 115.
34. Linderski, "The Augural Law," p. 2196, especially note 177, citing Servius, note to Aeneid 3.89.
35. See Livy, Book VI 41, for the words of Appius Claudius Crassus on why election to the consulate should be restricted to patricians on these grounds.
36. Linderski, "The Augural Law," pp. 2294-2295; U. Coli, Regnum Rome 1959.
37. Pliny, Natural History 18.14.: "when ears of wheat have already

formed but are still in the sheaths".

38. Liv. VI 41; X 81; IV 6

39. With the passing of the Lex Ogulnia. The first plebeian consul was elected in 367 BC in consequence of the leges Liciniae Sextiae.

40. L. Schmitz, entry on "Augur," in A Dictionary of Greek and Roman Antiquities (London 1875).

41. Jerzy Linderski, "The libri reconditi", Harvard Studies in Classical Philology 89 (1985), pp. 226-227; Robert Schilling, "Augurs and Augury", Roman and European Mythologies (University of Chicago Press, 1992), p. 116.

42. Schmitz, "Augur."

43. According to the Augustan historian Pompeius Trogus, who was himself a Celt of the Vocontii civitas, the Celts had acquired expertise in the practice of augury beyond other peoples (nam augurandi studio Galli praeter ceteros callent, as epitomized by Justin 42.4). Discussion of Celtic augury by J.A. MacCulloch, The Religion of the Ancient Celts (Edinburgh, 1911), p. 247.

44. Robert Schilling, "Augurs and Augury", Roman and European Mythologies (University of Chicago Press, 1992, from the French edition of 1981), p. 116.

45. W. Jeffrey Tatum, The Patrician Tribune: Publius Clodius Pulcher (University of North Carolina Press, 1999), p. 127.

46. Andrew Lintott, The Constitution of the Roman Republic (Oxford: Clarendon Press, 1999, reprinted 2002), p. 103 online.

47. John Scheid, An Introduction to Roman Religion (Indiana University Press, 2003), pp. 113-114.

48. H.S. Versnel, Triumphus: An Inquiry into the Origin, Development and Meaning of the Roman Triumph (Brill, 1970), p. 324 online et passim.

49. T. Corey Brennan, The Praetorship in the Roman Republic (Oxford University Press, 2000), p. 19 online.

50. Veit Rosenberger, "Republican nobiles: Controlling the res publica", in A Companion to Roman Religion (Blackwell, 2007), p. 293.

51. Cicero, De divinatione I 28.

52. Cicero, de Divinatione I 28; Cato the Elder, as quoted by Festus p. 342 L 2nd.

53. Festus sv. Silentio surgere, p. 438 L 2nd.

54. G. Dumezil La religion romaine archaique Paris 1974 part IV chapt. 4; It. tr. Milano 1977 p. 526

55. Pliny the Elder, *Natural History* 2, 13; Plautus, *Curculio* 438-484.
56. Festus, sv. *regalia exta* p. 382 L 2nd (p. 367 in the 1997 Teubner edition).
57. Livy I 20, 7.
58. Macrobius, *Saturnalia* III 20 3, citing Tarquitius Priscus: "It is necessary to order evil portents and prodigies to be burnt by means of trees which are in the tutelage of infernal or averting gods," with an enumeration of such trees (*Arbores quae inferum deorum avertentiumque in tutela sunt ... quibus portenta prodigiaque mala comburi iubere oportet*).
59. Varro, *De Lingua Latina* VII 102: "*Ab avertendo averruncare, ut deus qui in eis rebus praeest Averruncus.*"
60. Livy 1.32; 31.8.3; 36.3.9
61. William Warde Fowler, *The Roman Festivals of the Period of the Republic* (London 1925), pp. 33ff.; M. Kaser, *Das altroemische Ius* (Goettingen 1949), pp. 22ff; P. Catalano, *Linee del sistema sovrannazionale romano* (Torino 1965), pp. 14ff.; W. V. Harris, *War and imperialism in Republican Rome, 327-70 B.C.* (Oxford 1979), pp. 161ff.
62. Livy 9.1.10; Cicero, *Divinatio in Caecilium* 63; *De provinciis consularibus* 4; *Ad Atticum* VII 14, 3; IX 19, 1; *Pro rege Deiotauro* 13; *De officiis* I 36; *Philippicae* XI 37; XIII 35; *De re publica* II 31; III 35; Isidore of Seville, *Origines* XVIII 1, 2; Modestinus, *Libro I regolarum* = *Digesta* I 3, 40; E. Badian, *Roman Imperialism in the Late Republic* (Ithaca 1968, 2nd ed.), p.11.
63. Valerius Maximus 1.1.1.
64. Hendrik Wagenvort, "Caerimonia", in *Studies in Roman Literature, Culture and Religion* (Brill, 1956), pp. 84–101.
65. Hans-Friedrich Mueller, *Roman Religion in Valerius Maximus* (Routledge, 2002), pp. 64–65 online.
66. See Davide Del Bello, *Forgotten Paths: Etymology and the Allegorical Mindset* (Catholic University of America Press, 2007), pp. 34–46, on etymology as a form of interpretation or construction of meaning among Roman authors.
67. Wagenvoort, "Caerimonia", p. 100 online.
68. Isidore of Seville, *Etymologiae* 6.19.36 online.
69. Festus, p. 354 L2 = p. 58 M; Jörg Rüpke, *Religion of the Romans* (Polity Press, 2007, originally published in German 2001), p. 227 online.
70. Robert E.A. Palmer, "The Deconstruction of Mommsen on

Festus 462/464, or the Hazards of Interpretation", in *Imperium sine fine: T. Robert S. Broughton and the Roman Republic* (Franz Steiner, 1996), p. 83.

71. Capite aperto, "bareheaded"; Martin Söderlind, *Late Etruscan Votive Heads from Tessennano* («L'Erma» di Bretschneider, 2002), p. 370 online.

72. Robert Schilling, "Roman Sacrifice", *Roman and European Mythologies* (University of Chicago Press, 1992), p. 78.

73. *Classical Sculpture: Catalogue of the Cypriot, Greek, and Roman Stone Sculpture in the University of Pennsylvania Museum of Archaeology and Anthropology* (University of Pennsylvania Museum of Archaeology and Anthropology, 2006), p. 169.

74. 1 Corinthians 11:4; see Neil Elliott, *Liberating Paul: The Justice of God and the Politics of the Apostle* (Fortress Press, 1994, 2006), p. 210 online; Bruce W. Winter, *After Paul Left Corinth: The Influence of Secular Ethics and Social Change* (Wm. B. Eerdmans, 2001), pp. 121–123 online, citing as the standard source D.W.J. Gill, "The Importance of Roman Portraiture for Head-Coverings in 1 Corinthians 11:2–16", Tyndale Bulletin 41 (1990) 245–260; Elaine Fantham, "Covering the Head at Rome" Ritual and Gender," in *Roman Dress and the Fabrics of Culture* (University of Toronto Press, 2008), p. 159, citing Richard Oster. The passage has been explained with reference to Jewish and other practices as well.

75. Frances Hickson Hahn, "Performing the Sacred: Prayers and Hymns", in *A Companion to Roman Religion* (Blackwell, 2007), p. 236, citing also Michael C.J. Putnam, *Horace's Carmen Saeculare* (London, 2001), p. 133.

76. Sarah Iles Johnston, *Religions of the Ancient World: A Guide* (Harvard University Press, 2004), p. 367.

77. Georg Luck, *Arcana Mundi*, p. 510.

78. Bernadotte Filotas, *Pagan Survivals, Superstitions and Popular Cultures in Early Medieval Pastoral Literature* (Pontifical Institute of Mediaeval Studies, 2005), p. 256.

79. Compare Sanskrit s'ista.

80. M. Morani"Lat. 'sacer' ..." Aevum LV 1981 p. 38. Another etymology connects it to Vedic s'asti, 'he gives the instruction', and to Avestic saas-tu, 'that he educate': in G. Dumezil *La religion romaine archaique* Paris, 1974, Remarques preliminaires IX

81. Vergil, Aeneid, 6.661: "Sacerdotes casti dum vita manebat", in H. Fugier, Recherches... cit. p.18 ff.

82. See, for instance, mola salsa.
83. a b H.H. Scullard, A History of the Roman World: 753 to 146 BC (Routledge, 1935, 2013), p. 409.
84. John Scheid, An Introduction to Roman Religion (Indiana University Press, 2003), p. 80.
85. Servius, note to Aeneid 5.755.
86. Servius, note to Aeneid 7.612; Larissa Bonfante, "Ritual Dress," p. 185, and Fay Glinister, "Veiled and Unveiled: Uncovering Roman Influence in Hellenistic Italy," p. 197, both in Votives, Places, and Rituals in Etruscan Religion: Studies in Honor of Jean MacIntosh Turfa (Brill, 2009).
87. Cicero, In Verrem 5.21.53.
88. Horace, Carmen 1.35, 17, 18; 3.24, 6, 6.
89. Praetor maximus, the chief magistrate with imperium; T. Corey Brennan, The Praetorship in the Roman Republic (Oxford University Press, 2000), p. 21.
90. Festus, 49 in the edition of Linday, says that "the year-nail was so called because it was fixed into the walls of the sacred aedes every year, so that the number of years could be reckoned by means of them".
91. Livy, 7.3; Brennan, Praetorship, p. 21.
92. Livy, 7.3.
93. The Fasti Capitolini record dictatores clavi figendi causa for 363, 331, and 263.
94. H.S. Versnel, Triumphus: An Inquiry into the Origin, Development and Meaning of the Roman Triumph (Brill, 1970), pp. 271-272.
95. Brennan, Praetorship, p. 21.
96. Cassius Dio 55.10.4, as cited by Michael Lipka, Roman Gods: A Conceptual Approach (Brill, 2009), p. 108; Brennan, Praetorship, p. 21.
97. David S. Potter, "Roman Religion: Ideas and Action", in Life, Death, and Entertainment in the Roman Empire (University of Michigan, 1999), pp. 139-140.
98. Aulus Gellius, Noctes Atticae XV 27, 1-3, citing Laelius Felix in reference to M. Antistius Labeo.
99. George Willis Botsford, The Roman Assemblies from Their Origin to the End of the Republic (Macmillan, 1909), pp. 155-165.
100. Botsford, Roman Assemblies, p. 153.
101. Botsford, Roman Assemblies, p. 154.

102. Botsford, *Roman Assemblies*, pp. 104, 154.
103. George Mousourakis, *The Historical and Institutional Context of Roman Law* (Ashgate, 2003), p. 105.
104. In the Fasti Viae Lanza.
105. As summarized by Jörg Rüpke, *The Roman Calendar from Numa to Constantine: Time, History, and the Fasti* (Wiley-Blackwell, 2011), pp. 26–27.
106. Jerzy Linderski, "The Augural Law", *Aufstieg und Niedergang der römischen Welt* II.16 (1986), p. 2245, note 387.
107. Jerzy Linderski, "The libri reconditi", *Harvard Studies in Classical Philology* 89 (1985), pp. 228–229.
108. Cicero de Div. II 42
109. Festus, book 17, p. 819.
110. Serv. Dan. Aen. I 398
111. Livy, IV 31, 4; VIII 15, 6; XXIII 31, 13; XLI 18, 8.
112. Moses Hadas, *A History of Latin Literature* (Columbia University Press, 1952), p. 15 online.
113. C.O. Brink, *Horace on Poetry. Epistles Book II: The Letters to Augustus and Florus* (Cambridge University Press, 1982), p. 64 online.
114. Cicero, De domo sua 136.
115. Wilfried Stroh, "De domo sua: Legal Problem and Structure", in *Cicero the Advocate* (Oxford University Press, 2004), p. 341.
116. W.S. Teuffel, *History of Roman Literature*, translated by George C.W. Warr (London, 1900), vol. 1, p. 104 online.
117. Jerzy Linderski, "The libri reconditi", *Harvard Studies in Classical Philology* 89 (1985) 207–234, especially p. 216.
118. For example, Pliny, Natural History 18.14, in reference to the *augurium canarium*, a dog sacrifice. Other references include Cicero, Brutus 55 and De domo sua 186; Livy 4.3 and 6.1; Quintilian 8.2.12, as cited by Teuffel.
119. Linderski, "The libri reconditi", pp. 218–219.
120. Brink, *Horace on Poetry*, p. 64.
121. Adolf Berger, *Encyclopedic Dictionary of Roman Law* (American Philosophical Society, 1991 reprint), p. 399 online.
122. Jerzy Linderski, "The Augural Law", *Aufstieg und Niedergang der römischen Welt* II.16 (1986), 2231–2233, 2238.
123. Greek *stochasmos* (στοχασμός); Tobias Reinhardt, "Rhetoric in the Fourth Academy", *Classical Quarterly* 50 (2000), p. 534. The Greek equivalent of *conicere* is *symballein*, from which English

"symbol" derives; François Guillaumont, "Divination et prévision rationelle dans la correspondance de Cicéron," in Epistulae Antiquae: Actes du Ier Colloque "Le genre épistolaire antique et ses prolongements (Université François-Rabelais, Tours, 18-19 septembre 1998) (Peeters, 2002).

124. Jerzy Linderski, "The Augural Law", Aufstieg und Niedergang der römischen Welt II.16 (1986), p. 2249 online.

125. Cicero, De domo sua 139; F. Sini, Documenti sacerdotali di Roma antica (Sassari, 1983), p.152

126. Cicero. De domo sua 136.

127. J. Marquardt, Römische Staatsverwaltung III (Leipzig, 1885), pp. 269 ff.; G. Wissowa, Religion und Kultus der Römer, p.385.

128. Cicero, De Natura Deorum 2.8 and 1.117.

129. Clifford Ando, The Matter of the Gods (University of California Press, 2009), p. 6.

130. Ando, The Matter of the Gods, pp. 5–7; Valerie M. Warrior, Roman Religion (Cambridge University Press, 2006), p. 6; James B. Rives, Religion in the Roman Empire (Blackwell, 2007), pp. 13, 23.

131. Augustine, De Civitate Dei 10.1; Ando, The Matter of the Gods, p. 6.

132. Jerzy Linderski, "The libri reconditi" Harvard Studies in Classical Philology 89 (1985), pp. 218–219.

133. Sabine MacCormack, The Shadows of Poetry: Vergil in the Mind of Augustine (University of California Press, 1998), p. 75.

134. Clifford Ando, The Matter of the Gods: Religion and the Roman Empire (University of California Press, 2008), p. 110.

135. apud Nonius p. 792 L.

136. As recorded by Servius, ad Aen. II 225.

137. Festus De verborum significatu s.v. delubrum p. 64 L; G. Colonna "Sacred Architecture and the Religion of the Etruscans" in N. T. De Grummond The Religion of the Etruscans 2006 p. 165 n. 59.

138. Isidore of Seville, Etymologiae 15.4.9; Stephen A. Barney, The Etymologies of Isidore of Seville (Cambridge University Press, 2006), p. 310 online.

139. Servius, note to Aeneid 2.156; Robert Turcan, The Gods of Ancient Rome (Routledge, 2000), p. 44.

140. George Willis Botsford, The Roman Assemblies from Their Origin to the End of the Republic (Macmillan, 1909), pp. 161–162.

141. Servius, note to Aeneid 12.139.

142. David Wardle, "Deus or Divus: The Genesis of Roman

Terminology for Deified Emperors and a Philosopher's Contribution", in Philosophy and Power in the Graeco-Roman World: Essays in Honour of Miriam Griffin (Oxford University Press, 2002), p. 182.
143. Servius Aen. II 141: "pontifices dicunt singulis actibus proprios deos praeesse, hos Varro certos deos appellat", the pontiffs say that every single action is presided upon by its own deity, these Varro calls certain gods"; A. von Domaszewski, "Dii certi und incerti" in Abhandlungen fuer roemische Religion 1909 pp. 154-170.
144. Jörg Rüpke, Religion in Republican Rome: Rationalization and Ritual Change (University of Pennsylvania Press, 2012), p. 183.
145. As preserved by Augustine, De Civitate Dei VI 3.
146. Livy 8.9; for a brief introduction and English translation of the passage, see Mary Beard, J.A. North, and S.R.F. Price, Religions of Rome: A Sourcebook (Cambridge University Press, 1998), p. 157 online.
147. Carlos F. Noreña, Imperial Ideals in the Roman West: Representation, Circulation, Power (Cambridge University Press, 2011), p. 142.
148. C.E.V. Nixon, In Praise of Later Roman Emperors: The Panegyrici Latini (University of California Press, 1994), pp. 179-185; Albino Garzetti, From Tiberius To The Antonines (Methuen, 1974), originally published 1960 in Italian), p. 618. Paganism and Christianity, 100-425 C.E.: A Sourcebook edited by Ramsay MacMullen and Eugene N. Lane (Augsburg Fortress, 1992), p. 154; Roger S. Bagnall and Raffaella Cribiore, Women's Letters from Ancient Egypt 300 BC–AD 800 (University of Michigan Press, 2006), pp. 346-347.
149. Nixon, In Praise of Later Roman Emperors, p. 182.
150. Macrobius, Saturnalia 1.16.36; William Warde Fowler, The Religious Experience of the Roman People (London, 1922), pp. 28, 42.
151. Vernaclus was buried by his father, Lucius Cassius Tacitus, in Colonia Ubii. Maureen Carroll, Spirits of the Dead: Roman Funerary Commemoration in Western Europe (Oxford University Press, 2006), p. 172.
152. M. Golden, "Did the Ancients Care When Their Children Died?" Greece & Rome 35 (1988) 152-163.
153. Christian Laes, Children in the Roman Empire: Outsiders Within (Cambridge University Press, 2011), p. 66.
154. Jens-Uwe Krause, "Children in the Roman Family and Beyond," in The Oxford Handbook of Social Relations in the Roman World

(Oxford University Press, 2011), p. 627.
155. Caesar's Calendar, p. 148.
156. Feeney, Caesar's Calendar, p. 148.
157. Feeney, Caesar's Calendar, pp. 148–149.
158. a b Feeney, Caesar's Calendar, p. 149.
159. Regina Gee, "From Corpse to Ancestor: The Role of Tombside Dining in the Transformation of the Body in Ancient Rome," in The Materiality of Death: Bodies, Burials, Beliefs, Bar International Series 1768 (Oxford, 2008), p. 64.
160. Gary Forsythe, A Critical History of Early Rome: From Prehistory to the First Punic War (University of California Press, 2005, 2006), p. 131.
161. Michael Lipka, Roman Gods: A Conceptual Approach (Brill, 2009), p. 47.
162. Patricia Cox Miller, "'The Little Blue Flower Is Red': Relics and the Poeticizing of the Body," Journal of Early Christian Studies 8.2 (2000), p. 228.
163. H.H. Scullard, Festivals and Ceremonies of the Roman Republic (Cornell University Press, 1981), p. 45.
164. Cicero, Ad Atticum 4.9.1; Festus 268 in the edition of Lindsay; Jerzy Linderski, "The Augural Law", Aufstieg und Niedergang der römischen Welt II.16 (1986), pp. 2187–2188.
165. Jörg Rüpke, The Roman Calendar from Numa to Constantine: Time, History, and the Fasti, translated by David M.B. Richardson (Blackwell, 2011, originally published 1995 in German), pp. 151–152. The Fasti Maffeiani (= Degrassi, Inscriptiones Italiae 13.2.72) reads Dies vitios[us] ex s[enatus] c[onsulto], as noted by Rüpke, Kalender und Öffentlichkeit: Die Geschichte der Repräsentation und religiösen Qualifikation von Zeit in Rom (De Gruyter, 1995), p. 436, note 36. The designation is also found in the Fasti Praenestini.
166. Linderski, "The Augural Law," p. 2188.
167. Cassius Dio 51.19.3; Linderski, "The Augural Law," pp. 2187–2188.
168. Suetonius, Divus Claudius 11.3, with commentary by Donna W. Hurley, Suetonius: Divus Claudius (Cambridge University Press, 2001), p. 106.
169. Servius, note to Aeneid 4.453; Festus 69 (edition of Lindsay).
170. David Wardle, Cicero on Divination, Book 1 (Oxford University Press, 2006), pp. 178, 182; Jerzy Linderski, "The Augural Law", Aufstieg und Niedergang der römischen Welt II.16 (1986), p. 2203.
171. William Warde Fowler, The Religious Experience of the Roman

People (London, 1922), p. 59; Georg Luck, *Arcana Mundi: Magic and the Occult in the Greek and Roman Worlds* (Johns Hopkins University Press, 1985, 2006, 2nd ed.), passim.

172. The phrase is *Druidarum religionem ... dirae immanitatis* ("the malevolent inhumanity of the religion of the druids"), where *immanitas* seems to be the opposite of *humanitas* as also evidenced among the Celts: Suetonius, *Claudius* 25, in the same passage containing one of the earliest mentions of Christianity as a threat.

173. P.A. Brunt, *Roman Imperial Themes* (Oxford University Press, 1990, 2001), p. 485 online.

174. The phrase is used for instance by Servius, note to *Aeneid* 4.166.

175. Massimo Pallottino, "The Doctrine and Sacred Books of the *Disciplina Etrusca*", *Roman and European Mythologies* (University of Chicago Press, 1992, from the French edition of 1981), pp. 43–44.

176. Elizabeth Rawson, "Caesar, Etruria, and the *Disciplina Etrusca*", *Journal of Roman Studies* 68 (1978), p. 138.

177. Servius, note to *Aeneid* 5.45, also 12.139.

178. Servius is unclear as to whether Lucius Ateius Praetextatus or Gaius Ateius Capito is meant.

179. David Wardle, "*Deus* or *Divus*: The Genesis of Roman Terminology for Deified Emperors and a Philosopher's Contribution", in *Philosophy and Power in the Graeco-Roman World* (Oxford University Press, 2002), pp. 181–183.

180. Jörg Rüpke, *Religion of the Romans* (Polity Press, 2007, originally published in German 2001), p. 149 online.

181. Georg Luck, *Arcana Mundi: Magic and the Occult in the Greek and Roman Worlds* (Johns Hopkins University Press, 1985, 2006), p. 479 online.

182. Adolf Berger, *Encyclopedic Dictionary of Roman Law* (Transactions of the American Philosophical Society, 1953, 2002), p. 414.

183. James R. Harrison, *Paul's Language of Grace in Its Graeco-Roman Context* (C.B. Mohr, 2003), p. 284. See *Charites* for the ancient Greek goddesses known as the Graces.

184. Max Weber, *The Sociology of Religion* (Beacon Press, 1963, 1991, originally published in German 1922), p. 82 online.

185. Émile Durkheim, *The Elementary Forms of Religious Life* (Oxford University Press, 2001 translation), p. 257 online.

186. Festus 146 (edition of Lindsay).

187. Jerzy Linderski, "The Augural Law", *Aufstieg und Niedergang*

der römischen Welt II.16 (1986), pp. 2156-2157.

188. Robert Schilling, "Augurs and Augury," *Roman and European Mythologies* (University of Chicago Press, 1992), p. 115.

189. Daniel J. Gargola, *Lands, Laws and Gods: Magistrates and Ceremony in the Regulation of Public Lands* (University of North Carolina Press, 1995), p. 27.

190. Linderski, "Augural Law," p. 2274.

191. Mary Beard, J.A. North, and S.R.F. Price, *Religions of Rome: A Sourcebook* (Cambridge University Press, 1998), p. 41.

192. Nicholas Purcell, "On the Sacking of Corinth and Carthage", in *Ethics and Rhetoric: Classical Essays for Donald Russell on His Seventy*(Oxford University Press, 1995), pp. 140-142.

193. Beard et al., *Religions of Rome: A Sourcebook*, pp. 41-42, with the passage from Livy, 5.21.1-7; Robert Turcan, *The Cults of the Roman Empire* (Blackwell, 1996, 2001, originally published in French 1992), p. 12; Robert Schilling, "Juno", *Roman and European Mythologies* (University of Chicago Press, 1992, from the French edition of 1981), p 131.

194. Daniel J. Gargola, *Lands, Laws, and Gods: Magistrates and Ceremonies in the Regulation of Public Lands in Republican Rome* (University of North Carolina Press, 1995), p. 30. Elizabeth Rawson expresses doubts as to whether the evocatio of 146 BC occurred as such; see "Scipio, Laelius, Furius and the Ancestral Religion", *Journal of Roman Studies* 63 (1973) 161-174.

195. Evidenced by an inscription dedicated by an imperator Gaius Servilius, probably at the vowed temple; Beard et al., *Religions of Rome: A Sourcebook*, p. 248.

196. As implied but not explicitly stated by Propertius, Elegy 4.2; Daniel P. Harmon, "Religion in the Latin Elegists", *Aufstieg und Niedergang der römischen Welt II.16.3* (1986), pp. 1960-1961.

197. Eric Orlin, *Foreign Cults in Rome: Creating a Roman Empire* (Oxford University Press, 2010), pp. 37-38.

198. Mary Beard, J.A. North, and S.R.F. Price, *Religions of Rome: A History* (Cambridge University Press, 1998), p. 254.

199. Arnaldo Momigliano, *On Pagans, Jews, and Christians* (Wesleyan University Press, 1987), p. 178; Greg Woolf, *Becoming Roman: The Origins of Provincial Civilization in Gaul* (Cambridge University Press, 1998), p. 214.

200. George Mousourakis, *The Historical and Institutional Context of Roman Law* (Ashgate, 2003), p. 339 online.

201. Daniel J. Gargola, *Lands, Laws, and Gods: Magistrates and Ceremony in the Regulation of Public Lands* (University of North Carolina Press, 1995), p. 27; Jerzy Linderski, "The Augural Law", *Aufstieg und Niedergang der römischen Welt* II.16 (1986), p. 2273.

202. Clifford Ando, *The Matter of the Gods: Religion and the Roman Empire* (University of California Press, 2008), p. 184, citing Servius, note to *Aeneid* 2.351: "Pontifical law advises that unless Roman deities are called by their proper names, they cannot be exaugurated" (*et iure pontificum cautum est, ne suis nominibus dii Romani appellarentur, ne exaugurari possint*).

203. Livy 5.54.7; Dionysius of Halicarnassus 3.69.5; J. Rufus Fears, "The Cult of Virtues and Roman Imperial Ideology," *Aufstieg und Niedergang der römischen Welt* II.17.2 (1981), p. 848.

204. Clifford Ando, "Exporting Roman Religion," in *A Companion to Roman Religion* (Blackwell, 2007), p. 442.

205. Fay Glinister, "Sacred Rubbish," in *Religion in Archaic and Republican Rome and Italy: Evidence and Experience* (Edinburgh University Press, 2000), p. 66.

206. Jörg Rüpke, *Fasti sacerdotum: A Prosopography of Pagan, Jewish, and Christian Religious Officials in the City of Rome, 300 BC to AD 499* (Oxford University Press, 2008), pp. 530, 753.

207. Macrobius, *Saturnalia* III 5, 6, quoting a passage from Veranius, *De pontificalibus quaestionibus*: *eximias dictas hostias quae ad sacrificium destinatae eximantur e grege, vel quod eximia specie quasi offerendae numinibus eligantur.*

208. F. SiniSua cuique civitati religio Torino 2001 p. 197

209. Cicero, *De divinatione* 2.12.29. According to Pliny (*Natural History* 11.186), before 274 BC the heart was not included among the exta.

210. Robert Schilling, "The Roman Religion", in *Historia Religionum: Religions of the Past* (Brill, 1969), vol. 1, pp. 471–472, and "Roman Sacrifice," *Roman and European Mythologies* (University of Chicago Press, 1992), p. 79; John Scheid, *An Introduction to Roman Religion* (Indiana University Press, 2003, originally published in French 1998), p. 84.

211. Georg Luck, *Arcana Mundi: Magic and the Occult in the Greek and Roman Worlds* (Johns Hopkins University Press, 1985, 2006, 2nd ed.), p. 511.

212. Juvenal, *Satire* 2.110–114; Livy 37.9 and 38.18; Richard M. Crill, "Roman Paganism under the Antonines and Severans," *Aufstieg und*

Niedergang der römischen Welt II.16.2 (1976), p. 31.

213. Juvenal, Satire 4.123; Stephen L. Dyson, *Rome: A Living Portrait of an Ancient City* (Johns Hopkins University Press, 2010), pp. 228, 328; John E. Stambaugh, "The Functions of Roman Temples," ANRW II.16.2 (1976), p. 593; Robert Turcan, *The Cults of the Roman Empire* (Blackwell, 1992, 2001 printing), p. 41.

214. Anonymous author of the Historia Augusta, Tacitus 17.1: *Fanaticus quidam in Templo Silvani tensis membris exclamavit*, as cited by Peter F. Dorcey, *The Cult of Silvanus: A Study in Roman Folk Religion* (Brill, 1992), p. 90, with some due skepticism toward the source.

215. CIL VI.490, 2232, and 2234, as cited by Stambaugh, "The Function of Roman Temples," p. 593, note 275.

216. *Fanaticum agmen*, Tacitus, Annales 14.30.

217. See for instance Cicero, De domo sua 105, De divinatione 2.118; and Horace's comparison of supposedly inspired poetic frenzy to the *fanaticus* error of religious mania (Ars Poetica 454); C.O. Brink, *Horace on Poetry: Epistles Book II, The Letters to Augustus and Florus* (Cambridge University Press, 1982), p. 357; Marten Stol, *Epilepsy in Babylonia* (Brill, 1993), p. 121 online.

218. *Fanatica dicitur arbor fulmine icta*, apud Paulus, p. 92M.

219. Festus s.v. delubrum p. 64 M; G. Colonna "Sacred Architecture and the Religion of the Etruscans" in N. Thomas De Grummond *The Religion of the Etruscans* 2006 p. 165 n. 59

220. S. 53.1, CCSL 103:233–234, as cited by Bernadotte Filotas, *Pagan Survivals, Superstitions and Popular Cultures in Early Medieval Pastoral Literature* (Pontifical Institute of Mediaeval Studies, 2005), p. 68.

221. "What a thing is that, that when those trees to which people make vows fall, no one carries wood from them home to use on the hearth! Behold the wretchedness and stupidity of mankind: they show honour to a dead tree and despite the commands of the living God; they do not dare to put the branches of a tree into the fire and by an act of sacrilege throw themselves headlong into hell": Caesarius of Arles, S. 54.5, CCSL 103:239, as quoted and discussed by Filotas, *Pagan Survivals*, p. 146.

222. As for instance in Livy 10.37.15, where he says that the temple of Jupiter Stator, established by the wartime *votum* of the consul and general M. Atilius Regulus in the 290s BC, had already been vowed by Romulus, but had remained only a *fanum*, a site (*locus*) delineated by

means of verbalized ritual (effatus) for a templum.

223. Roger D. Woodard, *Indo-European Sacred Space: Vedic and Roman Cult* (University of Illinois Press, 2006), p. 150 online.

224. *Fíisnú* is the nominative form.

225. The form *fesnaf-e* is an accusative plural with an enclitic postposition.

226. Woodard, *Indo-European Sacred Space*, p. 150.

227. S.P. Oakley, *A Commentary on Livy, Books 6–10* (Oxford University Press, 2005), p. 378; Michel P.J. van den Hout, *A Commentary on the Letters of M. Cornelius Fronto* (Brill, 1999), p. 164.

228. Lawrence Richardson, *A New Topographical Dictionary of Ancient Rome* (Johns Hopkins University Press, 1992), p. 2.

229. Patrice Méniel, "Fanum and sanctuary," in *Celtic Culture: A Historical Encyclopedia* (ABC-Clio, 2006), pp. 229, 733–734 online.

230. See Romano-Celtic Temple Bourton Grounds in Great-Britain and Romano-British Temples

231. T.F. Hoad, *English Etymology*, Oxford University Press 1993. p. 372a.

232. Servius, note to Aeneid 2.54; Nicholas Horsfall, *Virgil, Aeneid 2: A Commentary* (Brill, 2008), p. 91.

233. Horsfall, *Virgil, Aeneid 2*, p. 91.

234. Elisabeth Henry, *The Vigour of Prophecy: A Study of Virgil's Aeneid* (Southern Illinois University Press, 1989) passim.

235. Jerzy Linderski, "Founding the City," in *Ten Years of the Agnes Kirsopp Lake Michels Lectures at Bryn Mawr College* (Bryn Mawr Commentaries, 2006), p. 93.

236. R.L. Rike, *Apex Omnium: Religion in the Res Gestae of Ammianus* (University of California Press, 1987), p. 123.

237. Cynthia White, "The Vision of Augustus," *Classica et Mediaevalia* 55 (2004), p. 276.

238. Rike, *Apex Omnium*, pp. 122–123.

239. Ammianus Marcellinus, *Res gestae* 23.1.7, as cited by Rike, *Apex Omnium*, p. 122, note 57; Sarolta A. Takács, *Vestal Virgins, Sibyls, and Matrons: Women in Roman Religion* (University of Texas Press, 2008), p. 68.

240. See Mary Beard et al., *Religions of Rome: Volume 1, a History* (Cambridge University Press, 1998), p. 370 online, in a Christianized context with reference to Constantine I's AD 314 address of the Donatist dispute.

241. Robert Schilling, "Roman Festivals," *Roman and European Mythologies* (University of Chicago Press, 1992), p. 92. So too R. Orestano, "Dal ius al fas," *Bullettino dell'Istituto di diritto romano* 46 (1939), p. 244 ff., and *I fatti di normazione nell 'esperienza romana arcaica* (Turin 1967), p.106 ff.; A. Guarino, *L'ordinamento giuridico romano* (Naples 1980), p. 93; J. Paoli, *Le monde juridique du paganisme romain* p. 5; P. Catalano, *Contributi allo studio del diritto augurale* (Turin 1960), pp. 23 ff., 326 n. 10; C. Gioffredi, *Diritto e processo nelle antiche forme giuridiche romane* (Rome 1955), p. 25; B. Albanese, *Premesse allo studio del diritto privat romano* (Palermo 1978), p.127.

242. Valerie M. Warrior, *Roman Religion*, Cambridge University Press, 2006, p.160 [1]

243. Michael Lipka, *Roman Gods: A Conceptual Approach* (Brill, 2009), p.113 online.

244. Vergil, *Georgics* 1.269, with Servius's note: "divina humanaque iura permittunt: nam ad religionem fas, ad hominem iura pertinunt". See also Robert Turcan, *The Gods of Ancient Rome: Religion in Everyday Life from Archaic to Imperial Times* (Routledge, 2000), p.5 online. and discussion of the relationship between fas and ius from multiple scholarly perspectives by Jerzy Linderski, "The Augural Law", *Aufstieg und Niedergang der römischen Welt* II.16 (1986), pp. 2203–04 online.

245. Schilling, *Roman and European Mythologies*, p. 92.

246. *The Oxford Latin Dictionary* (Oxford: Clarendon Press, 1982, 1985 reprinting), entry on fas p. 676, considers the etymology dubious but leans toward for, fari. The Indo-Europeanist Emile Benveniste derives fas, as a form of divine speech, from the IE root *bhā (as cited by Schilling, *Roman and European Mythologies*, p. 93, note 4).

247. Varro, *De Lingua Latina*, 6.29, because on dies fasti the courts are in session and political speech may be practiced freely. Ovid pursues the connection between the dies fasti and permissible speech (fas est) in his calendrical poem the Fasti; see discussion by Carole E. Newlands, *Playing with Time: Ovid and the Fasti"* (Cornell Studies in Classical Philology, 1995), p. 175 online.

248. Dumézil holds that fas derives from the IE root *dhē (as noted by Schilling, *Roman and European Mythologies*, p. 93, note 4). One ancient tradition associated the etymology of fas with that of Themis as the "establisher". See Paulus, epitome of Festus, p. 505 (edition of Lindsay); Ausonius, *Technopaegnion* 8, and *de diis* 1. For the

scholarship, see U. Coli, "Regnum" in *Studia et documenta historiae et iuris* 17 1951; C. Ferrini "Fas" in *Nuovo Digesto Italiano* p. 918; C. Gioffredi, *Diritto e processo nelle antiche forme giuridiche romane* (Roma 1955) p. 25 n.1; H. Fugier, *Recherches sur l' expression du sacre' dans la langue latine* (Paris 1963), pp. 142 ff.; G. Dumezil, *La religion romaine archaique* (Paris 1974), p. 144.

249. H. Fugier *Recherches sur l'expression du sacre' dans la langue latine* Paris, 1963

250. W. W. Skeat *Etymological Dictionary of the English Language* New York 1963 sv felicity, feminine

251. G. Dumezil *La religion romaine archaique* Paris 1974 part IV chapt. 2; *Camillus: a study of Indo-European religion as Roman history* (University of California Press, 1980), p. 214 online, citing Macrobius, Saturnalia 1.16.2.

252. Inc. Auc. de Praenominibus I apud Valerius Maximus X: "Fertorem Resium qui ius fetiale constituit"; Inc. Auc. de Viribus Illustribus V 4 apud Aurelius Victor p. 29: "(Ancus Martius) ius fetiale...ab Aequicolis transtulit quod primus Ferter Rhesus excogitavisse"; CIL VI 1302 from the Palatine (II-I century BC); Festus s. v. Ferctius p. 81 L; Propertius IV 105-146; Plutarch Marcellus 8. 4, Romulus 16. 6.

253. Livy I.18.9; Varro, De lingua latina V.143, VI.153, VII.8-9; Aulus Gellius XIII.14.1 (on the pomerium); Festus p. 488 L, tesca.

254. Joseph Rykwert, *The Idea of a Town: The Anthropology of Urban Form in Rome, Italy and the Ancient World* (MIT Press, 1988, originally published 1976), pp. 106–107, 126–127; Wissowa, *Religion und Kultus der Römer* (Munich 1912) 2nd pp. 136 ff.; G. Dumezil, *La religion romaine archaique* (Paris 1974) 2nd, pp. 210 ff.; Varro, De lingua latina V.21; Isidore, Origines XV.14.3; Paulus, Fest. epit. p. 505 L; Ovid, Fasti II 639 ff.

255. Discussion and citation of ancient sources by Steven J. Green, *Ovid, Fasti 1: A Commentary* (Brill, 2004), pp. 159–160 online.

256. Servius, note to Aeneid 1.334.

257. Hostibus a domitis hostia nomen habet ("the hostia gets its name from the 'hostiles' that have been defeated"), Ovid, Fasti 1.336; victima quae dextra cecidit victrice vocatur ("the victim which is killed by the victor's right hand is named [from that act]"), 1.335.

258. a b Char. 403.38.

259. Macrobius Sat. VI 9, 5-7; Varro Ling. Lat. V

260. Macrobius Sat. VI 9, 7; Festus s.v. bidentes p.33 M

261. Macrobius, Saturnalia III 5, 1 ff.

262. Nathan Rosenstein, *Imperatores Victi: Military Defeat and Aristocratic Competition in the Middle and Late Republic* (University of California Press, 1990), p. 64.

263. Robert Turcan, *The Gods of Ancient Rome* (Routledge, 2001; originally published in French 1998), p. 9.

264. Turcan, *The Gods of Ancient Rome*, p. 39.

265. Veranius, Iur. 7: *praesentanaea porca dicitur ... quae familiae purgandae causa Cereris immolatur, quod pars quaedam eius sacrificii fit in conspectu mortui eius, cuius funus instituitur.*

266. Aulus Gellius *Noctes Atticae* IV 6, 3-10 for *hostia succidanea* and *praecidanea*; also Festus p. 250 L. s. v. *praecidanea hostia*; Festus p. 298 L. s.v. *praesentanea hostia*. Gellius's passage implies a conceptual connexion between the *hostia praecidanea* and the *feriae succidaneae*, though this is not explicated. Scholarly interpretations thus differ on what the *feriae praecidaneae* were: cf. A. Bouché-Leclercq *Dictionnaire des antiquités grecques et romaines* III Paris 1898 s. v *Inauguratio* p. 440 and n. 1; G. Wissowa *Religion und Kultus der Römer* München 1912 p.438 f.; L. Schmitz in W. Smith *A Dictionary of Greek and Roman Antiquities* London 1875 s. v. *feriae*; P. Catalano *Contributi allo studio del diritto augurale* Torino 1960 p. 352.

267. Cicero, *De legibus* ii 8,20; Dionysius Halicarnassus II 22,3.

268. Livy XXVII 36, 5; XL 42, 8-10; Aulus Gellius XV 17, 1

269. Gaius I 130; III 114; Livy XXVII 8,4; XLI 28, 7; XXXVII 47, 8; XXIX 38, 6;XLV 15,19; Macrobius II 13, 11;

270. Cicero, *Brutus* 1; Livy XXVII 36, 5; XXX 26, 10; Dionysius Halicarnassus II 73, 3.

271. William Warde Fowler, *The Roman Festivals of the Period of the Republic* (London, 1908), p. 89.

272. In particular, Book 14 of the non-extant *Antiquitates rerum divinarum*; see Lipka, *Roman Gods*, pp. 69–70.

273. W.R. Johnson, "The Return of Tutunus", *Arethusa* (1992) 173–179; Fowler, *Religious Experience*, p. 163. Wissowa, however, asserted that Varro's lists were not *indigitamenta*, but *di certi*, gods whose function could still be identified with certainty; *Encyclopedia of Religion and Ethics* (unknown edition), vol. 13, p. 218 online. See also Kurt Latte, *Roemische Religionsgeschichte* (Munich, 1960), pp. 44-45.

274. Lactantius, *Div. inst.* 1.6.7; Censorinus 3.2; Arnaldo Momigliano, "The Theological Efforts of the Roman Upper Classes in

the First Century B.C.", Classical Philology 79 *(1984), p. 210.*

275. Georg Luck, Arcana Mundi: Magic and the Occult in the Greek and Roman Worlds *(Johns Hopkins University Press, 1985, 2006, 2nd ed.), p. 513.*

276. Matthias Klinghardt, "Prayer Formularies for Public Recitation: Their Use and Function in Ancient Religion", Numen *46 (1999), pp. 44–45; Frances Hickson Hahn, "Performing the Sacred: Prayers and Hymns", in* A Companion to Roman Religion *(Blackwell, 2007), p. 240; Nicole Belayche, "Religious Actors in Daily Life: Practices and Shared Beliefs", in* A Companion to Roman Religion, *p. 279.*

277. *The vocative is the grammatical case used only for "calling" or invoking, that is, hailing or addressing someone paratactically.*

278. Gábor Betegh, The Derveni Papyrus: Cosmology, Theology and Interpretation *(Cambridge University Press, 2004), p. 137.*

279. Jerzy Linderski, "The Augural Law", Aufstieg und Niedergang der römischen Welt *II.16 (1986), pp. 2253*

280. Luck, Arcana Mundi, *pp. 497, 498.*

281. *Pausanias gave specific examples in regard to Poseidon (7.21.7); Claude Calame, "The Homeric Hymns as Poetic Offerings: Musical and Ritual Relationships with the Gods," in* The Homeric Hymns: Interpretive Essays *(Oxford University Press, 2011), p. 338.*

282. *A. Berger* Encyclopedical Dictionary of Roman Law *Philadelphia 1968 sv. ius*

283. *Inst. 2, 2 ap. Dig. 1, 8, 1: Summa itaque rerum divisio in duos articulos diducitur: nam aliae sunt divini iuris, aliae humani, 'thus the highest division of things is reduced into two articles : some belong to divine right, some to human right'.*

284. *F.Sini Bellum nefandum Sassari 1991 p. 110*

285. *In Festus: ...iudex atque arbiter habetur rerum divinarum humanarumque: 'he is considered to be the judge and arbiter of things divine and human'... his authority stems from his regal (originally king Numa's) investiture. F. Sini Bellum nefandum Sassari 1991 p. 108 ff. R. Orestano Dal ius al fas p.201.*

286. *Ulpian Libr. I regularum ap. Digesta 1, 1, 10, 2: Iuris prudentia est divinarum atque humanrum rerum notitia, iusti atque iniusti scientia*

287. *Mary Beard, J.A. North, and S.R.F. Price,* Religions of Rome: A History *(Cambridge University Press, 1998), p. 105.*

288. Jörg Rüpke, Religion of the Romans *(Polity Press, 2007, originally published in German 2001), p. 130, citing Gaius,* Institutes

2.1-9.
289. William Warde Fowler, *The Religious Experience of the Roman People* (London, 1922), p. 122ff.
290. W.W. Skeat, *Etymological dictionary of the English Language* entries on legal, legion, diligent, negligent, religion.
291. For example in Livy, *Ab Urbe Condita*, 1.24.7, Jupiter is called on to hear the oath.
292. Serv. in Aen. III, 89: *legum* here is understood as the uttering of a set of fixed, binding conditions.
293. M. Morani "Lat. 'sacer'..." *Aevum* LV 1981 p. 38 n.22
294. For example, those dated to 58 BC, relating to the temple of Jupiter Liber at Furfo: CIL IX 3513
295. G. Dumezil *la religion romaine archaic* Paris, 1974.
296. P. Noailles RH 19/20 (1940/41) 1, 27 ff; A. Magdelain *De la royauté et du droit des Romaines* (Rome, 1995) chap. II, III
297. Paul Veyne, *The Roman Empire* (Harvard University Press, 1987), p. 213.
298. H.S. Versnel, *Transition and Reversal in Myth and Ritual* (Brill, 1993, 1994), pp. 62-63.
299. Jerzy Linderski, "The Augural Law", *Aufstieg und Niedergang der römischen Welt* II.16 (1986), pp. 2156-2157, 2248.
300. Robert Schilling, "Augurs and Augury," in *Roman and European Mythologies* (University of Chicago Press, 1992), p. 116.
301. F. Sini *Documenti sacerdotali di Roma antica* Sassari, 1983; S. Tondo *Leges regiae e paricidas* Firenze, 1973; E. Peruzzi *Origini di Roma II*
302. Francesco Sini, *Documenti sacerdotali di Roma antica. I. Libri e documenti* Sassari, 1983, IV, 10, p. 175 ff.
303. Cicero, *De Legibus* ("On Laws"), 2, 21.
304. M. Van Den Bruwaene, "Precison sur la loi religieuse du de leg. II, 19-22 de Ciceron" in *Helikon* 1 (1961) p.89.
305. F. Sini *Documenti sacerdotali di Roma antica I. Libri e commentari* Sassari 1983 p. 22; S. Tondo *Leges regiae e paricidas* Firenze, 1973, p.20-21; R. Besnier "Le archives privees publiques et religieuses a' Rome au temps des rois" in *Studi Albertario* II Milano 1953 pp.1 ff.; L. Bickel "Lehrbuch der Geschichte der roemischen Literatur" p. 303; G. J. Szemler *The priests of the Roman Republic* Bruxelles 1972.
306. Livy 41.14-15.
307. Robert Schilling, "Roman Sacrifice", *Roman and European*

Mythologies (University of Chicago Press, 1992, from the French edition of 1981), p. 79.
308. Jörg Rüpke, *Religion of the Romans* (Polity Press, 2007, originally published in German 2001), pp. 149–150.
309. Paulus Festi epitome p. 57 L s.v. capitalis lucus
310. Berger, Adolf (1953). Encyclopedic Dictionary of Roman Law. Transactions of The American Philosophical Society 43. Philadelphia: The American Philosophical Society. p. 546. ISBN 1584771425 Check |isbn= value (help).
311. CIL I 2nd 366; XI 4766; CIL I2 401, IX 782; R. Del Ponte, "Santità delle mura e sanzione divina" in Diritto e Storia 3 2004.
312. W.W. Skeat Etymological Dictionary of the English Language New York 1973 s.v. lustration
313. Stefan Weinstock, "Libri fulgurales," Papers of the British School at Rome 19 (1951), p. 125.
314. Weinstock, p. 125.
315. Seneca, Naturales Questiones 2.41.1.
316. Massimo Pallottino, "The Doctrine and Sacred Books of the Disciplina Etrusca," Roman and European Mythologies (University of Chicago Press, 1992), p. 44.
317. According to Seneca, NQ 2.41.1. See also Festus p. 219M = 114 edition of Lindsay; entry on peremptalia fulgura, p. 236 in the 1997 Teubner edition; Pliny, Natural History 2.138; and Servius, note to Aeneid 1.42, as cited and discussed by Weinstock, p. 125ff. Noted also by Auguste Bouché-Leclercq, Histoire de la divination dans l'antiquité (Jérôme Millon, 2003 reprint, originally published 1883), p. 845, note 54.
318. Pallottino, "Doctrine and Sacred Books," p. 44.
319. Weinstock, p. 127. See also The Religion of the Etruscans, pp. 40–41, where an identification of the dii involuti with the Favores Opertaneii ("Secret Gods of Favor") referred to by Martianus Capella is proposed.
320. Georges Dumézil, La religion romaine archaïque (Paris 1974), pp. 630 and 633 (note 3), drawing on Seneca, NQ 2.41.1–2 and 39.
321. Pallottino, "Doctrine and Sacred Books", pp. 43–44.
322. Auguste Bouché-Leclercq, Histoire de la divination dans l'antiquité: Divination hellénique et divination italique (Jérôme Millon, 2003 reprint), p. 873; T.P. Wiseman, "History, Poetry, and Annales", in Clio and the Poets: Augustan Poetry and the Traditions of Ancient Historiography (Brill, 2002), p. 359 "awe and amazement

are the result, not the cause, of the miraculum.

323. Livy 1.39.

324. George Williamson, "Mucianus and a Touch of the Miraculous: Pilgrimage and Tourism in Roman Asia Minor", in *Seeing the Gods: Pilgrimage in Graeco-Roman and Early Christian Antiquity* (Oxford University Press, 2005, 2007), p. 245 online.

325. Ariadne Staples, *From Good Goddess to Vestal Virgins: Sex and Category in Roman Religion* (Routledge, 1998), pp. 154–155.

326. Servius, note to Eclogue 8.82:

327. Fernando Navarro Antolín, *Lygdamus. Corpus Tibullianum III.1–6: Lygdami Elegiarum Liber* (Brill, 1996), pp. 272–272 online.

328. David Wardle, *Cicero on Divination, Book 1* (Oxford University Press, 2006), p. 102.

329. Varro as recorded by Servius, note to Aeneid 3.336, cited by Wardle, *Cicero on Divination*, p. 330 online.

330. Philip R. Hardie, *Virgil: Aeneid, Book IX* (Cambridge University Press, 1994, reprinted 2000), p. 97.

331. Mary Beagon, "Beyond Comparison: M. Sergius, Fortunae victor", in *Philosophy and Power in the Graeco-Roman World: Essays in Honour of Miriam Griffin* (Oxford University Press, 2002), p. 127.

332. As cited by Wardle, *Cicero on Divination*, p. 330.

333. Beagon, "Beyond Comparison", in *Philosophy and Power*, p. 127.

334. Michèle Lowrie, *Horace's Narrative Odes* (Oxford University Press, 1997), pp. 151–154.

335. Cicero, *In Catilinam* 2.1.

336. Gregory A. Staley, *Seneca and the Idea of Tragedy* (Oxford University Press, 2010), pp. 80, 96, 109, 113 et passim.

337. L. Banti; G. Dumézil *La religion romaine archaïque* Paris 1974 ,It. tr. p. 482-3.

338. M. Humm, "Le mundus et le Comitium : représentations symboliques de l'espace de la cité," *Histoire urbaine*, 2, 10, 2004. French language, full preview.

339. *Dies religiosi* were marked by the gods as inauspicious, so in theory, no official work should have been done, but it was not a legally binding religious the rule. G. Dumézil above.

340. Festus p. 261 L2, citing Cato's commentaries on civil law. An inscription at Capua names a *sacerdos Cerialis mundalis* (CIL X 3926). For the connection between deities of agriculture and the underworld, see W. Warde Fowler, "Mundus Patet" in *Journal of Roman Studies*, 2, (1912), pp.25-33

341. A. Guarino L'ordinamento giuridico romano Napoli, 1980, p. 93.
342. Olga Tellegen-Couperus, *A Short History of Roman Law*, Routledge, 1993. ISBN 978-0-415-07250-2 pp17-18.
343. Festus p. 424 L: At homo sacer is est, quem populus iudicavit ob maleficium; neque fas est eum immolari, sed qui occidit, parricidi non damnatur.
344. Livy, Ab Urbe Condita, 4.3.9.
345. Paul Roche, *Lucan: De Bello Civili, Book 1* (Oxford University Press, 2009), p. 296.
346. Servius, note to Aeneid 1.310, arborum multitudo cum religione.
347. Jörg Rüpke, *Religion of the Romans* (Polity Press, 2007), p. 275, noting that he finds Servius's distinction "artificial."
348. Fernando Navarro Antolin, *Lygdamus: Corpus Tibullianum III.1–6, Lygdami Elegiarum Liber* (Brill, 1996), p. 127–128.
349. Martial, 4.64.17, as cited by Robert Schilling, "Anna Perenna," *Roman and European Mythologies* (University of Chicago Press, 1992), p. 112.
350. Stephen L. Dyson, *Rome: A Living Portrait of an Ancient City* (Johns Hopkins University Press, 2010), p. 147.
351. Jerzy Linderski, "The Augural Law," *Aufstieg und Niedergang der römischen Welt* II.16 (1986), pp. 2159–2160, 2168, et passim.
352. S.W. Rasmussen, ''Public Portents in Republican Rome' online.
353. W. Jeffrey Tatum, *The Patrician Tribune: Publius Clodius Pulcher* (University of North Carolina Press, 1999) p. 127.
354. Beard, M., Price, S., North, J., *Religions of Rome: Volume 1, a History*, illustrated, Cambridge University Press, 1998, pp 109-10.
355. J.P.V.D. Balsdon, "Roman History, 58–56 B.C.: Three Ciceronian Problems", *Journal of Roman Studies* 47 (1957) 16–16.
356. Jerzy Linderski, "The Augural Law", *Aufstieg und Niedergang der römischen Welt* II.16 (1986), pp. 2232–2234, 2237–2241.
357. The etymology is debated. The older Latin form is osmen", which may have meant "an utterance"; see W. W. Skeat *Etymological Dictionary of the English Language* sv omen New York 1963. It has also been connected to an ancient Hittite exclamation ha ("it's true"); see R. Bloch *Les prodiges dans l'antiquite'* - Rome Paris 1968; It. tr. Rome 1978 p. 74, and E. Benveniste "Hittite et Indo-Europeen. Etudes comparatives" in *Bibl. arch. et hist. de l'Institut francais a,'Arch. de Stambul* V, 1962, p.10.
358. See Veit Rosenberger, in Rüpke, Jörg (Editor), *A Companion to Roman Religion*, Wiley-Blackwell, 2007, p.298; citing Cicero, De

Divinatione, 2.77.

359. Donald Lateiner, "Signifying Names and Other Ominous Accidental Utterances in Classical Historiography", Greek, Roman, and Byzantine Studies, (2005), pp.51-55, 45, 49.[2]. Paullus is said to have accepted the omen with the words, "accipio, mea filia, omen." ("I accept the omen, my daughter").

360. Donald Lateiner, "Signifying Names and Other Ominous Accidental Utterances in Classical Historiography", Greek, Roman, and Byzantine Studies, (2005), 49.[3]

361. "If we are going to accept chance utterances of this kind as omens, we had better look out when we stumble, or break a shoe-string, or sneeze!" Cicero De Divinatione 2.84: Loeb translation (1923) online at Bill Thayer's site [4]. In Pliny, Historia Naturalis, 15.83: ex hoc genere sunt, ut diximus, cottana et caricae quaeque conscendendi navem adversus Parthos omen fecere M. Crasso venales praedicantes voce, Cavneae. Teubner-Mahoff edn. transcribed at Bill Thayer's site [5]

362. Jerzy Linderski, "The libri reconditi", Harvard Studies in Classical Philology 89 (1985), p. 231–232.

363. Both are mentioned by Macrobius, Saturnalia 3.20.3 and 3.7.2; Nancy Thomson de Grummond, "Introduction: The History of the Study of Etruscan Religion", in The Religion of the Etruscans (University of Texas Press, 2006), p. 2.

364. Pliny, Natural History 10.6–42.

365. Ex Tarquitianis libris in titulo "de rebus divinis": Ammianus Marcellinus XXV 27.

366. Robert Schilling, "The Disciplina Etrusca", Roman and European Mythologies (University of Chicago Press, 1992, from the French edition of 1981), p. 44.

367. Varro quoted by Servius, note to Aeneid 3.336, as cited by David Wardle, Cicero on Divination, Book 1 (Oxford University Press, 2006), p. 330 online.

368. As cited by Wardle, Cicero on Divination, p.330.

369. Wardle, Cicero on Divination, p. 330; Auguste Bouché-Leclerq, Histoire de la divination dans l'antiquité (Jérôme Millon, 2003, originally published 1882), pp. 873–874 online.

370. Jerzy Linderski, "The Augural Law", Aufstieg und Niedergang der römischen Welt II.16 (1986), pp. 2150 and 2230–2232; see Cicero, De Divinatione, 1.72 and 2.49.

371. Festus rationalises the order: the rex is "the most powerful" of

priests, the Flamen Dialis is "sacerdos of the entire universe", the Flamen Martialis represents Mars as the parent of Rome's founder Romulus, and the Flamen Quirinalis represents the Roman principle of shared sovereignty. The Pontifex Maximus "is considered the judge and arbiter of things both divine and human": Festus, p. 198-200 L

372. H.S. Versnel, *Inconsistencies in Greek and Roman Religion: Transition and Reversal in Myth and Ritual* (Brill, 1993, 1994), p. 158, especially note 104.

373. De lingua latina 7.37.

374. Festus, p. 291 L, citing Veranius (1826 edition of Dacier, p. 1084 online); R. Del Ponte, "Documenti sacerdotali in Veranio e Granio Flacco," Diritto e Storia 4 (2005).[6]

375. Jerzy Linderski, "Q. Scipio Imperator," in *Imperium sine fine: T. Robert S. Broughton and the Roman Republic* (Franz Steiner, 1996), p. 168; Jonathan Edmondson and Alison Keith, *Roman Dress and the Fabrics of Roman Culture* (University of Toronto Press, 2008), p. 12.

376. Fred K. Drogula, "Imperium, potestas and the pomerium in the Roman Republic," Historia 56.4 (2007), pp. 436–437.

377. Christoph F. Konrad, "Vellere signa," in *Augusto augurio: rerum humanarum et divinarum commentationes in honorem Jerzy Linderski* (Franz Steiner, 2004), p. 181; see Cicero, Second Verrine 5.34; Livy 21.63.9 and 41.39.11.

378. Festus 439L, as cited by Versnel, Inconsistencies, p. 158 online.

379. Thomas N. Habinek, *The World of Roman Song: From Ritualized Speech to Social Order* (Johns Hopkins University Press, 2005), p. 256.

380. The noun derives from the past participle of pacisci to agree, to come to an agreement, allied to pactus, past participle of verb pangere to fasten or tie. Compare Sanskrit pac to bind, and Greek peegnumi, I fasten: W. W. Skeat *Etymological Dictionary of the English Language* s.v. peace, pact

381. As in Plautus, Mercator 678; Lucetius, De rerum natura V, 1227; Livy III 5, 14.

382. Jörg Rüpke, *Religion of the Romans* (Polity Press, 2007, originally published in German 2001), p. 81 online.

383. William Warde Fowler, *The Religious Experience of the Roman People* (London, 1922), p. 191.

384. Robert E.A. Palmer, "The Deconstruction of Mommsen on Festus 462/464 L, or the Hazards of Interpretation", in *Imperium sine fine: T. Robert S. Broughton and the Roman Republic* (Franz Steiner,

1996), p. 99, note 129 online; Roger D. Woodard, Indo-European Sacred Space: Vedic and Roman Cult (University of Illinois Press, 2006), p. 122 online.

385. Livy 8.9.1–11.

386. Compare Sanskrit cayati. See M. Morani "Latino sacer..." in Aevum LV 1981 pp. 30-46. Pius may derive from Umbrian and thus appear with a p instead of a q; some Indo-European languages resolved the original velar k(h) into the voiceless labial p, as did Greek and Celtic. Umbrian is one of such languages although it preserved the velar before a u. In Proto-Italic it has given ii with a long first i as in pii-: cfr. G. L. Bakkum The Latin Dialect of the Ager Faliscus: 150 Years of Scholarship p. 57 n. 34 quoting Meiser 1986 pp.37-38.

387. William Warde Fowler, The Religious Experience of the Roman People (London, 1922), p. 462.

388. Gerard Mussies, "Cascelia's Prayer," in La Soteriologia dei culti orientali nell' impero romano (Brill, 1982), p. 160.

389. Along with pater, "father." Hendrik Wagenvoort, "Horace and Vergil," in Studies in Roman Literature, Culture and Religion (Brill, 1956), pp. 82–83.

390. M. Morani "Latino Sacer..." In Aevum 1981 LV.

391. Varro Lingua Latina V 15, 83; G. Bonfante "Tracce di terminologia palafitticola nel vocabolario latino?" Atti dell' Istituto Veneto di Scienze, Lettere e Arti 97 (1937: 53-70)

392. K. Latte Römische Religionsgeschichte. Munich 1960 p. 400-1; H. Fugier Recherhches sur l' expression du sacree' dans la langue latine Paris 1963 pp.161-172.

393. First proposed by F. Ribezzo in "Pontifices 'quinionalis sacrificii effectores' , Rivista indo-greco-italica di Filologia-Lingua-Antichità 15 1931 p. 56.

394. For a review of the proposed hypotheses cfr. J. P. Hallet "Over Troubled Waters: The Meaning of the Title Pontifex" in Transactions and Proceedings of the American Philological Association 101 1970 p. 219 ff.

395. Marietta Horster, "Living on Religion: Professionals and Personnel", in A Companion to Roman Religion, pp. 332–334.

396. Macrobius, Saturnalia III 2, 3- 4: R. Del Ponte, "Documenti sacerdotali in Veranio e Granio Flacco" in Diritto estoria, 4, 2005.

397. Robert Schilling, "Roman Sacrifice," Roman and European Mythologies (University of Chicago Press, 1992, from the French

edition of 1981), p. 79 online.

398. Jerzy Linderski, "The Augural Law", Aufstieg und Niedergang der römischen Welt II.16 (1986), pp. 2232, 2247.

399. Claude Moussy, "Signa et portenta", in Donum grammaticum: Studies in Latin and Celtic Linguistics in Honour of Hannah Rosén (Peeters, 2002), p. 269 online.

400. Pliny, Natural History 11.272, Latin text at LacusCurtius; Mary Beagon, Roman Nature: The Thought of Pliny the Elder (Oxford University Press, 1992), p. 146.

401. Varro's passage is preserved by Servius, note to Aeneid 3.336, as cited by David Wardle, Cicero on Divination, Book 1 (Oxford University Press, 2006), p. 330 online.

402. Auguste Bouché-Leclercq, Histoire de la divination dans l'antiquité: Divination hellénique et divination italique (Jérôme Millon, 2003 reprint), pp. 873–874.

403. Blandine Cuny-Le Callet, Rome et ses monstres: Naissance d'un concept philosophique et rhétorique (Jérôme Millon, 2005), p. 48, with reference to Fronto.

404. For instance, Roman and European Mythologies (University of Chicago Press, 1992, from the French edition of 1981), pp. 43 and 98. Despite its title, S.W. Rasmussen's Public Portents in Republican Rome («L'Erma» di Bretschneider, 2003), does not distinguish among prodigium, omen, portentum and ostentum (p. 15, note 9).

405. Augustine, De civitate Dei 21.8: Portentum ergo fit non contra naturam, sed contra quam est nota natura ("therefore a portent does not occur contrary to nature, but contrary to what is known of nature"). See Michael W. Herren and Shirley Ann Brown, Christ in Celtic Christianity (Boydell Press, 2002), p. 163.

406. Pliny, Natural History 28.11, as cited by Matthias Klinghardt, "Prayer Formularies for Public Recitation: Their Use and Function in Ancient Religion", Numen 46 (1999), p. 15.

407. Jerzy Linderski, "The Augural Law", Aufstieg und Niedergang der römischen Welt II.16 (1986), p. 2246.

408. A.A. Barb, "Animula Vagula Blandula ... Notes on Jingles, Nursery-Rhymes and Charms with an Excursus on Noththe's Sisters", Folklore 61 (1950), p. 23; Maarten J. Vermaseren and Carel C. van Essen, The Excavations in the Mithraeum of the Church of Santa Prisca on the Aventine (Brill, 1965), pp. 188–191.

409. W.S. Teuffel, History of Roman Literature (London, 1900, translation of the 5th German edition), vol. 1, p. 547.

410. Pliny, *Natural History* 28.19, as cited by Nicole Belayche, "Religious Actors in Daily Life", in *A Companion to Roman Religion* (Blackwell, 2007), p. 287.
411. Linderski, "The Augural Law", pp. 2252-2256.
412. Steven M. Cerutti, *Cicero's Accretive Style: Rhetorical Strategies in the Exordia of the Judicial Speeches* (University Press of America, 1996), passim; Jill Harries, *Law and Empire in Late Antiquity* (Cambridge University Press, 1996), p. 36.
413. Fritz Graf, "Prayer in Magic and Religious Ritual", in *Magika Hiera: Ancient Greek Magic and Religion* (Oxford University Press, 1991), p. 189.
414. Robert Schilling, "Roman Sacrifice", *Roman and European Mythologies* (University of Chicago Press, 1992), p. 77.
415. Georg Luck, *Arcana Mundi* (Johns Hopkins University Press, 1985, 2006), p. 515.
416. Dirae is used by Tacitus (*Annales* 14.30) to describe the preces uttered by the druids against the Romans at Anglesey.
417. As in Lucretius, *De rerum natura* 5.1229. According to Emile Benveniste (*Le vocabulaire*, p. 404) quaeso would mean "I use the appropriate means to obtain"; in the interpretation of Morani,[citation needed] quaeso means "I wish to obtain, try and obtain", while precor designates the utterance of the adequate words to achieve one's aim.
418. Adolf Berger, *Encyclopedic Dictionary of Roman Law* (American Philosophical Society, 1991 reprint), p. 648; Detlef Liebs, "Roman Law", in *The Cambridge Ancient History. Late Antiquity: Empire and Successors, A.D. 425-600* (Cambridge University Press, 2000), vol. 15, p. 243.
419. Andrew Lintott, *The Constitution of the Roman Republic* (Oxford: Clarendon Press, 1999, reprinted 2002), p. 103 online.
420. Orlin, in Rüpke (ed), 60.
421. R. Bloch ibidem p. 96
422. Rosenberger, in Rüpke (ed), 297.
423. Rosenberger, in Rüpke (ed), 295 - 8: the task fell to the haruspex, who set the child to drown in the sea. The survival of such a child for four years after its birth would have between regarded as extreme dereliction of religious duty.
424. Livy, 27.37.5–15; the hymn was composed by the poet Livius Andronicus. Cited by Halm, in Rüpke (ed) 244. For remainder, see Rosenberger, in Rüpke (ed), 297.

425. See Livy, 22.1 ff.

426. For Livy's use of prodigies and portents as markers of Roman impiety and military failure, see Feeney, in Rüpke (ed), 138 - 9. For prodigies in the context of political decision-making, see Rosenberger, in Rüpke (ed), 295 - 8. See also R. Bloch Les prodiges dans l'antiquite'-Les prodiges a Rome It. transl. 1981, chap. 1, 2

427. Dennis Feeney, in Jörg Rüpke, (Editor), A Companion to Roman Religion, Wiley-Blackwell, 2007. p.140.

428. Festus s. v. praepetes aves p. 286 L "aves quae se ante auspicantem ferunt" "who go before the a.", 224 L "quia secundum auspicium faciant praetervolantes...aut ea quae praepetamus indicent..." "since they make the auspice favourable by flying nearby...or point to what we wish for...". W. W. Skeat An Etymological Dictionary of the English language s. v. propitious New York 1963 (reprint).

429. William Warde Fowler, The Religious Experience of the Roman People (London, 1922), pp. 265–266; Mary Beard, J.A. North, and S.R.F. Price, Religions of Rome: A History (Cambridge University Press, 1998), vol. 1, p. 40.

430. Charlotte Long, The Twelve Gods of Greece and Rome (Brill, 1987), pp. 235–236.

431. Jerzy Linderski, "The Augural Law", Aufstieg und Niedergang der römischen Welt II.16 (1986), p. 2180, and in the same volume, G.J. Szemler, "Priesthoods and Priestly Careers in Ancient Rome," p. 2322.

432. Clifford Ando, The Matter of the Gods: Religion and the Roman Empire (University of California Press, 2008), p. 126.

433. Cicero, De natura deorum 2.8.

434. Ando, The Matter of the Gods, p. 13.

435. Nicole Belayche, in Rüpke, Jörg (Editor), A Companion to Roman Religion, Wiley-Blackwell, 2007, p. 279: "Care for the gods, the very meaning of religio, had [therefore] to go through life, and one might thus understand why Cicero wrote that religion was "necessary". Religious behavior – pietas in Latin, eusebeia in Greek – belonged to action and not to contemplation. Consequently religious acts took place wherever the faithful were: in houses, boroughs, associations, cities, military camps, cemeteries, in the country, on boats."

436. CIL VII.45 = ILS 4920.

437. Jack N. Lightstone, "Roman Diaspora Judaism," in A Companion to Roman Religion (Blackwell, 2007), pp. 360, 368.

438. Adelaide D. Simpson, "Epicureans, Christians, Atheists in the Second Century," Transactions and Proceedings of the American Philological Association 72 (1941) 372-381.
439. Beard et al., Vol. 1, 217.
440. F. De Visscher "Locus religiosus" Atti del Congresso internazionale di Diritto Romano, 3, 1951
441. Warde Fowler considers a possible origin for sacer in taboos applied to holy or accursed things or places, without direct reference to deities and their property. W. Warde Fowler "The Original Meaning of the Word Sacer" Journal of Roman Studies, I, 1911, p.57-63
442. Varro. LL V, 150. See also Festus, 253 L: "A place was once considered to become religiosus which looked to have been dedicated to himself by a god": "locus statim fieri putabatur religiosus, quod eum deus dicasse videbatur".
443. Cicero, De natura deorum 2.3.82 and 2.28.72; Ittai Gradel, Emperor Worship and Roman Religion (Oxford University Press, 2002), pp. 4-6.
444. Massimo Pallottino, "Sacrificial Cults and Rites in Pre-Roman Italty," in Roman and European Mythologies (University of Chicago Press, 1992), p.33.
445. Clifford Ando, "Religion and ius publicum," in Religion and Law in Classical and Christian Rome (Franz Steiner, 2006), pp. 140-142.
446. Gian Biagio Conte, Latin Literature: A History (Johns Hopkins University Press, 1994, originally published 1987 in Italian), p. 213.
447. Herbert Vorgrimler, Sacramental Theology (Patmos, 1987, 1992), p. 45.
448. Jerzy Linderski, "The libri reconditi"," Harvard Studies in Classical Philology 89 (1985), pp.218-219.
449. Jörg Rüpke, Religion of the Romans (Polity Press, 2007, originally published in German 2001), p. 223 online.
450. Festus on the ordo sacerdotum, 198 in the edition of Lindsay.
451. Gary Forsythe, A Critical History of Early Rome: From Prehistory to the First Punic War (University of California Press, 2005), p. 136 online.
452. Festus, entry on ritus, p. 364 (edition of Lindsay): ritus est est mos comprobatus in administrandis sacrificis. See also the entry on ritus from Paulus, Festi Epitome, p. 337 (Lindsay), where he defines ritus as mos or consuetudo, "customary use", adding that rite autem significat bene ac recte. See also Varro De Lingua Latina II 88; Cicero De Legibus II 20 and 21.

453. G. Dumézil ARR It. tr. Milan 1977 p. 127 citing A. Bergaigne La religion védique III 1883 p. 220.

454. Jean-Louis Durand, John Scheid "Rites et religion. Remarques sur certains préjugés des historiens de la religions des Grecs et des Romains" in Arcives des sciences sociales des religions 85 1994 pp. 23-43 part. pp. 24-25.

455. John Scheid, "Graeco Ritu: A Typically Roman Way of Honoring the Gods", Harvard Studies in Classical Philology, Vol. 97, Greece in Rome: Influence, Integration, 1995, pp. 15–31.

456. Aulus Gellius, Attic Nights 7.12.5, discounting the etymology proffered by Gaius Trebatius in his lost work On Religions (as sacer + cella).

457. Varro, Res Divinae frg. 62 in the edition of Cardauns.

458. Verrius Flaccus as cited by Festus, p. 422.15–17 L.

459. Jörg Rüpke, Religion of the Romans (Polity Press, 2007, originally published in German 2001), pp. 183–185.

460. Dionysius Halicarnassus II 64, 3.

461. Varro, De res rustica, 2.1., describes porci sacres (pigs considered sacer and thus reserved for sacrifice) as necessarily "pure" (or perfect); "porci puri ad sacrificium".

462. M. Morani "Lat. sacer...cit. p. 41. See also Festus. p. 414 L2 & p.253 L: Gallus Aelius ait sacrum esse quodcumque modo atque instituto civitatis consecratum est, sive aedis sive ara sive signum, locum sive pecunia, sive aliud quod dis dedicatum atque consecratum sit; quod autem privati suae religionis causa aliquid earum rerum deo dedicent, id pontifices Romanos non existimare sacrum: "Gallus Aelius says that sacer is anything made sacred (consecratum) in any way or by any institution of the community, be it a building or an altar or a sign, a place or money, or anything that else can be dedicated to the gods; the Roman pontiffs do not consider sacer any things dedicated to a god in private religious cult."

463. ...si id moritur...profanum esto "if the animal dies ...it shall be profane": Livy, Ab Urbe Condita, 22.10. For the archaic variant, see G. Dumezil La religion romaine archaique Paris, 1974, Considerations preliminaires

464. F. De Visscher "Locus religiosus" Atti del Congresoo internazionale di Diritto Romano, 3, 1951

465. Warde Fowler considers a possible origin for sacer in the taboos applied to things or places holy or accursed without direct reference to deities and their property. W. Warde Fowler "The

Original Meaning of the Word Sacer" Journal of Roman Studies, I, 1911, p.57-63

466. As in Horace, Sermones II 3, 181,

467. As in Servius, Aeneid VI, 609: Dionysius of Halicarnassus, II 10, 3; Festus 505 L.

468. Festus, p422 L: "homo sacer is est quem populus iudicavit ob maleficium; neque fas est eum imolari, sed qui occidit, parricidii non damnatur". For further discussion on the homo sacer in relation to the plebeian tribunes, see Ogilvie, R M, A Commentary on Livy 1-5, Oxford, 1965.

469. H. Bennet Sacer esto.. thinks that the person declared sacred was originally sacrificed to the gods. This hypothesis seems to be supported by Plut. Rom. 22, 3 and Macr. Sat.III, 7, 5, who compare the homo sacer to the victim in a sacrifice. The prerogative of declaring somebody sacer supposedly belonged to the king during the regal era; during the Republic, this right passed to the pontiff and courts.

470. G. Devoto Origini Indoeuropee (Firenze, 1962), p. 468

471. John Scheid, An Introduction to Roman Religion (Indiana University Press, 2003), p. 129.

472. Scheid, Introduction to Roman Religion, pp. 129-130.

473. Lesley E. Lundeen, "In Search of the Etruscan Priestess: A Re-Examination of the hatrencu," in Religion in Republican Italy (Cambridge University Press, 2006), p. 46; Celia E. Schultz, Women's Religious Activity in the Roman Republic (University of North Carolina Press, 2006), pp. 70-71.

474. Varro. De Lingua Latina VI 24; Festus sv Septimontium p. 348, 340, 341L; Plut. Quest. Rom. 69

475. Festus sv Publica sacra; Dionys. Hal. II 21, 23; Appian. Hist. Rom. VIII 138; de Bello Civ. II 106; Plut. Quaest. Rom. 89; Christopher John Smith, The Roman Clan: The gens from Ancient Ideology to Modern Anthropology (Cambridge University Press, 2006), p. 44.

476. Plutarch Numa 14, 6-7 gives a list of Numa's ritual prescriptions: obligation of sacrificing an uneven number of victims to the heavenly gods and an even one to the inferi (cf. Serv. Ecl. 5, 66; Serv. Dan. Ecl. 8, 75; Macrobius I 13,5); the prohibition to make libations to the gods with wine; of sacrificing without flour; the obligation to pray and worship divinities while making a turn on oneselves (Livy V 21,16; Suetonius Vit. 2); the composition of the indigitamenta (Arnobius Adversus nationes II 73, 17-18).

477. Livy I, 20; Dion. Hal. II

478. Macrobius I 12. Macrobius mentions in former times the inadvertent nomination of Salus, Semonia, Seia, Segetia, Tutilina required the observance of a dies feriatus of the person involved.

479. Cic. de Leg. II 1, 9-21; Turcan, The Gods of Ancient Rome, p. 44.

480. William Warde Fowler, The Religious Experience of the Roman People (London, 1922), p. 86.

481. Livy 5.46.2-3; Clifford Ando, The Matter of the Gods: Religion and the Roman Empire (University of California Press, 2009), pp. 142-143; Emmanuele Curti, "From Concordia to the Quirinal: Notes on Religion and Politics in Mid-Republican/Hellenistic Rome," in Religion in Archaic and Republican Rome and Italy: Evidence and Experience (Routledge, 2000), p. 85; Robert E.A. Palmer, "The Deconstruction of Mommsen on Festus 462/464, or the Hazards of Interpretation", in Imperium sine fine: T. Robert S. Broughton and the Roman Republic (Franz Steiner, 1996),

482. Liv. V 46; XXII 18; Dionys. Hal. Ant. Rom. IX 19; Cic. Har. Resp. XV 32; Turcan, The Gods of Ancient Rome, p. 43ff.; Smith, The Roman Clan, p. 46.

483. Mommsen thought, perhaps wrongly, that the Julian sacra for Apollo was in fact a sacrum publicum entrusted to a particular gens. Mommsen Staatsrecht III 19; G. Dumézil La religion romaine archaique It. tr. Milano 1977 p. 475

484. Festus, p. 274 (edition of Lindsay); Robert Turcan, The Gods of Ancient Rome (Routledge, 2001; originally published in French 1998), p. 44; Smith, The Roman Clan, p. 45.

485. Legal questions might arise about the extent to which the inheritance of property was or ought to be attached to the sacra; Andrew R. Dyck, A Commentary on Cicero, De Legibus (University of Michigan Press, 2004), pp. 381-382, note on an issue raised at De legibus 2.48a.

486. Cicero, De legibus 2.1.9-21; Turcan, The Gods of Ancient Rome, p. 44.

487. Jörg Rüpke, Religion of the Romans (Polity Press, 2007, originally published in German 2001), p. 26.

488. Festus 146 in the edition of Lindsay.

489. Olivier de Cazanove, "Pre-Roman Italy, Before and Under the Romans," in A Companion to Roman Religion (Blackwell, 2007), p. 55.

490. Jörg Rüpke, Domi Militiae: Die religiöse Konstruktion des

Krieges in Rom (Franz Steiner, 1990), pp. 76-80.

491. D. Briquel "Sur les aspects militaires du dieu ombrien Fisus Sancius" in Revue de l' histoire des religions[full citation needed] i p. 150-151; J. A. C. Thomas *A Textbook of Roman law* Amsterdam 1976 p. 74 and 105.

492. Varro *De Lingua latina* V 180; Festus s.v. *sacramentum* p. 466 L; 511 L; Paulus Festi Epitome p.467 L.

493. George Mousourakis, *A Legal History of Rome* (Routledge, 2007), p. 33.

494. Mousourakis, *A Legal History of Rome*, pp. 33, 206.

495. See further discussion at *fustuarium*

496. Gladiators swore to commit their bodies to the possibility of being "burned, bound, beaten, and slain by the sword"; Petronius, *Satyricon* 117; Seneca, *Epistulae* 71.32.

497. Carlin A. Barton, *The Sorrows of the Ancient Romans: The Gladiator and the Monster* (Princeton University Press, 1993), pp. 14-16, 35 (note 88), 42, 45-47.

498. Apuleius, *Metamorphoses* 11.15.5; Robert Schilling, "The Decline and Survival of Roman Religion," in *Roman and European Mythologies* (University of Chicago Press, 1992, from the French edition of 1981)

499. Arnaldo Momigliano, *Quinto contributo alla storia degli studi classici e del mondo antico* (Storia e letteratura, 1975), vol. 2, pp. 975-977; Luca Grillo, *The Art of Caesar's Bellum Civile: Literature, Ideology, and Community* (Cambridge University Press, 2012), p. 60.

500. Ulpian, *Digest* I.8.9.2: *sacrarium est locus in quo sacra reponuntur*.

501. Ittai Gradel, *Emperor Worship and Roman Religion* (Oxford University Press, 2002), p. 10.

502. Robert E. A. Palmer, *The Archaic Community of the Romans*, p. 171, note 1.

503. R.P.H. Green, "The Christianity of Ausonius," *Studia Patristica: Papers Presented at the Eleventh International Conference on Patristic Studies Held in Oxford 1991* (Peeters, 1993), vol. 28, pp. 39 and 46; Kim Bowes, "'Christianization' and the Rural Home," *Journal of Early Christian Studies* 15.2 (2007), pp. 143-144, 162.

504. *Built of Living Stones: Art, Architecture, and Worship: Guidelines* (United States Conference of Catholic Bishops, 2005), p. 73. See also Wolfred Nelson Cote, *The Archaeology of Baptism* (Lond, 1876), p. 138.

505. Livy II 33, 1; III 19, 10
506. Dionysius of Halicarnassus VI 89, 3
507. Livy IV 3, 6; 44, 5;XXIX 20, 11
508. M. Morani Latino sacer..." Aevum LV 1981 p. 40
509. H. Fugier Recherches sur l'expression du sacre' dans la langue latine Paris 1963; E. Benveniste Le vocubulaire des institutions indoeuropeenees Paris 1939, p. 427 ff.
510. P.Krestchmer in Glotta 1919, X, p. 155
511. H. Fugier, Recherches, pp. 125 ff; E. Benveniste, Le vocabulaire, pp. 427 ff.; K. Latte Roemische Religionsgeshichte Muenchen 1960 p.127 ff.; D. Briquel "Sur les aspects militaires du dieu Ombrien Fisius Sancius" Paris 1978
512. Ulpian Digest 1.8.9: dicimus sancta, quae neque sacra neque profana sunt.
513. G. DumezilLa religion Romaine archaique It. transl. Milano 1977 p. 127; F. Sini "Sanctitas: cose, uomini, dei" in Sanctitas. Persone e cose da Roma a Costantinopoli a Mosca Roma 2001; Cic. de Nat. Deor. III 94; Festus sv tesca p. 488L
514. Gaius, following Aelius Gallus: inter sacrum autem et sanctum et religiosum differentias bellissime refert [Gallus]: sacrum aedificium, consecrato deo; sanctum murum, qui sit circa oppidum. See also Marcian, Digest 1.8.8: "sanctum" est quod ab iniuria hominum defensum atque munitum est ("it is sanctum that which is defended and protected from the attack of men").
515. Huguette Fugier, Recherches sur l'expression du sacré dans la langue latine, Archives des sciences sociales des religions, 1964, Volume 17, Issue 17, p.180 [7]
516. Servius glosses Amsancti valles (Aeneid 7.565) as loci amsancti, id est omni parte sancti ("amsancti valleys: amsancti places, that is, sanctus here in the sense of secluded, protected by a fence, on every side"). The Oxford Latin Dictionary, however, identifies Ampsanctus in this instance and in Cicero, De divinatione 1.79 as a proper noun referring to a valley and lake in Samnium regarded as an entrance to the Underworld because of its mephitic air.
517. Ovid, Fasti 2.658.
518. Ovid Fasti 1.608-9.
519. Nancy Edwards, "Celtic Saints and Early Medieval Archaeology", in Local Saints and Local Churches in the Early Medieval West (Oxford University Press, 2002), p. 229 online.
520. Robert A. Castus, CIcero: Speech on Behalf of Publius Sestius

(Oxford University Press, 2006), p. 416; Susanne William Rasmussen, Public Portents in Republican Rome (Rome, 2003), p. 163 online.

521. C.T. Lewis & C. Short, *A Latin Dictionary*, Oxford. Clarendon Press, 1879. Online at [8]

522. Pliny *Naturalis Historia* XXVIII 11; Seneca *De Vita Beata* XXVI 7; Cicero *De Divinatione* I 102; Servius Danielis *In Aeneidem* V 71.

523. Cicero *De Divinatione* II 71 and 72; Festus v. *Silentio surgere* p. 474 L; v. *Sinistrum*; Livy VII 6, 3-4; T. I. VI a 5-7.

524. Livy VIII 23, 15; IX 38, 14; IV 57, 5.

525. Jörg Rüpke, *Religion of the Romans* (Polity Press, 2007, originally published in German 2001), p. 206.

526. Thomas N. Habinek, *The World of Roman Song: From Ritualized Speech to Social Order* pp. 36–37.

527. For instance, a woman and her associates (*socii*) donated a lot with a "clubhouse" (*schola*) and colonnade to Silvanus and his *sodalicium*, who were to use it for sacrifice, banquets, and dinners; Robert E.A. Palmer, "Silvanus, Sylvester, and the Chair of St. Peter", *Proceedings of the American Philosophical Society* 122 (1978), pp. 237, 243.

528. Attilio Mastrocinque, "Creating One's Own Religion: Intellectual Choices", in *A Companion to Roman Religion* (Blackwell, 2007), p. 382.

529. Ammianus Marcellinus, 15.9.8; Georges Dottin, *Manuel pour servir à l'étude de l'Antiquité Celtique* (Paris, 1906), pp. 279–289: the *sodalicia consortia* of the druids "ne signifie pas autre chose qu'associations corporatives, collèges, plus ou moins analogues aux collèges sacerdotaux des Romains" (*sodalicia consortia* can "mean nothing other than corporate associations, colleges, more or less analogous to the priestly colleges of the Romans").

530. Eric Orlin, "Urban Religion in the Middle and Late Republic", in *A Companion to Roman Religion*, pp. 63–64; John Scheid, "Sacrifices for Gods and Ancestors", p. 268.

531. Gaius, *Digest* xlvii.22.4 = *Twelve Tables* viii.27; A. Drummond, "Rome in the Fifth Century", *Cambridge Ancient History: The Rise of Rome to 220 B.C.* (Cambridge University Press, 1989, 2002 reprint), vol. 7, part 2, p. 158 online.

532. J.-M. David, S. Demougin, E. Deniaux, D. Ferey, J.-M. Flambard, C. Nicolet, "Le Commentariolum petitionis de Quintus Cicéron", *Aufstieg under Niedergang der römischen Welt* I (1973) pp. 252, 276–277.

533. W. Jeffrey Tatum, *The Patrician Tribune* (University of North Carolina Press, 1999), p.127.
534. W. H. Buckler *The origin and history of contract in Roman law* 1895 pp. 13-15
535. The Hittite is also written as sipant or ispant-.
536. Servius, note to Aeneid X 79
537. In conjunction with archaeological evidence from Lavinium.
538. G. Dumezil "La deuxieme ligne de l'inscription de Duenos" in Latomus 102 1969 pp. 244-255; *Idees romaines* Paris 1969 pp. 12 ff.
539. Jörg Rüpke, "Roman Religion — Religions of Rome," in *A Companion to Roman Religion* (Blackwell, 2007), p. 5.
540. Mary Beard, J.A. North, and S.R.F. Price, *Religions of Rome: A History* (Cambridge University Press, 1998), vol. 1, pp. 215–217.
541. Maijastina Kahlos, *Debate and Dialogue: Christian and Pagan Cultures c. 360-430* (Ashgate, 2007), p. 95.
542. Seneca, De clementia 2.5.1; Beard et al, *Religions of Rome: A History*, p. 216.
543. Beard et al, *Religions of Rome: A History*, p. 216.
544. Yasmin Haskell, "Religion and Enlightenment in the Neo-Latin Reception of Lucretius," in *The Cambridge Companion to Lucretius* (Cambridge University Press, 2007), p. 198 online.
545. Beard et al, *Religions of Rome: A History*, pp. 217–219.
546. Beard et al, *Religions of Rome: A History*, p. 221.
547. Lactantius, Divine Institutes 4.28.11; Beard et al, *Religions of Rome: A History*, p. 216.
548. Frances Hickson Hahn, "Performing the Sacred: Prayers and Hymns," pp. 238, 247, and John Scheid, "Sacrifices for Gods and Ancestors," p. 270, both in *A Companion to Roman Religion* (Blackwell, 2007).
549. Veit Rosenberger, in "Religious Actors in Daily Life: Practices and Related Beliefs," in *A Companion to Roman Religion*, p. 296.
550. W. W. Skeat *Etymological Dictionary of the English Language* New York 1963 sv temple
551. Mary Beard, Simon Price, John North, *Religions of Rome: A History* (Cambridge University Press, 1998), vol. 1, p. 23.
552. Beard et al., "Religions of Rome," vol. 1, p. 23.
553. Servius Ad Aeneid 4.200; Festus. s.v. calls the auguraculum minora templa.
554. G. Dumezil *La religion romaine archaique* Paris, 1974 p.510: J. Marquardt "Le cult chez les romaines" Manuel des antiquités

romaines XII 1. French Transl. 1889 pp. 187-188: See also Cicero, *De Legibus*, 2.2, & Servius,*Aeneid*, 4.200.

555. Jerzy Linderski, "The Augural Law", *Aufstieg und Niedergang der römischen Welt* II.16 (1986), pp. 2266-2267 online, and 2292-2293. On legal usage, see also Elizabeth A. Meyer, *Legitimacy and Law in the Roman World* (Cambridge University Press, 2004), p. 80ff.; Daniel J. Gargola, *Land, Laws and Gods: Magistrates and Ceremony in the Regulation of Public Lands in Republican Rome* (University of North Carolina Press, 1995), p. 202, note 55 online.

556. Meyer, *Legitimacy and Law*, p. 62 online.

557. Hendrik Wagenvoort, "Augustus and Vesta", in *Pietas: Selected Studies in Roman Religion* (Brill, 1980), p. 211 online.

558. Matthias Klinghardt, "Prayer Formularies for Public Recitation: Their Use and Function in Ancient Religion", *Numen* 46 (1999) 1-52.

559. Jerzy Linderski, "The Augural Law", *Aufstieg und Niedergang der römischen Welt* II.16 (1986), pp. 2246, 2267ff.

560. The jurist Gaius (4.30) says that *concepta verba* is synonymous with *formulae*, as cited by Adolf Berger, *Encyclopedic Dictionary of Roman Law* (Amerian Philosophical Society, 1991 reprint), p. 401, and Shane Butler, *The Hand of Cicero* (Routledge, 2002), p. 10.

561. T. Corey Brennan, *The Praetorship in the Roman Republic* (Oxford University Press, 2000), pp. 131-132.

562. Augustine, *Confessions* 11.xviii, as cited by Paolo Bartoloni, *On the Cultures of Exile, Translation, and Writing* (Purdue University Press, 2008), p. 69 online.

563. For instance, Karla Taylor, *Chaucer Reads "The Divine Comedy"* (Stanford University Press, 1989), p. 27 online. For an overview of the Indo-European background regarding the relation of memory to poetry, charm, and formulaic utterance, see Calvert Watkins, *How to Kill a Dragon: Aspects of Indo-European Poetics* (Oxford University Press, 1995), passim, especially pp. 68-70 on memory and the poet-priest (Latin *vates*) as "the preserver and the professional of the spoken word". "For the Romans", notes Frances Hickson Hahn, "there was no distinction between prayer and spell and poetry and song; all were intimately linked to one another"; see "Performing the Sacred: Prayers and Hymns", in *A Companion to Roman Religion* (Blackwell, 2007), p. 236

564. Gian Biagio Conte, *Latin Literature: A History* (Johns Hopkins University Press, 1994, originally published 1987 in Italian), pp. 15-23; George A. Sheets, "Elements of Style in Catullus," in *A Companion to*

Catullus (Blackwell, 2011) n.p.
565. Katja Moede, "Reliefs, Public and Private", in *A Companion to Roman Religion* (Blackwell, 2007), p. 173.
566. John Scheid, "Sacrifices for Gods and Ancestors", in *A Companion to Roman Religion* (Blackwell, 2007), pp. 264, 266.
567. For the Taurobolium, see Duthoy, Robert, *The Taurobolium: Its Evolution and Terminology*, Volume 10, Brill, 1969, p. 1 ff, and Cameron, Alan, *The Last Pagans of Rome*, Oxford University press, 2011, p. 163. The earliest known Taurobolium was dedicated to the goddess Venus Caelestis in 134 AD.
568. Steven J. Green, *Ovid, Fasti 1: A Commentary* (Brill, 2004), pp.159–160.
569. Servius, note to Aeneid 1. 334.
570. *Victima quae dextra cecidit victrice vocatur*, Ovid, Fasti 1.335: ; *hostibus a domitis hostia nomen habet* ("the hostia gets its name from the 'hostiles' that have been defeated"), 1.336.
571. Mary Beard, J.A. North, and S.R.F. Price, *Religions of Rome: A Sourcebook* (Cambridge University Press, 1998), p. 368.
572. Katja Moede, "Reliefs, Public and Private", in *A Companion to Roman Religion* (Blackwell, 2007), p. 168.
573. Marietta Horster, "Living on Religion: Professionals and Personnel", in *A Companion to Roman Religion* (ed. Rüpke), pp. 332-334.
574. Therefore the election must have been vitiated in some way known only to Jupiter: see Veit Rosenberger, in Rüpke, Jörg (Editor), *A Companion to Roman Religion*, Wiley-Blackwell, 2007, p.298; citing Cicero, De Divinatione, 2.77.
575. David Wardle, *Cicero on Divination, Book 1* (Oxford University Press, 2006), p. 178.
576. Macrobius, Saturnalia III 2,12.
577. William Warde Fowler, *The Roman Festivals of the Period of the Republic* (London, 1908), p. 179'; Robert Turcan, *The Gods of Ancient Rome* (Routledge, 2001), p. 75.
578. John Scheid, "Sacrifices for Gods and Ancestors", in *A Companion to Roman Religion* (Blackwell, 2007), p. 270; William Warde Fowler, *The Religious Experience of the Roman People* (London, 1922), pp. 200–202.

LVCIVS VITELLIVS TRIARIVS

ABOUT THE AUTHOR

Lucius Vitellius Triarius, aka Chip Hatcher, is a Graduate (cum Laude) in Political Science, focusing in Ancient Mediterranean Political Systems, from the University of Tennessee at Knoxville and resides in the foothills of the Great Smoky Mountains in Eastern Tennessee.

He is also a member of Nova Roma (www.novaroma.org), the global Roman Reconstruction project, advocating the via Romana, or Roman Way, where he serves as a Pontifex and Senator of Nova Roma.

The Roman Way is the study and practical application of "Romanitas" and the "mos maiorum", the revival of all aspects of Roman life, culture, virtues, ethics and philosophies in our everyday lives.

It is as part of the *mos maiorum* that citizens are expected to take up Roman names for use within the society. Learning Latin, the language of Roman culture, is also an equally important step towards becoming a modern Roman.

One of the cornerstones of Romanitas are the Roman virtues; those qualities which define the ideal state of being and behavior of the Roman citizen.

He believes that we must remember and preserve the good parts of the past in the present, so that others will remember it in the future.

NOTES

NOTES

NOTES

NOTES

NOTES

NOTES

NOTES

NOTES

LVCIVS VITELLIVS TRIARIVS

f·i·n·i·s